IRISH STARS
OF THE OPERA

Gus Smith

Best wishes

Gus Smith

Wexford Festival

Oct 1996

Irish Stars of the Opera

MADISON PUBLISHERS LTD

Madison Publishers Ltd
5 Lower Abbey Street
Dublin 1
Ireland

CONTENTS

Introduction

‘ I realise that being
a singer and being able to
give your best to the public is a
great responsibility.
You have to be in good
physical shape and
very disciplined. I always
wanted a long career.
Not a short, glittering,
Callas – type thing,
but a long, solid, fine career
and the gratification of
knowing that the people who
come to my performances
now still go away feeling
satisfied and enriched.
That has always been my ideal.
So, I took care of myself
and sacrificed certain things.
You have to, if you want to last! ’

Nicolai Gedda

Author's Acknowledgements

In the preparation of this operatic text I wish to express my indebtedness to a number of people, particularly the following singers who made the book possible: Veronica Dunne, Bernadette Greevy, Ann Murray, Louis Browne, Peter McBrien, Josef Locke, Virginia Kerr, Kate McCarney, Mary Hegarty, John O'Flynn, Elizabeth Connell, Patricia Bardon, Regina Nathan, Alison Browner, Marie-Claire O'Reirdan, Suzanne Murphy, Tom Lawlor, Therese Feighan, Angela Feeney, Bruno Caproni, Frances Lucey.

My thanks also to Eithne Troy for her valuable reminiscences of her late husband, Dermot Troy; Liam Breen for his quiet commentary on his unique John McCormack Museum; James Shaw for memories of his friend, the late James Johnston; Maureen Lemass for making available press cuttings collected by her late father, William Lemass, about his colleague, baritone Walter McNally; Derek Walshe for useful information with regard to Irish singers of the past, and Lord Harewood, who recalled for me James Johnston's days at the Royal Opera House Covent Garden.

There are others I'm indebted to for their generous recall: Brendan Cavanagh, soprano Renée Flynn, Col. J.M. Doyle, Dr. Havelock Nelson, Jeannie Reddin, Mildred O'Brien, Patrick Brennan (DGOS Opera Ireland for tapes and photographs), Nancy Calthorpe, Joan Roughneen, Barra O Tuama, Kevin Hannon (Limerick), Hubert Valentine, Terence Molloy, Anne-Marie O'Sullivan, Jerome Hynes (Chief Executive, Wexford Festival Opera), Henrietta Hewson, Noel Smith, Mrs. P. Collier, Donnie Potter (DGOS), Angela McCrone (DGOS Opera Ireland), Assumpta Lawless (Opera Theatre Company) and Ray Lynott (RTE) for useful interview with James Johnston, and Joe Lynch.

Agencies who lent useful assistance include Covent Garden Archives Department, Welsh National Opera, English National Opera, RTE Tapes

Department, *Irish Times* Library, Irish National Library, Trinity College Library, *Opera* magazine; and the editors of the following newspapers for their permission to quote from reviews of opera and special features: *Irish Independent, Evening Herald, Sunday Independent, Irish Press, Sunday Press, Sunday Tribune, Irish Times, Cork Examiner, Limerick Leader, The Times of London, The Financial Times, Daily Telegraph, Belfast Telegraph, Belfast News Letter, Irish News Belfast, The Guardian*.

I wish also to acknowledge the following authors and their publications: *Opera at Covent Garden* by Harold Rosenthal (Victor Gollancz Ltd.), *Welsh National Opera* by Richard Fawkes (Julia MacRea Publications), *Prima Donna - History by Rupert Christiansen* (Penguin Books Ltd.), *Monte Carlo Opera 1910-1915* by T.J. Walsh (Boethius Press), *Bravo* by Helena Matheopoulos (Victor Gollancz), *Diva* by Helena Metheopoulos (Victor Gollancz), *Kathleen - the Life of Kathleen Ferrier* by Maurice Leonard (Hutchinson), *I Hear You Calling Me* by Lily McCormack (W.H. Allen), *Verdi* by Charles Osborne (Pan Books Ltd.) *5000 Nights at the Opera* by Rudolf Bing (Doubleday, New York), *The Great Irish Tenor* by Gordon Ledbetter (Duckworth & Co. London), *A Bank of Violets* by Havelock Nelson (Greyston).

Introduction - The 27

Who are the 27? They are, in a word, the singers I have chosen through which to highlight Ireland's achievements at home and abroad in the world of Grand Opera. True, the number could as easily be 50 or even 100, but in the final analysis 27 was the figure agreed.

Sadly, a number of the singers profiled have passed on, others quietly retired, the majority, though, have continued to find success in their chosen profession. Restrictions of space alone prevented the inclusion of profiles of different generations of singers, such as May Davitt, Patricia Black, John Lynskey, J.C. Browner, Robert Irwin, Limerick-born Francis Egerton, John Carolan, Mary Sheridan, Frank O'Brien, Brendan Cavanagh, Ruth Maher, Patrick Ring, Ethna Robinson, Nicola Sharkey and Colette McGahon.

In the case of tenors, Michael Kelly and John O'Sullivan and soprano Catherine Hayes, I decided to profile them, albeit briefly, because of their unique achievements in a golden age of opera. Undeniably, they set an example for future generations of Irish artists destined to make their mark in the opera houses of Italy, Germany, Austria and Switzerland.

Michael Kelly was born in Dublin on Christmas Day 1762, and by the age of 17 had made his operatic debut in Piccini's *La Buona Figliola*. His father was urged to send his son to Italy for voice training; young Michael was conspicuous by his blond hair and fair complexion. After minor engagements in Florence and Venice, the young tenor made his way to Vienna and was taken on by the Court Theatre. The next four years were to prove the most eventful of his life, and those for which he is mainly remembered.

He sang Almaviva in Paisiello's *Barbiere di Siviglia* during August 1783, and in December of that year appeared as Pylades in a revival of *Iphigenie en Tauride*, rehearsed by Gluck himself. Incidentally, the Paisiello opera caused a furore when presented at the Wexford Festival in the autumn of 1993, mainly due to a tasteless production.

Apart from his singing, Kelly on occasions displayed a quick Dublin wit and gift at mimicry. Elizabeth Forbes, in her account of the singer's career for *Opera* magazine, wrote: 'One evening at the composer Stephen Storace's lodgings when both Paisiello and Storace's librettist Casti were present, Kelly so successfully imitated a notorious old Viennese miser, Varese, singing his favourite canzonetta in a thin, quivery voice, that he was given the role of Gafforio in Paisiello's new opera *Il Re Teodoro*, in which he would score a resounding success.'

The year 1786 was a milestone for the popular tenor. Mozart and da Ponte together provided him with his claim to immortailty with *Le Nozze di Figaro*, skilfully adapted from the famous Beaumarchais play dealing with the delicate relationships between the different social classes. Kelly sang the roles of Don Basilio and Don Curzio in the premiere, and Nancy Storace, Stephen's sister, was the Susanna.

The tenor was friendly with Mozart and they often dined in Vienna's most fashionable restaurants; at other times they played billiards together. The story goes that Mozart always won, being much the better player, but Kelly in typical Irish style, was regarded as a sporting loser. He had cause, though, to remember the first night of *Le Nozze di Figaro*, not only because of its enormous success but for Mozart's reaction.

He wrote in his *Reminiscences* in 1826: 'When the performance was over, Mozart came on stage to me, and shaking me by both hands, said, "Bravo! young man, I feel obliged to you, and acknowledge you to have been in the right, and myself in the wrong". You see, I had played the part of the stuttering judge, but in rehearsal Mozart asked me to desist from stuttering during the Sextet as it would spoil his music. I protested and eventually got my way. The enthusiasm of the audience showed I was right.'

Kelly won further fame in Stephen Storace's opera *Gli Equivoci*, with a libretto by da Ponte based on *The Comedy of Errors*. This work was received with enthusiasm at the Wexford Festival of 1992 in an English translation by Arthur Jacobs. The producer was Giles Havergal. It was to be the tenor's last role in Vienna. Shortly afterwards he set out for England with Stephen and Nancy Storace, arriving in London on 18 March 1787. After making his English debut, he made a long overdue visit to Dublin to see his parents, in particular his mother who was seriously ill.

While in Ireland he found time to sing in concerts in Cork and Limerick where, we are told, his 'stylish singing and polished artistry' were greatly appreciated by audiences. Later, on his return to London, he announced his decision to spend the rest of his professional life in the city. He sang Macbeth in *The Beggar's Opera* in April 1789, and when the new Drury Lane Theatre was opened he was one of the stars of the musical *Lodoiska*; in time he would become the threatre's musical director.

In 1799, performances of his operas, *A Friend in Need* and *Bluebeard* were presented there with no great success. He continued to accept singing engagements as well as to manage the King's Theatre, which was an indication of the man's exemplary energy. Unfortunately, Drury Lane was burnt down on the night of 24 February 1809 and scores of 60 of his operas were destroyed.

Michael Kelly's last appearance on any stage was in Dublin on 1 October 1811. He continued, though, to write operas for another decade and his last, *The Lady and the Devil* was presented at the re-built Drury Lane on 3 May 1820.

As an operatic composer his reputation never rose above the ordinary. According to Elizabeth Forbes, the tenor's last years were unfortunately marked by gout and ill-health and he was confined to a wheelchair. When he died in 1826, he had outlived Mozart by 35 years. He is buried in the graveyard of the actors' church, St. Paul's, Covent Garden.

Twenty years on, Limerick-born soprano, Catherine Hayes, was to achieve international acclaim; in fact, the year 1846 saw her at her peak, a firm favourite with La Scala audiences for her unfailing beauty of tone and resplendent coloratura. During the season she sang the title roles in Donizetti's *Lucia di Lammermoor* and his *Linda di Chamounix* and Desdemona in Rossini's *Otello* as well as Violetta in Mercadante's *Il Braco*.

During the 1840s and '50s she was greatly in demand in European opera houses, and in April 1849 made an immediate impression at Covent Garden in *Linda di Chamounix*. In July of the same year she partnered the renowned Italian tenor, Giovanni Mario in Meyerbeer's *Le Prophète*. Years afterwards Margaret Burke Sheridan would pay tribute to Catherine Hayes' achievements: 'She paved the way for me in Italy. Italian audiences adored her.'

She was born at 4 Patrick Street, Limerick in October 1825, the third daughter of Arthur Hayes, who was Bandmaster in the Limerick City Militia. He deserted his family and left them in very poor circumstances with the burden of bringing up the family falling on their mother, Mary Hayes, who eked out a living by making straw hats.

The story of young Catherine's discovery is reminiscent of Cinderella. She was in the habit of accompanying her cousin, a Mrs. Carroll, to Lord Limerick's house in Henry Street where she worked as a char. On one occasion, Dr. Knox, the Church of Ireland Bishop of Limerick, who lived next door, was enjoying a siesta in his garden when he was awakened by the traditional air *Jemmy, mo mhíle stór*, sung by the 'most beautiful voice he had ever heard.' Looking over some shrubs, he spied the frail-looking girl 'thrilling the air with the sweetest of melody'

After making enquiries, the bishop with the assistance of friends in the local commercial and musical life of the city, had Catherine sent to Dublin for voice training with Antonio Sapio. She gave her first public concert in Dublin at the Rotunda in May, 1839 and at a recital in the Theatre Royal Limerick she thrilled the audience with her pure, sweet-toned soprano voice although she was still inexperienced as a stage performer. Within a few years she would become known as the 'Swan of Erin' and the 'Irish Nightingale.'

Catherine later went to Milan where she studied with Signor Roncono, an authority in the Italian school of singing. She made her continental debut at Marseilles in May, 1845 in a performance of Bellini's *I Puritani*, and toured the continent as 'La Hayes', winning growing acclaim. She was soon engaged as *prima donna* at La Scala, Milan where her performance in Don Donizetti's *Linda di Chamounix* established her supremacy as an interpreter of Italian opera, and she appeared in works by Ricci, Mercadante, Rossini and Verdi in Venice, Vienna and London where she sang in April, 1849 with the Royal Italian Opera. Mile-long queues formed to hear her and she was invited to Buckingham Palace by Queen Victoria. By the time she returned to Limerrick, she was an international celebrity.

News of her success at Covent Garden in *Linda di Chamounix* had already reached Limerick, so that when it was announced that she would sing in opera there in March, 1850 there was a clamour for tickets. The Theatre Royal was filled to capacity on the opening night of Bellini's *La Sonnambula* with Catherine Hayes singing the role of Amina. Next day, the *Limerick Chronicle* reported: 'Limerick has rarely seen a more splendid display of rank, fashion and beauty as that assembled for the occasion. It must indeed have been a gratifying moment for Miss Hayes when every hand, voice and heart present united in one of the most enthusiastic welcomes that ever our theatre has witnessed.'

The newspaper described her singing as 'the perfection of vocalism' and her acting as 'charmingly natural.' The excited audience made the diva encore Amina's romance, "Ah, non credea mirarti" and at the final curtain the stage was showered with flowers. During the same week she sang the title role in *Norma* and again her radiant voice thrilled the audience. 'Another glorious triumph for Miss Hayes' stated the *Limerick Chronicle*. 'Never have we heard her in better voice, never was her acting more convincing.' Catherine also sang outside St Mary's Parish Chruch where she had been baptised, a song especially composed for her by Harvey :

When roaming on a foreign strand
I fancy still my steps were here:
Home of my heart, my native land.

Later, she undertook arduous tours of North and South America, as well as Australia. Catherine was particularly taken by the warmth of the reception accorded her in San Francisco. A local newspaper reported: 'A most enthusiastic audience threw necklaces, gold trinkets and other gifts at her feet on stage.' Her agent in the USA was William Avery Bushnell who had also acted for Jenny Lind on her American tours. Tickets for Catherine's recitals sometimes cost $1,150 and in San Francisco, from November 1852 to May, 1853 her fees averaged £650 per month.

Her arrival in Sydney aroused 'an excitement wholly unparalleled in the theatrical annals of the colony.' Audiences were impressed by her bravura operatic arias but were more affected by her singing of such ballads as "Home sweet home" and Irish airs. Her repertoire on these tours consisted primarily of the great Italian operas by Bellini and Donizetti with their unsurpassed opportunities for virtuoso coloratura singing.

Shortly after her return to Britain, she unwisely undertook an exhaustive concert tour but on medical advice was persuaded to cut her engagements. Constant travel and overwork had exhausted her and impaired her health, which was never robust. In 1857 she decided to settle in London where she married her manager, William Bushnell. She continued to sing in London and on provincial tours, but restricted her performances after her husband's death in France in July, 1858, aged thirty-five. She died in August, 1861 in London and was buried in Kensal Green cemetery, leaving an estate of £16,000. There is a small plaque erected on the house in Limerick where she was born, but the great soprano is worthy of a more impressive memorial.

It is true to say that tenor, John O'Sullivan, is not widely known in Ireland, yet in view of his world renown he deserves a plaque to his name. Born in County Cork in 1878, he is reputed to have left the country to live with an aunt in the French provinces and later trained as a singer at the Paris Conservatoire. His career really took off in July 1914 after his success as Raoul in *Les Huguenots* at the Paris Opera and in the following 19 years he sang all the heroic tenor roles at the Opera; he was also much in demand at the leading Italian opera houses and in August 1926 made his debut at Arena di Verona as Manrico in *Il Trovatore*. His Covent Garden debut in 1927 was less impressive when he sang Raoul in a revival of *Les Huguenots*; one English critic described the performance as 'disastrous.'

But O'Sullivan, a forthright individual, quickly put the experience behind him and went on to sing with great success at La Scala and at the Colon, Buenos Aires. Dr. Tom Walsh, founder of the Wexford Festival, and a respected writer on opera matters, observed: 'Italian tenors who had sung with O'Sullivan declared his voice to be the most exciting they had ever heard. Unfortunately when he made recordings of arias from Verdi's *Otello* prior to 1925 the voice sounded rough-hewn, not helped by the inadequate recording techniques of the time. Yet, I've no doubt he made a thrilling impression in dramatic roles in big opera houses.'

Listening to O'Sullivan's recording of "Eultate!" and "Ora e per sempre addio" from *Otello* I was forcibly reminded of the renowned Italian tenor, Mario del Monaco. Ringing top notes, powerful projection and fine range were hallmarks of both tenors. O'Sullivan was to become a celebrated exponent of the role of Arnold in Rossini's *Guillaume Tell* and sang it with increasing success throughout the world.

Late in his career he became friendly with James Joyce in Paris; Joyce, it will be remembered, once came third in the tenor section at the Dublin Feis Ceoil. Soon the eminent Irish writer was telling his friends: 'John O'Sullivan has the most wonderful voice in the world. It is not the sweetest, but he can do with it more than any man alive can do with his voice.'

Backing his enthusiasm with his money, Joyce bought bundles of tickets for the performance of *Guillaume Tell* and distributed them around Paris. He insisted that his large party should sit in various parts of the house so that the applause for O'Sullivan should come, not only from one group, but from all over the theatre.

Dr. Walsh takes up the story: 'Joyce's reason was that he believed the tenor was being suppressed by an international group of tenors, and that all Irishmen should rally round him. What in fact occurred was that O'Sullivan was sharing the role of Arnold with the young Giacomo Lauri-

Volpi. This generated tense rivalry, provoking O'Sullivan to write a challenging letter to the critic, Louis Schneider. But it was an unequal contest which Lauri-Volpi, because of his age, was bound to win.'

O'Sullivan, in spite of his very busy schedule, visited Ireland for a recital at the Theatre Royal, Dublin in 1930. News of his friendship with James Joyce had preceded his arrival at Dun Laoghaire and an irate Dublin Jesuit endeavoured to have the concert banned, but his misguided effort failed. The tenor thrilled a full and enthusiastic house with his powerful voice, particularly in arias from *Trovatore* and *Otello*. He was paid a fee of £120.

By the time he retired in 1938, O'Sullivan had enjoyed a successful career spanning over 30 years. He died on 9 February 1948 in Paris. Perhaps it is fitting that the final tribute be paid by his friend, James Joyce. Commenting on the tenor's performance as Arnold, he stated: 'The role has never been sung in its entirety since the days of Tamagno. I have been through the Rossini score of the opera and I discovered that O'Sullivan sings 456 Gs, 93 A flats, 92 As, 54 B flats, 15 Bs, 19Cs and 2 C sharps. Nobody else can do it.'

There were others, such as Allan James Foli – or Allan Foley as he was known in his native Cahir, Co. Tipperary where he was born in 1835. He had a magnificent bass voice, but the musical snobbery of the time declined to recognise true artistry except in a Continental and he met with little success. When he changed his name to Signor Foli, he was immediately acknowledged as a splendid singer. He died on 20 October, 1899, and is buried at Southport, Lancashire. Tenor Barton McGuckian was trained in Dublin and Milan and made his debut with the Carl Rosa Company and went on to become the first tenor to sing the title role in English in Verdi's *Otello* at Covent Garden. His repertoire comprised 150 operatic roles, among them Manrico, Radames, Don Jose and Thaddeus in Balfe's *The Bohemian Girl*. McGuckian died in England in the year 1913.

Dublin-born Michael Balfe, was not only a prolific composer but the possessor of a baritone voice much admired by Rossini, in whose opera *Il Barbiere di Siviglia* he sang Figaro. Balfe, along with fellow countryman, Vincent Wallace, had the distinction of seeing their operas performed regularly at Covent Garden; in October 1848, in fact, there were performances of *The Bohemian Girl* and *The Enchantress*, while Wallace's most popular opera, *Maritana* was also staged during the same month.

In the early decades of the Nineties, John McCormack and Margaret Burke Sheridan sang with some of the most outstanding singers of their day. Regrettably, most Irish people never have had the pleasure of either seeing the tenor or the soprano in their finest operatic parts. It is a situation that, unfortunately, has continued, particularly in the case of Ann Murray whose successes at Salzburg, La Scala and other venues, her own people have perhaps only read about but seldom, if ever, had the opportunity to enjoy. How nice it would be if DGOS Opera Ireland could engage her for a Handel, Mozart or Rossini production. Surely the Society could find the money from some source to bring her to Dublin?

Hubert Valentine has been living in America since the late Thirties and for some years now the veteran tenor has had his own radio show on a 24-hour classical music station in Boston. He has always aimed to promote young Irish singers and musicians. After singing the roles of Faust and Rodolfo, he toyed with the idea of an operatic career, but as he told me once on a visit to Dublin, 'I wasn't keen on the acting side. I felt more at home on the concert stage, so I never went back to opera.'

Another Irish tenor, Terence Molloy was to make his home in California and during the last 30 years has sung with some leading opera companies, including the Bernardino City Grand Opera with whom he sang Canio, Chenier, Don José and Don Ottavio in *Don Giovanni*. One critic was particularly impressed by Molloy's singing of "Il mo tesoro" while his Edgardo in *Lucia di Lammermoor* has won much praise. The tenor, who is a native of Dublin, once gave an operatic recital at the Opera House in Cork.

The list of singers does not end there. Soprano Heather Harper, from Belfast, progressed from the chorus at Glyndebourne to leading roles at

Covent Garden, Bayreuth, Buenos Aires and the Metropolitan. Similarly, Norma Burrowes, a lyric soprano from Bangor, County Down, has performed with distinction at the Aix Festival, with English National Opera and at the Salzburg Festival; she is, in fact, one of a tiny band of Irish-born singers to have sung at this elite festival.

At home in the late Thirties, the Dublin Opera Society provided Irish singers with the chance to further their careers. For example, mezzo Patricia Black sang leading roles in *La Favorita*, *Lohengrin*, *Carmen* and *Trovatore*. As Azucena in the Verdi opera, one critic wrote, 'Ms. Black played the Gipsy mother with a passionate abandonment that is thrilling in its realism.'

Soprano May Devitt, mezzo Geraldine Costigan and baritone John Lynskey displayed vocal talent above the ordinary; Lynskey as the jester in *Rigoletto* and Count di Luna in *Trovatore* proved a natural actor/singer with a high degree of musicality. Devitt's Butterfly - the delight of Dublin audiences at the time - was close to international standards. While the Dublin Operatic Society depended on British guest artists like Heddle Nash, Leslie Jones, Elena Danieli, Ben Williams and Florence Austral to fill some key leading roles, the Irish artists could be said to be indispensable.

Opera buffs could certainly not complain about the scope of the seasons offered to them, for it was not unusual during a single week to have the following choice of operas: *The Magic Flute*, *La Boheme*, *L'Elisir d'Amore*, *Rigoletto* and *Der Freischutz*. Unlike today, Wagnerian lovers were catered for and either *Lohengrin* or *Die Meistersinger* could be relied upon to pack the Gaiety Theatre. The neglect of Wagner's operas in the past 25 years in Dublin must be regarded as nothing short of a scandal and underlines how far the capital has slipped since even the late Thirties. Which inevitably prompts the question: when can we expect a Wagner revival?

Came World War II, and the scene changed. Grand Opera would be performed as usual but without the luxury of guest artists from overseas. Fortunately, Dublin had a sufficient number of singers to present at least the popular repertory. After the war the hunger for opera continued and, as always, this was reflected in the box office receipts at the Gaiety. Undoubtedly, the biggest operatic event of the Fifties was the launch of the Wexford Festival, the brainchild of dynamic local doctor, Tom Walsh; he was supported by his friends, in particular Dr. Des Ffrench, Eugene McCarthy, owner of White's Hotel; Seamus O'Dwyer, a postal worker with a wide knowledge of opera, and the novelist, Compton MacKenzie.

Balfe's *The Rose of Castile* was the first production in 1951, and it is now history that Tom Walsh and a few helpers knocked on doors in the compact streets of the town to ensure that the opera didn't play to empty houses during its four nights' run. The festival, however, survived its teething troubles and Dr. Tom – as he was affectionately known – saw it gather momentum with the subsequent sparkling productions of *L'Elisir d'Amore*, *Don Pasquale* and *La Sonnambula*. Soon it became the fashionable thing to visit Wexford and its friendly festival.

Although Alfro Poli, Nicola Monti, Elvina Ramella and Christiano Dallamangas gave the event a truly international dimension, Irish singers, including Ruth Maher, Patrick Ring, Mary Sheridan, Francis Egerton, Sean Mitten and Colette McGahon bravely played their part. Neilli Walsh, sister of Dr. Tom, sang in the chorus of *The Rose of Castile* and only retired in the early Nineties, a proud record indeed. When I talked to this good-humoured woman on a recent visit to Wexford, she remarked, 'All of us in the chorus sang for the sheer pleasure of singing, and it was wonderful, too, to meet the star singers. I think in my heart that Dr. Tom always felt the festival would succeed. It became his life's interest.'

Like most music festivals, Wexford has had its critics. From time to time, Irish artists complained of being overlooked by the various artistic directors, yet I can say that some of our most talented singers have performed there. The word 'elitism' has been used to describe the festival, but here again it is an inaccurate description, for in the case of Elaine Padmore she has succeeded in making it a people's festival, socially and musically. Despite criticism of rising ticket prices, the event nonetheless remains popular with the public, both with Irish and overseas visitors, and this, I feel, can be mainly attributed to the excellent 'mix' of professional and voluntary personnel; the event could not conceivably go on without these loyal and selfless Wexford volunteers. Furthermore, the refurbishment of the quaint 19th century Theatre Royal in the autumn of 1993 was surely a marvellous act of faith in the festival's future.

Compared with Wexford, the Castleward Opera Festival – a summer event – is a mere infant, yet it quickly caught on since it was founded in l985 and during that short span has staged operas by Mozart, Purcell, Donizetti and Verdi. An exceptional achievement as the theatre itself is a converted stable with a tiny stage measuring only 15 feet by 10, and seating for a mere 220 people. It is the overall setting, however, that captivates the visitor. Castleward House is set amid trees and greenery in the heart of County Down and it is reached by travelling by road from Belfast to Portaferry and taking the ferry across the picturesque Strangford Lough.

The 1993 programme consisted of *Lucia di Lammermoor* and *La Belle Helene*, with the Donizetti work not surprisingly attracting most of the attention. Nicola Sharkey was cast as the doomed heroine. Against all the odds, designer Adam O'Neill transformed the living-room sized stage into the house and grounds of Ravenswood Castle with stylish sets and neat optical illusions. On this imaginative showing, one can only say that Castleward's £15,000 grant from the Arts Council of Northern Ireland was well deserved. The overall cost of presenting the festival is around £165,000. To the visitor like myself, Castleward House exuded charm and elegance and as the opera buffs dined during the long interval on the lawn outside, I was reminded of Glyndebourne's grandeur, even if only in a miniature way. I can see this festival becoming an essential date in the Irish operatic calendar.

Staying in Northern Ireland, the achievements of the Belfast- based Opera Northern Ireland cannot be overlooked. Despite the Troubles, the company has courageously carried on, though the periodic bombing of Belfast's Grand Opera House has been a particularly cruel blow. Due to severe structural damage caused to the building in 1993, the company was obliged to cancel performances there of *Eugene Onegin* and *The Turn of the*

Screw, though the latter opera was toured successfully in the province in November. Looking back, the company enjoyed some fruitful years, with 1992 one of the high points with its production of *Faust*, directed by Bliss Herbert, highly praised by the Belfast and Dublin critics.

Opera Theatre Company, based in Dublin, is funded by the Republic's Arts Council and concentrates on touring small-scale productions, often with piano. Founded in 1986, it has presented works as varied as *The Rape of Lucretia* and *Falstaff* and provided welcome employment for a galaxy of young singers, such as Regina Hanley, Paul McCann, Peter Kerr and Fionnuala Gill. In the winter of 1993 the company toured widely with *Jenufa*, whose storyline woven round an unwanted baby, appealed even to casual opera lovers. In the past, a number of OTC's more avant-garde choices drew some severe criticism from the paying public and one suspects that this did not go unheeded; the company has a role to play in Irish opera as some of its more imaginative works have shown.

Significantly, when *Jenufa* was presented for two nights at the Samuel Beckett Theatre TCD, it played to full houses, which seemed to bear out a theory of mine that Dublin needs a small theatre as a permanent home for opera. OTC's productions tend to attract an increasing number of young opera lovers, so one can appreciate the importance to them of more regular operatic performances of the kind they wouldn't experience at DGOS Opera Ireland's Gaiety seasons.

It is ironic, though, that at a time when Ireland has an abundance of vocal talent the opportunities in opera for singers have seldom been fewer. Because of inadequate funding, DGOS Opera Ireland has in more recent years been restricted to two short seasons, Spring and Winter, each consisting of eight performances of two different operas, which as Elaine Padmore, the Artistic Director up to 1993, pointed out to me, was unacceptable in a city the size of Dublin. She has taken over as artistic head of the Danish Royal Opera which presents more than 100 nights of opera in the year.

Lack of adequate funding has also meant that certain operas by Wagner, Massenet, Verdi and Gounod cannot be staged, which for opera-lovers remains a great disappointment. In operatic terms, too, it has caused musical stagnation and unless the trend is reversed large-scale Verdi works will have to be sacrificed for 'repeats' of *Boheme*, *Butterfly*, *Carmen* and *Traviata*. Nonetheless, there are a few more hopeful signs on the operatic horizon. The 1993 Winter Season was a financial and artistic success, with a number of people failing to get tickets for the popular production of *Boheme*. The success of Delibes' *Lakmé* also augured well for the future, and suggested that the French repertoire could be exploited.

However, as the year 2000 approaches, it would appear that Irish artists will, for the most part, have to continue to look for opportunities overseas and live outside their own country, but at least they are qualified to hold their own with their foreign colleagues. In the chapters ahead, you will read how a number of them have succeeded in Britain and the Continent. In another respect, if this book inspires a new generation of Irish singers to emulate the achievements of the past as well as the present generations, it will have achieved one of its main purposes.

Chapter One

Joseph O'Mara

THE 'IRISH CARUSO'

'**M**y early life was wild, harum-scarum. A devil-may-care was I, and I fear the passing years have not materially changed me but, after all, I come from Limerick.'

Years ago, famous tenor, Joseph O'Mara, made this frank admission when asked by T.P. O'Connor, his London-Irish parliamentary friend, to contribute to his paper. And in the same vein, O'Mara added, 'I was convinced that a life on the ocean wave was the only life for me, so I shipped as an apprentice on board a liner sailing from Dundee to Calcutta. I saw myself as captain of a Cunarder in a year or two. I will not dwell on all I endured on that voyage, suffice to say I returned home totally cured.'

James O'Mara, his father, was the owner of a prosperous bacon factory in Limerick and had hoped that his son would join it, but early on he became only too aware of Joseph's restless disposition.

The O'Mara home was a happy one. 'I was born with a great love of music', the boy would say later on in life. 'I remember my mother's voice which though untrained, was full of purity and sweetness. Hearing her sing folk songs was a delightful treat that never failed to lure me away from the nefarious pursuits upon which I was usually engaged.'

He was born on 16 July 1864, the second youngest of a family of 13 and became a pupil of the local Jesuit College. Despite his wild escapades, he found time to sing in a church choir and was encouraged by his teachers who recognised the potential in his voice.

Joseph was only 14 when his mother died. It was a cruel blow and he took time to get over the trauma. After his short-lived sea voyage, he accepted his father's offer to join the family bacon factory and also resumed singing with St. Michael's Choir. However, he saw a notice of a forthcoming examination for a scholarship at the Royal College of Music, London, and without telling his father he crossed over to England and presented himself for examination.

He was the first of the 30 candidates to sing and was afterwards asked by Sir George Groves whether in the event of his getting the scholarship his father would be able to support him during his career at the college. O'Mara's angry response amused the examiners. 'My father', he retorted, 'could support every student in the college.' They had been impressed enough by his singing to ask again, 'You are quite sure Mr. O'Mara that your father will pay everything necessary?' Unguardedly, young O'Mara replied, 'Oh! I have no doubt he will if I ask him.' He then had to admit that he had come over without his father's knowledge.

He afterwards said, 'I do not know that I would have won the scholarship, but certainly the doubt about my father's willingness to support me destroyed any chance I had.'

However, he had done well enough to justify him in thinking that he might succeed as a singer. He told his father all that had happened and asked permission to follow his true vocation. James O'Mara was sympathetic and saw the futility of keeping his son in the bacon business, but at the same time he pointed out to him the precarious life before him. He feared also that he was not robust enough for such an arduous career.

At this time, Joseph fell in for a small legacy, so feeling very independent – and with his father's blessing – set off for Milan on New Year's Day, 1889. He soon found an able voice coach in Signor Moretti who came to admire his natural tenor voice. Joseph's life fell into a fixed pattern and he grew to like the volatile and warm-hearted Italians. He kept in close touch with home.

'My days are full', he wrote his father. 'I get up early every morning, breakfast at eight o'clock, then go for a walk. Afterwards, I have books in Italian to study and before noon I have voice lessons with Signor Moretti. I have another walk, then luncheon followed by more lessons. Dinner is at six. Four evenings of the week, I take myself to opera at La Scala.'

In March 1890 he experienced his first crisis. He wrote home: 'Last week I was within a pip of throwing in the sponge and going home. I went to my lesson one day and didn't have the vestige of a singing voice. There and then I told Signor Moretti I'd give up singing and shake the dust of Milan off my shoes. I was in the deepest blues. Moretti argued, scolded and cajoled until I was persuaded to remain a week and test, which I did. Thank goodness my voice is restored and I'm ready for work to-morrow.'

After two years in Milan, O'Mara returned to Limerick more determined than ever to get on with his career. Hearing of a new opera being put on by the D'Oyly Carte in London, he applied for an audition. This was arranged and took place before Richard Carte, founder of the company. When O'Mara asked him for his verdict, Carte said, 'Promising ... very promising indeed. I would like you to come back to-morrow and sing for Sir Arthur.'

'Sir Arthur whom ...?'

'Sir Arthur Sullivan, of course.'

Despite his faux pas, O'Mara was successful. He was engaged to share the title role in Gilbert & Sullivan's new opera, *Ivanhoe* with Ben Davies – then Britain's finest tenor. It was the breakthrough he needed and soon his voice attracted wide notice and he received many concert engagements. He decided, however, to return to Milan to complete his training in Italian opera and took lessons from Signor Perini.

In 1893 while on holiday in Limerick he received a telegram from Sir Augustus Harris asking him to contact him at once. O'Mara lost no time and was told he was wanted for productions of *Cavalleria Rusticana*, *Pagliacci* and *Faust*, apparently having to go on without rehearsals. On tour with the company he also sang in *Carmen, Lohengrin* and *Meistersinger*. In October 1893 the company crossed the Channel to present a season at

Dublin's Gaiety Theatre. O'Mara was delighted with the opportunity to sing opera before his own people, and although the baritone in the performance of *Carmen* was hissed, the critic of the *Freeman's Journal* praised the tenor's singing of the Flower Song and his dramatic acting in the final scene.

As a company member, O'Mara was popular with his colleagues who enjoyed his puckish sense of humour and warm, if forceful character. He clashed with Sir Augustus Harris when he refused to take the leading role in Irish composer Sir Charles Standford's new opera, *Shamus O'Brien* because he considered it an almost entirely acting part. Sir Augustus was highly indignant and spoke of 'young puppies who did not know on which side their bread was buttered.' Rather than be thought ungrateful, the tenor agreed to play the role if Stanford would write in a special song for him. This was how "Oh! Ochone when I used to be young" came to be written.

In that same year 1896 he married a Miss Power from Waterford, of whom little is known. O'Mara was 32 and, as a singer, enjoyed growing popularity. A year later they set sail together for America where O'Mara was engaged to sing the tenor lead in *The Highwayman*. From all accounts his fine voice and acting ability so impressed impresarios that he was offered attractive concert and operatic work but turned the offers down; he longed to be nearer Ireland.

Back in Britain he was not short of engagements. It was the age of oratorios, concerts and musical 'at homes' and he soon sang in houses of note. One of these musical evenings was given by the Duchess of Manchester, at which O'Mara was introduced to Prince Edward, to be crowned Edward VII shortly afterwards. The artists at the evening's concert included Melba, Paderewski, Kubelik and O'Mara. And around this time, he was associated with the outstanding singers and instrumentalists of the day – Patti, Jean and Edouard de Reszke, Caruso, Tosti, John Coates, Clara Butt, Hamilton Harty, Sir Henry Wood and Coleridge Taylor.

But opera was really the tenor's first love and in 1902 he joined the Moody-Manners Company, one of the most respected in Britain and toured with them for some years. From Germany came Herr Richard Eckhold, the Wagner conductor who brought with him Toni Seiter as leading mezzo, and the Dutch tenor Philip Brozel who was outstanding. O'Mara appeared with the company in the autumn season at Covent Garden, September 1902, during which he sang Firmiano in one new work, Pizzi's *Rosalba* with Fanny Moody and Francis Maclennan, and Manrico in *Il Trovatore* and *Faust*. The following year he sang there again in *Maritana*, *Romeo et Juliette* and in a new native opera, *The Cross and the Crescent*. In Dublin in 1903 he was the tenor lead in *The Tinker and the Fairy* by Esposito, at the time professor of piano at the Royal Irish Academy of Music. Always a firm favourite with Irish audiences, he went on to achieve a number of operatic 'firsts' in Ireland. He was the first tenor to sing Enzo in *La Gioconda* and in 1908 the first Rodolfo in *La Bohème*. Later he was the first to sing Cavaradossi in Ireland and in the same season was in the Irish premiere of *Samson et Dalila*.

Ever on the move, O'Mara, accompanied by his wife, returned to New York to take the tenor lead in a musical *Peggy Machree* and received such enthusiastic notices in the press that two Dublin papers quoted from them at length.

Under the heading, IRISH TENOR'S TRIUMPH, Ashton Stevens in the *New York Journal* wrote:

'There is an Irish Caruso at the Broadway Theatre and his name is Joseph O'Mara and in a ballad he can sing a sure straight note that hits the heart; he is a real tenor, something of the reedy sweetness of the clarinet, sweetness without cloying his treble voice. He is a virile singer and most of his music in *Peggy Machree* is recruited from the good old virile love songs of Ireland.'

The *Journal of Commerce* commented: 'One of Joseph O'Mara's first lines in *Peggy Machree* is "Ye'll not get such a welcome as that outside of Ireland", but the warmth of the welcome given him last night at the Broadway Theatre by the loyal Irish and others must have made him very doubtful of that statement; in fact in a little curtain speech at the end of the second act he said "it was worth coming from Ireland for" and was presented with a wreath - a green one - with intertwined Irish and American flags."

But even O'Mara must have been amused by the review of the musical in *The World*, which described him as 'the only Irish comedian of the present day, alleged or real, whose songs have the flavour of the shamrock and convey to his hearers the aspirations, hopes, joys and sorrows of the land from which he spring.'

The *New York Herald*, whose critiques were generally highly valued, remarked, 'If there is any Irish man or woman in New York who was born in Ireland or whose ancestors were Irish, or who ever was in Ireland, that man or woman ought to go to the Broadway Theatre, to see and listen to Mr. O'Mara's presentation of Patrick Bidwell's new romantic musical comedy. When the clever Irish actor-singer was forced by an enthusiastic audience to make a speech he said that he and his company had tried to present a play that was good, clean and wholesome. He might truthfully have added that they had been entirely successful.'

Apart from the nostalgia the musical evoked among the Irish in particular, there was no mistaking the splendid impression O'Mara had made. 'A voice full of feeling', wrote one music critic, and a colleague added, 'A voice rare in its appeal.' There is no doubt that if the tenor had cared to stay in America for a year or more, he would have become a wealthy man. He agreed to sing in the musical at the Park Theatre in Boston and during his stay in the city he and his wife were special guests of the Gerald Griffin Club which was composed of Limerick men and women.

On his return to London, he joined the Thomas Beecham Company in 1909 and a few months later was back on the Covent Garden stage singing in *The Tales of Hoffmann* - a role he shared with Walter Hyde - and *Faust*. In that same year Beecham revived *Shamus O'Brien* at His Majesty's Theatre and the *Irish Times* London correspondent commented: 'Mr. Joseph O'Mara returns to play the part of Mike, the informer, and his fine voice was heard to the greatest effect. In the "Begging Song" he scored a notable success and was several times recalled at the end of the act and a wreath of laurels was presented to him.'

As a concert artist, he was also in demand. The same paper reported on a 1909 London concert appearance: "Mr. Joseph O'Mara, who received a hearty reception contributed a group of Irish songs, "The Birds Fly South", "My Lagan Love" and "The Heather Glen". As a song interpreter his well-known gifts are highly appreciated, the tenderness which he infused into the strains of "The Birds Fly South" sinking to the faintest pianissimo sounds was a revelation to the audience, and the singular brightness of his vocalism in "The Heather Glen" evoked applause from every part. After the interval he sang "Celeste Aida" with highly dramatic effect and was obliged to add an encore, "I'll sing thee songs of Araby."

For touring purposes he formed his own concert party. Monday, 20 February 1911 found him at the Town Hall, Ballina, Co. Mayo. His party included Angelo Fronani, the celebrated pianist. He was loudly applauded when he sang "On the Road to Castlebar" and as an encore "Believe Me". On the operatic side the tenor gave an intensely dramatic rendering of "On with the Motley". In the same week he and his party, which included the Covent Garden soprano Edith Evans and New Zealand contralto Irene Ainsly were accorded a rousing reception at the Theatre Royal in Limerick.

The year 1912 was to be a highlight in Joseph O'Mara's career. Limerick people rejoiced when he was accorded the Freedom of the City, an honour they felt he richly deserved, for in their eyes he was their ambassador of song. Bands played at the railway station to greet his arrival and he and his wife were conveyed in an open, horse-drawn carriage through the city streets. The tenor counted the experience as one of the proudest moments of his life.

In the same year he formed the Joseph O'Mara Opera Company and recruited a number of Irish singers, including Henry O'Dempsey, tenor, and his soprano wife, Kathleen McCully, mezzo Florence Cahill and baritone John Browne. They were cast with O'Mara in *The Lily of Killarney*, where in the kitchen scene the tenor always interpolated an Irish ballad, more often than not "Oft in the Stilly Night" or "The Derry Air".

For his first Dublin season, October 1913 he opened singing Raoul in *The Huguenots*. The company missed Dublin in 1914 because of the out-break of war. In February 1915, however, he returned for two weeks with the special attraction of Zelie de Lussan as guest artist in her renowned role of Carmen, which she sang four times, supported by O'Mara, Lewys James and Florence Morden. De Lussan had been singing the part since the 1880s and was now on her final tour.

By 1919 the O'Mara Company was so popular in Dublin that it was engaged for four weeks in February and another four in June and this con-tinued for several years, despite the fact that the Carl Rosa Company also gave three weeks opera in the autumn. From this period onwards O'Mara produced many interesting works, notably Puccini's *Manon Lescaut* in which he also sang; *Mignon*, *A Masked Ball*, *La Wally* (Catalani), *Tristan and Isolde*, *Orpheus* (Gluck) and Mozart's *Seraglio*. Another revival was Balfe's *The Rose of Castile* which proved quite a hit. During these years the O'Mara Company appeared with great success at the Opera House, Cork and the Theatre Royal, Limerick. Usually on arrival at the railway station in Limerick he and the company were welcomed by a brass band and the tenor himself sometimes sang an aria from *The Bohemian Girl* or *Maritana* to the waiting crowd.

The year 1924 saw him introduce a complete novelty in *Der Evangelimann* by the Austrian composer Wilhelm Kienzl, which had a splendid singing/acting role for O'Mara, who produced it for a few sea-sons but as with *La Juive*, a good deal of its success was due to the tenor's masterly characterisation. When the company visited Liverpool the local Rabbi went to see *La Juive* and was so thrilled by O'Mara's acting as the old Jew Eleazar that he presented him with a Jewish garment and jewelled dagger which the tenor afterwards always wore when doing the role.

Considering that opera today is heavily subsidised, the question will inevitably be asked as to how the O'Mara company managed to operate on box-office receipts alone. The fact was that in Dublin, Cork and Limerick the company normally performed to full houses. Was the staging then substandard?

'There was nothing shoddy about the O'Mara productions', a Dublin lady, Mrs. Harriet Simpson, would recall later. 'They were well dressed, the scenery was perfectly adequate, and taken all round were satisfactory performances of a very big repertoire. For a touring company, O'Mara's was a first-class show all round.'

By now he was acknowledged as an outstanding actor-singer. His Canio was unforgettable. As one critic wrote, 'With his heart-broken sobs, he could tear passion to tatters and at the same time never exaggerate the character.' Like many artists who excelled in tragic parts, the tenor could also extract the last ounce of humour from roles that lent themselves to mirth, such as Myles na-gCopaleen in *The Lily of Killarney* and Mike Murphy in Stanford's *Shamus O'Brien*. Sir Charles Stanford told of one occasion when he was conducting his opera and O'Mara was in exuberant form and so funny were his antics that Sir Charles became quite doubled up with laughter and unable to conduct. He had to lay down his baton, the orchestra ceased playing and also commenced to roar with laughter along with the entire audience; and only when all had recovered and the uproar ceased could the opera proceed.

Yet the critic of the *Irish Times* in February 1918 observed: 'Mr. O'Mara's Lohengrin is to my mind one of his best parts; it is not hurricane passion like Tannhauser, it demands a purer vocalism, a quiet dignity, a calm and spiritual character, and yet, at the back of it all, an abundance of reserve power. This is what we get from Mr. O'Mara; we never lose sight of the fact that his Lohengrin has come from another sphere and that no earthly Prince has power to restrain him, O'Mara sang his music with such dignity.'

The tenor went on to sing the title role in Harold A. White's new-opera, *Shaun the Post* to such effect that White, then a prominent Dublin music critic, stated, 'O'Mara's success as Shaun was electrifying. He gave the character more humour, more romance, more dramatic significance than I ever dreamt could be put into it.'

O'Mara had evidently prepared the role meticulously, and in numbers such as his "Leprechaun" song in the first act and the meditation in prison, where he sang "The Derry Air", his performance was excellent.

He was by now in his middle fifties and Shaun the Post was the last new role he attempted. But his voice remained in good shape, as was evidenced in a revival of *Shamus O'Brien*, when one Dublin critic wrote, 'Seeing and hearing Mr. O'Mara last night, it was easy to understand the popularity of this opera and the extent of the tenor's reputation when both were at their biggest.'

Such was his secure vocal technique that he experienced no real difficulty in tackling either light or dramatic roles. Occasionally his puckish Limerick humour got the better of him, as when he sang Myles na-gCopaleen he liked to pull funny faces at the prima donna whenever possible without the audience seeing him. Once, as one of the lovers in *Romeo et Juliette*, he stood before the Friar to be married and persisted in tickling the poor Friar's bare feet with the long feather in his hat.

On another occasion, he was singing Faust and wasn't feeling very well, so he sent his dresser out for brandy. It was close to closing time and the pubs were shut by the time the dresser got there. Back in the theatre, he waited in the wings until O'Mara caught his eye and he indicated to him 'no brandy.' At that moment as Martha sang, "Oh, distressing news ... grief beyond expression", O'Mara burst into laughter and was obliged to finish the scene with his back to the audience.

Altogether he sang in 67 operas. A prodigious worker, he was blessed with an exceptional musical memory. He could prompt either soprano, contralto, baritone or bass in any one of the operas in which he sang. Because of his innate acting ability it was agreed that if ever he lost his voice he could have earned a good living as an actor. During the peak of his career, he never lost touch with Ireland. He judged singing competitions several times in Dublin and Sligo and to this day the O'Mara Cup is competed for at the Dublin Feis Ceoil.

After he retired the company was taken over by Cynlaid Gibbs (who had been a tenor in it) and run under his name. Still later it reverted to the

O'Mara Opera Company and as such made its last appearance at the old Cork Opera House. Incidentally, it was in Cork years before that O'Mara gave his first operatic recital, singing excerpts from *Trovatore*. 'A voice of rare quality', summed up one local critic. 'Mr. O'Mara can look forward to a very bright future.'

When he died in Dublin on 5 August 1927 the newspapers stated, 'Death has removed the greatest figure in the Irish musical world, a great singer and the greatest force behind grand opera in Ireland.'

Unfortunately, he left behind few, if any, worthwhile recordings, certainly none by which to assess the true merit of his operatic singing. Listening to him sing, for instance, "The Heather Glen" gives no clue to a voice that we are told thrilled audiences in roles such as Don Jose and Manrico; no hint either of the tenor who so impressed Covent Garden audiences in *The Cross and the Crescent* in September 1903. One can only assume that O'Mara's voice possessed the range, depth and colour to cope with such contrasting roles as Samson, Canio, Hoffmann and Lohengrin. Looking at old photographs of the tenor, showing a solid frame and broad shoulders, one feels he had the physical stamina for Wagnerian roles.

O'Mara's manager, it appears, was bitterly disappointed with the quality of his recordings. 'They are libels on that lovely voice' he once declared.

In the final analysis, the tenor has to be judged on his stage record and there is no denying its merit. He sang with many of the finest singers of his day and more than held his own. In addition, he was the quintessential Irishman who thought nothing of accepting a concert date in Ennis while at the same time rehearsing a new operatic role for Covent Garden.

In Limerick his name is not entirely forgotten, though he is surely worthy of greater recognition. A small plaque on the facade of the house where he was born, and which today is known as Ozanam House, the headquarters of the local St. Vincent de Paul Society, is the only reminder of one of Limerick's most famous sons.

Would not a bursary in his name, awarded, say, annually to a talented young Limerick singer or instrumentalist, be more lasting and appropriate?

Chapter Two

John McCormack

MUSEUM IN HIS HONOUR

If Liam Breen was money-minded, he could undoubtedly have cashed in on his unique private John McCormack Museum. This amiable County Wexford man has preferred instead to share the pleasures of the museum with his friends and genuine music-lovers; in fact, he is always happy to act as their unpaid guide.

It was an April afternoon in 1994 and we were talking in the sitting room of his bungalow home in Sutton, County Dublin. 'It's time', he said eventually, 'that I showed you round the museum.' I had heard vaguely about it but had no idea what it looked like.

Proudly he led the way into the hallway and from an aperture in the ceiling overhead a small steel ladder dropped onto the floor beside us. Breen's was the first foot on the rung. For a man of 80, who more than a decade before had suffered a heart attack, he climbed easily to the top of the ladder. In a moment I joined him above and together we surveyed the scene.

At a glance, it resembled an Aladdin's cave, except that in this case it was packed with John McCormack memorabilia; it was more spacious than one could have imagined, yet retained an engaging intimacy. The windows in the relatively low ceiling let through ample light to allow a thorough inspection of the interior.

Breen, in a softly-spoken voice, began a quiet commentary: 'I myself converted this attic into a museum, mainly because I had no place else in the house to display all the items you see before you. It has taken me thirty-six years to collect them and I can personally thank the McCormack family for making many of them available to me. John's son, Cyril, was very generous and gave me some priceless items, including his father's gold wedding ring. It's inscribed Giovanni, which is John in English. And one afternoon at his home in County Wicklow, where my wife and I used to go for Sunday lunch, he dropped into my hand Count John's Prince Albert gold watch chain. It was his thanks to me for keeping his father's memory alive in Ireland.'

As he spoke, he proudly held the gold chain in his hand, then passed over to me McCormack's gold wedding ring. At a nearby stand he pointed to a silver matchbox the tenor had won playing a friendly game of tennis in California. There was the gold-plated cigarette case presented by him to his wife, Lily McCormack, as well as his own pigskin wallet; and on a small stand the original copy of the famous song, "I Hear You Calling Me" dated May 1914. It would become synonymous with McCormack who rarely left it out of a concert programme.

There were reminders around us of people and places in his life and career: a photograph of a crowded concert hall in Melbourne with Dr. Vincent O'Brien, his celebrated accompanist, at the piano; close by a photograph of violinist, Fritz Kreisler with the inscription, 'To dear John McCormack from a devoted friend, Fritz Kreisler'; a fine photograph of popular Italian tenor Beniamino Gigli, and others of Teddy Schneider, his American piano accompanist in many overseas recitals; renowned boxer, Jack Dempsey, and Irish film actress, Maureen O'Sullivan whom the McCormacks first met in Hollywood and afterwards became firm friends.

As Liam Breen picked out a striking photograph of the tenor singing at his farewell concert at the Albert Hall in November 1938, he remarked with typical good humour, 'I have a story about that suit John is wearing. A few years ago a young tenor from England called here to see the museum and when he tried on the jacket and trousers they fitted him like a glove. He offered to do a charity concert without a fee for me if I loaned him the outfit for the evening. All I can say is that we had a wonderful concert and he even told the audience in the Mansion House, Dublin how he came to be wearing the suit.'

He reached across to a wardrobe and took out the suit and asked me to try on the jacket; it was a good fit. For its age, the suit was in good condition, if somewhat faded. 'Cyril McCormack gave me that as well as those operatic costumes you see over there', he said. One of the costumes was worn by the tenor when he sang his first Faust in Dublin in 1907: the other was for the role of Edgardo in Donizetti's *Lucia di Lammermoor*. But the most striking costume on display showed him as Cavaradossi in Puccini's *Tosca*, wearing a long cape, tightly-fitting trousers and top boots.

Neatly displayed on a long stand in the middle of the room were copious press cuttings, including reviews of concerts in America, Japan and European cities. There were newspaper reminiscences by Lily McCormack recalling her husband's early years in Dublin and London and his Covent Garden debut as Turriddu in *Cavalleria Rusticana*, which had made McCormack at 23 the youngest tenor ever to sing a major role in that opera house.

We made our way to the far corner of the room where were hung a number of papal uniforms, a solemn reminder of the many honours heaped upon McCormack. Pope Benedict XV has, for example, made him a Knight Commander of the Order of St. Gregory the Great, also of the Order of the Holy Sepulchre.

'I count myself fortunate to have some of these uniforms', Breen said as he took one carefully from a hanger. 'It was in the Eighties and I remember Cyril McCormack telling me one day that some papal uniforms had been stolen and he was concerned about them. Not long afterwards, I got a 'phone call at my home and a young man with a rough-edged voice said to me, "Aren't yous the fella that runs the John McCormack Society? I want yous to know that I have his uniforms."'

'He had taken me by complete surprise. He wanted to know if I was interested in buying them. I told him I'd have to see them first. He agreed to meet me the following day in Crumlin. In the meantime, I telephoned Cyril McCormack and told him the uniforms had surfaced and if I should inform the garda authorities. He asked me to make no fuss about the matter. If you want to buy them, he said, you have my permission to do so, so I replied, fair enough.

'As arranged, I visited the man's home a week later and was met at the door by a large woman. I explained my business, but she gave me a curious look and said her son was at work. Then, she blurted, "Oh, God, his father will kill him for this!" She muttered something about her husband having the uniforms in a tin box. I felt I was being conned.'

Breen drove home to Sutton convinced that this was the last he would hear about the uniforms. He was disappointed as he wanted them for his museum. However, a year later he was surprised to receive a 'phone call from a man who enquired if he was still interested in the uniforms. He said he was and the caller agreed to come to his house within days. Eventually he arrived with a second man in a Toyota car and parked outside the bungalow. One man got out, opened the boot, and took out a bundle of clothing.

'I recognised the papal uniforms immediately', Breen recalled. 'Inside the house we talked about a price and one man said, "We don't want them, they should be yours." He agreed to hand them over to me for the price of a few drinks. Since I wasn't a drinking man all I could do was reach in my pocket and take out a ten pound note and asked if that was enough. I enquired where they had got the uniforms and they explained that they had been asked to empty one of the rooms in Cyril McCormack's wine store in the village of Blackrock and came across the uniforms. Believing that no one wanted them, they took them away.'

Breen looked at them and saw they were crumpled but not damaged. A good dusting down and some needlework would make them look respectable enough to display in the museum. It was the closest he had come to losing valuable memorabilia. He was ever on the lookout for McCormack items. As he said, 'Anything, even a bus ticket, I was prepared to have.'

We had not yet finished inspecting the museum. Going across to a small corner stand, he picked up two pencil sketches executed on the back of restaurant cards, depicting McCormack's head in a wine glass and Caruso's in another. He explained that as the tenors were dining together, either in Boston or London, Caruso saw a reflection of McCormack's face in one glass and his own in the other and could not resist the temptation to sketch them.

'I know that John treasured these sketches', Breen said. 'Cyril gave them to me for safe keeping.' The McCormack sketch bore the neat inscription, 'to my friend, McCormack.'

Among the most interesting memorabilia on display were the numerous posters recalling McCormack's operatic appearances in London and New York. Lily McCormack had confirmed years before that her husband's favourite role was Rodolfo in *La Boheme*.

At that moment Liam Breen pointed to a photograph of the tenor in Rodolfo's costume, and said, 'As you see, he has his hands in his pockets and this gives the photo a natural pose. Unlike other roles he sang, he considered the poet Rodolfo a down-to-earth human being. It is no secret that John didn't enjoy most of the roles he performed, mainly I understand because he regarded opera as false. Maybe his own moderate acting ability compounded this impression.'

I read with interest the posters recalling his performances at the Manhattan Opera House, New York, where his Alfredo in *La Traviata* was praised by the critics. His Violetta was the famed Italian soprano Luisa Tetrazzini and the elder Germont, the baritone Mario Sammarco. The trio had sung together in numerous operatic productions.

'John's happiest operas were with Tetrazzini, 'Lily McCormack recalled in her biography, *I Hear You Calling Me*, and she added:

'She was quite taken by my handsome young tenor and never tried to hide it, even from me. John was tremendously flattered by the Diva's attentions and their mutual regard worked out admirably for them both. They sang some of the most superb performances I have ever heard, breath for breath, note for note.'

She went on to tell the story of one particular Traviata performance:

'Tetrazzini was always very tightly laced and corseted. One evening for some unknown reason she left her corsets off. In the last act, when she is dying, John rushes in and grabs her in his arms. This particular evening he rushed in and grabbed, as he said himself, a huge bundle of fat, or what seemed like a couple of 'Michelin Tyres.' The surprise on his face started her laughing; then he started. He said he never knew how they got to the end of the act.'

New York critics expressed surprise at his repertoire for 'so young a tenor'. They listed his chief roles as Cavaradossi, Almaviva, Rodolfo, Alfredo, Duke of Mantua, Faust, Edgardo, Tonio (*La Fille du Regiment*) and Gerald (*Lakmé*). When he was first engaged by the Manhattan Opera in 1909, the critic of the *Telegraph* remarked, 'John McCormack has a real tenor voice handled with unusual skill and taste; it is of unusual richness, freshness and musicality. Be it understood that it is not either rapacious or explosive, but essentially lyric and tender. The impression he made on the audience was more than favourable, for the Americans love a good voice and order and self-repressive demeanour and obvious taste and training.'

To Liam Breen, it was an accurate assessment of the tenor's voice and it was true that he loved singing with Tetrazzini. 'There's a story told about her', he said, 'that she wouldn't always allow him to sing a top C where she could do it. Just open your mouth and let me sing', she'd say. 'You must save your voice and seemingly she meant it. It was not that she wanted the applause for herself; she was really thinking of John.'

Predictably in the copious newspaper and magazine reports displayed in the museum there was no whiff of scandal to tarnish the tenor's reputation; no reported clashes with malicious or vindictive prima donnas which, in themselves, would evoke little surprise in an operatic scene that even then abounded with spite and gossip. Breen felt that Lily McCormack's influence was a major factor in her husband's career and their happy marriage a decided help.

He said that McCormack as the years rolled on became a public celebrity and made friends with people outside the profession of singing. 'John lived an extraordinary full life as you can see from all those pho-

tographs around you. They show him at concerts in Berlin and Paris and
the Carnegie Hall. I don't think gossip or scandal greatly interested him.
In those early days in London and New York he lived for his family and for
singing.'

There was a photograph showing him in conversation with Sir Edward
Elgar. The caption on the photograph, which had been sent by the tenor
to the composer, read: 'With the affection and admiration of one who is
very proud to call you, Sir Edward, friend – John McCormack.'

When the men first met, the atmosphere was not cordial. Elgar went
backstage after a Birmingham performance of the *Verdi Requiem* in 1912
and told the soloists it was the worst interpretation he had ever heard.
'Who the hell is this major- general type?' snapped McCormack of a fellow soloist. On being told it was Elgar, he added, 'Thank God his music
is better than his manners!'

It was late afternoon by the time we descended the ladder and retreat-
ed to his tiny music-room on the ground floor. Different McCormack
biographies filled a row of shelves on a wall opposite and on a stand by the
window were scores of LPs and cassettes. 'Maybe it's time we heard John's
voice', Breen said with undisguised enthusiasm. As the first notes of "Una
furtiva lagrima" echoed in the room, I was reminded again of what the
great Jean de Reszke once said about McCormack, 'You are the true
redeemer of bel canto.'

Later, over coffee, he traced for me his association with the John
McCormack Society, which he said was founded in a Dublin public house
in the 1950s. 'In those days all of us were avid record collectors with
dozens of old McCormack 78s. We were determined to keep his memory alive and at the same time put strong pressure on record companies to
re-issue his best recordings. In time, we achieved this, so that today you
have available on CD the best of McCormack.'

From the outset, he said, the McCormack family were behind the new
society. Lily McCormack, John's widow – John had died at the age of 61
in Dublin in September 1945 – became their first president and Cyril

McCormack its first patron; Gwen McCormack, Cyril's sister, also took an active interest. Monsignor Arthur Ryan, a personal friend of the tenor, was happy to become a member of the society. Usually, he welcomed the tenor on his concert visits to Belfast and for years both men kept up a regular correspondence.

The society managed to create fresh interest in John McCormack. When Lily McCormack gave a talk to the society's members, Liam Breen remembered that she stressed her husband's human facets, like his love of family, his lifelong love of Ireland, and the sheer joy that singing – in particular concert work – afforded him.

'Lily always referred to him as "her John",' he said. 'Cyril was somewhat shy of publicity and preferred to keep out of the limelight, but we could always depend on his support. He was an excellent raconteur and an entertaining host.'

In time, Breen would become the society's treasurer and later its chairman. Soon he was busy giving talks up and down the country and was astonished by the interest in McCormack's life and singing career. He tried to vary the talks; one was titled, 'Around the World with John McCormack', another, 'The Life of John McCormack.' He used slides to illustrate the talks and the musical programme consisted of the tenor singing Irish ballads, popular songs and operatic arias; a few people requested his Leider repertoire.

Organisations sometimes invited him back a second time and he was amazed to discover that their enthusiasm even surpassed that of his previous visit. 'I couldn't understand it,' he recalled. 'They would listen for hours to John singing Victorian ballads and songs like "Kathleen Mavoureen", "I Hear You Calling Me" and "Somewhere a Voice is Calling". Opera only appealed to a minority of the audience, though they loved to hear him sing "When Other Lips" or arias and duets from *Traviata*, *Boheme* or *Carmen*.'

When RTE began to research a documentary on the tenor's life, Breen was asked to be an advisor and suggested to Tony Barry, the director, that Italian tenor, Guiseppe di Stefano, be among those interviewed. The interview took place in Savona where McCormack had made his operatic debut in the leading role of Mascagni's *L'Amico Fritz* in 1906.

Through the Seventies and Eighties Breen was satisfied that McCormack's name was being kept before the Irish public. Scarcely a week passed without a request to him to give a talk about the great tenor. In the early Nineties he went one better, when a truck conveyed his museum to Summerhill College in Sligo where it would go on view. Once again, he was astonished by the interest shown by the public. Years before he had supplied McCormack memorabilia to the National Concert Hall and more for display in Athlone, where the tenor had been born on 14th June, 1884. One of his greatest regrets is that the townspeople failed to preserve the house of his birth. As he said, 'It was an opportunity lost.'

Among the names in the museum's visitors' book was that of Dennis O'Neill, the Cardiff-based tenor who is popular with Irish audiences. Not only was he fascinated by the McCormack memorabilia on display, but downstairs listened enthralled to records of the tenor he had not heard before. Breen played for him arias by Delibes, Gounod, Verdi and Rossini, but two tenor arias from *Lucia di Lammermoor* merited most of his attention.

'One of them, "Fra poco a me" is a great favourite of mine', Breen said, 'and Dennis was absolutely taken by it, mainly because of John's mastery of the bel canto style, his breath control and lovely legato. He was convinced that he was an outstanding operatic singer and I was delighted to hear him say so, for too many people express their reservations of him in this respect.'

Which brought me to a question that I knew interested him. Why did he think McCormack retired before the age of 40 from the operatic stage?

'In his heart John felt that opera was false. There were other factors of course. He wasn't a very convincing actor and rehearsals never appealed to him. Vocally, he had no problems.'

I agreed. Yet it was puzzling that he should give up opera at the peak of his career. Today, Placido Domingo has operatic dates in his diary that will see him singing Verdi and Puccini operas after the age of 60. In view of that McCormack's decision is all the more surprising.

One can only assume that he did not need the money from opera, particularly since his phonograph recordings were already achieving phenomenal sales. In 1918, for instance, his royalties from that source amounted to 180,000 dollars, which was said to exceed even those of Caruso. His total income, it was claimed, was over 300,000 dollars a year. With Caruso and Kreisler, he was the mainstay of the ECA Company's Red Seal catalogue for a period of 25 years.

'There's another explanation', Liam Breen said. 'John wanted to devote all his spare time to concert recitals and to make more records. He was at the time singing to huge audiences.'

The tenor chose to make his farewell appearance with the Monte Carlo Opera in the year 1923. 'McCormack's appearance was eagerly awaited', recalled Dr. Tom Walsh, writing about Monte Carlo's 'opulent opera period' between the years 1920-1934. 'There was a glamour and glitter about the seasons there that was hard to match anywhere else in Europe, and of course they attracted a galaxy of stars.'

McCormack did not disappoint his admirers. The first performance ever in Monte Carlo of *Die Zauberflote* was distinguished by his singing as Tamino. One leading French critic described him as 'an impeccable artist with an excellent method and lovely style.'

After his performance as Cavaradossi in *Tosca*, a visiting critic stated: 'We must say at once that those of us who have been privileged to hear this impeccable singer at concerts were not disappointed. The voice is not large, it is the voice of a light tenor, extraordinarily well placed, to which study has given incredible suppleness, a voice which the artist used to perfection. The manner in which he sang the last act was a real feast of delicacy.'

During the same season he sang Pinkerton in *Butterfly*, Lionel in *Martha* and Almaviva in Rossini's *Barber,* but surprisingly it was in the first production of *La Foire de Sorotchintzi* by Mussorgsky that he excelled. The critic André Corneau wrote that McCormack had found his best role of the season. 'This opera provoked an enormous response, a tempest of cheers and bravos.'

It was McCormack's last performance on the operatic stage. 'Few singers have been acclaimed more perceptively or more fervently on their farewell appearance,' wrote Dr. Tom Walsh years afterwards. Which invites the question, why in his hour of operatic glory did the tenor turn his back on opera? Lily McCormack, in her biography, makes no reference to her husband's decision, despite the fact that he had written to her from Prague where he had given a recital before going on to Monte Carlo. Was his mind still undecided at the time? Or did Lily feel such a sensitive matter was best left to John himself? It is argued that John was finding difficulty in controlling his weight and was more conscious of it on the operatic than the concert stage; whatever the real reason he did, unlike some other tenors, get out as audiences clamoured for more. Perhaps he was wise.

After his death at his home in Dublin in 1945 more light was cast on his operatic career by way of tributes from colleagues. Edwin Schneider, his regular accompanist, recalled: 'I heard a performance of *Don Giovanni* when he sang with the Philadelphia Opera Company in Boston in 1913, and vividly remember conductor Felix Weingartner put down his baton and join in the applause after John's singing of "Il mio tesoro".'

To Dr. Vincent O'Brien, his first voice teacher in Dublin, his performance in the same opera, this time in London, was unforgettable. He was convinced that John was a great Mozartian singer. He also felt that his voice blended most beautifully with Nellie Melba's.

'He used to say to me that to listen to Melba's phrasing in "Mimi chiamamo" was one of the most wonderful experiences. He was like that in his appreciation. He selected something essential and revealing from the work of the artist and he could always repeat it. If he hadn't been the great artist he was he would have made a fortune as a mimic. He'd choose a cast for an opera, Melba, Caruso, all the great ones, and then he'd sit down at the piano and give us them all, a little of each, perfect imitation; he'd go up into the top register of the soprano, and he'd conduct it all. And the conductor would always be Toscanini. Toscanini was his idol. I remember once Toscanini was conducting *Aida* at the Met; Caruso was the

23

Radames. John bought three seats, right behind the conductor. He put me in the middle, Lily and himself on each side of me. He was entranced and wanted me to see every movement Toscanini made.'

On a broader note, the famous English critic Ernest Newman felt McCormack was the supreme example of the art that conceals art. 'I never knew him in public or his private singing to be guilty of a lapse of taste, of making an effort for mere effort's sake. He was a patrician artist, dignified even in apparent undress, with a respect for art that is rarely met among tenors.'

Singers today usually like to autograph programmes after their concert recitals, but not so McCormack who preferred to do so back in his hotel. Gerald Moore, who occasionally accompanied him on the piano, recalled: 'John was away and out of the hall in his car almost before the applause had subsided. It was in his hotel that his friends and admirers would gather; there I have met renowned conductors, singers, violinists, pianists, ambassadors, statesmen, writers, actors and actresses, even tennis players.

'On the day of a concert, John was unapproachable. He would not see anybody except his own immediate circle. Lily ensured that he had all the newspapers around him and his books. He conversed in whispers (an iron restraint on his part, for he was a vehement and explosive conversationalist). I'd tap on his door when the car arrived to take us to the concert; he would drink a cup of black tea and off we'd go - with me doing most of the talking to monosyllable replies from John. On arrival, he'd go through a crowd of autograph hunters like a knife through butter, as he refused to stand out in the cold and damp signing autographs just before he was due to sing - the programmes could be sent in to him and he'd sign them in his dressing-room.'

To Liam Breen the tenor was above all else a generous man, though like myself he had heard that McCormack was often too generous with his money to the bookies at Irish race meetings. 'They say he lost a small fortune', he said, breaking into a short laugh. But he was quick to add that the tenor had donated the proceeds of some of his Irish concerts to charity, and that included one in Athlone.

It was time to leave the friendly bungalow and its unique museum. There would be others eager to follow in my footsteps and identify with the country's greatest tenor. To Liam Breen, John McCormack was a thoughtful man, so I decided the best way, perhaps, to end this piece was to recall the words of Dorothy Caruso shortly after the death of her husband:

> I remember my first Christmas without Enrico. I did not know John McCormack well at that time, yet of all the millions who mourned my husband, it was John whose strong and simple sympathy lifted me from despair. He telephoned on Christmas Eve, and said, 'In case you are sitting alone tonight, Lily and I would like you to go with us to St. Patrick's midnight Mass and come back for a bit of supper afterwards. I went, and from that moment I no longer felt lost.

Chapter Three

Margaret Burke Sheridan

AN AFFAIR OF THE HEART

On her arrival in London from Milan in the early summer of 1925 Margherita Sheridan was greeted by the press as an established operatic star. As she stepped from the train at Victoria Station, she was quizzed by reporters about her background and her successes at La Scala, the San Carlo and other leading opera houses in Italy.

Six years before she had slipped into London a virtual unknown singer, but her performance in the title role of Mascagni's new opera *Iris* attracted the favourable attention of the critics who agreed that she stole the vocal honours of the evening. 'Margherita Sheridan's success as *Iris* augurs well for her career as a singer and actress,' noted *The Times*. In that same Covent Garden season of 1919 she scored a popular and artistic triumph as Mimi in *La Boheme*. With more experience, she was clearly a singer to watch in the future.

She was now 36 and her return to Covent Garden was eagerly awaited. In an accent, unmistakably Irish, she expressed delight at being back at the Garden and was quick to remind the reporters present that years before her compatriot John McCormack had triumphed there. Managing director of the theatre, Colonel Eustace Blois had engaged her to sing in *Madama Butterfly* and *Andrea Chenier*. The 48-year-old Blois, who had known her for a short time, was attracted to the soprano not only because of her beautiful voice but her shapely figure, quick wit and lively personality. For her part, she was taken by his love for music, especially opera, good humour and military bearing. From the outset, they discovered much in common and gradually their friendship developed into an affair. During his army days Blois had served with his regiment in Ireland and was taken by the Irish wit and spirit he encountered.

The only snag in their relationship was the Colonel's marriage and he was determined to remain a married man. This aspect of their affair began to trouble Margaret Sheridan, as she was known to her Irish and English friends, and induced in her a feeling of moral hang-up. She had had lots of admirers, but the tall, distinguished-looking Blois, with his cultured English accent and appealing grey-blue eyes, was a different matter. In no time he was advising her on business matters and opera house contracts.

To the extrovert Miss Sheridan, he was a steady and reassuring influence. However, his determination to keep their affair secret upset her and hurt her pride. But there was little she could do about it. Blois was a man of strong character who was accustomed to getting his own way. Aware how emotional entanglements could affect singers, she tried to compartmentalise her life, though she knew it wouldn't be easy.

Staying at the Savoy Hotel, she was in demand for newspaper interviews and she tried to be helpful. She recalled her days in Ireland, how within five years of her birth in Castlebar, County Mayo in 1889, she was left an orphan and for the next few years was reared by relatives; how she came to be a boarder of the Dominican Convent in Eccles Street, Dublin, and the good influence exerted on her by Mother Clement, who gave her singing lessons and taught her voice technique. It was a friendship that would endure for years.

For the pretty girl from Castlebar, they were carefree and happy days. In 1908 she entered for Dublin's Feis Ceoil and won the mezzo-soprano award. Her voice was regarded as 'very promising' by no less a musician than Dr. Vincent O'Brien. She went to London with powerful letters of introduction. Thanks to the active interest of T.P. O'Connor, Father of the House of Commons, she was heard and praised by an increasing number of influential people. She completed two years' study in the R.A.M. in July 1911.

Four years later, at the age of 26, Marconi, the renowned radio engineer, brought her to Rome, where he placed her in luxurious living quarters, after which he presented her to the celebrated teacher Alfredo Martino. His verdict on the Irish soprano's voice was that it had strong potential, but mainly because of faulty training, she had developed several bad habits, one of which was straining in the upper register. He promised her that if she did exactly as he directed he could eradicate those faults. She agreed she would, and so the hard grind began.

Margaret's first opportunity came in 1919 when famed soprano Lucrezia Bori, who was to sing Mimi in Rome, fell ill. The director of the opera house had heard the Irish singer and believed she could sing the Puccini part if she was prepared to rehearse and be note-perfect in time. Martino felt his pupil was being rushed. 'She is not yet ready', he protested. But the head- strong soprano accepted the offer and was a success in the opera. It was the beginning of her love affair with Italy. Not only did she commence lessons in Italian, but went back to her scales.

Shortly afterwards her Butterfly was acclaimed in Naples, and when she sang it at the Dal Verme in Milan the great Toscanini heard her and forecast that in time she would become one of its finest interpreters. More success followed. Billed as Margherita Sheridan in Italy, she sang in a revival of Catalani's *La Wally* at La Scala as well as Liu in *Turandot* and Lauretta in *Gianni Schicchi*. The critics liked her in all three productions.

Puccini went to Rimini to hear her in *Andrea Chenier*, which she sang with a promising new tenor named Gigli. The composer believed she would make an ideal Manon Lescaut and decided to coach her in the part. The premiere of the opera took place in August 1923 in Rimini and once again the Italian audience wildly applauded La Sheridan in the role of Manon. Puccini was said to be 'immensely pleased' by her performance, especially by the beauty of her singing in the fourth act.

Her career had taken on a new momentum. She was by now an acknowledged interpreter of Puccini's music and her striking good looks and warm personality endeared her to the Italian people. She moved in the best operatic and social circles. Toscanini booked her to appear again at La Scala and soon her presence there became a talking point. She had been interviewed in a Milan newspaper, during which she had expressed gratitude to Mussolini's government for allowing her, a foreigner, to make a career in Italy. Toscanini detested Il Duce for many reasons, not the least of them being that the Fascists were thwarting his own political ambitions.

During a rehearsal the soprano was not singing very well. While she was in the middle of an aria Toscanini banged the rostrum and called out, 'If you spouted less in political interviews you would be a better singer than you are.'

La Sheridan lost her temper. 'And if you dabbled less in politics you might be a greater conductor', she replied angrily.

By the time she arrived in London for the 1925 Covent Garden Italian season the story had preceded her. Privately she hoped her outburst would not affect her relations with La Scala, and in newspaper interviews tried to avoid the subject altogether. Her return to Covent Garden came about as a result of Nellie Melba's realisation that at 64 she was beyond singing young soprano parts.

The season was also significant for another reason - the out- standing Austrian soprano Maria Jeritiza would sing Tosca and Fedora. But Margaret's press notices would match those of Jeritiza. Commenting on her Butterfly, *The Times* critic wrote: 'How experience has ripened Margherita Sheridan's style. She sang the music finely and her whole treatment of the part grew in dramatic interest as the opera progressed.' Other critics referred to her 'beautiful singing' as well as 'the depth of the character she created.'

A few weeks later she sang Maddalena in *Andrea Chenier* with the tenor Giacomo Lauri-Volpi who was making his Covent Garden debut. The critics noted how together they thrilled the audience in the final dramatic scene. The opera was the highlight of that season and Margaret Sheridan's return to Covent Garden was hailed as an undeniable triumph.

Off-stage her love affair with Colonel Blois continued to occupy her mind and time. Although some friends and colleagues in London's social and operatic circles were aware of it they exercised discretion. The strain began to tell, however, on Margaret Sheridan, for such secrecy was alien to her outgoing personality and typical Irish loquaciousness. But Blois remained unmoved; he was not prepared to risk his marriage.

She confided in T.P. O'Connor, who told her, 'It is natural that you should think of love, that is human nature. It is in accord with all life. But don't let it get an obsession with you as I think it is getting to be.'

O'Connor's perception was correct. Margaret had become almost obsessional about the relationship and her moral dilemma was further evidenced by her words, 'I am suffering at the thought that I could become the lover of a married man.' Blois's letters to her compounded the dilemma even more, for he came to call her 'Peggy' and 'Paddy Darling' and his affection appeared unquestionable.

'Margaret's love for Blois was real', claimed Anne Chambers in her biography of the singer. 'Indeed, there was almost a sense of desperation about it, as if she were making one final attempt to capture an elusive dream. Her need for love and affection was great.'

Obviously T.P. O'Connor suspected the agony the singer was experiencing, when he wrote her, 'I pray that love may come and in the right way, the wrong way will never suit you and it would be a tragedy.'

He was no doubt thinking of her Catholic background and her possible scruples. He felt, too, perhaps that Blois would eventually divorce his wife for Margaret Sheridan and this was something he did not want to see happen. While he appreciated her private and deep sexual frustration, it was in his eyes more acceptable than an unhappy future.

When the late Conor O'Brien, the well-known Dublin journalist and opera-lover, profiled the soprano for *The Record Collector*, he was sceptical about the 'love affair'. I quote:

At this point the matter of Sheridan's 'romance' should be clarified if only to get rid of some of the fantasies that have grown up and have been published over the years. There was no lover, and certainly there was no Italian nobleman who entered a box in La Scala while she was singing and shot himself! The truth is far less colourful. An opera administrator at Covent Garden tried to persuade her into a live-in affair. He was married, so with Peggy's convent upbringing his chances of success were never strong. Nevertheless, she must have found him attractive, because she did not reject him straight away. Indeed, she obviously got into a moral tangle with her conscience.

O'Brien always held that Mother Clement's influence over Margaret Sheridan was profound and that she had set down the moral guidelines for the singer. As he said, 'In later years as Peggy was making a reputation in Italy, Mother Clement's pleasure was greatly modified by her anxiety for her moral welfare, and she prayed constantly that her protegee would be delivered safely from the fleshpots of Milan and Rome. This is not to mock her. It was the perfectly normal reaction of a caring guardian in those days and, knowing Peggy's flighty nature better than most, she had cause to be worried. Between two utterly different people there was the deep and abiding love of a mother and daughter, and it was this love rather than singing that was the dominant factor in their relationship.'

Whether Margaret Sheridan discussed her dilemma with Mother Clement we do not know, but the nun, one suspects, would have frowned on any improper relationship, especially the likelihood of Peggy ever marrying a divorced man. It was to T.P. O'Connor the soprano turned and wrote to him when she could or met him during her seasons at Covent Garden. He worried about the emotional strain the affair was obviously causing her.

Fortunately, it was not affecting her singing. Colonel Blois engaged her to open the Covent Garden summer season of 1926 in *La Boheme*, in which she was to score another popular success. King George V came to this production and afterwards met the singers. He struggled to make conversation with the largely Italian cast and then turned with some relief to Margherita Sheridan, as she was billed on the programme.

'Well, you have no language difficulty', the King said. 'You are English.'

She replied with some asperity, 'Sire, I am Irish!'

During that year she made some recordings for HMV, including "Ave Maria" from Verdi's *Otello* and "Un Bel Di Vedremo". Colonel Blois not only conducted the orchestra but signed the contracts for the singer with HMV. She had by now come to rely on Blois more and more in her business affairs.

On her return to Italy she sang performances of *Madama Butterfly* at the San Carlo in Naples, but a recurrence of her nose and throat infections tended to make her stay in the city uncomfortable. To her annoyance, she was also putting on weight and already the critics questioned her future suitability for roles such as Mimi and Butterfly. Nonetheless, she was heartened by offers from some leading opera houses in America. It had always been a source of puzzlement to her Italian colleagues that America wasn't a priority with her, as the majority of them jumped at the opportunity to sing in opera there.

The problem lay with Colonel Blois; he was set against the idea. 'I want you Paddy Darling for Covent Garden,' he would reassure her. In his letters he still pledged his love and liked to recall their happy times together on the Continent. He now regarded America as a threat to their continued happiness and refused to discuss the offers with her. For Margaret it was a golden opportunity lost to increase her earnings and ensure her future. What she needed was a strong agent to overrule the persuasive Colonel Blois, but in some respects she was naive. Later on she talked somewhat enviously of the 'fortune made by John McCormack in America' and one can only assume that she had enormous regrets.

She continued to divide her time between engagements in Italy and at Covent Garden. She sang 10 performances of Manon in *Manon Lesaut* in Brescia early in 1926, and in the spring was back at Covent Garden for three performances of Mimi in *La Boheme* and one of Lauretta in *Gianni Schicchi*. 1927 was a comparatively quiet year for her; in January she sang performances of Butterfly at the San Carlo and was as popular as ever. Later on in the year she was present at Covent Garden for John

O'Sullivan's debut there as Raoul in *Les Huguenots* and despite the poor production of the opera she was said to be impressed by the tenor's tonal quality and exceptional range. A year later she sang Mimi there partnered by one of her favourite tenors, Aureliano Pertile; she also sang Liu to the Turandot of Eva Turner, an artist she greatly admired.

'When I went to La Scala in 1924 Margaret was already established there and had made a great success especially in *La Wally*,' Miss Turner said later. 'She was very good-looking and had a most attractive personality.'

In 1929 Margaret Sheridan was back at Covent Garden in a highly important season for her. She sang Manon there for the first time in a revival of *Manon Lescaut* and with a cast that included the tenor Pertile. The critics' response was enthusiastic, with *The Times* noting 'how Miss Sheridan highlighted the subtle qualities of the character'. Another daily newspaper critic commented, 'Last night Margaret Sheridan and Signor Pertile gave their duets in superb style, each artist in splendid voice and blending their singing most effectively.'

The death in September 1929 of her friend T.P. O'Connor was a blow, for the veteran parliamentarian had always listened sympathetically to Margaret's troubles, even if she had ignored his advice to break with Colonel Blois. In recent months Blois's behaviour had caused her growing anxiety. As the Covent Garden squabbles with Sir Thomas Beecham and Bruno Walter took up more of his time, she saw less and less of him. He seemed to be solely preoccupied with his work to the exclusion of almost everything else.

The inner anguish she suffered appeared to take the sheen off her operatic successes in London and in Italy. For the first time she felt a sense of embitterment towards the man she loved. Blois sensed this embitterment. After a short holiday together in Italy, he wrote her, 'If our future is to be what we have planned it to be, it must not, Paddy darling, be subjected to the risk of embitterment.' And, as usual, he ended his letter with a pledge of love: 'I told you that I love you, as I always have and that there had never been anyone else for me and that there never would be and that, therefore, in spite of all our obstacles, I wanted as much of you and your life as was possible.'

The relationship was still on his terms. At no time had he discussed a possible divorce from his wife; indeed, he was not above reminding Margaret Sheridan that his marriage remained the biggest obstacle to their total happiness together. While he selfishly played with her emotions, he continued to advise her on her business affairs. He saw to it that she sang with the finest singers of the day at Covent Garden, and in the summer of 1930 she was engaged to sing in *Andrea Chenier* opposite Beniamino Gigli. The evening was a triumph for both singers.

She went on to sing Butterfly to some mixed reviews. Due to illness she was forced to retire after the first act. But she recovered in time to take over from Iva Pacetti in Verdi's *Otello* and won over the critics with her 'pure singing' as Desdemona. It would be her last performance at Covent Garden.

She was now 41 and entering the final chapter of her career. Back in Italy, she had been asked to sing in Puccini's *Gianni Schicchi* at a gala performance in Rome in honour of a royal wedding. It was an occasion of glittering social splendour attended not only by royalty, but also by many of the giants of Italian music. La Sheridan cracked unexpectedly over several high notes and at the end of the opera she collapsed. She never sang in public again.

She was obliged to cancel important concert dates, but was able to record a few Irish songs for HMV. She continued to be dogged by nose and throat complaints and in 1932 had a throat operation in Milan. In London she no longer stayed at the Savoy Hotel but with her close friends Sir Samuel and Ginnie Courtauld. By now she had become totally disenchanted with Colonel Blois and felt it was at last time to consider ending their relationship.

Margaret Sheridan had become disillusioned by his pledges of love and above all his refusal to make real sacrifices on her behalf. He continued to carry on the affair in his own way. Yet, in the final analysis, the question must be faced that if Blois had agreed to divorce his wife for his 'Paddy darling' as he never ceased to call Margaret, would she have dared to join him in matrimony? I have received conflicting answers to that question and not surprisingly so, for the soprano often seemed perplexed by her religious obligations on the one hand and on the other her deeply felt emotional needs.

In one of her last letters to Blois, she wrote with a strange mixture of bitterness and disillusionment: 'I messed up everybody and everything just to dedicate myself to you and this against my judgment, my principles, religion, life, everything.'

In the middle of her trauma, she turned to prayer. In Soho one day she went into St. Patrick's Church where she prayed for guidance. When she emerged into the street she looked back towards the church and saw the sun directly behind the cross. She decided this was the divine sign she had been looking for, and so ended the affair. She described it as 'the most important decision of her life'.

Colonel Blois had his own problems at Covent Garden contending with the whims of the autocratic Beecham and his own failing health. In the middle of planning the 1933 international season he was taken ill and died suddenly. The musical world was shocked. Margaret Sheridan, who was still not over the ending of their affair, hardly knew what to think. Her friends assured her that he had loved her. All she could think was the emotional strain the affair had caused her.

Determined to sing again, she was persuaded to visit a voice clinic in Salzburg (Lehmann was there at the same time), but if this did anything for her it cannot have been enough. By 1934 she was in London and in the care of E. Herbert-Caesari, a singing teacher and a prolific writer on vocal technique. To judge by his writings on the soprano he was totally besotted by her singing and her personality. He described how 'a devastating emotional upheaval had obviously shattered all faith in herself and her will to return to public performance.'

This conclusion must have been no less than the truth. In fact, years later in Dublin people would talk of the singer 'losing her nerve'. She stayed under Caesari's care until the outbreak of the second World War, when she returned to Dublin.

Writing about her progress in 1939, he stated: 'Her voice was as sound as a bell with not the slightest symptom or sign of wear or age in it. The quality was truly exquisite and more than ever evident as a result of her technical studies.'

In the next sentence, Caesari came to the real source of the problem: 'If only certain inhibitions could have been uprooted and mental adjustments crystallised there was nothing whatever to prevent her returning to her well-loved opera stage. The desire was now there, but not the full will. At times, where singing was concerned, she could be revealed as fearful, hesitant, self- doubting, everything the exact opposite of herself.'

On her return to Dublin she renewed acquaintance with Mother Clement, but by now the nun was old and in poor health. To the dismay of friends Margaret cancelled a big concert tour organised by theatre man Louis Elliman. The excuse she gave was that she was 'resting'. Not long after this her self-confidence must have been restored somewhat, for she agreed to record some songs, though she insisted she did not want it talked about. Terry O'Connor, an astute musical judge, assembled a small orchestra with as much secrecy as possible.

During the preliminaries Margaret Sheridan told Terry that her top notes had gone and all her songs would have to be brought down. When the recordings began the transpositions were, in fact, quite considerably down. Terry recalls: 'I had expected a mezzo sound and that she would probably be in trouble above and below. She wasn't too secure on top, which I think was due to a lack of confidence, what really surprised me was the richness of her voice in the lower passages. She produced a genuine contralto sound without the slightest difficulty.'

When the war ended she was 56. Needing the loyal and comforting reassurances of Caesari, she went to London where, for almost a year, she visited the studio regularly. Her singing continued to captivate him. In his searching profile of the soprano for *The Record Collector*, Conor O'Brien recalled her return to Dublin in 1946:

It was probably the start of the most demoralising period of her

life. Apart from her lack of money, there was a total lack of purpose in her life. Without even the deluding fantasies that she
might sing again, the realities of her situation closed in around her.
Dublin's wartime isolation had spawned the very worst type of
narrow provincialism. It had become a city that suffocated its
young writers and artists and ignored the older ones. Margaret
Sheridan was far from being an intellectual, but she thrived in the
superficial bohemianism that is usually found on the fringes of
artistic and intellectual life. Often she would sit in the foyers of the
Gresham and Shelbourne Hotels, a striking, plump little woman,
heavily made up and, by the standards of Dublin at that time, flam-
boyantly dressed. It was to be understood on these occasions that
she was willing to be brought to lunch. In fairness, many who
invited her into the dining room were usually thrilled to do so and
were vastly entertained by her rewarding flow of anecdotes.

The routine was broken when she received an invitation in 1950 to
visit New York and join a committee of the Arts Foundation which had
been formed to search for promising singers. The fee was substantial and
the expenses generous. She was there for four weeks and worked very
hard on auditioning boards. The most celebrated Irish diva of her time, as
one American columnist described her, should have been giving serious
thought to living out the rest of her life in New York where she had made
a true friend in the wealthy Ruth Axe.

Mrs. Axe and her husband Emerson owned a thriving investment
company and lived in Tarrytown Castle, overlooking the Hudson River.
Margaret Sheridan stayed with them and the Axes in turn introduced her
to the rich and famous and she accompanied them to the opera where
they had their own box.

Irish tenor Hubert Valentine had got to know Margaret during his
visits to Dublin and they were now in touch with one another in New
York. He felt that she should have settled in the city, though because of
her temperament and unpredictability he couldn't be sure if this would

work out. True, the Axes had already placed at her disposal a Fifth Avenue apartment and a private maid and couldn't be more helpful, yet he sensed she was restless and sometimes bored, not only with Tarrytown Castle but with life in her apartment.

'I don't think she got on well with Emerson Axe,' recalled Valentine, 'for during her stay in the castle she occasionally telephoned me that she was unhappy and asked if I'd take her out to dine.' It was said, however, that Emerson Axe, for his part, found her 'a magnetic personality, a woman who drew adventure to her'.

Her last trip to New York was in October 1956. She had not been feeling well, but she fulfilled her engagements. Ruth Axe persuaded her to see a doctor who sent her immediately to a clinic where cancer was diagnosed. After several weeks her condition seemed to improve and the doctors hoped they had arrested the growth. Although she was getting expert treatment and was surrounded by kindness and friendship, she wanted to get home. So, in April 1957, she sailed for Ireland.

When her friends in Dublin expressed concern at her appearance she said she had been working too hard and needed only a long rest. But this was one fiction she could not sustain, because she knew the truth. Fourteen years previously Mother Clement had faced the same truth with a tranquility that Margaret had never forgotten. Now she herself prayed with great fervour that she could do the same. But she did not die until 16 April 1958, the evening before *Manon Lescaut* was due to be sung in her honour at the Gaiety Theatre. Fittingly, excerpts from the *Verdi Requiem* were sung next day at the Mass in University Church, St. Stephen's Green, the singers being Gloria Davy and Ebi Stignani. The nation as a whole mourned her passing. She would be always remembered as Maggie from Mayo.

Chapter Four

Walter McNally

ACCLAIM AT THE EMPIRE

In 1918 as the first World War raged relentlessly throughout Europe with heavy casualties at the Battle of the Somme - many Irishmen among them - life in Dublin proceeded at a leisurely pace, though the controversial issue of conscription was hotly debated in the newspapers. In March the death of veteran parliamentarian John Redmond was mourned by many Irish people.

In spite of the universal gloom cast by the war, the musical and theatrical scene in Dublin was vibrant ; plays by Lady Gregory, Lennox Robinson and T.C. Murray helped fill the Abbey Theatre, the Queen's attracted lovers of melodrama, and theatres such as the Empire (now re-named the Olympia Theatre) the Gaiety, Tivoli and the Royal provided a mixed diet of musicals, variety, classical drama and opera.

In February the popular O'Mara Opera Company presented a two-week programme of operas at the Gaiety Theatre, including *Rigoletto, La Traviata, Lohengrin* and *Carmen*. Shortly afterwards the same theatre was again packed for the visit of the D'Oyly Carte Company with Gilbert & Sullivan's *Utopia Ltd*.

The announcement in May, meanwhile, that Walter McNally was forming his own operatic company was warmly greeted. Dark-haired and handsome, McNally possessed a natural baritone voice of rich timbre and vocal strength. Born in Scranton, Pennsylvania in 1884, of County Mayo parents, he came with them to Ireland in the year 1906 and within a few months his father had set up a butcher's shop in the town of Westport. Soon his fine singing was admired by the locals - particularly Molly Staunton - who was quickly taken by his affable manner and good looks. When eventually they were married on Christmas Day, Molly's people reckoned their daughter had married 'a little beneath herself'.

The happy couple decided to emigrate to America where Walter worked at a number of different jobs without apparently any notable success. Prompted by letters from home, they returned after a few years to County Mayo with their two young children, Patrick and Mary. Molly's father, a generous and kindly man, set them up in a guesthouse-cum-bar business in the village of Clonbur, near Ashford Castle.

Walter McNally was anxious to have his voice trained and fortunately found a wealthy patron in Ballinrobe who agreed to fund his singing lessons in Dublin. He trained with Dr. Vincent O'Brien and in 1915 won the Feis Ceoil gold medal in the baritone section. O'Brien, an astute judge of a voice, believed that McNally was good enough to make singing his career. Soon he was getting concert engagements, so many offers in fact that he and his wife Molly decided to sell their business venture and settle with their children in Dublin. Their house, Addison Lodge, in Botanic Road would quickly become known to the musical fraternity of the capital.

McNally was fortunate to be able to call on some splendid singers for his new company, people such as tenor Harry O'Dempsey, who had guested with the O'Mara Company, Dublin baritone William Lemass, soprano Kathleen McCully, contralto Florrie Ryan and mezzo-soprano Joan Burke. Dr. Vincent O'Brien doubled as musical director and conductor. One of the avowed aims of the company was to encourage talented Irish singers. Because of limited resources, the company mostly, though not always, performed concert versions of operas.

It was launched in the spring of 1918 at the Empire Theatre with a week of operas by Wallace and Benedict. For Walter McNally, it was a dream realised, but to his intense disappointment he was unable to sing at the performances of *Maritana* and *The Lily of Killarney*. During the rehearsals of the latter, he was stricken by influenza and ordered to bed by his doctor. The newspapers gave full coverage to the story.

McNally was replaced in the role of Danny Mann by a Mr. John Neilan and the performance was given before a packed Empire Theatre audience. The flu virus also struck the cast of *Maritana* and William Lemass had to be replaced at the last moment in the part of Don Jose. In the case of McNally, the papers followed his medical progress and by the end of the week the *Evening Mail* reported: 'His numerous friends in Dublin, all through Ireland, and even outside Ireland, will be glad to know that the popular Walter McNally is once again fully restored to health. His was a nasty knock-down. The demon influenza just gripped him hard, bowled him over. It was the first time in his life that he was laid up in bed.'

When the company played a fortnight's season at the Empire Theatre in June, Walter McNally was able to take his place in the cast of *Maritana*. The other operas presented were *Faust, The Lily of Killarney* and *The Bohemian Girl*. Newspapers reported that people were turned away almost every night and that the season was without exaggeration 'the most successful local enterprise yet attempted in Ireland'. The report concluded: 'A finer chorus has probably never been heard in grand opera in Dublin since the days of the Quinlan Company. In *Lurline* and again in *Faust,* they achieved their greatest successes. As I anticipated, the public demand for *Faust* has been so general and so insistent that the company had no option but to cancel *The Bohemian Girl* and substitute the melodic work of Gounod whose centenary (he was born in 1818) occurs about this time.'

In September Walter McNally decided to present a full stage version of *Pagliacci* at the Empire. It was the company's first production of this popular work and not surprisingly it merited a gread deal of attention. One morning newspaper wrote:

It was a big compliment to actor-manager Mr. Walter McNally that every seat in the auditorium was filled at the first house a quarter of an hour before he came on clad in his motley garb to ring up the curtain. He might have prepared us in the old traditional style by sticking his head through the folds of the curtain. In his singing here, as throughout the night, he gave free play to dramatic gesture. He gave us a Tonio with a heart 'just like you men'. The McNally stamp of quality was over all the work.

The critic felt the rest of the principals were somewhat over-anxious, though he praised Harry O'Dempsey's Canio and his fine singing of 'On with the Motley', Kathleen McCully's well- drawn portrayal of Nedda and William Lemass's convincingly sung Silvio. And he concluded: 'The great, pleasing encouraging fact is that grand opera of this intricate character can be done with such excellence by a purely Dublin company.' He attributed much of the success to musical director and conductor Dr. Vincent O'Brien.

The company did not confine its efforts to Dublin. Regular visits were made to Limerick, Waterford, Cork and Sligo. The programmes varied and often consisted of songs in the first half and, after the interval, scenes from popular operas. At the Theatre Royal in Limerick a full house in late October 1918 warmly applauded *Maritana* and the cast that included McNally, Lemass, Florrie Ryan and Kathleen McCully.

When the company opened for a week in Waterford there was limited standing room only in the packed Coliseum. 'Walter McNally was, of course, the real attraction,' stated a report in a local newspaper. 'He was hardly ever in better voice, and despite the arduous time he is having, he is still gilt-edged as ever. His well-measured notes were poured forth as only this famous baritone can do it. No wonder he got a tremendous reception. His first numbers were "Farewell in the Desert", "The Floral Song" and "Molly Brannigan". These, however, are by no means the best of his repertoire, and one longed to hear him give some of his favourites that really show him at his best, such as "The Trumpeter", "The Colleen Bawn" and "Father's Love" from *Lurline*.'

It was obvious during those years that there was a great demand for singing, especially opera, not only in Dublin but all over the country. The company also gave concerts in Glasgow and other Scottish cities and the programme usually included Irish ballads and operatic arias. It was a busy time for McNally. In February 1919, he guested with the J.S. O'Brien Choral & Operatic Society for a performance of *Faust* in Derry where he scored a personal triumph as Valentine. He visited Dundalk for three nights with his own concert group and packed the Town Hall. On this occasion he concentrated on songs and the local paper reported the rousing applause accorded him for "The Cornish Dance"and"TheTrumpeter". William Lemass, Harry O'Dempsey and Joan Burke sang arias and duets from *Faust* and *Trovatore*.

He was accompanied by the same singers in a performance of the Sullivan oratorio *The Prodigal Son* at Dublin's Theatre Royal. 'The performance reflected much credit on the McNally Company, especially on Walter McNally who is to be complimented not alone on his enterprise, but on the high level attained, with the devotional spirit of the work being carefully preserved,' stated the *Evening Herald* critic.

For the spring season of operas at the Empire Theatre, the baritone chose two Verdi works *Traviata* and the rarely performed *Ernani* as well as *Lurline* and *Maritana*. He was taking a risk with *Ernani* as it was the first time it was staged by the company. He need not have worried; the Empire was packed for every performance. The reviews suggested that the opera was under rehearsed, with one critic stating, 'There were weaknesses that constant and conscientious study and rehearsal could have overcome. The orchestra seemed to be reading the parts at times.'

McNally played Don Carlos, the King of Spain and, as the *Evening Mail* put it, 'In his dramatic rendering of the part he was as effective as ever, and realised faithfully the heroic and pathetic qualities of the unhappy king.' The critic recalled his two fine arias. 'These were "Since the day I first beheld thee," in which 'he was rather more free perhaps than the score intended', and his aria in the catacombs - one of the best numbers heard during the performance, and the one which the audience called for again and again, but did not get.'

While tenor William Mulcahy was described as weak in the title role, William Lemass's Don Silva was stated to be consistently good and his singing of the aria, "How I trust Thee" won deserved applause. The star of the production, however, was Miss Kitty Fagan in the role of Elvira.

'From first to last Miss Fagan was word and music perfect,' stated one critic, who also singled out the chorus: 'Their "Hail to the King" was splendid, but was only one of the chorus numbers which evoked a burst of applause from a critical and delighted audience.'

Ernani closed the season on a Saturday night before a crowded house. It was the company's custom to present an early and a late night performance, which must certainly have been extremely taxing on the principals. On this particular night, guest tenor Gwynne Davies was singing the title role and next day the *Evening Mail* critic stated: 'Mr. Davies was never in worse voice. The strain of two houses nightly has told severely on this excellent and justly popular tenor. His voice showed obvious symptoms of wear and tear after a strenuous three weeks, and all the time he was struggling against this handicap. He deserves, and his friends hope, he will take a good rest.'

From all accounts the audience at the second house was a boisterous one and loud ovations were accorded to Walter McNally, William Lemass and Kitty Fagan. At the final curtain McNally, in response to calls for a speech, announced that in the autumn he hoped to be able to produce operas in full once nightly and prove to Dublin people and visitors that an all-Irish opera company could give as good a performance of the principal popular operas as any company from abroad.

Around this time William Lemass married Miss Lucy Leenane. She was the very talented accompanist for the McNally concert troupe which was inundated with offers to perform in and outside of Dublin. McNally added new names such as soprano Eily Murnaghan, mezzo Bridie Moloney and bass Ted Kelly. The popularity of the concerts was such that in Sligo on one occasion people queued for hours for tickets but were to be disappointed.

Reporting on the event, the *Sligo Champion* stated: 'Mr. McNally was, of course, the main attraction of the bill. His pleasing baritone has lost none of its power and sweetness and his singing drew rounds of applause. He was remarkably good in arias from *Faust* and *The Lily of Killarney*, yet we are puzzled why he omitted singing "The Colleen Bawn".

McNally showed no hesitation in going North with his concert party. He was by now a firm favourite in Belfast and Derry and their programme consisted of songs and arias. Audiences at the Belfast Empire responded enthusiastically to scenes from *Travatore, Maritana* and *Faust* when the other artists included Florrie Ryan, Kathleen McCully, Harry O'Dempsey, William Lemass and McNally. On one return visit in early 1920 a local critic commented: 'We have never heard McNally in more effective vein. He excels in the rendering of native melodies, whether plaintive or romantic, and as an operatic artist his appearance and expression count almost as much as his sonorous and expressive vocalism. He is not merely an artist, however, for he is also an organiser with a fine faculty for diagnosing the popular taste.'

Likewise, at the Opera House in Derry he was a particular favourite as much as for his singing of songs as operatic arias. Once, when he and his party played at the theatre the local newspaper remarked: 'This was a Walter McNally week - very much so, and the result artistically and financially is equally gratifying. Everybody in the party seemed to be at the top of their form. Mr. McNally, as usual, excelled in scenes from the operas, as did his colleagues.'

On the evening of 17 May 1920, the Empire Theatre in Dublin was full to capacity for a concert by the McNally party. It was an emotional occasion as news had already filtered through musical circles that the baritone would soon leave for Italy for further voice training and to acquaint himself with the Italian approach to opera management. He hoped, he said, on his return, to bring a concert group on a tour of America.

'The warm place this popular artist occupies in the affections of the people was very strikingly demonstrated last night,' wrote an evening newspaper critic. 'After his Irish song scene with Miss Eily Murnaghan, the pair were recalled again and again. Through the scene, in which several Irish melodies and ballads are strung together in storied form, applause frequently burst forth, only to be hushed lest any part of the music feast should be missed. At the close Mr. McNally graciously thanked the audience for their cordial reception.'

He was by now 34, which seemed rather late to embark on a trip to Italy; he was also married with a young family, but he felt he had much to learn about musicianship and Italian operatic techniques. Inside a few months he was talking the language and he was happy also with progress in his vocal studies. He began to follow the glittering career of Margaret Burke Sheridan and was in Naples on 28 February 1921 when she sang her first Madama Butterfly at the famous San Carlo Opera House. He recalled that the atmosphere was electric. 'I shall never forget her performance. It was thrilling; it made one lose oneself to be in the audience and hear a great mighty roar of thousands of people standing up in their seats shouting "Brava, Brava," and crying aloud, "Sheridan, Sheridan."'

In due course he got some operatic engagements in Italy. Due to his dark good looks and fluent Italian he was often taken for a native of that country. On one occasion, he was standing in the foyer of a provincial opera house when a small group of Irish tourists approached him and enquired about seats for that night's opera. They were surprised when he answered their questions in an Irish accent.

Back in Dublin in 1922, McNally wrote to Margaret Burke Sheridan inviting her to sing with him in a celebrity concert in November at the Theatre Royal. He reckoned it was high time that the diva was heard in her own country where her fame was already talked about in musical circles. Indeed, she had not been home since she went to Rome in 1916 and a lot had occurred in the meantime in Ireland. It was said, however, that she had kept in touch and was well acquainted with political developments.

It was not perhaps the most opportune time for her homecoming; a bitter civil war raged and Dublin, like the rest of the country, was embroiled. McNally assured her that she would be safe and that the concert promised to be a sell-out. It was undoubtedly the musical event of the year in the capital, a fact not lost on the *Evening Mail*. It reported: 'Maybe all roads lead to Rome for Margaret Burke Sheridan, but certainly all routes led to the Theatre Royal yesterday. All kinds of people comprised the audience – from the wives of the staff of the National Army to the active members of the opposing forces, from constant attenders at the "old Castle drawing-rooms" to a "Red" sister imported from Russia.'

The audience was not disappointed. Walter McNally introduced the diva to enthusiastic applause and remarked how happy she was to be home in Ireland. She quickly endeared herself to the audience by her regal stage presence and lovely singing. The critics were impressed. 'Miss Sheridan is a true interpreter,' wrote the *Evening Mail*. 'She lives the part she is acting. She has a voice of immense power, of great range and ravishing beauty.' A daily newspaper critic expressed the hope that Dublin would one day see Miss Sheridan in her operatic roles.

Earlier, she had confided in Walter McNally that she was nervous coming to Dublin, or as she put it, 'I did not feel half as nervous when appearing at La Scala. I can best and most completely express myself in opera.' To McNally who sang songs and ballads at the concert, Margaret had exceeded all expectations. 'She was overwhelmed by the warmth of the Dublin reception and she was in outstanding voice.'

In the following year, he presented matinee performances of *Hansel and Gretel*, Humperdinck's fairytale opera, at the Theatre Royal. He himself shared the role of Peter, the children's father, with William Lemass and Joan Burke sang the Witch. Casting the Dew fairy posed a problem but eventually the role was given to a Miss Renée Flynn, an 18-year-old soprano, who in a few years would sing a small role in Wagner's *Die Walkure* at Covent Garden. When I talked to her early in 1994 she was quietly celebrating her 89th birthday, but recalled with pleasure the production of *Hansel and Gretel*: 'I do remember that Joan Burke was terrific as the Witch and that Walter McNally sang and acted superbly. To a young woman like me, he was a striking-looking man and could be taken for a foreigner. He had also a fine stage presence. The production was excellent and the audiences loved it.'

In 1924, McNally travelled to America with his wife Molly and youngest child Joan for a series of concert performances. While over there he was engaged to sing in *The Student Prince* in Chicago where the musical ran for months. In the ensuing years he became friendly with the Kennedys, Joe and Rose, and occasionally when he visited their home Rose would accompany him on the piano.

Eventually he left America for good and returned home to Adison Lodge. While in the U.S. he had acquired a real interest in cinema and reckoned it offered bright possibilities in Ireland. This judgment was correct and before long he was running his own cinemas. Count John McCormack performed the official opening of McNally's Savoy Cinema in Galway, where Renée Flynn once sang in the stage show prior to the screening of a movie, and later in 1927 the popular baritone decided to retire from singing. But first he planned a farewell concert at the Theatre Royal and invited Margaret Burke Sheridan to be his special guest artist. To his intense disappointment, she asked to be excused, saying she could not leave Italy.

It came as a surprise to his friends that he was retiring at the comparatively early age of 43, particularly as his voice was still in fine shape. But his mind was made up; he wanted to devote all his time to the cinema business, which in time would prove far more lucrative than all the effort he had put into organising concerts and operatic performances.

Mrs. Joan Roughneen, the only surviving member of the McNally family, remembered being brought by her mother to the Theatre Royal for her father's farewell concert. 'I think we all felt very excited and very proud. I remember he sang Irish songs as well as operatic arias and the audience responded enthusiastically. Walter was always a very popular performer, a real showman I suppose you could say. I can still hear the applause as he sang his final song. Joan Burke and Willie Lemass were also on the programme. Giving up the stage had nothing to do with his health; my father began to do really well in the cinema business and I also think he felt he had sung enough.'

Joan Roughneen lives today in Glenageary and is a regular opera-goer at the Gaiety Theatre. She remembered her father saying that he was not in favour of any of his children taking up acting or singing, something she found difficult to accept at the time. 'I know that he was always nervous going on stage to sing,' she said, 'and usually held in his hand a medal. He was a bundle of nerves.'

Later on she and her father would occasionally have afternoon tea with Margaret Burke Sheridan in the Gresham Hotel, and once the diva said to her, 'Joan, why didn't you ask me to sing at your wedding?'

Joan McNally had married J.P. Roughneen, a businessman from Kiltimagh, County Mayo, and Dr. Vincent O'Brien had played the organ at their wedding. When Joan mentioned to her father Walter what Margaret Burke Sheridan had said, he shrugged his head. 'I don't know if she would have sung at your wedding,' he said. He had come to regard Margaret as difficult and temperamental and was perhaps thinking also of how she had turned down his invitation to sing at his own farewell concert, a fact that still rankled with him.

'My father was a lovely man,' reflected Joan Roughneen. 'On and off-stage he had charisma and a warm personality. In later years, when his health wasn't good he loved being with the family. He did very well in the cinema business and a restaurant he ran in Dublin's O'Connell Street made him a good deal of money. He continued to take interest in young singers and remained friendly with John McCormack.'

One of the young singers Walter McNally helped was Hubert Valentine. They first met in August 1936 when McNally arranged an audition for him with Dr. Vincent O'Brien.

'I first met Walter McNally through an introduction by Miss Nora Jennings, who had heard me sing in Our Lady of Refuge Church, Rathmines,' recalled Valentine. 'Miss Jennings told him of my singing and the quality of my tenor voice. I remember that the audition was held in Vincent O'Brien's home in Parnell Square, and among those present were McNally, William Lemass, Lucy Linnane, Kitty McCullough and the critic Harold White.

'I sang "I Hear You Calling Me", "The Snowy Breasted Pearl" and "Panis Angelicus" and afterwards Vincent O'Brien agreed to accept me as his pupil. I could see that Walter McNally was delighted and a week later he arranged to have me make my first public appearance on a Dublin stage and that was in the Grand Central Cinema. It was one of the many movie houses McNally was connected with or owned. I sang three performances daily during the week, with Lucy Linnane as my accompanist.

'The week was a great success and was the beginning of my musical career which I credit to Walter McNally. He had a powerful baritone voice in his younger days, according to William Lemass, who was a close friend of the McNally family. Walter had such a great love of opera that he formed his own company. Though he was not a great musician, nevertheless he would learn the opera scores to the last note or more and add his own version of the leading baritone arias. Lucy Linnane, who was the official accompanist for the company, used to say, "You never knew what to expect from Walter. One time singing "Di Provenzo" from *La Traviata* he could not finish the aria as written, so he added some more notes to the run and she gave up. Nonetheless, the house would go wild. Just one of the many things he would do during the opera company tours.

'I met Walter many times prior to my departure for the United States in 1939. He had given up public singing appearances and was concentrating on his business. He was a very handsome man, always dressed smartly with bow tie and spats. Privately, he still loved to sing. I had the pleasure of singing with him the big duet from *The Lily of Killarney* during one of his musical evenings at Adison Lodge, where his wife Molly and their friends made one feel so much at home.'

Walter McNally was only 55 when he died in August 1945. The newspapers of the time gave extensive coverage to this passing. The *Evening Mail* wrote: 'Death has rung down the curtain on a colourful career, and Dublin has lost a vivid personality in Walter McNally, opera singer turned film distributor. Few persons, even among his personal friends, were aware that he was born in America, but as a matter of fact, his singing career may be said to have commenced in his native town of Scranton, Pennsylvannia, where he sang in the choir of St. Patrick's Cathedral.'

The paper's final comment was more than interesting:

'It was a curious decision for an operatic star who had studied in Milan and sang operatic roles in Italy to abandon his musical career at its height and spend the remainder of his life in film renting and cinema ownership. But he proved as successful in business as he had in opera, and handled very large interests with the utmost efficiency.'

McNally's name would endure in musical circles. Florrie Ryan, a leading member of his operatic company, recalled those exciting touring days whenever she was interviewed by the press or by radio reporters. Florrie married George Hewson, a young chemist, and settled in Ballina, County Mayo, where she continued to sing in the church choir.

Hubert Valentine was in America when he heard of McNally's death. On frequent visits home to Dublin he likes today to recall the singer. 'I shall always remember Walter McNally as a great artist, a great man and a dear friend.'

Mrs. Joan Roughneen summed up: 'I am sure that it was Walter's personality as much as his voice that endeared him to audiences in Dublin and throughout Ireland. It is a pity that the old 78s do not do justice to his voice.'

Chapter Five

James Johnston

CLASH WITH CALLAS

James Johnston had become a principal tenor at Covent Garden in 1950, singing with increasing success such roles as Pinkerton, Cavaradossi, Alfredo and the Duke in *Rigoletto*.

During Coronation year (1953) the house's general administrator, David Webster, engaged Maria Callas for three operas, *Aida*, *Norma* and *Il Trovatore*, but when tenor Gino Penno cancelled Webster asked Belfast-born James Johnston to sing Manrico in *Trovatore*.

'I had only sung the role in English', the tenor recalled, 'and it now meant I would have to learn it in Italian at short notice. I asked to be released from other operatic engagements, but the request was only partly granted, which left me little time to study the part in Italian.'

Callas, meanwhile, took a suite in the Savoy, which in time would become known as the 'Callas Suite'. She was already a star, acclaimed for her performances in *Lucia di Lammermoor* and *La Gioconda*. A few months before she had sung Leonora in *Trovatore* at La Scala with a steller cast that included Stignani, Penno and the baritone Carlo Tagliabue as the Count di Luna.

In the course of his review in *Opera*, Peter Dragadre stated, 'This *Trovatore* was worth waiting for, and had the success that it merited. The success was not due to the usually dominating figure of Manrico, but to the almost unforgettable singing of Leonora and Azucena taken by Maria

Callas and Ebe Stignani.'

It was the period when Callas was fighting a weight problem and this tended to make her irritable and temperamental. She was determined to become slim and elegant-looking and was in the middle of a dieting programme that featured green salads, almost raw meat and electrical massages. But as one critic put it, 'Audrey Hepburn seemed a long way off.'.

James Johnston was not unaware of the stories of the prima donna's short fuse and her well-publicised tiffs with colleagues and opera house managements. But he had not heard of her overweight problem, although newspaper photographs showed her as plump, even on the fat side. The cast for *Trovatore* was not as strong as La Scala's, yet apart from Callas and Johnston, it did include the brilliant mezzo-soprano Giulietto Simionato, who would sing the role of the gipsy woman Azucena.

As rehearsals began, Johnston was not slow to notice Callas's stand-offish manner and her display of arrogance. She seemed intent on showing her colleagues the amount of energy and dedication she brought to rehearsals. Unfortunately what it succeeded in doing was to create unnecessary tensions among the cast and Johnston quickly got the impression that the fiery diva did not particularly like him. Maybe she is disappointed, he thought, because the Italian is not singing Manrico. His Irish blood began to boil. Colleagues knew that beneath his wit and gift of mimicry the tenor could be a blunt and no-nonsense Ulsterman.

During one scene in the opera when Manrico accuses Leonora of being false to him, he pushed her away from him and she fell on the stage. 'At this time', Johnston recalled, 'Callas was roly- poly and she rolled into the prop box. Slowly she got to her feet and shook herself and proceeded to call me all the names she could think of, so I called her a few fancy ones back. I told her we could do the opera without her and that if she wanted to get me sacked, as she did to other singers in the past, to go ahead and do so.'

Enraged, she said she wouldn't take any cheek from a 'whipper snapper like Johnston', but as she stormed off the rehearsal stage, he shouted after her, 'Go back to Brooklyn.'

Baritone Jess Walters and bass Michael Langdon stood aside and hardly knew what to say. Like the tenor, they wondered if Callas would carry on or ask to be released from the production. To their surprise, she resumed rehearsals after lunch as though the incident had never happened.

Johnston was puzzled. 'I had no idea what made her change her attitude', he was to say later. 'She was friendly to me and I could only conclude that something had happened during lunchtime. Then a chorus member remarked to me, "Jimmy, I hear you apologised to Maria Callas and sent her a lovely bouquet of flowers." I told him I did nothing of the sort. "Oh, indeed, you did, Jimmy" said another chorus member. After rehearsals I tackled Webster and asked him what he had done. He looked at me disarmingly, and said, "Not a thing, Jimmy, not a thing." I told him that somebody had sent flowers and signed my name to them. He looked at me and replied, "As long as the feud is over, it's alright."'

Although the Covent Garden audience warmly applauded the first night performance, Callas was said to be disappointed not only with the shabby sets and the conventional production, but with the rest of the cast. People attributed her unrelenting attitude to her punishing work schedule and strict dieting programme. Predictably, the critics devoted most of their reviews to her performance. 'Her voice was a source of unending amazement', summed up Cecil Smith later in *Opera*. The rest of the cast could hardly have been pleased by *The Times* comment: 'Mme. Maria Callas sang and acted everyone off the stage.'

The critics did not unduly worry James Johnston; he was confident that his own career had taken off and he had no fears for the future. There is a story told that after one particular performance of *Trovatore* he was relaxing with friends in his dressing-room when Callas walked past the door. The tenor, on an impulse, shouted after her, 'Maria, there are people in here who want to meet you.' She ignored the call. Even then, the diva valued her privacy above most things.

It was her imperious manner that annoyed the earthy Belfast tenor. He had not found a trace of it in Victoria de Los Angeles, whom he had partnered the previous year in *Madama Butterfly* at Covent Garden, nor for that matter in Gre Brouwenstin when he sang with her in *Aida*. For another reason, that performance was particularly pleasing to him, as one critic commented, 'As a Verdi singer, James Johnston has few equals. The timbre of his voice is ideal for this style of singing.'

He was asked to sing Alfredo opposite Elisabeth Schwarzkopf at less than 24 hours' notice. He accepted after explaining that he had not sung the part for three years. The performance was a triumph, except for one thing, recalled the tenor: 'In the last act I completely forgot the duet with Violetta and poor Miss Schwarzkopf had to sing it alone.!'

Later, he was engaged to sing the tenor lead in Sir Arthur Bliss's opera, *The Olympians*. He learned the role in eleven days. He regretted that he was never asked to sing the role of *Faust* at Covent Garden. As he said, 'It was one of my ambitions to do so, especially since I had sung it in other theatres and with Vic Oliver conducting on one occasion. In the "Jewel Song" scene Marguerite is supposed to hand me the jewel case but this night she must have been nervous because she refused to hand it over. We had a tug-of-war until finally Marguerite put the jewel case down almost in the footlights. At the end of the act the curtain came and as it went up again for us to take our bow the jewel case went up with it. There was a shriek of laughter from the audience. The cast had a hearty laugh too.
'

Growing up in Belfast, where he was born in 1903, Jimmy Johnston was a hardy youngster and from an early age became a butcher's boy, learning the animal slaughtering skills from his father. At Sunday School he began to take an interest in singing and later joined a local choir in which he either sang baritone or bass, although when the choir was short of tenors he shifted to that position.

After he had won all the awards possible in vocal competitions in Belfast and elsewhere in the province, one adjudicator hold him, 'I can't give you the baritone award because you're not a baritone, you're a tenor.'

Young Johnston thought the man was talking nonsense; he simply didn't want to be a tenor. As he later explained, 'I associated tenors with pansies, but after hearing them sing in competitions I remember saying to myself, "Maybe not all tenors are, after all, pansies", so I decided to sing tenor.' After working long days in his father's butcher shops he looked forward to singing as a welcome diversion. He was encouraged to take lessons with an English-born tutor, John Vine and was amused when he enquired about the fees to be paid. Vine said to him, 'I don't want a fee from you, Jimmy; instead when the electricity bill comes to me, I want you to pay it.'

Vine was a singer who specialised in oratorio and he quickly recognized that young Johnston's voice was ideally suited to this vocal art form. Later, when his pupil began to sing Irish songs and ballads in a voice as near as possible to Gigli's, Vine became excited. 'Jimmy, I've been trying to get you to sing like that for months. That's the tone I want.'

Around this time a wealthy Belfastman, who had heard Johnston sing in oratorio, offered to send him to Italy to study the Italian language and learn opera technique. When Jimmy, excited by the prospect, told his father, he was shattered by his reaction. 'No son of mine', his father bellowed', is going on the stage, for it is a sure way to hell.'

Johnston, senior, was in his son's opinion 'a very good Methodist' and detested the bohemianism connected with the stage. It was an opportunity James Johnston would regret for the rest of his career, for a knowledge of Italian was, he felt, necessary when he came to tackle major roles in Italian opera.

He was singing in Edward German's *Merrie England* in Derry in the early 1940s when he was approached by Bill O'Kelly, chairman of the Dublin Grand Opera Society, who invited the tenor to sing with the society. 'We are desperately short of tenors', O'Kelly told him.' We can put some good parts in your way.'

'I'll write to you', promised Johnston. He rather took to the down-to-earth O'Kelly who was an army officer by profession. The only opera Johnston had seen up to then was *Rigoletto* and by now was able to sing a few arias from the opera. He telephoned John Vine in Belfast about the Dublin offer to sing *Faust,* but Vine urged caution. Eventually, the tenor wrote to O'Kelly, saying he wanted to sing the Duke in *Rigoletto.* The

DGOS chairman had no option but to agree.

Johnston had just six weeks to learn the part. 'You'll never do it, Jimmy', said John Vine, with a hint of a stammer. The tenor would later say, 'John was nearly right. I had to work every day on the part, but it helped that I was to sing it in English.' The Dublin critics praised the rich quality of his voice. 'At least we have got a tenor who sings Verdi music as Verdi wrote it', commented the *Irish Independent* critic. And he added: 'It's a pity though that the tenor's acting was non-existent.'

On another occasion when Johnston was engaged to sing Faust with the DGOS, he was met at Amiens Street railway station by Bill O'Kelly. Looking up, Johnston spied his name on a large poster under the name of Faust. O'Kelly remarked slyly, 'Do you see anything else on that poster, Jimmy?' The tenor looked again and to his astonishment saw he was billed to sing Alfredo in *La Traviata*.

'I can't sing Alfredo', he protested. 'I don't know the part, it's as simple as that, Bill.'

With typical bluntness, O'Kelly replied, 'You will, Jimmy and you have only ten days to learn it!'

For years afterwards Johnston would talk about the ordeal. 'I had to stand on a chair for the drinking duet in Act I and as I wore tights I could see my knees shake; I hoped nobody else did. It was the first time on stage that I was really frightened, but I got through the opera, despite the fact that by the end I was nearly hoarse. May Devitt was a very good and reliable Violetta.'

Although his acting was still as poor as John McCormack's, he went on to sing *Carmen*, *Don Giovanni* and *Cavalleria Rusticana & Pagliacci* with the DGOS and became one of the most popular operatic artists to sing in Dublin. Distinguished piano accompanist Jeannie Reddin recalled that he sang Faust beautifully and had no problem with his high Cs; he was equally good in more dramatic roles such as Manrico and Don José. Offstage, she found his sense of humour infectious and his mimicry very amusing. His contribution to opera in the Dublin of the Forties was, she said, very important.

Around 1944 James Johnston was in his butcher's shop one afternoon in Belfast when a man walked in and introduced himself as Tyrone Guthrie from the Sadler's Wells Opera Company. He said he had heard Johnston sing in Dublin and thought he should advance his career in London. 'We are very short of tenors', he added.

To the tenor, Guthrie looked exceptionally tall and gangling, but he spoke in a soft, cultured accent. He explained to the director that since opera singing didn't pay very well he was cautious about a move to London. 'I must tell you that I'm making a fair living here', he stressed, 'and I don't want for singing engagements in my spare time.'

Guthrie towered over the stockily-built tenor. 'I'm afraid that we won't be able to pay you very much; at the most I would say between £25 and £30 a week.'

Johnston said that he was making four times that amount every week working in his brother's butcher shop. Guthrie was persuasive and pointed out that it was the waste of a fine voice and that he had no doubt he would in time earn considerable money singing in London. 'Give it a try', he urged him. 'You have the voice.'

Johnston liked to be straight with people. 'I'll go over for six months and if I don't like it, and if Sadler's Wells doesn't like me, I'll come home again to Belfast.'

He quickly settled in London and made an early impression as Jenik in *The Bartered Bride* in 1945. He was always good at playing country boys - the title role in Vaughan Williams' *Hugh the Drover* would soon be another of his successes. The critics commented favourably on the purity of his tenor voice, its effortless range, and rich tonal quality.

He was not long at Sadler's Wells, however, until it became clear that the big Italian roles were the ones Johnston enjoyed most and his Manrico was particularly acclaimed. He won many new admirers after he sang the role of Gabriele Adorno in the first British performance of Verdi's *Simone Boccanegra*. Purists hold that it is one of Johnston's finest recordings, showing him in glorious voice.

He found time to record the *Messiah* and *Elijah* and these in due course became bestsellers. It was becoming increasingly clear that his future lay at Covent Garden where he would get an opportunity of singing with world guest stars – and in Italian. He made his debut there on March 11, 1950 as Pinkerton and inside the next few years he would sing the Duke in Rigoletto, Mario Cavaradossi (*Tosca*), Alfredo, Calaf (*Turandot*), Radames (*Aida*) and Gustavus III (*Un Ballo in Maschera*).

Critics noted that his acting was variable: he was not a tall man and was by then nearly 50, so he needed a careful make-up.

The drama was mainly in the voice. 'When he was going for a top C you always knew he was going to do it', a colleague said. And that was what his considerable fan club wanted. Among his best roles at Covent Garden were Don Jose and Calaf. However, the policy of opera in English, which ruled for part of his stay at this house, did not always suit – the Belfast accent never left him.

The critic Elizabeth Forbes thought that the finest of his Puccini roles was Cavaradossi, although the tenor was always greatly applauded as Calaf, particularly for his ringing "Nessun dorma". On the other hand, as the Duke in *Rigoletto* he lacked, in her opinion, 'the ideal elegance for the part', but as Radames he appeared in his element, vocally secure, dramatically convincing. In the Nile scene he invariably generated excitement. His Manrico, whether in English at Sadler's Wells or in Italian at Covent Garden, was equally effective.

From 1950 to 1958 he sang in all 275 performances at Covent Garden, including Rodolfo in *Boheme,* Max in *Der Freischutz* and Hoffmann in *Les Contes d'Hoffmann.* His final performance there was as Radames in June 1958. Afterwards he was asked by both Sir David Webster and Reginald Goodall to prepare himself for German roles in the following season, in particular David in *Die Meistersinger.* 'I was to sing the part in German', Johnston later said', and for six weeks sweated blood trying to get it right. But I was too old by then to learn the German repertoire. I felt I had gone far enough.'

Webster was not totally convinced that this was the end of the popular Belfast tenor. He sent a note to his dressing-room, 'Hope to have you next year.' But Johnston had no intention of changing his mind. Although at 55 his voice was in good shape, he had become somewhat disenchanted with Covent Garden. Seeing guest stars being paid exorbitant fees while others, like himself, got a good deal less money, was a source of annoyance to him. Not surprisingly, he decided to return to the Belfast he loved.

During the Fifties, Lord Harewood was attached to the Covent Garden administrative staff and recalled for me the circumstances surounding Johnston's departure which differ somewhat from the tenor's own version.

'I remember that Jimmy left in 1957 suddenly, without any warning, and in some dudgeon. He came to see me to say that he had just been to resign and that he was leaving within days. It seemed that the reason was the arrival of Jon Vickers, who was immediately favoured by management and public for the sheer conviction and brilliance of his performances as much as for his voice, which was very strong but not Italianate. Jimmy felt threatened, said firmly that he thought Vickers would never sing *Turandot* (which he never did), but that we would now have to do without his services. He was off back to Ireland.

'It was a sad ending but somehow nobody held it against him as he was extremely popular and his sheer charm made one forgive him whatever would otherwise have seemed out of order. I suppose his most successful role at Covent Garden in many ways was Calaf in *Turandot* which he sang quite often after Walter Midgley had left and which he sang excellently. Again, it was his top register which was his great strength in this role.'

Dr. Havelock Nelson, the conductor and pianist, thought that the war restricted James Johnston's true development, for it meant he arrived on the London operatic stage relatively late. His greatest memory was seeing the tenor partner Victoria de Los Angeles in *Madama Butterfly*. 'I can remember their voices blending beautifully in the big duet in Act I and Jimmy sounded really Italian. Near the end of his career at Covent Garden I suspected from talking to him that he didn't like the politics in the theatre. Belfast audiences loved him, whether in opera or oratorio. In spite of the fame he enjoyed in London, Jimmy never got above himself.'

To Havelock Nelson, it was Johnston's generous spirit that stood out, especially the way he tried to help young singers. He would tell them, 'Learn foreign languages and be able to sing in these languages; learn new music and, above all, learn the piano.' He, himself, was once conducting a Saturday night concert in Belfast with the tenor as the soloist, when shortly before it began he had a 'phone call from Jimmy to say he would be delayed and if he could possibly get someone to deputise for him in the first half.

'Luckily we had a deputy in a young singer called Joe McCarthy, with whom I had rehearsed the programme, so Joe agreed to go on. When I went to the Green Room at the interval I discovered that Jimmy Johnston had arrived in the hall quite early, but seemingly sat out of sight so that Joe McCarthy could do the whole first half of the concert. What is more, he insisted that Joe sing a song in the second half.'

James Shaw, who today teaches singing in Belfast, first met the tenor in the early 1940s when he was asked to take the place of an indisposed bass in a performance of the Messiah. He was a teenager and remembers that James Johnston complimented him on his singing, though careful to add, 'But you have a lot to learn.'

Soon he found himself getting engagements in Belfast and elsewhere in the province on the tenor's recommendation. He sang with him quite often and was greatly encouraged by him and his practical approach to his craft. Later, he visited him at Sadler's Wells and Covent Garden. He found Jimmy's sense of humour infectious – there was nearly always a twinkle in his eye – and together they talked often about opera.

'Of all the roles he played, perhaps his favourite was Calaf', Shaw recalled. 'I think it was Edward Greenfield who wrote that when Johnston sang this role, certainly no one slept. He was also particularly pleased, as were the critics, with Gabriele Adorno in *Simone Boccanegra*. He rarely spoke harshly about anyone, although never kindly about Callas. He admired her talent but did not seem to get on well with her personally.

But then, who did?

'He told me he enjoyed working with the young Sutherland, Amy Shuard and Joyce Gartside and, of course, Victoria de Los Angeles. I was in Covent Garden in 1951 when she made her debut in Butterfly with Jimmy as Pinkerton; that had a happy sequel years later – in 1986 when she gave a recital in the Opera House in Belfast. I invited Jimmy to come to it and he had a wonderful reunion with the diva.'

When the tenor came home from London to settle in Belfast in 1961, he and James Shaw would see a lot more of each other. Shaw visited his large house in the suburbs and sometimes found Jimmy gardening. About 1980 the veteran tenor moved to a bungalow at Crumlin, near where he was born. He inherited a neglected garden but soon put his own stamp on it. Later on, he moved again, to Jordanstown, near Belfast, on the shores of Belfast Lough.

'Jimmy liked listening to his own recordings, but generally you had to ask to hear them', said Shaw. 'He did go to opera but again somebody usually had to suggest it to him. Dublin was very dear to him; he felt he owed a lot to the DGOS because the society gave him his first taste of opera and it was there that Joan Cross and Tyrone Guthrie first heard him sing. When he returned to live permanently in Ireland he intended to teach singing, but never did; I doubt if he would have had the patience. He was, though, always willing to listen to young singers.'

Johnston did regret, Shaw says, that he was unable to broaden his operatic career, perhaps sing in American and European opera houses. But in those days it was not essential to sing opera in England in the original language, so it was a drawback to his international prospects. 'I feel his limitations were due to the fact that he did not go into opera full-time until he was over 40. Certainly his Italianate voice suited the Italian language as it had a resonant ring to it, rare to singers in these islands. The only time I heard him sing a complete opera in Italian was Macduff in Verdi's *Macbeth* at Glyndebourne and it sounded wonderful.'

Shaw appreciated Johnston's decision to leave Covent Garden when he did. As he said, 'At that time, the administration there were contemplating more Wagner and eventually "The Ring" cycle. I think it was Reginald Goodall who first asked Jimmy to consider undertaking this task in German. Jimmy was not keen to embark on what he felt was a new career at his age, so he decided to retire and come home. After all he was a master butcher and still had his own shops in Belfast. In fact, the last thing I sang with him was *Messiah* and I recall collecting him at his shop in Sandy Row on the way to Enniskillen Cathedral.'

When the celebrated tenor died in November 1991, he was 88. Tributes poured into his home from friends and opera-lovers everywhere. A thanksgiving choral evensong was planned for St. Anne's Cathedral where James Johnston was once a choir boy. Television ran a documentary on the career of the tenor and it made an abiding impression in both north and south of the country. It helped to remind people how outstanding a tenor he was in opera and oratorio.

Commented James Shaw: 'Johnston, the singer, was to me the most naturally gifted vocalist I have worked with or, indeed, have heard. His rich resonant quality was rare in these islands; he would undoubtedly have been successful in Italy if he had a chance there earlier. He did not claim to be an actor, but he was more than competent. One of his great assets was his total commitment to whatever he was singing – the listener never failed to be involved. As an individual, he was modest but confident in his own ability.'

Lord Harewood remembered him as 'a graceful singer, easy on the stage with what I suppose one would call the "common touch". At Sadler's Wells, he had been remarkable in difficult Italian roles, such as Adorno in *Boccanegra* and the title role in *Don Carlos*, to say nothing of things like Manrico and the Duke of Mantua. The one truly Italianate thing about him was the ring at the top of his voice, and he was really better suited to mid-European or even English roles (his Hugh the Drover was outstanding).

'I remember that the great Italian conductor Vittorio Gui, who had him in his cast for *Macbeth* at Glyndebourne (or at least heard him there),

was totally mystified at the English liking for what was to him so obviously a voiceless tenor. Italians tended not to relish him in the theatre, but I
remember too that in 1974 I attended a Verdi Congress in Chicago and, in
my short talk about *Boccanegra* in England, played the recording Jimmy
Johnston made of the great aria. Afterwards, more than one Italian came
up to ask who was the magnificient tenor in the recording and was he still
active and available!'

To Lord Harewood, his lack of international fame was in fact due to an
inherently non-Italian quality in the Italian roles he mainly sang. Certainly
he came to opera rather late in life, having auditioned during the war to
Joan Cross and Sadler's Wells and being immediately engaged. Possibly
that is why he retained the freshness of voice until the end of his singing
career.

'I am sure he enjoyed his singing and he was also the kind of singer
who, as you suggest, never let one down. His Manrico opposite Callas in
1953 has left me with few memories, though I am sure it was decently
sung. But when he took it over a year or two later at short notice with
Zinka Milanov as Leonora, that was another story. To begin with, the
whole enterprise had seemed doomed from the start. One singer after
another fell ill and Kurt Baum was the one least satisfactorily covered. He
had reported sick on the day of the performance in question and Jimmy
Johnston was rehearsing. When he heard that Baum would not sing, I was
deputed to find Johnston and ask him to go on that evening. I did, at the
top of the building, pleased but exhausted after having just sung full voice
the role of Hoffmann which he was due to take over a little later! He said
he didn't know if he had any voice left in him for the evening but he would
do his best, which was what he managed, although it was not what he or
anyone else would have hoped for. But he was a Trojan and he went on.

'I liked him very much in roles like Jenik in *The Bartered Bride*-
and I now cannot remember why he did not sing it when it was put on
for Kubelik at Covent Garden in 1955. I think he just refused to, out of
some element of pique, and that nothing would persuade him to change
his mind! But what caused the pique (if I am right) I cannot now remem-

ber.'

Havelock Nelson was asked to give the eulogy at the thanks- giving choral evensong. He opened by describing Jimmy Johnston as 'a darlin' man' and went on to recall that when he first heard his voice it made a wonderful impression on him. 'I can recall, too, when the Northern Ireland Grand Opera Society staged *Carmen* for the first time in 1969, Jimmy put his services at our disposal and his advice proved of great value.

'Every major singer of the time I had the privilege of working with had good things to say of Jimmy. Isobel Baillie, for example, told me that, in her opinion, nobody sang the tenor arias in *Messiah* and *Creation* as well as he did – and I, myself, truly agree with that.'

He read letters of sympathy from tenor Ull Deane and Kenneth Montgomery, Artistic Director of Northern Ireland Opera, who disclosed that in future they would name the tenor bursary offered by the company after James Johnston.

Deane wrote: 'When I was a teenager I idolised Jimmy Johnston and even went to wait for him outside the BBC late one night, where he was doing a live broadcast. I wanted his autograph. He came out, put me in his car and brought me to his house where he talked and talked about the world of singing until my head swam with the need to sing like him and enjoy life as he did. Years later he told me he had heard me sing on the radio from London quite a few times, and gave me praise. He was one of the greats.'

The memorial service ended with the voice of James Johnston filling the cathedral in a recorded excerpt from *Elijah*. As Havelock Nelson solemnly told the congregation, 'No further words are necessary – this magnificient singing sums up it all.'

Chapter Six

Joseph McLoughlin

PINKERTON FROM DERRY

Joseph McLoughlin, a young Derry-born tenor with the striking appearance of a screen actor and a voice in the Richard Tauber mould, enlivened the dull war years in the Dublin of the early 1940s with his exuberant singing of "You Are My Heart's Delight", "O Maiden, My Maiden" and other vocal favourites on show bills at the Theatre Royal. He was usually partnered in duets by an attractive Dublin soprano, May Devitt, who was keen to pursue an operatic career.

It was a time when Captain Bill O'Kelly was still on the lookout for tenors for the DGOS and had heard good reports of McLoughlin. One evening he slipped into the Theatre Royal to hear him sing and afterwards told Captain J.M. Doyle, the DGOS's musical director that the singer had operatic potential. Heddle Nash, the popular English lyric tenor was unable to sing Pinkerton in the society's new production of *Madama Butterfly* because of wartime passport restrictions, leaving the society in a dilemma. They could not ask James Johnston as he was already cast that season as Faust, Don Jose and the Duke of Mantua. O'Kelly decided to approach May Devitt to 'sound out' Joseph McLoughlin.

The young tenor, who is better known today as Josef Locke, remembered being astonished by the invitation to sing in grand opera. 'I told May that I had never seen an opera, never mind sing the role of Pinkerton. But she refused to take no for an answer. "I'll teach the part to you, Joe", she said. And she did. between Julia Grey – the society's repetiteur – and herself they taught me the words and music. Since Pinkerton isn't all that big a part – he doesn't appear at all in Act II of the opera – I felt I could manage it, but I had only two weeks to learn it.'

Captain J.M. Doyle had conducted two operas, *The Lily of Killarney* and *Faust* (with Heddle Nash singing the title role) for the old Dublin Operatic Society, but after the 'split', which resulted in the formation in 1941 of the Dublin Grand Opera Society, he was invited by his Irish Army colleague, Bill O'Kelly, to conduct for the DGOS. Doyle thought that the tall and slim Joseph McLoughlin would cut an impressive figure as Pinkerton, the U.S. Naval Lieutenant.

When I talked with him in the early 1990s at his home in suburban Dublin, he said with a wry sense of humour, 'We hammered the role of Pinkerton into Joe McLoughlin. May Devitt and Julia Grey worked very hard on him and it paid off. Julia had done the same with James Johnston, for when he arrived in Dublin to sing in *Rigoletto* he was a novice in operatic terms. She was thorough and very patient and in the case of young McLoughlin spent hours teaching him the notes. It wasn't easy work.'

More experienced singers filled the other principal parts. The reliable John Lynskey was cast as Sharpless, the American Consul, Michael O'Higgins as Boze, a Japanese priest, and May Devitt the geisha Cio-Cio-San. The production got a good press. The *Irish Times* critic wrote: 'The DGOS would have to go a long way to find a better combination than May Devitt and Joseph McLoughlin.'

The singers were praised for their expressive love duet in Act I, and the majority of critics agreed that May Devitt's "One Fine Day" and her farewell in the final act, "Beloved Idol" were movingly sung. In the Dublin operatic circles of the time, her Butterfly was regarded as a portrayal of international stature and is still talked about today in glowing terms.

Although his acting in no way matched that of May Devitt, Josef Locke says today, 'I got away with it. I felt I had sung the role of Pinkerton quite well. I remember the Gaiety audience gave May and myself a great hand at the final curtain. She was wonderful to sing with and our voices blended well.'

He was next cast as the poet Rodolfo in *La Boheme* and like *Madama Butterfly* the opera would be sung in English. Julia Grey and May Devitt again got to work on the tenor and did not let up until he knew the part. Even as he and May Devitt walked side by side in Grafton Street or O'Connell Street she would be humming the music or going over with him the words of the love duet in Act I.

'We were glad to have him at the time', recalled Col. J.M. Doyle years later. 'We had plenty of baritones but a real scarcity of tenors. But Joe was, I'm afraid, a lazy singer as far as opera was concerned. He loved to sing the big arias and hit B Flats or high Cs, but learning recitatives proved a tedious exercise for him. However, he mastered the roles he attempted, even if on occasions I had to pull him up at rehearsals when he got the words mixed up. That could be sometimes very amusing and it was as well that the audience didn't hear some of the verbal slips!.'

While the Gaiety audience received the first night of *Boheme* enthusiastically, the critics for the most part expressed their reservations about the production. In a brief review in the *Irish Press*, 'P.T.' stated that 'May Devitt was as good as ever as Mimi, with the additional virtue of much reserve in the quieter passages. Joseph McLoughlin's Rodolfo was not his best work: the singer was evidently troubled by a cold.'

'Taken all round it was a meritorious production by the DGOS', observed the *Irish Times*, 'not perfect but thoroughly enjoyable, with May Devitt always acting in character and her singing was intensely dramatic – at times almost too passionate.

'Playing opposite her was Joseph McLoughlin as Rodolfo, the poet. It was his debut in the part and he came through the ordeal creditably. His movements were to the point and his singing had a fine ringing tone, especially in the well-known aria in the first act. There were odd moments in the ensemble singing when he seemed uncertain, but he pulled through alright.'

The critic praised John Lynskey's acting and singing as Marcel, the painter and described him as 'the life and soul of the quartet of

Bohemians.' The *Irish Independent* critic 'J. O'Neill' was more critical of the production than any of his colleagues and went on to outline the merits as well as the blemishes. He praised the performances by May Devitt and John Lynskey but stated that the DGOS set Joseph McLoughlin a difficult task by casting him as Rodolfo.

'Vocally the part is well within his scope', he observed, 'but much more than ability to sing the notes is required. An accurate appreciation of time values, a sense of poetry, and a Bohemian romanticism, must all be used for a full interpretation of the part. The duet with Marcel was spoiled by the tenor's failure to observe a pause note entering the second verse.'

He was critical of the chorus work in Act II, and stated there were 'many uneasy moments'; the playing of the orchestra was, in his opinion, disappointing. Unlike his colleagues, he did not take into sufficient consideration the fact that Joseph McLoughlin was new to the part of Rodolfo, a role acknowledged as one of the most demanding vocally in the tenor repertoire.

Looking back, Josef Locke could not recollect suffering from a cold on the first night of *Boheme*. He was encored for 'Your Tiny Hand is Frozen' in Act I and felt he sang with greater ease than in *Madama Butterfly*. As he said, 'The part suited my high tenor to perfection and I thought the audience reaction, especially at the end of Act I, was tremendous. The critics didn't worry me. I was happy enough helping out my friend Bill O'Kelly, even if the financial rewards were paltry.'

By now he had become friendly with James Johnston and once or twice sat in a Gaiety Theatre box to hear him sing in *Carmen* or *Rigoletto*. He admired him greatly as a singer and never failed to be moved by the feeling he brought to the "Flower Song" in *Carmen*. 'Jimmy Johnston and myself never had a wrong word', he recalls today. 'I knew he admired my voice and said so to colleagues, but I recognized that as a singer he was far superior to me. I used to joke him about his butcher shops in Belfast, telling him that he could afford to sing in opera and that I really couldn't. He had a grand sense of humour and to him Protestants and Catholics were all alike. Jimmy made a great contribution to opera during the war years in Dublin.'

In 1944 the DGOS decided to put on Ponchielli's spectacular opera, *La Gioconda*, mainly as a vehicle for the society's outstanding mezzo, Patricia Black. May Devitt was cast as Gioconda and, to the surprise of some opera buffs, Joseph McLoughlin as Enzo Grimaldi, a Genoese prince, a role first sung in Dublin by Joseph O'Mara. The action is set in Venice and the music is melodic, the story itself passionate and dramatic. The opera was first performed at La Scala, Milan, in 1876.

The production caused a stir in Dublin and booking was exceptionally brisk. The *Irish Times* described the production as 'an enormous success for the DGOS' and added that it was truly lavish and spectacular. 'Typically Italian, the opera is full of flowing melodies with wonderful choral effects, while the ballet music is brilliant. There was a first-rate team of principals, headed by May Devitt, who gave a passionate study of the ballad singer. Her acting is forceful and her singing had a great urgency. Patricia Black, as Laura, had one of those dramatic parts in which she revels and she rose to splendid heights.'

Joseph McLoughlin must have been heartened by what the *Irish Press* critic wrote about his performance: 'Joseph McLoughlin had the exciting tenor role of Enzo, the Genoese nobleman. He has improved enormously and though his acting is still somewhat stilted, one forgot it in listening to his resonant voice. His rendering of the big aria, "Heaven and Ocean" was highly artistic.'

'The tenor part in *La Gioconda* abounds in graceful music', stated 'J.O'N' in the *Irish Independent*, but Joseph McLoughlin did not make the most of his opportunities as often his tone was muffed by varying methods of vocal production.'

The critic was obviously more impressed by the performances of May Devitt and Patricia Black and pointed out that the dramatic situations in which they figured were convincingly carried. Both sang, he said, with fire and colour and their duet in Act I raised the first thrill of the evening.

Today Josef Locke has mixed feelings about the occasion. 'John McCormack, I do remember, was the DGOS's guest of honour and he and his wife, Lily, occupied a box overlooking the stage. After the applause had died down at the final curtain, he was invited on stage to meet the cast and chorus. I was standing centre stage as he walked past me to congratulate May Devitt and tell her how well she had sung Gioconda. Then he went along the line and shook the hands of Patricia Black, Michael O'Higgins and Nora Finn. When he came to me I expected him to congratulate me too; instead, he looked at me and remarked, "As for you McLoughlin, grand opera is not your forte." I was taken aback, indeed puzzled why he should say such a thing. Bill O'Kelly, who had accompanied him on stage, obviously heard the remark and must have wondered if I'd go on singing the role that week. I reckoned I'd sung the part well; at least the audience thought so; I had had to encore the big area "Heaven and Ocean" for them.'

Although now in his 80s, Col. J.M. Doyle, the conductor, remembered the occasion clearly and agreed that Joseph McLoughlin had sung the role of Enzo wholeheartedly, but that the real stars of the opera were Patricia Black and May Devitt. He had watched from the podium as McCormack met the principals and chorus. 'I remember him shaking May Devitt's hand and smiling as he congratulated her. She, like himself, was a pupil of Dr. Vincent O'Brien. In my opinion, May had sung a difficult part exceedingly well. Naturally McCormack made a fuss of her, as he did in the case of Patricia Black. Because of this, maybe Joe McLoughlin felt he was being ignored and became upset. Although McCormack could be very blunt when he wanted to be, I don't believe he would deliberately snub a fellow artist. He might have said to Joe in a whisper to confine himself in the future to operetta or songs and ballads. Or that he did not think grand opera was really for him. I would have said the same thing. You need to be a musician to sing opera, you must possess a special vocal technique and know how to preserve your voice over a two or three hour stretch. I felt at the time that Joe would make an excellent interpreter of the musicals of Lehar, Sullivan, Offenbach and Johann Strauss. I suspect that where grand opera was concerned he was aware of his limitations, though that is not to suggest he let down the DGOS. Far from it. He did very well for us and got us out of a dilemma.'

McLoughlin's mixture of charm and sparkle appealed to the Dublin public. Bill O'Kelly was convinced that with a few years vocal training in Vienna the tenor would have emulated Richard Tauber and become an operetta star in his own right. As he said, 'Joe's got the notes, all he needs is the technique and the discipline.'

To Col. J.M. Doyle, James Johnston was always the more likely to be a success in opera, for unlike McLoughlin he arrived in Dublin from Belfast with voice training behind him. He conducted him in DGOS performances of *Faust* and *Rigoletto* and regarded his singing of Faust as superb.

To Dublin opera buffs it came as no surprise when in 1945 the society cast Joseph McLoughlin and May Devitt as the lovers in *Romeo et Juliette*. They looked a handsome pair and their voices blended appealingly; off-stage, they were lovers and this provided added interest for audiences who by now regarded them as popular stage stars. Offstage, they were sometimes seen travelling together in a horse-drawn carriage through Dublin's streets. 'Joe and May liked to do things in style,' recalled an oldtimer.

Joseph McLoughlin confided in May Devitt that Romeo was the most difficult operatic role he had tackled; in particular, his attempt to pick up the notes from the orchestra. Usually she or J.M. Doyle gave him musical cues. The opera was a resounding success when premiered in Paris in April 1867, but the DGOS was staging it for the first time and it would be sung in English. The Gaiety audiences responded warmly, clearly captivated by the mellifluous music.

The *Irish Times*, in a short critique, observed: 'May Devitt and Joseph McLoughlin in the leading roles were convincing; their singing in the garden scene of the second act and the vault scene of the last act were among the best things they have done.'

'E.H.W.' in the *Irish Independent*, commented: 'The sincerity of May Devitt's acting as Juliette and the beauty of her singing were the chief contributing factors in the success of the production. Her powers as an actress were seen to best advantage, notably in the scene in Juliette's bed chamber.

'Joseph McLoughlin was a romantic Romeo. His reading of the part was on the whole rather too restrained as compared with Miss Devitt's intense acting, but he did rise to dramatic heights in the duel scene and his farewell to Juliette.'

A few nights later, Bill O'Kelly watched from the wings and concluded that on this occasion the young tenor was being over-amorous and tended to spoil at least one love scene. O'Kelly, who was known to take no nonsense from either tenors or divas, tackled Joseph McLoughlin after the final curtain.

'Cut out that business on the settee, Joe', he said with undisguised anger. 'It's a bit too bloody much.'

'Bill meant every word he uttered', said Josef Locke, recalling the scene with amusement. 'I was leaning over May Devitt as I sang, while at the same time I kept sliding her arm away from under her to make her lie back further on the settee. By now as I lay across her I was almost touching her lips. To Bill O'Kelly, it was obvious that I was too ardent a Romeo.'

The warm, sensuous timbre of his voice seemed ideally suited to Gounod's music, and his use of *mezzo voce* produced some honeyed tones. Nonetheless, when his voice is discussed today in opera circles some professional judges of singing express the view that the top of his voice was too light and too thin to cope with big operatic roles. Others claim that with adequate training he could have won fame in lyrical Donizetti, Rossini and Bellini roles.

Pianist Jeannie Reddin, who accompanied Josef Locke in concerts, thought that with the right discipline and dedication he could have been successful in opera and have been Ireland's answer to Heddle Nash. She felt, however, that with his larger- than-life personality an operatic career would have been too restrictive and certainly less remunerative than top of the bill in variety.

Dr. Havelock Nelson remembered James Johnston telling him how good a voice Josef Locke possessed. 'Joe has a better voice than myself.' He himself thought it a well-focused high tenor voice that often throbbed with feeling for the songs he sung.

Hubert Valentine was convinced that the Derry singer had done the right thing in pursuing a career on the variety stage and instanced his great successes at the London Palladium and later in Blackpool.' Joe was made for that kind of show business career', he said. 'He once told me he loved the glamour and the excitement – and the money was very, very good. And he was shrewd enough to look after it. I don't think he would have had the patience and dedication to pursue an operatic career. It is a different world altogether. As a star variety act he had the charisma – and the voice – that audiences loved.'

Soprano Renée Flynn was impressed by his singing of Pinkerton and believed that had he come to opera earlier and been trained in voice technique he would, perhaps, have made a success as an opera singer. 'Joseph McLoughlin had a better voice than some other tenors who followed a career in opera', she said.

To Renée, Joe was 'a bit of a character' and once to her astonishment, met him 'parading down a corridor of the Gaiety Theatre in full Pinkerton regalia'. She stopped him in his tracks. 'I looked at him and said crossly, "Where do you think you're going, Joseph McLoughlin?" It was during the first interval of *Madama Butterfly* and he said he was dying for a cup of tea. I reminded him that performers never mingled with the audience in this way. He took my advice and sauntered back to his dressing-room.'

She had sung Violetta to James Johnston's Alfredo in *Traviata,* but her favourite role remained Nedda in *Pagliacci*. She regarded May Devitt as the perfect Butterfly and an under-rated Tosca. She has no doubt that given the opportunity to study in Italy, May would have emulated Margaret Burke Sheridan.

To Col. Doyle the tenor was also 'a character'. During a performance of *Romeo et Juliette* at the Opera House Cork, he found him having a sip of champagne with May Devitt at the interval. It always struck him that Joe liked the good life, though as a performer he worked very hard and in that way was a good professional. Gaiety Theatre audiences loved his Romeo and Pinkerton, too, and his appearance in an opera was worth a few hundred pounds at the box office. One old Dublin opera buff told me,

'Sure we used to go to the Gaiety to see Joe's clinches with May.'

Together they starred in *Show Boat*, one of the big Dublin musical successes at the time. With the war over, McLoughlin began to think of spreading his wings. He turned down an offer from Bill O'Kelly to sing Mario Cavaradossi in *Tosca* in DGOS's spring season in 1946; he also told his friend James Johnston that he had decided against making opera his career. When Johnston showed surprise, Joe remarked, 'For God's sake, Jimmy, the money's no good. I'd to death starve on it.'

Impresarios began to show an interest in his singing act with May Devitt and word had reached London of the pair's popularity in Dublin. Col. Bill O'Kelly expressed no surprise when Joe McLoughlin told him that he and May were leaving to sing in variety in London. O'Kelly was to tell me later, 'I knew we couldn't keep him in Ireland and that opera would never be his goal. He was made for the variety stage. But he hadn't let me down and for that I was very grateful. Without Joe and Jimmy Johnston we would have been hard put to put on wartime opera in Dublin.'

Joseph McLoughlin had come to the opera stage in a curious way. As a boy he lived just outside St. Eugene's Cathedral in Derry where Professor Joe O'Brien - Dr. Vincent's brother - was the organist. 'I got the job of singing the *Credo*,' he recalled, 'so that meant no more pumping the organ for Joe! I was about twelve and my soprano voice hadn't broken. It was considered a good voice and I had already won feis awards, though my oldest brother Paddy's voice was better than mine; he won the tenor award on three consecutive years.

'Being a bit of a wild young fellow, I was caught a few times looking for bald heads in the congregation beneath me, so I was quickly dispatched to again pumping the organ. After my father's cattle business fell on tough times, I left school at fourteen and, in truth, I think the Christian Brothers were glad to get rid of me. To make ends meet, I worked for a while in small jobs that paid paltry wages.'

Eventually, he joined the Irish Guards and was posted to Cairo. At 18, he was the youngest sergeant in the Guards. He was a drill instructor with, as he good-humouredly recalled, 'a high-pitched voice that could be heard for miles around.' In Cairo, he began to sing at open-air concerts with the band of the Irish Guards and a number of the concerts were broadcast by the BBC.

On his return to Northern Ireland, he joined the RUC in Belfast, but came to hate the job. He had already gained a reputation in the force as a singer of songs and ballads and was determined to make singing his career. He was told that Dublin comedian Jimmy O'Dea, whose variety company was playing Belfast for a week, was holding auditions for a singer and he immediately decided to go along. He had no music with him but O'Dea, a small, soft-faced man, listened attentively as he sang, "I'll Walk Beside You"; he was then asked to sing something with a high note and belted out "Ave Maria".

'I'm hiring you McLoughlin', Jimmy O'Dea told him. 'When can you start? I'm prepared to pay you £6 a week if you come to work for me.'

He explained to the comedian that he would have to apply to get out of the police force. It wouldn't be as easy as Joe reckoned. When the tall Derry singer informed his senior officer that he intended to be a full-time singer, he was told he wouldn't be allowed to leave. He persisted and eventually joined the O'Dea Company that included Noel Purcell, Vernon Hayden and a little dancer called Maureen Potter.

Young McLoughlin quickly discovered that a show business life wasn't all glamour, especially when you travelled by truck from place to place. You were expected to prepare the stage, borrow props such as chairs, tables, furniture, even china. In Loughrea, County Galway, the hall belonged to an undertaker and the company members had to build the stage on top of empty coffins. He decided he had had enough. He complained to the company manager that he had joined as a singer and not as a furniture remover. And when Jimmy O'Dea said they would be leaving at a specified time in the morning, McLoughlin snapped, 'I'll not be there.'

He felt he had done well on the short tour with the company. People were enthusiastic when he sang "Count Your Blessings" and "Toselli's Serenade" and called for encores. In Dublin he was met by Harry O'Donovan, a talented scriptwriter who tried to persuade him to go back to the O'Dea Company. Eventually he did rejoin it in a show in the Gaiety Theatre billed as 'So What!' He became a particular favourite with women, singing highly romantic numbers like "Love's Last Word Is Spoken" and "A Tear, A Kiss, A Smile".

But it was not until he sang in opera that people took him seriously as a singer. Strangely at the time he had no fears about tackling opera, though he admits that he probably would have had later. 'I suppose I was too young to have real fears. Nor do I remember having been nervous on the stage. Singing operatic roles gave me the utmost satisfaction, especially with May Devitt. I suppose my biggest thrill was singing the great love duet in Madama Butterfly. I was a big strong fellow and instead of caressing Butterfly and walking her into the bedroom, I just lifted her like a butterfly and carried her in. The audience warmly applauded.'

He was introduced to Margaret Burke Sheridan during this time and she proceeded to give him some advice on how to sing Pinkerton. 'She was always nice to me', says Josef Locke today, 'and was present on the first night of *Butterfly*. She used to say to me, "Mind your voice, Joseph, it is a good voice." May Devitt, for her own reasons, avoided her.'

Joseph McLoughlin's first date in London was at the popular Victoria Palace in a variety show with some of Britain's top stars. When it came to billing him on the programme impresario Jack Hilton decided the name McLoughlin was too long and changed it to Locke, and similarly Joseph to Josef. 'I had no objection', he recalled. 'I did object, though, when Jack wanted soprano Pat Kirkwood to partner me. I told him that May Devitt was better than myself and he looked at me and remarked, "Well, if that is so, get her to come over and sign a contract."'

Their appearance on the show, in which they would close the first half, was a big hit. Josef Locke would soon be in the big money. Later, as a solo artist he was engaged to sing at the Palladium. Soon he deputised for Beniamino Gigli in a concert at the Albert Hall, an experience that he was not likely to forget.

'It was, I remember, a black tie affair with lots of celebrities in the audience, as well as my own Palladium fans. Jimmy Johnston was seated in the first row and when I came on he gave me a smile. I began to sing "Questo o quella" in English and got through the first verse alright, but I totally forgot the words of the second. Ivor Newton was accompanying me and suddenly realised my dilemma, but he kept playing the piano in the hope that the words would come. At the same time Jimmy Johnston was trying to prompt me, but I couldn't hear him. In desperation, I sang the second verse in pidgin Italian and must have got away with it for there wasn't a boo to be heard in the house.'

He was introduced to Richard Tauber in London and in Glasgow met Gigli who was staying at the same hotel. In conversation, the renowned Italian tenor expressed surprise that he hadn't pursued a career in opera. Josef Locke told him he was earning £2,000 a week as top of the bill. Gigli wasn't impressed. 'I earn that for a single concert', he said.

He was seldom out of the news. He ran into difficulties with the British Revenue Commissioners and for a time left Britain altogether, but after a few years wisely settled with them. In the Seventies and early Eighties the name Josef Locke was once again prominent in Dublin variety. Whenever he wanted, he packed the Olympia Theatre in Dublin, singing the songs synonymous with his name, "Blaze Away", "I Did It My Way" and "Festival of Roses".

Today he lives quietly with his charming wife Carmel in the cosy village of Clane in County Kildare, but as ever his ebullient personality seems to attract publicity. In the early Nineties, for instance, it was a film based loosely on his career - *Hear My Song* - that once more brought newspapermen and TV cameras to his door. Eventually they found him happily ensconced in an armchair by the front window of Jones' lounge bar in the main street of Clane with a pint of Guinness before him on the table.

The film, a great hit in Britain and Ireland, featured many of Josef Locke's favourite songs and when a CD was released of them it quickly sold in thousands. Locke, surrounded by press and friends, joked about his new celebrity status. He talked about his glory days at the Palladium and at Blackpool and other highlights of his 40-year career. Although in his late seventies, he travelled to England for a television programme *This Is Your Life*, based on his life and times. He was introduced to royalty and invited to America, where *Hear My Song* had taken off in a big way.

On Irish radio listeners heard the voice of Locke sing songs from his popular CD. One particular number, "Take A Pair of Sparkling Eyes" from Sullivan's *The Gondoliers* confirmed what Col. J.M. Doyle and other good judges had said years before, 'Joseph Locke can make a fine operetta singer.'

Interestingly, in the wave of fresh publicity about his career few, if anyone, referred to his operatic career in the Forties. During my interview with him in Jones' lounge bar, he said he felt very proud of his days with the DGOS and as if to remind 'the crowd drinking next door in the bar', that he was once an opera star, burst into an aria from *La Boheme* that brought cheers when he hit a high C with all his old gusto. 'See', Joe said gleefully, 'I can still do it!'

It didn't worry him that a younger generation had never heard of his Romeo or Rodolfo; that he had sung the parts was all that mattered to a man as legendary in his own way as the great Luciano Pavarotti. He drinks three pints of Guinness a day, then he will rise and walk back to his bungalow in the village and to his wife Carmel. 'D'you know', he said, 'Carmel's favourite tenor has always been Gigli. Imagine that!'

Chapter Seven

Veronica Dunne

SOJOURN IN ROME

'I fell in love with all my Rodolfos', declared Veronica Dunne with an impish smile.Singing Mimi, the role that would make her famous, she always found an emotional experience, for in the opera she and Rodolfo quickly fall in love at their first meeting in the cold Parisian attic.

'You can fall in love on stage', mused Ronnie – as she is affectionately known – 'especially if your Rodolfos happen to be handsome.' She recounted with typical frankness the story of Oreste Kirkop who was one of her Covent Garden Rodolfos; he had just made a Hollywood musical, *A Vagabond King* and on his arrival in London was met by press reporters and photographers.

'So there I was, lying on my deathbed in the last act of the opera, and he was to lift me up', recalled Veronica Dunne. 'He had this wonderful head of hair, so I thought, "I know, I'll run my fingers through it; very romantic. And next thing – oh, God – my fingers came out the far side, and I couldn't understand why his hair was so sticky underneath until it came off in my hand. And I said, "Oh, I'm terribly sorry" and stuck it back on his head. I nearly died, and so did my love for Rodolfo!' ·

She remembers other Rodolfos, John Lanigan, Rowland Jones, Charles Craig, Richard Verreau and James Johnston, whose voice she described as magnificent, though she facetiously added, 'Jimmy was always trying to flirt with me. I used to push him off and joke with him, 'You're a married man, Jimmy, go away outa dat for God's sake. My God, tenors are all the same!'

Singing her first Mimi at Covent Garden provided her with one of her most memorable operatic moments, for among the audience that night in 1952 was Margaret Burke Sheridan who in the 1920s had sung Mimi on the same stage on numerous occasions.

Veronica Dunne acknowledged the diva's assistance in her preparation of the part. 'Margaret went through the entire opera with me, every movement, every subtlety. She showed me how to cry and how to express many of the more psychological aspects inherent in the character of Mimi.'

After the performance she came backstage and kissed and hugged the young Dublin soprano in her dressing-room. 'Margaret liked my Mimi, in fact she told me she loved it. There was no hint of jealousy that I had emulated her achievement. I think she was proud of my success. To her it was simply an Irish singer's success.'

Veronica came to adore the role of Mimi. 'You need to be young to be Mimi, to throw yourself totally into this puppyish love and then after you've died on the bed, not to want to come back to life again.'

Like 'Maggie from Mayo', she had been educated in a Dublin convent. Brought up on the north side of the city, she was reared with as much music and horse riding as her father - a building contractor - could contrive to find for her. 'I had two ponies and went hunting four days a week. My father kept all his racehorses with Tom Taaffe - and he also had a lovely baritone voice, as had my brother William Dunne. And so, too, my seven uncles. We were allowed to stay up to listen to Margaret Burke Sheridan on radio. It was a singing family but then those were the days of musical evenings. You never went to a party without your music and your party-piece ready. A party was always drink, supper and then songs from 20-odd guests and duets and trios and quartets.

'My father's piece was one of Mario's arias from *Tosca,* but usually most guests went for Balfe's *Bohemian Girl, Maritana* and *The Lily of Killarney.* The lovely Balfe aria, "I dreamt I dwelt in marble halls" was always a popular item, and of course those were the days when it was possible to get vassals and serfs to attend you; money certainly bought more.'

School, she remembered with mixed feelings. She once recited a verse that went, 'One month married, all goes well. Three months married tummy begins to swell. Six months married, tummy begins to crack. Nine months married out comes Jack.'

For reciting those rather harmless lines the 13-year-old Veronica Dunne was expelled from Eccles Street Convent. Worse than that, her parents were no help; they, too, felt the shame of the forbidden words. 'My parents' attitude was that I had disgraced the family. My father was furious with me and did not speak to me for six months.'

As a young girl she was strong-minded and stubborn, but she would say later that at the time she did not understand the words that caused her expulsion; what were called the facts of life were still a mystery to her. At the convents which followed Eccles Street she paid no attention to the classes or the teachers. From being a star pupil she became an academic non- entity. Paradoxically her academic failure set her life on the course of success, for on leaving school she felt she had a point to prove. Certain characteristics were now noticeable. She had an appetitie for physical haz-ard, a desire to romp like a boy, a tendency that caused her to be nick-named 'Ronnie'. And she was an ardent young huntswoman with a qual-ity that she still retains today, which is an ability to make clear-minded, irrevocable decisions.

Most important of all, she was blessed with an exceptional singing voice. It was really big by the time she left school. She studied in Dublin with Hubert Rooney who advised the young soprano to go to Italy for further study and to work in a true operatic atmosphere. Taking his advice, she went to Rome in 1946. For a 19-year-old it was a daunting task.

Veronica Dunne had moved from post-Emergency unrationed Dublin to dire post-war Rome where food was scarce and poverty everywhere. Her first breakfast in the convent where she was staying consisted of a piece of dry bread and coffee made from the grounds of roasted orange peel. It had been a chance meeting with Monsignor Hugh O'Flaherty, known by then as the Pimpernel of the Vatican for his hiding of Allied PoWs from the Nazis, that had brought her there. Her next problem was finding a coach.

Since all the best voice teachers were gone – most of them to America – it wouldn't be easy. Eventually, she found the elderly Contessa Calcagni, who enjoyed an illustrious reputation. Vernoica's voice lessons started with the Contessa at 8 a.m. but from 11 to 2 p.m. she also had a repetiteur carefully taking her over all the best-known operatic roles. Every evening she attended either an opera or a classical concert, just the same routine that Margaret Burke Sheridan had followed years before in the Eternal City.

For the next two years she found time to travel to other opera houses outside Rome to hear outstanding singers. She attended performances of *La Boheme* with Magda Olivero as Mimi in order to write down the diva's every stage movement and expression and learn them all by heart.

Although the post-war austerity in Italy was not easy to accept, she did not complain for the simple reason that her father would have dragged her home to Ireland. Furthermore, she felt insulated living in a convent in Rome. As she said, 'I was carefully protected by Irish priests, especially Monsignor O'Flaherty who made it his business to ensure that I never went out with Italians. Probably a wise thing, too; can you imagine how easy it was for all those green Irish girls in Rome to get into trouble surrounded by all those gorgeous young Romans? I mean, I thought you had to have an operation to have a baby!'

Her fascination with opera grew. Once she went to a performance of Massenet's *Werther* and like many others waited at the stage door afterwards to congratulate the tenor Tito Schipa who had sung the title role. 'As he signed my programme I remember he asked me what I was doing in Rome and I told him I had come to study there. He had a superb vocal technique and when I asked him how long it would take to learn it, he replied, 'My dear, I am over 60 and I am still learning; every day I am learning more and more.'

On another occasion she went to the Argentina Theatre to hear the

Verdi's *Requiem* with Toscanini conducting. The tenor was Gigli, the soprano Maria Caniglia and the mezzo Ebe Stignani. Afterwards, when she was introduced to Beniamino Gigli, he smiled as he said, 'Ah, La Sheridan! What a wonderful singer she was and what a marvellous Butterfly. I can still hear her beautiful voice.' Then Signora Stignani joined their company and recalled hearing the diva sing Butterfly at the San Carlo in Naples. 'The Neopolitans loved her because she sang from the heart.'

Listening to these tributes made young Veronica Dunne feel intensely proud of La Sheridan. As she says today, 'I have heard many recordings of the famous Butterfly duet but none of them can compare to that made by Margaret with the tenor Pertile. I never tire of playing it over and over again. When I'm asked how good an artist Margaret was I tell people to listen to that recording. It is superb.'

Returning to Ireland in 1948, Veronica started practising for a musical festival at Southport where she won first prize in the soprano section. In Dublin she was in demand for concert and oratorio work and in 1949 made her operatic debut with the Dublin Grand Opera Society as Micaela in *Carmen*.

Anxious to complete her studies in Italy, she went back to Rome and for the next 13 months studied under Fernando Calcatelli. Years later asked about that experience, she was to say, 'As a vocal teacher, I always develop voices top and bottom, but they never exploited my top in Italy and so I never had the psychological comfort of knowing there were four or five notes more to go above my highest.'

On her return to Dublin she sang Ravel's *Sheherazade* in a radio symphony concert and later in the year was heard in *Messiah*. Singing Marguerite in *Faust* for the DGOS really brought her to the notice of the Dublin operatic public. 'I'll never forget the ovation I got from the Gaiety Theatre audience', she recalled. 'At the final curtain they simply rose to me, applauding for minutes on end. It was my first experience of personal excitement in the opera house and I loved the feeling. It was as if the audience wanted me to do well. For a young singer, acclamation like this can be an undoubted stimulus.'

She was back in Italy again at the beginning of 1952 to take part in a competition for operatic singing in Milan and got through all the preliminary rounds successfully. A visit to Dublin to sing Mimi in *La Boheme* with an Italian company intervened and that June she was summoned back to Milan for the final round of the competition. In this, she received an award entitling her to sing the part of Mimi in an Italian opera house. Three performances of *Boheme* at the Teatro Nuovo, Milan, resulted and after an audition at Covent Garden, she joined the company in September 1952.

For Veronica Dunne, who was 25, it was an ambition achieved. She made her debut as Sophie in *Der Rosenkavalier* and it was in her own words 'a nerve-racking experience.' She was already under- studying a number of roles when news came through that the original Sophie had fallen ill. Forced to learn Richard Strauss's complex, if beautiful score, in two weeks, she made a knee- trembling entry on the Covent Garden stage.

'The scene where Octavian presents the rose to Sophie - it has gorgeous music, you know... Well, Constance Shacklock was singing Octavian. She always reminded me of somebody playing hockey - "bully, darling, jolly good show", that kind of person - but she was a marvellous Octavian. Anyway, she presented me with the rose, and she was to hold my hands in her hands for a long moment. I started to shake, and I was shaking so much that she started to shake, too. So there we were, shaking away, until eventually she said, very briskly, "My dear - give it back to me." Nerves are dreadful. You never get over them, no matter how long you sing.'

They were austere days for the young soprano. She earned £10 per week, had a ration card which permitted only one rasher, one egg and one chop a week, and indulged herself in a weekly treat with Joan Sutherland of sausages and chips at Lyons Corner House for one shilling and three-pence. In a relatively starless Covent Garden, however, her repertoire expanded and her confidence grew.

Early in 1953 came her big opportunity. Sir John Barbirolli chose her for the important role of Euridice in Gluck's *Orfeo ed Euridice* alongside the contralto Kathleen Ferrier (Orpheus) and Adele Leigh (Amor). The conductor was determined that Ferrier's Orpheus would be the finest ever produced, and he had secured the best possible production talent. Although she was suffering from cancer, Kathleen Ferrier 'had this overpowering desire to sing in the opera' and said she would go ahead.

Everyone, including Veronica Dunne, considered the English contralto extremely courageous. The first performance went without a hitch, however, and the critics showered praise on the production. 'Kathleen Ferrier's Orpheus is a wonderful achievement,' stated the *Observer*.

'I knew I was in the presence of greatness,' recalled Veronica Dunne. 'It was a sensation I would never forget. Kathleen's voice was even better on stage than on record and when she sang "Che faro senza Euridice" you could hear a pin drop in the opera house.'

It was during the second performance on 6 February a crisis arose. In the second act, as she went to move, Ms. Ferrier experienced 'a searing pain and her leg ceased to function'. Barbirolli suddenly realised that something terrible had happened, but felt powerless. Adele Leigh said, 'I could see something was dreadfully wrong with Kathleen, but I was unable to get to her to help.'

Disregarding her stage instructions, Veronica Dunne moved over beside her. 'I could immediately see she was in intense pain and must be got off the stage. As the orchestra played, Kathleen whispered to me, "Veronica, I can't stand the pain." I begged her to hold on. I put out my hand, palm upwards, in the classical Greek manner and she took it. By supporting her like that she was able to drag her leg along, and I helped her from the stage. She was perspiring.'

Amazing as it may seem, the great contralto forced herself back on the stage for the closing music. The cast, including Veronica Dunne, were dumbfounded. 'All I could do was to stand back, astonished. Like the others, I hadn't realised how ill she was until this moment. Kathleen had never mentioned her illness.'

For the Dublin soprano, there would be less poignant operatic memories. Singing Susanna to Joan Sutherland's Countess and Geraint Evans's Figaro afforded her great satisfaction, but she was not to achieve one of her greatest ambitions and that was to sing Desdemona in Verdi's Otello. As she explained, 'I suppose the reason was that so few productions of the opera were presented in my time at Covent Garden or for that matter, in Dublin. It was a role that appealed to me greatly.' She did add to her repertoire, however, the role of Floria Tosca and sang some performances opposite Otakar Kraus's Scarpia which she counted a thrilling experience.

'I remember in rehearsal that he advised me to stay as passive as possible in my scene with Scarpia. His words were, "Stay put. You are supposed to be frightened of this man, this cruel Chief of Police, so much so that you are afraid to move. Think of the Gestapo."'

Kraus's dramatic intensity and innate interpretative powers were, she said, matched by the marvellous flair of Geraint Evans in comic roles. 'You were conscious of their star quality and singing on stage with them was an inspirational experience.' But just as her own career looked certain to scale new operatic heights Veronica Dunne's thoughts turned to love and marriage.

In 1953 she married Peter McCarthy, whom she had known since she was 16. He was a progressive young businessman and the couple decided to settle in Dublin. She was 26 and for an artist was making the ultimate sacrifice. In retrospect, she says, 'I was too young really to get married. My international career was about to take off and London was the place to be.'

In future she would have to fit in her career with her marriage. Soon she became a commuter between Dublin and London and elsewhere, and after her children were born, the burden of combining two careers wasn't easy. 'I became one of the first weekly commuters, boarding the 7 a.m. DC3 flight each Monday to London and trying to keep my stomach while the two Wright Cyclone engines hammered through the fuselage. That sort of life played hell with my voice.'

Furthermore, the weekly farewells 'played hell' with her emotions, as

Monday after Monday she left behind two tearful, resentful children. But she managed, even if she was to admit later that marriage curtailed her career. She continued, however, to fulfil engagements at Covent Garden and with the DGOS. In November 1957 she was called on at very short notice by the society to sing Antonia in *Tales of Hoffmann*, while on the same evening James Johnston, the Hoffmann, was confined to bed with 'flu. Edgar Evans hastened from London to replace him and only arrived at the Gaiety Theatre with 15 minutes to spare.

If the performance itself was regarded by some critics as 'no better than a dress rehearsal in the circumstances,' Veronica Dunne emerged with much praise. 'I hope to goodness we'll soon see Miss Dunne in a more cheerful role,' stated the *Evening Press*. 'Her voice is now at its richest and fullest and she is a skilful actress who would, I believe, excel in the high comedy vein.'

In the *Irish Independent*, Mary MacGoris commented: 'Our Miss Dunne covered herself with glory – she was completely convincing as the love-struck Antonia : she looked absolutely delightful and she gave us consistently the best singing of the night.'

In 1962 the soprano was invited by Dr. Tom Walsh, the Artistic Director of the Wexford Festival, to sing Suzel in Mascagni's *L'Amico Fritz* opposite Nicola Monti, the outstanding Italian lyric tenor who was a tremendous favourite with festival audiences. The opera appeared a year after the resounding success of the same composer's *Cavalleria Rusticana* and was first performed in Rome in 1891.

Her success in the part prompted at least one Dublin critic to ask why Dr. Walsh had not used Veronica Dunne before. It was a valid point, for her voice, with its penetrating top and rich middle register, coped effortlessly with Mascagni's music. An RTE recording exists of the stage performance and either singing individually or with Monti her performance provided immense pleasure.

In that same year at Wexford the brilliant young Italian soprano, Mirella Freni, made her festival debut as Elvira in Bellini's *I Puritani*. She was instantly hailed as a discovery. Veronica Dunne remembered the soprano for another reason. 'Mirella asked me to act as her interpreter when she approached Dr. Walsh for a first-class ticket home to Italy at the end of the festival. It seems Tom had allowed her only a third class ticket on the journey from Italy. I remember she said to me, "Veronica, how do I say these things in English"? I think I proved a good interpreter on her behalf! As a singer, Mirella had what I like to call star quality and a glorious voice.'

Back in Dublin, she herself was engaged by the DGOS to sing Manon in Massenet's opera. If the critics differed on the overall merits of the production, there was unanimity about the quality of the soprano's singing.' The soaring phrases and constant warmth of Veronica Dunne's voice made every point in the composer's case for Manon,' observed Mary MacGoris in the *Independent*. 'She gave us the character from her sprightly gaiety and brittle vanity to the dramatic climax in Saint Sulpice and her last, lost cry on the road to Havre.'

Charles Acton in the *Irish Times* found the English translation of Manon stilted. 'I am a strong advocate of opera in the vernacular,' he pointed out, 'but as that is a minority opinion in these islands, it is obvious that opera in English must be given superb presentations with first-class singers and utterly clear diction.'

With the exception of Miss Dunne, all the singing had depressed him, and he went on to describe them as 'threadbare voices, full of wobble without the artistry to make up for lack of quality. On the other hand, he said that Miss Dunne's Manon became a real character and her singing was beautiful from Act II onwards.

To Brian Quinn in the *Evening Herald*, Manon was an ideal vehicle for her luminous voice and the soprano clearly loved the role. He wondered, as had other critics, why she had not expanded her French repertoire by adding to it Marguerite and Louise. But in the Dublin of the time opportunities for such expansion were limited.

She became a regular guest artist with Welsh National Opera, singing Mimi and Tosca in Cardiff and on tour. She added the role of Nedda in *I Pagliacci* and scored a personal success. There was a surprise in operatic circles when she continued to ignore Verdi. In conversation with the soprano I put the question to her. 'I was afraid of Verdi,' she admitted. 'I preferred to concentrate on Puccini, although I did once sing Aida in a concert version of the opera in Neath in Wales.' She could say of course that Margaret Burke Sheridan also ignored Verdi, except for the role of Desdemona.

She recalled with a hint of nostalgia the occasion she sang Carmen in Kilrush, Co. Clare in the sixties and considers the Bizet role as one of the most exciting in the operatic repertoire. 'Kilrush was great and had lots of atmosphere,' she said, 'and introduced to Ireland, singers, who though in the veteran class, did not lack excellent artistry. It's a pity that these venues had to vanish from the operatic map.'

When I asked her about some of her other memories, Veronica did not hesitate to mention May Devitt's Butterfly. 'May was a fine actress and every inch Puccini's conception of Butterfly. And she sang it so beautifully, too. She was also a very convincing Tosca as well as an Aida.'

She admired tenor Charles Craig's voice enormously and she thought that Oreste Kirkop was the most romantic Rodolfo she partnered, and that baritone Otakar Kraus was the finest individual artist.

Mixing the roles of mother and opera star was, she discovered, increasingly difficult and although she counted herself fortunate in having an able home help, the conflict in her mind remained. As the children reached the ages of 10 and 12 she felt her place as mother was in the home, or at least in Dublin near them.

'I loved my children,' she said, so living out of a suitcase was for her emotionally draining. For the sake of them and her marriage, she was prepared to see her career suffer and consequently restricted her appearances in opera and oratorio.

In the early 1960s she added a new dimension to her life by accepting a role as a singing teacher. Henceforth she would mostly concentrate on imparting knowledge to Ireland's aspiring divas and tenors. For the next 25 years her dedicated work at the College of Music in Dublin would bring her deep respect and the gratitude of many young singers. She admitted that at the outset the transformation from singer to teacher was a gradual one.

'One day I realised quite suddenly that I was content in myself as a teacher. I couldn't go on travelling, but I could relive my life through these young people – by showing them, through the mistakes which I had made – how to be successful.'

As a teacher, she relied for the most part on the Bastini technique which she had acquired in Italy. At the same time she transmitted to her students a burning ambition to succeed, even at the price of abandoning conventional education, much as she had done herself for different reasons. Her personality was forceful, totally individualistic – so much so that her pupils were sometimes referred to as the 'Ronnies' and her classes as the 'dream factory'.

Gradually her dedication became almost obsessional. Teaching was her life to the point where she took home some pupils to live in her home. Once she told me, 'Sometimes my two children were quite bitter about this. They made jokes about making appointments to see me. And I suppose it is true that you cannot make a career out of music and be a wife and mother. Of course the rules were different in my day, but now I encourage my students, "Live with him, my dear, but don't marry him".'

In the 1990s when she went public to air this philosophy it caused quite a stir not only musically but morally. Was her statement too sweeping? Surely there were exceptions to the rule? For instance, English dramatic soprano Josephine Barstow has been quoted as saying, 'The single girls in this profession are to be pitied – even on the most mundane level. Where, for example, does a woman alone go to eat in a strange city? Hopefully, as her career progresses she will eventually acquire a caucus of friends in most operatic capitals, but this takes time.'

Soprano Kiri Te Kanawa has said that her happy home life has gone a long way in alleviating the pressures of her career. As she put it, 'The children need me a lot so the pressures of work are left out of the front door and are only encountered again the next day. I feel lucky because I know I am one of the few singers to combine a completely satisfying working life with a happy home life. But it means having no social life at all – just a very few close friends.'

While the majority of singers I talked to were in favour of marriage, others were prepared to put their careers first, mainly because singing being today so competitive they could more easily cope without a permanent partner. There were female singers who agreed with Veronica Dunne's theory that marriage must wait if a career is to be successfully launched internationally. Singers know what is required of them if they are to climb the ladder; in a word, they've got to be skilful networkers, patient, resilient, ambitious, disciplined and ready when an unexpected opportunity arises. You will find that the word relationship is often more commonly used than marriage, particularly in the case of the younger generation of singers, which probably suggests that for their own reasons they are in no hurry to tie the knot. Who can blame them, for the opera world, to take but one aspect of a singer's career, has never been more competitive and it takes exceptional talent to make it. Yet, as this book shows, the Irish are not faring badly in this respect but they have got to work tremendously hard to achieve success.

Young Irish singers have been fortunate in the good teachers at their disposal. Veronica Dunne, for example, has followed the fortunes of her students all over the place. I have met her in Cardiff, Bristol and London and such is her caring attitude that she not only shares their successes but their frustrations and failures as well. 'Ronnie pulls no punches,' one young soprano told me in Cardiff. 'If she thinks you could have done better she's the first to tell you. But when you've done well she's the first to hug and kiss you. Ronnie's wonderful to have around you.'

Undoubtedly one of the most moving moments in her long career arrived on a June evening in 1990, when to mark her retirement at the age of 65 from the College of Music in Dublin her pupils and past students came together to pay Ronne, as they called her, a very special tribute. It was soon evident that some thorough preparation had gone into the organisation of the concert. Suzanne Murphy flew in from Cardiff, Anna Caleb from her home in Switzerland, Angela Feeney from Munich and

Andrew Murphy from Vienna where he was singing with the Vienna Chamber Opera. The concert proved a delightful affair, featuring arias, duets and trios sung by Nicola Sharkey, Marie Walshe, Therese Feighan, Ciaran Rocks, Suzanne Murphy and Angela Feeney. At the conclusion of the concert Ronnie Dunne joined the artists on stage and the audience, including her husband Peter stood in silence to listen to the Balfe aria "I dreamt I dwelt" recorded years before by the soprano. It was a fitting climax to an emotional evening.

Nearly a year later when she was invited to speak in the Concert Hall of the RDS, Veronica Dunne delivered one of the most comprehensive talks on music heard in the capital. She reminded the big attendance of what another well known singing teacher Jean Nolan had said in the past:

> The singer's career in Ireland is fraught with grave financial uncertainty. Unlike the instrumentalist there are no means open to the singer of obtaining constant employment and too few opportunities of public performance. It is, therefore, not surprising that few Irish students can afford to spend years in studying for a profession which can offer them little prospect of eventually earning a living in their own country.

Veronica Dunne conceded, however, that the art of singing in Ireland had reached a very high level indeed and each year strove to reach greater heights. Dealing with the complexities of the human voice, she remarked, 'The voice, the most delicate of all musical instruments, needs very careful guidance. It must develop slowly and master a fine technique which will sustain the singer throughout a long career. They must become first class musicians. Knowledge of a vast repertoire not only in opera but Lieder, French song, English and Irish songs and of course oratorio is essential.

She went on to outline other requirements: 'Acting skills are most important to help singers enhance their operatic roles. One can no longer walk on stage and stand there like a block of cement. Deportment and presentation on and off stage are vital. They must be also fluent in two languages and have a knowledge of at least two others. Not only do they learn the music of the eminent composers like Schumann, Schubert,

Mahler and Strauss, but they must learn about the poets whom they the composers had chosen for their songs.

'When they study an operatic role they must also learn not only the music but the libretto, what period it took place in and what events happened in that era. On a more personal aspect, breath control is essential for singers, and that does not happen overnight. Every day it is imperative that they do one hour's exercises to develop their lungs and rib cage. The energy a singer needs to project sound is unbelievable. When a singer stands on an operatic stage that singer must project his/her voice over an orchestra which is spread across the full width of the stage with the possibility of a 100 or more musicians in the pit.

'In the past singing was never as specialised as it is now. Today a singer must be very versatile - we have to move with the times. It used to be that the singer would stay for the month or six weeks during an opera season, now they fly in, sing the role and fly on to another opera house. Alfredo Kraus is the only singer in the world who refuses to jet to and fro, with the result that he is now in his middle 60s and singing superbly. He lives on his interest not on his capital, and that is what you teach our young singers.'

To the young singers among the attendance it must have come as a surprise to hear Veronica Dunne declare that 'it takes eight years or more to develop a voice that will endure six hours a day over a period of three or four weeks rehearsing for a major operatic role.' But she did add, 'It is possible of course to do it in four or five years, which nowadays is essential because of limited finances. Between the cost of vocal tuition, opera and Lieder coaching, learning of languages and a singer's keep, we are talking in the region of £7,000 per annum; so over a period of four years, we arrive at a figure of £28,000. When God gives them voices on the law of averages he doesn't provide them with money.

'How then do we approach the problem? Mainly by government grants or sponsorship from industry and commerce. I personally would favour a mixture.' She said she was greatly encouraged by the number of Irish singers who had left the country and were more than capable of competing with the best in concert halls and opera houses.

By early 1993 she was teaching in the Leinster School in Dublin and planning with her young students a production of *The Magic Flute*; not only that - she was advocating a new opera house for Ireland, a place that Irish singers could call their home. As she told the RDS gathering on that March afternoon in 1993, 'Our actors and actresses are well catered for with the Abbey and Gate theatres; they at least have a home. It is time now to find one for our singers and unless the powers that be realise this, the wealth of voices we have on this island, is all lost for the future of our young singers.'

She admits the pull for performance is strong. 'I miss it still, I miss the excitement. I remember when I used to play Mimi the audience receded and it was as if they were not there. I entered into the part totally and when those curtains came down I had great difficulty returning to the present time, and sometimes even cried, such was the sense of loss coming back to reality.'

However, she is as energetic as ever. As she told me, 'I'm in the Leinster School of Music at 8 a.m. so that people can begin the day with their breathing exercises. Some of them are on my route, so I pick them up on my way in. There are more opportunities for singers today, but more competition also.'

A long time ago she discovered she was a good teacher and says it must be a gift that God gave her. 'I can spot a good voice and realise its potential. What I cannot predict is someone's commitment to study, to discipline.'

At 67, she still works nine hours a day, six days a week. It is a rare commitment.

Chapter Eight

Dermot Troy

SUCCESS IN GERMANY

Michael O'Higgins had called him his 'white hope' when he first began to give him singing lessons in the late 1940s at the Royal Irish Academy of Music. From the beginning, he had been impressed by Dermot Troy's light, expressive tenor voice and in no time he turned out to be a keen and earnest student, not just content to do the work demanded, but someone who searched for knowledge on his own initiative.

Young Troy, who was born in Tinahely, Co. Wicklow, on 31 July, 1927, faced up to the problems of learning foreign languages, which O'Higgins, a respected teacher, believed were essential for any singer with serious international ambitions. Around this time he formed all his students, including Gerald Duffy, Austin Gaffney, Arthur Agnew and Eithne McGrath into 'The Thirteens', for the specific purpose of giving them practical experience in ensemble singing. As a choral group they won the Culwick Cup at the Feis Ceoil in 1950.

O'Higgins' next step was to prepare them for a presentation of *The Magic Flute*. He had a genuine belief in the musical discipline of Mozart. In the opera, Dermot Troy would make his debut as Tamino, with Eithne McGrath as The Queen of the Night and Austin Gaffney as Papageno and Gerald Duffy as Sarastro.

Dermot Troy made an immediate impression. As O'Higgins later wrote, 'He sang the beautiful music with almost professional élan. I think I can say that all who took part in the performance were imbued with the Mozartian spirit.' The young tenor was even more successful in the society's *Don Giovanni*; his "Il mio tesoro" was encored. He had taken the rather surprising step of singing the aria in Italian, although he had sung the rest of the opera in English.

As a personality Troy was popular with his colleagues. His lively sense of humour and warmth of character made him particularly welcome in 'The Thirteens'. Michael O'Higgins was proud of the *esprit de corps* that existed in the society. He had brought in Dermot on a free scholarship and it was something he did not regret. Other Irish tenors he found aped after McCormack, but young Troy stood apart; it was a voice that was universal in tone and quality. Austin Gaffney was to agree. 'From the beginning, I felt he was destined for greatness. I admired his tenacity and his application to work.' Gerald Duffy thought that for a singer with no vocal training whatsoever he applied himself marvellously to the learning process. 'When he guested early on in a Sunday night concert I was presenting, it was quite obvious to me that Dermot was an exceptional singer with a golden tenor voice.'

The only time he tended to get annoyed was when colleagues joked about his weight or called him 'the big, fat tenor.' But for the most part he had a placid temperament and as Michael O'Higgins said, 'reserved his fire for stage performances.'

At this time the tenor's idol was the Italian lyric tenor Tito Schipa and almost every week he went off in search of his records, usually to shops along the Dublin quays. To Veronica Dunne, Troy's was an exciting voice and possessed a rare quality that was new to Irish tenors: a totally distinct vocal timbre. Once when she sang Lehar duets in the Phoenix Hall with him, she was taken by his easy style. 'Dermot struck me as good-humoured, a man who loved people.'

By now romance had blossomed between Dermot Troy and Eithne McGrath. Eithne, who had come to the academy on a scholarship at the age of 11, first met Dermot in 'The Thirteens' and it struck her almost immediately that he looked rather sad. It was then she learned that he had buried his sister Peggy and it was plain that her death had deeply affected him. Although he did not come from a musical background, she was impressed by the way he adapted himself to study at the academy, especially to foreign languages. He told her he had been in the RAF in England for more than three years and loved the experience; in fact, it was only family commitments that brought him back to Dublin.

Ironically, it was while singing at the RAF Club in Dublin that his talents were first recognised and friends persuaded him to have his voice trained. 'Dermot was handsome and intelligent and a very special person,' recalled Eithne McGrath. 'Listening to him sing, I knew he had a special quality in his voice, but there was also a sadness in it. I mentioned this to Michael O'Higgins and he attributed it to the sorrow Dermot had experienced in his early life, losing his sister and his father, both of whom were dear to him.'

In 1952, when the *Sunday Independent* ran 'The Great Caruso Contest' in conjunction with Metro-Golden-Mayer Film Company and London impresario Harold Fielding, he was declared the winner of the Irish section. Accompanied by Anthony Hughes, he sang the lovely aria "Spirto Gentil" from Donizetti's *La Favorita*, and looking back, Hughes says, 'Musically, it's a demanding aria but Dermot gave a mature performance for a young singer and adapted himself well to the bel canto style. I was very impressed and became more confident than ever about his future prospects. And the unaffected beauty of his singing proclaimed him a worthy winner in the final.'

In the overall final in Britain he came runner-up. An indication of the high standard of the contest was underlined by the fact that baritone Peter Glossop came only fifth; Glossop would go on to become one of his country's finest Verdi interpreters.

For his excellent showing, Dermot Troy was awarded a special British scholarship. Remaining in London, he studied with Dino Borgioli and found time to sing with a touring company formed by the British Arts Council. He was by now engaged to be married.

'We were very much in love,' says Eithne Troy today, 'and Dermot was looking forward to settling down. I was determined to do all I could to further his career, even if it meant giving up my own interest in singing.'

An accomplished pianist, she realised that musically she could be of assistance to him and was determined to help him achieve his ambition in a sphere that she had no illusions about. 'I knew that singing was an arduous life and that he needed the back-up to achieve international status.'

In 1954 he accepted an invitation from Jani Strasser, the chief coach of the Glyndebourne Festival Opera Company to become a member of the chorus and in addition to act as understudy to Peter Pears in the role of Evandre in Gluck's *Alceste*. From the outset, he was very happy in the idyllic surroundings of Glyndebourne. Conductor Bryan Balkwill was on the Glyndebourne music staff at the time and remembers coaching him for Mozart and Richard Strauss roles which he was either performing or covering, and even played cricket with him in a team drawn from the singers, directors and other staff at the opera house. 'Dermot worked very hard, but he also could enjoy himself. I regarded him as a promising Mozart singer.'

'He had come to the right opera house', said Eithne Troy. 'There were some eminent artists there and it had a reputation for style and technical perfection. Dermot was so eager to see all the operas performed in the small theatre that he was prepared to act as usher. Eventually he was invited to join the Covent Garden Company but much to his frustration Glyndebourne would not release him, claiming they wanted him for other main roles.'

In October of 1954 during one of his trips to Dublin to broadcast for Radio Eireann and fulfil concert dates, Dermot Troy was married to Eithne McGrath. Many of their musical friends attended the wedding reception. A few months later the couple travelled to America on a three month tour with a talented group of Irish artists under the direction of Kitty O'Callaghan.

Later, Dermot Troy received another invitation to join the Covent Garden Company as a principal tenor and on this occasion the

Soprano Catherine Hayes...
the 'Irish Nightingale'

Tenor Joseph O'Mara... given
the freedom of Limerick

INSIDE THE ATTIC MUSEUM... LIAM BREEN DISPLAYS JOHN MCCORMACK'S PAPAL SWORD

GUS SMITH SIGNS THE VISITORS' BOOK... 'OBLIGATORY', SAYS LIAM BREEN

JOHN McCORMACK RETIRED EARLY FROM THE OPERA STAGE

BARITONE WALTER MCNALLY RELAXES IN MILAN WHERE HE WENT FOR VOICE COACHING

MARGARET BURKE SHERIDAN...
AS MIMI IN 'LA BOHEME'

TENOR JOHN O'SULLIVAN...
FRIEND OF JAMES JOYCE IN PARIS

TENOR JAMES JOHNSTON...
POPULAR ARTIST WITH THE DGOS
IN THE 1940'S, LATER ACCLAIMED
AT COVENT GARDEN

JOHNSTON AS PINKERTON IN 'MADAMA BUTTERFLY',
ONE OF HIS BEST ROLES

JOHN LYNSKEY
A SPLENDID VERDI BARITONE

FROM TOP: JOSEPH MCLOUGHLIN; MAY DEVITT; PATRICIA BLACK; SOPRANO RENE FLYNN; MAIN PHOTOGRAPH IS LT.-COL. BILL O'KELLY... BROUGHT JAMES JOHNSTON TO DUBLIN FOR THE DGOS

May Devitt... her 'Butterfly' was loved by Dublin audiences

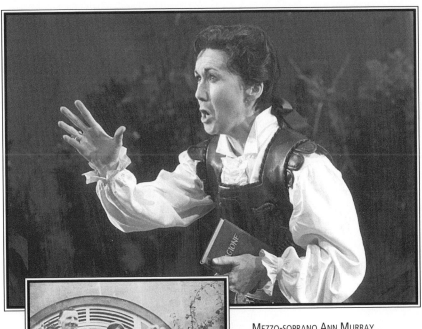

MEZZO-SOPRANO ANN MURRAY...
IN HANDEL'S 'ALCINA' AT COVENT GARDEN
IN THE 1990S

SCHOOL-GOING ANN WITH HER
PARENTS IN DUBLIN

ANN MURRAY, 1994

ANN MURRAY (STANDING) AND VESSELINA KASAROVA IN A SCENE FROM
MOZART'S 'LA CLEMENZA DI TITO' AT THE 1992 SALZBURG FESTIVAL

VERONICA DUNNE SINGS MIMI TO
ORESTE KIRKOP'S RODOLFO IN
'LA BOHÉME'

SOPRANO
VERONICA DUNNE...
RELAXES AT HOME

SOPRANO SUZANNE MURPHY... AS THE PUCCINI HEROINE TOSCA WITH WELSH NATIONAL OPERA
INSET: SUZANNE OFF-STAGE

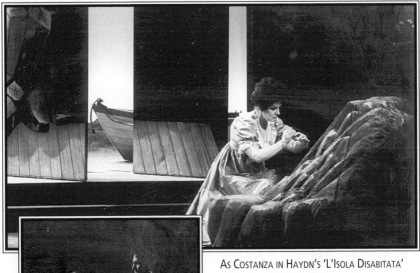

AS COSTANZA IN HAYDN'S 'L'ISOLA DISABITATA'
(1982 WEXFORD FESTIVAL)

MEZZO-SOPRANO BERNADETTE GREEVY AS
FEDERICA IN VERDI'S 'LUISA MILLER' AT THE
WEXFORD FESTIVAL IN 1969

BERNADETTE SANG THE TITLE ROLE IN HANDEL'S
'ARIODANTE' (1985 WEXFORD FESTIVAL)

BERNADETTE GREEVY

DERMOT TROY... AS OTTAVIO IN 'DON GIOVANNI', ONE OF HIS FAVOURITE ROLES

TENOR DERMOT TROY
AS TAMINO IN
'THE MAGIC FLUTE'
WITH PILAR LORENGAR,
PARIS, 1961

DERMOT TROY AND
EITHNE MCGRATH
ARE MARRIED IN DUBLIN

Glyndebourne management agreed to release him. During the summer recess, however, he sang with the Glyndebourne Company in Verdi's *Falstaff* at the 1955 Edinburgh Festival.

'We settled down eventually in Barnes', recalled Eithne Troy, 'and straight away Dermot worked very hard to make a success of his Covent Garden contract. What really brought him to the fore were two contrasting roles: Vasek in *The Bartered Bride* and David in *Die Meistersinger*. He had taken over from Peter Pears in *The Bartered Bride* and it was felt that his Vasek would not be of the same high standard, but Dermot gave the role an entirely different interpretation and scored a personal triumph. He refused to play Vasek as the fool – and it worked.'

The critics agreed on this point. J.H.E. in the *Guardian* wrote: 'Vasek was admirably done by Dermot Troy, who exposed the character's absurdity without descending into excess of caricature.' Another English critic stated that Troy resisted the temptation to be merely funny as the stuttering and slow-witted Vasek, and his blend of serio-comic and semi-pathetic was perfectly performed making this bashful swain both lovable and entirely convincing.'

Ernest Newman, one of the most distinguished critics of the day, wrote in glowing terms of the tenor's singing as the sailor in the revival of Berlioz's *Les Troyens* and again for his beauty of tone as David in *Die Meistersinger*. Indeed, Eithne Troy is convinced that his success as Hylas in the Berlioz work was the turning point in his career.

'I remember that Dermot was only on stage a short time, but his singing was exquisite and the audience responded enthusiastically. It was a fine cast that included Jon Vickers, Richard Verreau, Amy Shuard and bass Forbes Robinson, who a few years before had beaten him in the final of the British Voice Competition.'

Eithne knew that Dermot was disappointed that Covent Garden had refused to cast him as Tamino in *The Magic Flute*. 'More than anything else he wanted to sing this role, but nothing would move them. After his success, however, in *The Trojans* I knew it would not be long before he was asked to sing major parts.'

Cork-born tenor John Carolan, a contemporary of Dermot's was at Covent Garden for the performance of *Les Troyens* and says he has never forgotten the impact made on him by his singing in the scene at the beginning of Act 5. 'I remember Dermot sang the sailor's aria with plaintive and compelling tone, beautifully reflecting the sailor's nostalgia for his homeland. As he sang, there wasn't a sound in the packed house. His singing was quiet and persuasive, but filled every corner of the opera house. It had a profound affect on me and others who heard it.'

It was during his spell at Covent Garden that his deafness came to light, when a visiting conductor noticed that the tenor sometimes experienced difficulty hearing the orchestra. He was completely deaf in one ear, which was caused by an explosion while he was serving in the RAF in England. Dermot remained very sensitive about the fact. He first confided in his wife Eithne and henceforth the handicap proved a very delicate matter with him. He just didn't want people to know about it and never wanted to discuss it.

'Dermot managed to live with it,' says Eithne Troy, 'and the deafness never seriously affected him. I think it would have taken more than that to hold him back. He was always very determined.'

It was a busy time for the young couple. By now they had two children, Alanna and baby Mabel. But Eithne was happy and found time to entertain Dermot's musical friends. When she could, she attended his performances at Covent Garden, and although many of the roles he sang like Borsa in *Rigoletto* and Flavio in *Norma* were minor ones, she had the satisfaction of watching his vocal improvement. For instance, when he sang Monastatos in *The Magic Flute*, the critic A.M. in *The Stage* commented, 'Only Dermot Troy of the cast seemed near the true spirit of the work.' Occasionally she worried for fear that he was working too hard. There were times when he rehearsed in the morning and in the early afternoon and that night performed either in *Carmen* or a Strauss opera. Sometimes she noticed how desperately tired he was on arrival home and wondered if he was being pushed too much. 'I'd advise him to take it easy and not exhaust himself, but there was little he could do about it as the programme was set out for him.'

He became a record collector and she remembers him going out on Saturday mornings in search of 78s of Gigli, McCormack and Schipa which he was able to purchase for a few pence. At home she sometimes accompanied him on the piano in tunes synonymous with Richard Tauber, a tenor he much admired. He returned to Dublin to sing Don Ottavio in the DGOS spring season and was warmly received to Gaiety Theatre audiences.

'It says a great deal for Dermot Troy that he made so much of the difficult and inherently colourless part of Don Ottavio,' stated the *Irish Times* critic. 'As this is his first major professional role in Dublin it was all the more pleasing. "Il mio tesoro" was beautifully sung and I congratulate him on his recovery in "Dalla sua pace" from a slip that could happen to anyone in the circumstances.'

On his return to London, he was asked by the illustrious soprano Elisabeth Schwarzkopf to sing the part of The Italian Singer in a new recording by HMV of Richard Strauss's opera *Capriccio*. Seemingly, the invitation came about after the soprano had read sometime before Ernest Newman's praise of the young tenor in *The Trojans*. He was now in exalted company, for his colleagues included Fischer-Dieskau, Hans Hotter and Anna Moffo. Better still, he spent some time in Salzburg rehearsing and recording the opera. It was an experience that stayed with him for a long time. It sowed the first seeds in his mind that perhaps Germany would suit his style of singing. He began to discuss the subject with Eithne and his close friend at Covent Garden, the German bass Frederick Dalberg.

In due course, Dalberg told him that Mannheim was looking for a principal lyric tenor. 'I remember him ringing Dermot and asking him to apply immediately for an audition,' says Eithne Troy. 'I knew that my husband always loved a challenge and wasn't afraid to meet one, so I thought to myself that this is it. Singing Mozart in Germany would also be important to his career and help him master the Mozart style and vocal technique so essential to do full justice to the composer's operas.'

Frederick Dalberg, who by now had returned to live in his native Germany, was present in 1958 at Troy's audition in Mannheim and years later recalled, 'I can still remember the outburst of applause he caused when he sang "Una furtiva lagrima". Although Dermot was actually needed for the following season, the management of the opera house engaged him on the spot'.

Shortly afterwards the Troys were accorded a warm welcome by Dalberg and his wife Ellen when they arrived in Mannheim to begin a new life. It was soon apparent to Dermot Troy, however, that the staff and singers at the opera house did not particularly like 'outsiders' coming in and taking the leading jobs there. It was known that principal tenors did not speak to each other in some German houses and there was a definite resistance to foreign singers.

'When Dermot explained what was happening, I was naturally taken aback,' recalled Eithne Troy. 'Because he was appointed first lyric tenor there were objections and eventually it led to an industrial dispute between the Intendant and the opera house singers. A meeting was held and the Intendant told the strikers that if they could nominate a better candidate than Dermot he was prepared to consider him. Since there was no one of his calibre in Mannheim there the matter rested. I can't tell you how relieved Dermot and I felt.' After he had made his debut in the house as Belmonte in Mozart's *Il Seraglio* there was little doubt that he would become a favourite with audiences.

For Eithne Troy and the children life was comfortable and when she found time she attended his performances in *Cosi fan tutte*, *Don Giovanni*, *The Magic Flute* and *The Barber of Seville*. His Ferrando in *Cosi fan tutte* was described by one German critic as 'faultless, with the tenor in complete command, in the recitative as well as in the arias – a delightful Ferrando.'

With his flair for languages, he quickly mastered German, so well in fact that some people in Mannheim believed he was German. Eithne Troy remembered how he worked hard on achieving proper pronunciation of the language and perfect diction. 'Sometimes he'd come home after a rehearsal, or indeed a performance, and go straight to the bookshelf for a dictionary to check words. He was a great student and for someone who had left school at fourteen years of age in Dublin, was acquiring a fund of knowledge. But he never got above himself.

'He was always careful not to allow fame to go to his head. After a year in Mannheim he was being described as the perfect Ottavio and a singer wonderfully suited to Mozart, but he always felt he had more to learn. He was now being classified as a Mozart tenor and that in Germany was a considerable honour. I knew that as an interpretative artist and as an actor he had considerably improved; his musicianship and vocal artistry had never been in doubt. I had always admired his musical understanding and his search for perfection.'

During his second year in Mannheim, he began to guest in some leading German opera houses, including Hamburg State Opera where he was to be engaged as leading lyric tenor under unusual circumstances. He had appeared in a performance of *Il Seraglio*, stepping straight onto the stage without any preliminary rehearsals. In the first interval the General Manager Rolf Liebermann offered him a contract for the next three years.

The tenor's name was being mentioned in the same breath as that of Fritz Wunderlich. Essentially a Mozart singer, Wunderlich was being acclaimed in all the German houses for his Tamino, Ottavio, Belmonte and Ferrando, though his repertoire extended also into Rossini, Smetana, Janacek and Donizetti.

'Dermot talked a good deal about Fritz Wunderlich' said Eithne Troy. 'He came to know him in Hamburg and made no secret of his admiration for him. He once told me that Fritz had the edge on him, that he had a unique vocal quality, a kind of honeyed tone as he described it. He never envied him his place in Germany. As he would say with a smile, "Dear, there's room for Wunderlich and Troy in Germany".'

To Eithne, there was a humility about her husband that was matched only by his innate charm. 'I never heard Dermot say once that he was famous; he left it to others to judge him. All the time he wanted to be better. His wasn't a big voice, but it projected well in an opera house. He would invariably ask me how he sang and I would be truthful with him.

For instance, I thought his Tamino was ahead of his Duke of Mantua. Joining the Hamburg State Opera meant a tremendous lot to him; it was though he had reached some kind of summit in his career. He was recognized as a star; people waited outside the opera house for his autograph. I felt immensely proud of him and his achievements.'

At times, though, she worried about his excessive smoking and the deep fatigue that came over him. Since she first knew him in Dublin he had seldom, if ever, let up on cigarettes in spite of advice from well-meaning friends and, indeed, a stiff warning from his doctor in London. His singing career could also be stressful, what with lengthy rehearsals, actual performances and travel. Eithne's own maxim is that as a singer you live on stress anyway. With the birth of their third child Vivienne she became even more aware of her husband's health and welfare.

Yet when he suffered a totally unexpected heart attack in June 1961, just shortly before he was about to take up his contract in Hamburg, she was shattered. 'It was a great shock to me, to everyone,' she says today. 'I was utterly unprepared for it. In those days heart attacks at the age of thirty-four were rare, though in Dermot's case there was a heart history in the family.'

The news spread through the music world rapidly. His friends in Dublin were incredulous. Later, the American baritone Thomas Tipton would recall what exactly happened. He had first met Troy in Mannheim and they became friends and also sang together in a number of operas, notably in *Cosi fan tutte*, *Don Giovanni* and *Rigoletto*.

'My first awareness of Dermot's heart condition was in an *Otello* performance, where I sang the role of Iago and he the part of Cassio. In a scene, which appears in the first act, Cassio has a very strenuous duel and it was in this scene that I first saw the pain in his face. I was afraid that he would not be able to finish the act. Despite the pain in his chest he did continue. A doctor was called immediately and his pain was relieved.'

After the performance, he was rushed to hospital and a cardiograph was taken. Eithne Troy, who had arrived there by now, was informed that her husband had suffered a heart attack. He would have to rest and give up singing for a while. She decided that it was best perhaps that he convalesce in Dublin, so she made arrangements for them to leave Mannheim. In the meantime they were told that Hamburg was prepared to leave his contract open, which was indicative of their high regard for him.

Dermot Troy put on a brave face in Dublin. He managed to laugh and smile with old musical friends, but everyone knew it wasn't easy for him. 'I really felt for him,' says Eithne Troy. 'Singing was his life and I knew he derived tremendous pleasure and satisfaction whether singing in the bath or in an opera house. He was told that on no account must he sing until he was passed medically fit again.'

He tried to be patient and resigned, but it wasn't easy for him. As the months passed he and his wife discussed the possibility of returning to Germany. Medical opinion indicated that he would be able to sing again. Just as Eithne Troy felt that her husband would not be able to take much more of the passive life in Dublin and his endless days of waiting, he received medical advice that he could return to Hamburg. To his wife, he seemed enormously relieved, a new man. With a wife and three young children, he had become more conscious of the economic aspect and worried about the future. In addition, he had eaten into savings during his convalescence in Dublin.

In April 1962 the Troys arrived in Hamburg and soon the tenor embarked on a busy operatic schedule. He sang some of his favourite roles in Mozart operas as well as Lensky in a new production of Tchaikowsky's *Eugene Onegin*. He longed one day to sing Rodolfo in *La Boheme*, but his wife felt he could not now sustain this role. There were times in the following months when he looked tired and not his old zestful self. He probably wasn't feeling terribly well during this period, for in late August 1962 he went for a medical check-up and insisted on seeing his doctor alone. Had he in fact a premonition of death?

Around this time Eithne Troy's father died and she returned to Dublin to attend his funeral. It was during her absence that Dermot suffered a fatal heart attack. He died on 6 September 1962 at the age of 35. Coming on top of her father's death, Eithne Troy was grief-sticken. For months she had been deeply concerned about him, but death had never once entered her mind. He just seemed to her too young to die.

When news reached Dublin of his sudden passing, the operatic world was stunned. People presumed that he had got over his heart condition and would sing for years. It was noticeable in the many tributes that emphasis was put on Dermot Troy's warm personality and infectious sense of humour. Michael O'Higgins summed up, 'The death of Dermot Troy at the peak of his career is tragic for those who love him; it is equally tragic for Irish music. He was the first tenor to break through to the world outside since McCormack, and in doing so he reflected credit on our musical standards and good taste.'

Had he lived, the tenor in the following year was to have fulfilled engagements in Covent Garden (as Tamino in *The Magic Flute*) and was to have sung in a number of operas for the Vienna Staatsoper.

James Johnston recalled his first meeting with the singer at Covent Garden and said he had been impressed by his pleasant personality and resemblance to John McCormack. When he sang, there was no doubt in his mind about the beautiful quality of his voice, his instinctively intelligent approach to music and technique.

'I doubt if Dublin ever heard the best of his singing,' added Johnston. 'He seemed to react with sympathy and projection to the London audiences and it was at Covent Garden that his gifts developed and that his wonderful voice was heard at its best. When he was offered an engagement in Germany, I advised him to take it. He was born to sing Mozart and one cannot say that about every tenor. I will always remember his singing as David in *Die Meistersinger*. This was, I think, the crowning achievement of his career at Covent Garden.'

In Germany his death was deeply mourned. Frederick Dalberg, his loyal friend in Mannheim, was to write later: 'Critics and conductors were unanimous in their praise of his beautiful voice, his musicianship and acting ability. He had a truly Irish voice full of warmth and sweetness. His singing of arias like "Dies Bildnis ist bezaubernd Schön" from *The Magic Flute* was truly unique; he was recognized as one of the leading Mozart tenors on the Continent.'

Dalberg recalled the feeling in Germany after Dermot Troy's death: 'His colleagues found it difficult to sing in the operas in which he had performed. He seemed to be present when they were being performed.'

'As his director at Mannheim, I greatly admired him for his capability to portray and interpret so many difficult and divergent operatic roles,' wrote Ernst Poettgen in a special tribute in *The Capuchin Annual*. 'Whether as the helmsman in *The Flying Dutchman* or the shepherd boy in *Acis and Galathea* or the amorous Italian nobleman, Don Riccardo in *The Triumph of Love* or Cassio in *Otello*, he gave a musical and artistic portrayal. His performances which I loved were always polished and will be forever remembered by me and by very many others.'

German artist Heinz Hoppe, in the same magazine, remembered his first meeting in Hamburg with Dermot Troy and believed that his real career began there. The lyrical parts of Mozart's operas were the tenor's forte and very soon Hamburg's opera lovers knew him as one of Mozart's best interpreters.

'I have in mind one first night when he sang Don Ottavio. The baritone was Hermann Prey, a very popular German baritone. The performance had the most delightful harmony and Dermot's part still lives in my memory so wonderfully did he interpret and capture the nuances of Mozart's music. Another part which Dermot himself loved and which he sang extremely well was Lenskey in *Eugene Onegin*. He seemed to live in the music.' Dr. Anthony Hughes recalled that he last heard the tenor sing in Dublin in Bach's great *B Minor Mass*. 'Dermot's singing exquisitely pure, classically restrained, in his solo, "Angus Dei", touched every heart as it reached its tranquil conclusion in "Dona nobis pacem"'.

The tenor's remains were brought back to Dublin for burial. Today, in her brightly lit sitting-room in her house in Upper Glenageary, Co. Dublin, Eithne Troy has her husband's photographs proudly displayed.

In conversation she talked quietly about their days together and her greatest regret that he died so young and at a time when the operatic world was at his feet. 'Dermot was a romantic and gentle person,' she reflected. 'He had a lovely cheerful laugh. I can hear him laugh now. I think of him as a special person rather than as a singer. He was different, a man full of honour.'

Music is still a part of her life. She gives Lieder lessons in the College of Music, something very dear to her. Unfortunately Dermot did not leave many recordings behind. Apart from an LP issued in the Sixties and that included popular songs, there exists only some privately made tapes and two operatic performances recorded for North German Radio in Hamburg. These are Haydn's *L'infedelta delusa* and Mozart's *Zaide*.

After her husband's death, Eithne Troy was particularly comforted by a letter from John Roynane, who at the time was leader of the RTE Symphony Orchestra, in the course of which he wrote, 'Dermot had realised in his short life what most people don't realise in a normal life's span.'

Chapter Nine

Ann Murray

SUCCESS IN SALZBURG

'The atmosphere of Salzburg is saturated by beauty, playfulness and art', wrote Max Reinhardt when he founded the Salzburg Festival with Hugo Hofmansthal and Richard Strauss in 1920. Ann Murray would agree, I've no doubt, with that poetic description, for this baroque Austrian city on the Salzach River remains one of her favourite places, and understandably so. She has enjoyed great success there in Mozart, Monteverdi and Rossini roles and has been quoted as saying, 'Since opera houses close for the summer, managements come to Salzburg and things happen from there.' But she was quick to add, 'In Salzburg, though, you work such long hours you haven't time to work out if you're a star or not. I haul my luggage around there just like everybody else. I don't have cars sent for me.'

She made her festival debut in the summer of 1981 in *Les Contes d'Hoffmann*, singing the part of the faithful Nicklause with Placido Domingo in the title role. James Levine conducted and the production was regarded by the critics as one of the successes of the season. During the duration of her stay in Salzburg, Ann and her husband, Philip Langridge, the English tenor, were joined at their rented house by their young son, Jonathan, and his private nurse as well as Molly Murray, who enjoyed travelling with her famous daughter and son-in-law.

To Molly, a vivacious and friendly woman, Ann's debut was 'very exciting.' She remembers her on stage with Domingo who was in wonderful voice. 'When I look back on my visits to the festival I count this production as my favourite. From the beginning, Ann told me she loved the atmosphere of the city and considered it a showcase for singers.'

A year later Ann was back at the festival singing in the same opera and with much the same cast. This was the Herbert von Karajan era when contracts were handed out to some of the greatest stars in the world, among them Domingo, Pavarotti, Carreras, Baltsa, Ludwig and van Damn. For the next few years she would figure in the new festival production of *Cosi fan tutte* with Riccardo Muti conducting, and managed to make the part of Dorabella her own. In this respect, she was fortunate to have as her Fiordiligo the exceptionally talented Margaret Marshall. As one visiting critic put it, 'These well matched singers have now arrived at perfect cohesion. Ms. Murray and Ms. Marshall have both beautiful voices and also – essential to this score – complement each other perfectly.'

Ann Murray looked forward to her, by now, annual visit to Salzburg just as much as her mother. 'If Ann wanted me to join her there with Philip and Jonathan, I was happy to pack my bags in Dublin and go', said Molly Murray. 'Usually the weather was lovely and I'd take in coach tours or go shopping. Most times I was able to attend Ann's first nights.'

Ann's next festival engagement was in the 1987 production of Monteverdi's *Il Ritorno d'Ulisse in patria*, in which she sang Minerva, a soprano role that fitted her high mezzo. If the opera's libretto is mediocre, the characters are well-drawn and the composer's genius ensured musical variety. But it was not regarded as by any means the success of the season.

The real challenge for her would come in the summer of '88 when she was cast as Angelina in Rossini's *La Cenerentola*, a role greatly revered by mezzos like Teresa Berganza, Agnes Baltsa, Lucia Valentini Terrani and Frederica von Stade. Four years before she had made her La Scala debut in the opera and in somewhat unusual circumstances. She had never sung the part in Italian and the prompter, she recalled, nearly had a heart attack when she told him so. Furthermore, she had no orchestral rehearsal and ended up, in her own words, 'feeling frozen stiff with fright' on the afternoon of the first night.

Molly Murray had made the trip from Dublin for the occasion and Philip Langridge and her London agent also made the trip. Against all the odds, the night was a triumph for her and the reception accorded her by the Milanese audience enthusiastic. But Ann was the first to confess, 'If Philip and my agent and my mother hadn't been there, I wouldn't have made it.'

Molly was again in Salzburg as Ann prepared for *La Cenerentola* and later told me, 'Ann was looking forward tremendously to singing this, her favourite role, at the festival, but a few days before opening night on 28 July she picked up a virus and I really felt she wouldn't make it. I knew, however, that she would go on if at all possible, as she's very determined.'

Despite her illness, she decided to sing but first the audience was asked to excuse her vocal condition. Plainly she struggled through the performance but was able to take a bow at a final curtain. She had not improved sufficiently to finish on the second night and Martha Senn stepped in and completed it. By the third night, 5 August, she felt much better, though one local critic remarked that 'she lacked her customary freedom and ease, and sounded and looked a bit nervous.'

With Riccardo Chailly on the podium drawing a superb sound from the Vienna Philharmonic, the production was a popular success with festival audiences; for Ann Murray it was a brave triumph over adversity. Indeed, it was a festival that she liked to forget for another more poignant reason. The premature death of producer Jean-Pierre Ponnelle touched her deeply; as friend and mentor his influence on her was considerable and had an important bearing on her career. During that season she had sung in his acclaimed production of *Le nozze di Figaro*, with Thomas Hampson getting rave notices for his masterful Count Almaviva.

A year later she was back in Salzburg to repeat the title role in *La Cenerentola*, but it was to be for everybody, both the artists and the administration, a strange event, one dominated by a single event - the death of Herbert von Karajan on 16 July,

Eleven days before it was due to open. As one paper observed 'In death as in life, Karajan was everywhere: his photographs in all the shop

115

window displays, edged in black.' He was scheduled to conduct the new production of *Un ballo in maschera*, but this was now undertaken by Solti.

Ann Murray was in much better voice on this occasion, and though Ralf Weikert was a far less inspiring conductor of the Rossini work than Chailly, she made a sympathetic heroine and was vocally secure in the florid coloratura passages. Later, however, Charles Osborne reviewing for *Opera* stated, 'The role of Angelina calls for a warmer vocal timbre than Ms. Murray displayed.' There were critics in Salzburg who thought otherwise.

The von Karajan era may have ended, but for the Dublin mezzo it was clear that the new festival regime, headed by the Belgian-born Gerard Mortier, wanted her back again. She returned in the 1990s to sing Sextus in *La clemenza di Tito* under conductor Riccardo Muti. With only a week to go to rehearsals, however, Muti withdrew, maintaining he could not collaborate on a production with whose interpretation he fundamentally disagreed.

Ann Murray was determined not to let the off-stage drama affect her performance, so it seemed was the rest of the stellar cast. The production was hailed as one of the big successes of that season's festival. 'Ms. Murray, whose voice really blooms in the Kleines Festspielhaus, showed herself a world-class Sextus and stopped the show with her great arias', wrote Hugh Canning for *Opera*.

By now Ann's husband, Philip Langridge, had become an established festival star following his success in the title role of Mozart's *Idomeneo*. The couple welcomed the opportunity to be together in the idyllic setting of Salzburg, for during the year they were often separated by their operatic engagements. Molly Murray continued to join them there and by now young Jonathan was able to go walking with her through the quaint, narrow city streets or stroll in the lovely flower-filled parks.

At other times she enjoyed meeting the glitterati that surrounded every festival. She was usually introduced as Ann's mother, or in the words, 'This is Molly Murray, Ann's mother.' With typical good humour, she will tell you, 'I don't mind being introduced like that, but I'd prefer to be known for myself.' Not that she doesn't take justifiable pride in her daughter's brilliant achievements. When she talks about Ann it is with affection and intense pride. They share an obvious zest for life and are both infectious personalities. Although Molly has been a widow for 20 years, she sees life as a celebration and derives her greatest fulfilment and joy sitting in an opera house listening to her daughter sing. She has no hesitation in saying that Ann's performance as Charlotte in *Werther* at the Vienna State Opera afforded her her most memorable operatic moment. As mother and daughter, they are close, yet Molly appreciates the pressures Ann has got to contend with and does not intrude. 'I'm there when she wants me', is her philosophy.

Wellfield House is the engaging home today of Ann Murray, her husband and son and is situated in Brook, a picturesque area of Surrey, and is over an hour's drive to central London. The house derives its name from the well at the end of the garden. In her spare time, Ann tends to the flowers or mows the grass but mostly this is left to the gardener.

Molly Murray is a fairly frequent visitor to Wellfield House and says it exudes peace and serenity. When Ann suggested that perhaps she should move there and sell her home in Dublin, Molly thought about it but decided not. 'My roots are in Ireland', she said, 'and though I appreciated Ann's kind offer, I wanted to be near my old friends.' She pointed out that Ann and her husband had their own music room in the house and this was cut off from their living apartments.

Molly is aware of the gruelling demands singing can make on individuals. A soprano in her early years, she was trained at the College of Music in Dublin, but sang only for pleasure. Musical evenings at home were the fashion in those days and she loved to sing along with her family and friends. She will now tell you proudly that Ann sang her first notes in the cot and after that there was no stopping her. Thinking back, she says, 'When I put her to bed as a child, she'd look up at me and ask, "Can I sing, Mummy?" I had no problem with her growing up.'

Later on she noticed how well she mimicked tunes she heard on the radio and brought her to be auditioned at the College of Music, where Denis Cox took her on when she was only four. Not surprisingly, her musical education included such trodden paths as St. Louis Convent, Rathmines, where she was one of the original Young Dublin Singers, and the Chatham Street College of Music, where she continued her studies with Denis Cox and, after his death, Nancy Calthorpe.

Nancy taught Ann for eight years. 'Ann was always an artist', she recalled. 'From the time she was ten and studied musicianship with me, and took lessons in the harp, she was able to hold an audience in the palm of her hand. In those early years she was a high soprano, never a mezzo, and even today I regard her as a dramatic soprano. I do believe that she was born to sing and I remember her successes in various competitions, in fact anything she went for she won. Her voice had clarity and beauty of tone, and her breath control was exemplary. Ann's mother, Molly, was always very supportive of her and I often met them together at recitals and concerts. She ensured also that she attended every lesson with me.'

Nancy was amused once when she took Ann to a performance of *Messiah* at - of all places - Dublin's National Boxing Stadium, for during the interval the girl spotted a young male friend and to Nancy's dismay vanished with him. 'I was raging when she didn't return for the second half of the oratorio. I had planned to bring her back to my place for supper so that we could discuss the night's performance. She could play tricks on you sometimes. Next day Molly Murray sent her in to apologise to me.'

When Ann was enrolled as a boarder at the St. Louis Convent, Monaghan she found that the nuns were very good at exploiting talent. There were choirs, end-of-term musical presentations and a generally healthy music environment which she enjoyed. Later, at university in Dublin she showed an interest in becoming a surgeon but was persuaded by her mother and Nancy Calthorpe to continue with her singing lessons, and in this respect won almost every competition she entered. 'I believed Ann's true vocation was singing', recalled Nancy. 'I tried to persuade her to go abroad.'

Ann was in luck. She was offered a scholarship by the Manchester College of Music and with assistance from Player Wills cigarette company in Dublin was able to accept the offer. Molly Murray would later say, 'Manchester was the greatest thing ever to happen to Ann.'

She studied with Frederick Cox and made steady progress. The death of her father in Dublin was to prove a shattering experience for as a father/daughter relationship it was close. He had enjoyed their musical evenings at home when either Ann's Uncle Tom or her mother played the piano and Ann sang. Sometimes she accompanied her uncle in piano duets. Soon it was time to leave Manchester and thanks to another tobacco company, Peter Stuyvesent, she was able in 1972 to continue her studies at the London Opera Centre. During her term there, she was the only singer to be awarded a three year Gulbenkian Fellowship for further studies.

By now she was recognised as a high mezzo-soprano with a voice of fine flexibility. She achieved her first breakthrough in 1974 when engaged to sing the title role in Gluck's *Alceste* for Scottish Opera at the Aldeburgh Festival. In the mid-Seventies she made her Covent Garden debut as Cherubino in *Le Nozze di Figaro* and also sang Siebel in Gounod's *Faust*, but she managed to make little impact with either Scottish Opera or at Covent Garden. Recalling those formative years, she can be disarmingly candid: 'I was green, as green as can be. I think I was too shy and negative on stage. In fact, I was way out of my depth at Scottish Opera and certainly way out of my depth when I first sang at Covent Garden. I mean, I just didn't know what I was doing. I felt so stupid – as though I'd lost it for good. I can just see myself as Siebel pulling those blasted flowers out of the wall. It was frightful. And the longer I stayed at Covent Garden the smaller the parts got.'

In conversation with the critic, Alan Blyth, she reflected that at the time she was far happier with oratorio and song, and that it was the English Music Theatre, now sadly defunct, that really lifted her up. Performing Rossini's *Cinderella* with them set her on the right path, particularly working with conductor Steuart Bedford, and she welcomed the sense of teamwork.

'I like to know the people with whom I'm working', she told Blyth', otherwise I tend to turn up at rehearsals a bundle of nerves.'

During the Seventies Thomson Smillie, the Artistic Director of the Wexford Festival, invited her to sing the role of Myrtale in Massenet's *Thais* and she made an immediate impression, for apart from her stylish singing her stagecraft was above the ordinary. She was back again the following year as Laodicea in Cavalli's opera *Eritrea*, singing Eurimidonte. In the same production was Philip Langridge. Before they left this small and friendly town it was clear they were romantically attached. 'I was happy for Ann's sake', says Molly Murray. 'I felt they would one day marry.'

Not unlike some of her colleagues, Ann Murray believes that you need luck to get on in the business. 'No matter how talented you are, a great proportion of your career depends on luck. I know many talented soloists, both instrumental and vocal, who sit at home working very little. The market is flooded and luck gives you the boost to get on the road.'

Reflecting on why for most of the Seventies she was not accepted on the London operatic scene, she said, 'Not everyone can like you. A producer or a conductor may prefer someone else. That's fine, and in a way it has been a boon. You see I might have ended up doing many small or unimportant roles at Covent Garden. I would have been stuck in a rut and unambitious.'

March 1979 marked a significant turning point in her career. It arose out of an offer from Cologne and the time is clearly etched in her memory. 'They were wonderful to me. Music Director Gyorgy Fischer was my guiding light there until I found my feet. He conducted most of the pieces in which I was involved - mainly Mozart it was. He gave me confidence and cared for me. We had a marvellous time. I did very much learn the trade there. I learned that I had to go out there and do it myself. I made my debut with no rehearsal whatsoever. I'd never sung *La Cenerentola* in German before. I spoke no conversational German. So I thought, this is it - I'm going to have to learn it, otherwise I won't know what people are saying about me!'

Not only had she come to the right opera house but in its Director of Productions Ann Murray met a man, as Edward Seckerson pointed out in the *Gramophone*, who 'gave her her first real taste of theatrical creativity'. Jean-Pierre Ponnelle was held in the highest esteem in the opera world and was envied by other German houses. He cast her as Dorabella in *Cosi fan tutte* and the Cologne critics enthused about her performance, in particular her command of the stage and her flexible voice. Just as Steuart Bedford's English Music Theatre had provided the mezzo with the opportunity to try new things, Jean-Pierre Ponnelle's inspired direction was what she needed at this time.

'He was aggressive and so demanding', she remembers. 'There was no question that you couldn't do something – you just did it. You know, there are many people along the way who are instrumental in guiding one's career; you never forget them and in my case it was really through Ponnelle that my career took off. Through him I was able to get to Zurich and through Zurich to Salzburg. I got to the Met in a Ponnelle production, and through that I went to Milan, and through Milan to Vienna.'

In 1981, her life took on a new meaning with her marriage to Philip Langridge. He was quite established at the time and she herself had begin to make it on the Continent. 'Our house in London', she recalls with amusement, 'was a disaster area, like a railway station – always a case packed and waiting by the front door. It was all good fun at the time – we both travelled to see one another and became each other's most trusted critics, and we both knew the stresses and strains of the profession so we could accommodate each other's ups and downs.'

Five years later in 1986, Ann had her first child, Jonathan, and the responsibility brought with it all sorts of difficult decisions. 'Having a child with both parents travelling around on busy engagements all over the world was, I found, quite a strain. It was difficult for the marriage, because Philip and I were both under a lot of pressure with heavy schedules at the time, and my career was by now moving on a different level to when we'd first met. I suppose I was making a rod for my own back, but I've tried to be a full-time mother as well as a full-time singer as much as I could.'

They made a conscious decision that at least one of them should be at home at any given time, so that Jonathan got to spend some time with his parents as he grew up. It worked well as a whole. Having her life organised is important to Ann Murray, though she admits she worries about small things in everyday life which, she says, 'isn't great if you're an opera singer away from home so often: it leaves you a lot to worry about. The big things - well, if they happen they happen, there's nothing you can do about them. But those niggling things that go wrong really upset me. I like to have everything worked out and right - I don't like being taken unawares.'

In a world more synonymous with glitter and glamour than meditation and prayer, Ann Murray confesses she does sometimes rely on her Catholic upbringing and finds time for prayer. She describes herself as 'a convenience prayer' and on her way to an opera house may utter a prayer at the wheel of her car. It was the nuns who first instilled in her a practical attitude to life and today she is inclined to shun the hype of the singing world.

'I don't like the frills. I like to go and give my best on stage and be judged on that, not by the way I behave at the reception afterwards. I like the challenge of taking a piece of music and interpreting so that an audience today can really understand what's going on, emotionally and intellectually. And how well I work depends on the atmosphere in rehearsals. I rely on my colleagues to be generous and imaginative in their interpretations. You've got to be able to laugh together, to play around together on stage, to experiment with ideas in order to really get to the heart of an opera and give a good performance.'

In Salzburg, meanwhile, she sang for conductor James Levine in a Ponnelle production and Levine got her to the Metropolitan Opera House where she was heard in *La Clemenza di Tito* and *Cosi fan tutte*. 'It was a wonderful experience', she told me. 'It's a huge house with huge staffs. The company is run efficiently, yet it has the friendliest atmosphere I have ever encountered. People talk of Irish hospitality but believe me, the Americans gave me a fantastic welcome. My husband Philip was singing another role and we were both being asked to so many parties and dos, we couldn't possibly accept them all.'

When Riccardo Muti first heard her sing he liked her voice and as in the case of Ponnelle, became her mentor. She sang Dorabella in *Cosi* for him at La Scala, and then at the Salzburg Festival, though he was shocked that she had no Italian. He was said to have 'given orders' to both she and Margaret Marshall to learn the language before reporting back to the following year's festival.

For Ann Murray, working with Muti was an immensely rewarding experience. The conductor, in her own words, was wonderfully faithful to her musically and personally since 1981. 'One wants to do well – and not just because he's Muti. It's true that he has very strong ideas of his own about the shape of a piece, the way this or that phrase should go. But at the same time if I do something and it's not precisely the way he sees it, he waits until we work it through. He respects my ideas. Sometimes I'll try something and he'll say – okay, if you have the breath control to do it that way, I'd like to make even more of it. And so on. He has a marvellous sense of what I can do and he's prepared to stretch me, too.'

Although she was by now extending her repertoire, she continued to avoid Verdi and Puccini, and in typically forthright manner stated that the roles were not for her. As she explained, 'I don't have that sort of steel in the voice. The colour isn't right. I wouldn't be excited if I heard myself singing Verdi. It's no use chasing repertoire for big bucks if it's wrong. My voice is limited. There are certain things I simply would not sing. I'm a great believer in repertoire finding a singer.'

She was happy to improve on her chosen roles, such as Octavian, Charlotte, Idamante, Cenerentola, Cherubini and Elvira. She sang the part of Nichlausse in EMI's star-studded new recording of *Les contes d'Hoffmann*. Georg Solti became a friend through working with him in Salzburg and she likes to recall the good advice he gave her. 'He said to me, for as long as you can, sing Cenerentola and Cherubini and those roles will keep your voice young and fresh. He's right. When you listen to Berganza, for example – the most beautiful unfussed, unpushed sound: absolute natural velvet. OK, so it was a different era for her, in a sense. These days you are expected to do everything. She made a career from five or six roles, and sang them all wonderfully. There's a lesson in there somewhere. Indeed there is.'

Her growing fame had not gone unnoticed and soon offers began to come in from English opera managements. Naturally she was delighted to have her achievements overseas recognised, not least because it gave her more time to be with her young son and husband Philip. As Alan Blyth was to state in the *Daily Telegraph*, 'For an artist not fully recognised in Britain until the mid-Eighties, Ann Murray remains remarkably buoyant. Her Irish wit and spirit have seen her through difficult times in her career, and helped to achieve deserved triumphs in the past couple of years in such renowned operatic centres as Milan, Munich, New York and Cologne.'

When she was engaged in 1988 as the Child in Ravel's *L'Enfant et les Sortileges* in John Dexter's production, the critics claimed it was too long a gap for her to be absent from the Covent Garden stage.

After an absence of five years she accepted a recital engagement at the National Concert Hall, Dublin, and it brought together old friends, including Nancy Calthorpe who took deep satisfaction in her former pupil's glittering achievements on the operatic and concert stages of the world. Her programme consisted of songs by Schubert, Schumann, Berlioz, Barber and Richard Strauss. That the Concert Hall was not nearly full could be attributed either to an inexplicable lack of interest in Lieder or that the Dublin public had failed to keep up with the mezzo-soprano's achievements abroad. The critics, though, were enchanted by her performance.

Mary MacGoris in the *Irish Independent* echoed the feelings of most of them when she stated: 'A rare visitor returned to give the William O'Kelly Memorial Concert Recital by the DGOS in the National Concert Hall.

Partnered with delicate and sometimes dramatic sympathy by Steuart Bedford at the piano, Ms. Murray conceded no popularity handicap in a programme of seldom-heard German, French and American songs, all of considerable interest. Her full and wide ranging mezzo with its high impressive register was used with feeling and intelligence and she deployed a sensitive musical line with a high regard for the verbal content if not the clearest diction. The exquisitely controlled soft singing she brought to Schubert's "Nacht und Traume" was marvellously expressive.'

While Molly Murray was moved by the warmth of the response from the small attendance, she expressed her disappointment to me later about the organisation of the event. There was no taxi employed to collect Ann at Dublin airport on her arrival from London, and after her final song in the recital no one thought of presenting her with a bouquet of flowers. Mrs. Murray admitted she was upset and felt that Ann deserved better treatment for going out of her way to make herself available to sing in Dublin.

For my part, I feel it would be wrong to suggest that Irish music lovers had entirely forgotten about the singer, for over the years I know of a number of them who have attended her performances at Covent Garden and at English National Opera. The truth is that interest has waned in Lieder recitals, as was indicated a few years ago when the German baritone Hermann Prey sang to a half empty National Concert Hall and to an apathetic audience.

As the 1990s approached it was an increasingly hectic time for Ann Murray. She sang Rosina in Covent Garden's *Il Barbiere di Siviglia* and Charlotte in ENO's new production of Massenet's *Werther* at the Coliseum, and in between jetted to the Continent for performances of Mozart and Strauss operas. It was clear, though, that Handel remained one of her favourite composers despite the problems his operas pose to make them work dramatically. Essentially their oratorio-based 'stand still and sing' construction make them more suited to record than the operatic stage.

Nevertheless, she has scored some of her greatest triumphs in his operas, notably in the title role of *Xerxes*, which received a classic production by ENO at the Coliseum in 1992. 'One critic described her interpretation as 'masterly'. Later, *Gramophone* was to reflect: Nicholas Hytner's ENO production proved her best possible baptism in the art of making Handel, and especially the form of the *da capo* aria, dramatically convincing on stage, winning her a reputation as a Handel singer, she claims, "by pure chance"; she has since added only Ariodante and Julius Caesar to her Handelian stock. Before *Xerxes* she had sung Bradamante in *Alcina* at at Aix-en-Provence - "But badly, because it was too low for me".' I caught up with her in January 1993 when she sang the role of Ruggiero in Covent Garden's production of *Alcina*, a work that saw Handel score his last big operatic success in his lifetime. On the evening of a performance it is customary for her to drive from her home in Surrey and arrive at the opera house at about 4.15 p.m. After collecting her mail and messages she will proceed to her dressing room and relax for a while over toast and tea and chat with colleagues. This leaves her with ample time for make-up and getting into costume.

The curtain rose at exactly 7 o'clock and one was instantly struck by Stephen P. Lynch's stage design, depicting an exotic island scene dominated on one side by a large tree and its branches. It is here that men have lingered under the spell of Alcina and become her lovers. Attired in dark trousers, leather jacket and white blouse, Ann Murray cut a striking figure. Vocally her finest moments arrived in Act II, in her two reflective arias, "Mi lusinga" and "Verdi prati"; in the latter she is contemplating the paradise she is about to leave and sung in sotte voce the aria sounded ravishing.

The curtain eventually came down at 10.30, making the evening I'm afraid too long for some people in the stalls. Musically I found the performance rewarding, though dramatically there were dull passages. To my surprise, Ann Murray looked relaxed and cheerful when I talked to her afterwards, and she was obviously undeterred by her long hours in the theatre. She arrived smiling and holding a large bouquet of flowers in one hand and greeted friends with a handshake. She spoke in fluent German with a couple from Cologne. When I asked her if her mother Molly had seen the opera, she said she expected her in London later on. We talked about *Alcina* for a while, then we arranged to talk on the following Sunday morning.

In conversation, she is forthright and witty and her Dublin accent is unmistakable. Although having lived in England for 20 years, she takes pride in her Irish passport and recalled her childhood as thoroughly happy. 'I've never forgotten my roots', she mused. 'I can still see myself walking the pier in Dun Laoghaire and waving to friends. Philip and I once thought of having our son Jonathan educated in Ireland but we decided it wouldn't be practical in view of our careers. We wanted to be as near as we could to him. I hope to retire there, though, in Dalkey or Dun Laoghaire and I hope I can persuade Philip.'

For a star she can project engaging humility, as when she remarked, 'Composers are the real geniuses in our business. If Mozart, Rossini or Handel hadn't written their beautiful music, where would we singers be? There is too much adulation of singers, too much hype; we are no greater than ballet stars or people in other walks of life. As I see it, we are paid to do a job and it's up to us how we do it. I enjoy singing, it's a wonderful life and it has been marvellous to me, but I'm not carried away.'

She admitted that she takes advice from her husband with regard to certain operatic roles. 'I think it's good to have a critical eye at hand, and like myself Philip can be very honest when it comes to music.' They have enjoyed singing in opera together, though it is not very often. One of the occasions was Berlioz's *Beatrice and Benedict* in a new English translation for English National Opera. *Opera* reviewer was quick to point out that since Ann Murray and Philip Langridge 'are husband and wife in real life they took their bantering duets in confidently practised style.'

To Molly Murray, fame hasn't changed her daughter. Nor has her fixation about punctuality. 'Ann cannot stand anyone who is late for an appointment. I, myself, was once two minutes late and she looked at her watch. Otherwise, nothing really has changed. I know that some singers do not like to have in-laws around them when they are performing in opera, but Ann doesn't mind. I think she appreciates the way I have supported her in her career.'

Suddenly Molly will break into a laugh as she says, 'We have our little tiffs of course and differences, but we leave it at that. Sometimes I might find it hard to get through to her on the 'phone, as she can be very busy, and it annoys me. I'll tell her I'll make an appointment. She can be generous and thoughtful, too. If I fancy a new dress in a London boutique, she'll think nothing of buying it for me for Christmas.'

Molly was back in London in May 1993 for Ann's appearance in the title role of Handel's *Ariodante* at the Coliseum. She was to witness one of Ann's biggest successes and at the end of the performance was emotionally drained. 'I was so proud of her acting and singing', she told me later.

For my part, I found *Ariodante* more exciting dramatically that *Alcina*, mainly because Handel created a drama of conflicting emotions that is as charged as any in opera. In fact, it was worth going to the Coliseum alone to hear Ann Murray sing Ariodante's central aria "Scherza infida". The audience was held spellbound by the sheer beauty and power of her voice as she plunged the depths of confusion and despair.

Critic Clive Manning considered it to be one of the vocal highlights of the year, and added, 'I'm convinced that Ann Murray is one of our finest mezzo-sopranos.' *Financial Times* critic Max Loppert summed up, 'Ann Murray enjoys the latest of her London triumphs.'

There was no let-up for her. There were recitals in Britain and abroad, and in July she was off once more to the Salzburg Festival to sing the role of Cecilio in Mozart's *Lucio Silla* in a cast that included Anthony Rolfe Johnson as Lucio Silla. She was joined by Philip Langridge who was singing Nerone in Monteverdi's *L'Incoronazione di Poppea* and their son, Jonathan, who is now studying the piano. They rented a large apartment and during the course of the festival were joined by Molly Murray in buoyant spirits; as usual she took in Ann's and Philip's first nights in the opera house. She would be introduced in the days ahead to their music friends as 'Ann's mother', but she no longer minded, and she looked forward to meeting Sir Georg Solti who by now she found 'great company'. In spite of the mixed weather she visited Salzburg's myriad shops or took Jonathan, her grandson, on walks through the parks.

Ann Murray, too, was totally at home in the city. Work sometimes prevented her from enjoying her stay there to the full, but she managed to have a good time. She had achieved most of her ambitions; she has sung with conductors such as Kubelik, Muti, Haroncourt, Levine and Solti and with the greatest orchestras in the world; her records, *Sweet Power of Song* and *On Wings of Song* have sold exceedingly well and she was about to record a new album of Irish songs.

Irish critic Marese Murphy recalled that some of those who heard Ann sing in Dublin as a girl regarded her as a promising young soprano, but events had proved otherwise. Today she was acknowledged as a mezzo *virtuosa*, supreme mistress of the fiendish vocal pyrotechnics devised by Handel and Rossini, and in much demand with international opera houses. For years she has been a favourite at Salzburg, first in the role of Nicklausse in *Hoffmann*, later scoring success of a different order in Rossini's *La Cenerentola* - a performance which reached wider audiences by virtue of television.

To Ms Murphy, the mezzo-soprano achieved a significant breakthrough with her stunning performance in the Chereau production of Mozart's *Lucio Silla* in the enchanting little Theatre de la Monnaie in Brussels. 'Suddenly there was, I remember, a new dramatic quality in the voice, and this has been fostered ever since, with technical expertise to match, making her study, for instance, the role of Ariodante at the London Coliseum, a major achievement of the operatic calendar in 1993. And her most recent success was in *Moisé in Egitto* at Covent Garden, where despite some strain in the upper register on opening night, her flawless command of Rossini's taxing vocal idiom made it clear that this Dublin singer remains in the forefront of the world's operatic stars.'

While opera still continues to take up most of Ann Murray's time, she makes it her business, she says, to think about recital work, and in this respect either joined by her husband Philip Langridge or by soprano Felicity Lott she is a great crowd pleaser. 'If divas Murray and Lott did not sing a note between them, they could still be enjoying a brilliant career as the best comedy duo since Gert and Daisy,' wrote Rodney Milnes in the London *Times*. For his conversation with the divas left him 'helpless with laughter'. He tried to explain: 'Murray's technique is based on a poker face, a marginally raised eyebrow and salty putdowns (sometimes of herself), delivered with super-dry Dublin inflections); Lott is a mistress of timing, of the split second pause before the deflationary one-liner.'

The pair first sang together in *Der Rosenkavalier* in 1987 and they were seen to work well. Their duet concert series grew out of Graham Johnson's Songmakers' Almanac and since then they have recorded two recital discs for EMI.

'We do enjoy singing together,' says Ann Murray, and, they confirmed, almost in unison that, 'It's all about the joy of making music with someone you know and respect.'

Wherever she goes, she is invariably asked about her up- bringing in Ireland and why she emigrated. In New York once she supplied the answer: 'In order to pursue my career, I had to emigrate. I think if I had stayed at home I would have ended up a concert and Lieder singer. As fate opened up certain prospects for me, my visions and expectations improved. Perhaps improved isn't the word. Broadened. I think that perhaps my voice settled when I stopped apologizing for myself and when I stopped feeling subordinate. Feeling inadequate, and feeling very Irish. I remember an Irish colleague of mine saying that the problem with us all is that we were born saying, "Sorry!" And it's absolutely true'.

Chapter Ten

Suzanne Murphy

A CALL FROM VIENNA

On a bitterly cold morning in early March 1987, Suzanne Murphy joined me for coffee at a small cafe opposite the Vienna State Opera. On the previous night, along with some friends from Limerick, I had attended a performance of Mozart's *Idomeneo*, in which she sang the role of Elettra.

Despite the icy weather, she was relaxed and in cheerful mood, and when I asked her how she came to be singing in Vienna she was typically forthcoming: 'I suppose the opportunity initially arose when I stepped in for Margaret Price to sing the title role in *Norma* in Munich. That was about eighteen months ago, and in the meantime the Vienna State Opera were looking for an Elettra. One day, the Intendant of the opera house here mentioned my name in connection with Munich and, as it happened, Irish soprano Marie-Claire O'Reirdan was in his office. When he asked her if she thought I could sing Elettra, she answered unhesitatingly, "No problem at all." She told the Intendant she was a good friend of mine and he seemed very interested.

'Marie telephoned me in Cardiff and told me to expect a call from Vienna; they, in turn it seems, contacted Munich and checked my Norma performance there. Shortly afterwards I was engaged to sing in six performances of *Idomeneo*. I agree it was an opportunity for me, but it was something I had not thought about, or said to myself, "I want to do that." The fact is that some Mozart roles suit my voice, others do not. I've got to be choosy. I am glad I came; I'm awfully happy here.

'I first came over in early January for the start of rehearsals, and in all we have had about seven weeks' work preparing the opera. I didn't expect it to be so long in a big house like this, but they like to do things that way. We had a number of rehearsals with piano, and a number in costume with orchestra. It's all extremely thorough, nothing is left to chance. We worked six hours every day. Up to now most of my repertoire has been Italian, so tackling Mozart in Vienna is a new challenge for me. A lot is expected of singers here, standards are uniformly high.

'There has been a very good working relationship within the cast and with conductor Nikolaus Harnoncourt; a few touchy moments did arise but that is part and parcel of creating an opera. Furthermore, all the staff through the house, from dressing room to reception, have been very help-ful, so the atmosphere is good.

'Nikolaus Harnoncourt is the "in" conductor in Vienna at the moment and a great favourite with both singers and the public. For me it has been a wonderful experience working with him in *Idomeneo*; I can truly say he opened a window and let in a breath of fresh air on Mozart; he simply lets the music breathe and the sound he gets from the orchestra is incredible. And the cast, of course, is excellent; Peter Schreier, from Dresden, is a singer I greatly admire and, in my opinion, his Idomeneo could scarcely be bettered.'

When I recalled that her singing from a box high up overlooking the stage looked spectacular, she explained it could have been a hazardous experience for her. 'Last night, for instance, the tail of my full-length dress suddenly got caught in one of the light bulbs and I was terrified for a moment for fear it smashed the bulb and started a fire. As it was, part of my dress came away and I walked into the box and tried to sing as calmly as I could. I knew there was a fireman on duty and that there was a fire extinguisher nearby, but when you're going out to perform you haven't got time to think of everything.'

For the most part, however, she counted her Vienna experience a memorable one. In the course of the run of *Idomeno*, she was visited by soprano Angela Feeney, who made the rail journey from Munich, and Ingrid Surgenor, who has accompanied her at concerts, flew in from Cardiff. Earlier, her mother arrived from Limerick and spent a few days sight-seeing and shopping.

The positive response of the critics to her debut at the Vienna State Opera was an obvious source of satisfaction to her. She was, in the words of one leading critic, 'a lyrical and dramatic Elettra' and another remarked on her 'musically assured performance and purity of voice.'

As ever, her tall, striking figure made her a compelling stage per-former, and as far as I could see from my seat in the stalls, she displayed no visible hint of nerves. The brilliantly imaginative staging of the final scene made up for lack of dramatic action in the opera itself, one of the reasons why it is so difficult to stage.

Limerick friends with me proudly reminded me that the last Limerick soprano to storm Continental opera houses was the celebrated Catherine Hayes, a name not unfamiliar to Suzanne. In Vienna she entered into the spirit of this remarkable musical city and even went along in costume to the glittering Opera Ball. 'The Viennese men are such fine dancers,' she wryly remarked to me later. She is a woman of fine *joie de vivre*.

For Suzanne Murphy, the road to Vienna was a circuitous one. Years before she began singing with the Dublin-based WE 4, a folk group that went all over Ireland playing one-night stands. The group sang Crosby, Simon and Garfunkel and Peter, Paul and Mary songs, and even at unfash-ionable venues the men, Larry Hogan, John Harrington and Donal Lunny wore evening dress.

Looking back, she says, 'I suppose it was very good for me, it tough-ened me up and then I knew from there on what an audience was and how they could respond. Often we played to half-drunken parties and rowdy Christmas dances. And we used to do Friday evenings with the Chieftains in the Chariot Inn in Ranelagh. It was wonderful - they were fantastic nights - and why we never taped any of them, I'll never know.

Maybe there were no tape recorders. Or maybe someone somewhere has a pirate tape.'

From an early age, she had fallen in love with music. She suspected that her parents must have thought her strange to be 'so mad about music'. Her father was in the hardware business and the family lived in the Limerick suburbs. Sometimes she wondered where she inherited her love of music and concluded that it was hearing her grandparents singing parlour songs around a piano. Her parents had met at a concert in Bruff Convent, where her grandmother had also been a pupil. She was sent with her sister, Noelle, to the same convent, and Noelle turned out to be a good singer.

School plays were her big moments, and today she thinks that even then the stage was calling her. Learning the piano also provided her with much satisfaction. But music and acting were, she thought, only for people abroad. 'I never thought it could be for the likes of me. I suppose, however, I had it in me and it had to come out.'

Eventually, when she moved to Dublin to take up a secretarial post she met up with the people in WE 4. The sound appealed to her; it was integrated and melodic, so her voice didn't stand out particularly in the group, but she was noticed. Harry Christmas, the EMI boss in Dublin, told her she had a promising voice and that she should do something about it.

Later, she met Veronica Dunne at a dinner and they talked briefly about music and other current topics. It would be months before she plucked up enough courage to ask her to take her on as a pupil.

'When Suzanne first came to me', recalled Veronica Dunne, 'I thought the voice had a fine quality, but I quickly pointed out to her what I'd expect if I took her on. Naturally she was nervous and I got the impression that she believed she would never be good enough for a solo career. I remember her saying to me, "I just want my voice to be neat and tidy." She went away and didn't come back for a whole year.'

One day, however, she rang up and said, 'Will you take me back, Ronnie?' Veronica Dunne agreed. 'I knew that Suzanne had stayed away because she hadn't realised her own potential. She lacked self-confidence as far as singing was concerned. I under- stood her reaction. I intimated to her that if lessons went well she would have to think about leaving the WE 4 and becoming a full-time singer. I left her in no doubt that training for a singing career required sacrifices.'

After a few months, the WE 4 broke up, leaving Suzanne Murphy free to pursue her vocal studies. Sometimes, Veronica Dunne would ring her at 7.30 a.m. and ask her if she was up yet and would she come in for an hour's singing. Before lunchtime there would be another session. Suzanne entered for the Sligo Feis Ceoil and was successful.

To Veronica Dunne, the soprano's voice was by now more secure and better focused and had fine agility. And she was a most dedicated worker. 'I had no doubt that in time Suzanne would make it. I have an instinct about these things. Every week I could see her voice developing; it had a lovely quality and good range and an improving coloratura. Her confidence had grown and I knew she was ambitious enough to become a professional singer.'

Around this time in the Sixties the Irish National Opera Company was formed to support Irish singers and give them an opportunity to sing in opera. The men behind the company were Tony O'Dalaigh, Edwin Fitzgibbon, Gerald Duffy and Austin Gaffney. Veronica Dunne recalls that each of the four donated £10, so with £40 and not knowing what lay ahead, they put their plans into operation. The first production was *The Marriage of Figaro*, which Martin Dempsey produced with Colman Pearce as musical director. The date was 3 January 1965, the venue, Athlone. The company continued their tour that year all over the country, with three performances over every second weekend.

Suzanne Murphy joined the company in the Seventies and sang the title role in Rossini's *La Cenerentola*, in which she displayed operatic potential, and in 1975 Elisetta in Cimarosa's *Secret Marriage*. 'What a marvellous opportunity for any young singer to be given', said Veronica Dunne, 'I mean, the chance of performing a major role 30 or 50 times a year. It was a tremendous achievement. I know that in Suzanne's case it was a wonderful experience for her, not only vocally, but as a confidence builder. It was the same with other pupils of mine at the time – they all benefited.'

The Limerick-born soprano had discovered a new and fascinating musical world. Touring with the INOC, she learnt the basics of opera production, how to look after her make-up and perform several nights in a row at different venues and at weekends. Singing in duets, trios and quartets gave her a useful insight into the different vocal techniques required.

'When Suzanne first came to me her voice was small because she had been using a microphone with WE 4', said Veronica Dunne. 'But I managed to get her up a few octaves until she sounded like a fully-fledged soprano. The beauty was that at any register her voice never lost its sheen.'

'Ronnie was so enthusiastic – that's what made the difference to me', reflected Suzanne. 'When I first started going to her for lessons I was only treating it as a kind of pastime, really – but she was so enthusiastic that I got caught up in her enthusiasm and the fire that was in her. Actually she frightened the life out of me. I didn't believe I could do it, but she did. And she worked so very, very hard – she is a workaholic.'

It was time, she decided, to progress further as she could not hope to pursue a full-time career in Ireland. She was encouraged by Veronica Dunne and singers like tenor Edwin Fitzgibbon and Gerald Duffy who had recognised the potential in her voice. She tried Covent Garden but was politely told, 'to come back in a year.' She turned to the New York City Opera; again the answer was in the negative.

Hearing that Welsh National Opera were looking for someone for the chorus, she applied and was accepted for an audition. After she had sung two arias, they asked her to hold on while they fetched in some others to listen to her sing again. A month later a contract arrived. She was surprised and thrilled. 'It was all I'd been working for, a piece of paper to show my parents and Ronnie to say, "Look, I've made it!"

1976 was an eventful year to be joining the company. Not only was it celebrating 30 successful years in existence but a new artistic director, Brian McMaster, had been appointed; he would have a profound influence on the company's future progress. Unfortunately, a cloud was thrown over the celebrations when a fire destroyed about £400,000 worth of props and costumes in Cardiff.

Suzanne saw her future in Cardiff and quickly set about making her home in Wales. She bought a cottage some miles from the city and was happy in her new surroundings. A single woman, she was able to devote almost all her time to music, though she greatly enjoyed her little spare time. With her friendly disposition, she fitted comfortably into the company and was popular with her colleagues.

Welsh National Opera had a growing reputation and its standards were high. She would be singing with singers of the calibre of Thomas Allen, Stuart Burrowes, Geraint Evans, Richard Van Allan and Terence Sharpe, most of whom guested with the company. Work was constant, which in her case as a virtual opera beginner, was a great advantage.

Her first role was Constanze in Mozart's *The Seraglio*, which because of the disastrous fire, had to be performed in make-shift sets. She would have to wait, however, until the spring of 1977 for her first starring part and it was as Amalia in Verdi's *I Masnadieri*; it hadn't been performed in Britain since 1847. With a somewhat absurd plot, much depended on the chorus and principals to bring the opera alive. Apart from Suzanne Murphy, they consisted of tenor Kenneth Collins, baritone Terence Sharpe and bass Richard Van Allan.

Despite favourable press notices, the Welsh did not support the production in any great numbers. For Suzanne Muprhy, however, it was a milestone. The audience responded to her wholehearted singing. 'Miss Murphy took time to settle as Amalia', stated one critic, 'but went on to reveal a voice of exceptional strength, richness and agility, marred only by a tendency to scoop and by poor diction.'

In that same year, she got an opportunity to sing her first Gilda in *Rigoletto* opposite the fine American tenor Neil Shicoff, who earlier had had a problem getting Equity permission to perform in Wales. The *Western Mail*, the country's most influential paper, noted that she displayed confidence and considerable technical skill and was a soprano to watch.

It was a most encouraging start for her and she was prepared to learn as she went along. Her versatility as a singer paid dividends when she switched successfully from Verdi to Britten; her Helena in *A Midsummer Night's Dream* did not go unnoticed. She was also heard as Leonoro in *Il Trovatore*, a role that at the time seemed too heavy for her voice.

Elizabetta in Verdi's *Don Carlos* is a role admired and loved by sopranos, not only because of its beautiful music, but the moral strength of the heroine herself. It's written for a mature singer, as Elizabetta's music is quite heavy. Was Welsh National Opera wise then in casting a newcomer like Suzanne Murphy in the role? To find out, I flew to Bristol where I was joined by a number of London newspaper critics, no doubt attracted by the company's revival of the opera and the fact that Thomas Allen was singing his first Rodrigo.

Not surprisingly, they were to devote most of their reviews to his performance and the baritone was showered with plaudits. But all of them, without exception, noted Suzanne Murphy's convincing portrayal and her ability to sustain the role. For my part, I thought she sang with consistently beautiful tone throughout a memorable evening in the theatre. For the first time she had been heard by most of the London critics.

Next day, when I talked to her she was generous in her praise of Thomas Allen, a fact that underlined her own generosity towards colleagues, and said she looked forward to singing with him again. As always, she was relaxed and good-humoured and it was obvious she was pleased with life in Wales. She had by now fully repaid the trust placed in her by Welsh National Opera.

Next, she sang the Queen of the Night in *The Magic Flute*, followed by her first Violetta in *La Traviata*, a role that had long attracted her. Although the cast as a whole did not please the critics, she emerged as a star; indeed, Tom Sutcliffe, who can be an acerbic critic, penned the kind of notice in the *Guardian* every singer dreams about:

Miss Murphy exceeded the expectations whetted by her virile, passionate Queen of the Night and emerged as an operatic star who will make her mark on the international market. It may be

138

rash to base such a prediction on one beautifully sung Violetta ... But Miss Murphy is not just a pretty voice. She possesses an instrument of great tonal character. She commands the vocal heights with strength, excitement and a ravishing quality of sound. The individuality of the voice lies in a quality she shares with the late Callas – a kind of wedge-shaped hollowness in the tone of each note that, with a slight upping of the pressure, fills generously and thrillingly with colour, vitality and piercing resonance.

In those days Welsh National Opera presented a week's summer season at the seaside resort of Llandudno and it invariably attracted Irish opera lovers. With some friends from Limerick and Dublin, I made the sea and rail journey to the resort and in the unlikely setting of the Astra Cinema saw Suzanne's Violetta.

If the production itself was unimaginative and dull, the soprano's singing was totally committed as usual and her development of the character commendable. Vocally, she was in full command, her death scene being moving and intense. In John Treleaven she had a tenor as tall as herself; on other occasions it could be a problem when she figured in love scenes with tenors whose heads scarcely reached her bosom. She was amused when once I drew up the subject, but was able to see the funny side of it.

Verdi continued to take up much of her time. In the autumn of 1979 she was cast as Elvira in *Ernani*, with Kenneth Collins in the title role, Richard Van Allan as de Silva and Cornelius Opthof as Don Carlos. The producer was the gifted Elijah Moshinsky, who today is one of the most sought after Verdi interpreters in the world. The opera had not been seen in Britain since a production at Sadler's Wells in 1967.

Elvira's costumes looked stunning and tailor-made for her dignified and tall figure. And she scored another personal triumph in the role. 'Her voice did everything she required', stated critic Hugh Canning. 'If she can maintain this superb form she will have few rivals.'

Handel was not a composer associated with WNO, but in 1981 it was decided to present his *Rodelinda* and Suzanne was cast in the title role. She welcomed the opportunity to extend her repertoire and though a new-comer to Handel, performed convincingly. The performances were con-ducted by Julian Smith, who was an important cog in the company's music department.

Veronica Dunne had always felt that Suzanne Murphy's agile voice was ideal for bel canto and she was to be proved correct, when in 1982 the soprano was handed a plum role in the shape of Elvira in Bellini's *I Puritani*. In fact the company was mounting the opera especially for her, which was a sure indication of the enormous esteem in which she was by now regarded. She would be directed by the outstanding Romanian-born Andrei Serban; he was convinced that the opera, for all its lyric beauty, was more dramatic than imagined. He was determined to make it real and not just a platform for singing.

Serban sought to bring out the background of the Civil War between the supporters of Cromwell and the Stuarts against which the theme of the opera is set. He was aided in this respect by the brilliantly evocative stage sets of Michael Yeargan. Not surprisingly, the opening night in Cardiff was a remarkable success. The principals, including Suzanne and Dennis O'Neill won unstinted praise. 'Miss Murphy's performance was little short of magnificent', stated William Davies in the *Classical Times*. 'It's an impersonation that will long remain in the mind's eye.'

O'Neill's Arturo was sung against the advice of two doctors yet he matched the soprano in intensity and passion. As the influential critic, Desmond Shawe-Taylor, remarked in the *Sunday Times*, 'Many a tenor in robust health has given less satisfaction.'

Eventually I caught up with the production at the Dominion Theatre, London, and I remember that seated beside me that evening was the late Harold Rosenthal, editor of *Opera*. Serban's staging of the work had aroused considerable interest, in particular the symbolism attached to the wedding veil; it was the loss of the veil that would ultimately unhinge Elvira.

The Dominion Theatre is big and impersonal, but on this evening there was an undoubted buzz. The high point was reached in the Mad Scene in Act II, and here Suzanne Murphy was vocally and dramatically at her best. John Higgins in the London *Times* stated that her performance was little short of magnificent.

It's not often that a stage set gets applauded, but when the curtain rose on the final act Michael Yeargan's design drew spontaneous applause. The scene depicted a battlefield with a stagecoach stranded in a snowstorm. The sense of realism was overwhelming. It was a white and icy setting indeed for the lovers Elvira and Arturo to meet and sing of their mutual love.

Clearly Harold Rosenthal enjoyed the performance and told me so. He would write in that month's *Opera*: 'Past stagings of *Puritani* have at their worst been little more than concerts in costume and at their best unviable dramatically. This Welsh National Opera production has changed all that.'

Veronica Dunne was to share my own opinion that Suzanne Murphy had done nothing better than this with WNO. 'There were moments of greatness in her performance', she said, 'and I'm thinking particularly of the Mad Scene.'

Later in that same year, 1983, she was cast as Amelia in *Un Ballo in maschera* with Dennis O'Neill as Gustav and Donald Maxwell as Anckarstrom. The Cardiff audience received the production enthusiastically. If O'Neill stole the honours with some thrilling singing, Suzanne Murphy brought typical commitment to her role and together they were worthy protagonists. As a Verdi heroine she was by now one of the most respected in Britain.

It was hard to imagine that in six short years she had achieved so much with the company. It was inevitable that one day she would sing the title role in Bellini's masterpiece, *Norma*. After the enthusiastic reception for *Puritani*, Welsh National Company decided in 1985 to do *Norma* with the same production team of Serban, Yeargan and conductor Julian Smith. Suzanne Murphy prepared earnestly for her first Norma, a role so revered by Callas and Sutherland.

While the critics expressed reservations about Serban's production, especially his use of masks to symbolise the difference between private and public utterances, the singing of the principals was praised. John Higgins in the *Times* summed up: 'Suzanne Murphy had one or two cloudy moments vocally, but for most of the evening it was a thrillingly full-throated performance, lacking neither stamina nor the control for the start of "Casta Diva."'

Despite her success and celebrity status, she did not get above herself. Irish friends were welcomed warmly whether in Cardiff, Bristol or London and invited to her dressing room. Her mother, a charming Limerick woman, became her best fan. And Suzanne never lost her spontaneous sense of humour. She had good friends in Wales and Cardiff, among them Dennis O'Neill and piano accompanist Ingrid Surgenor.

In the meantime, she had not forgotten Ireland, nor for that matter had Ireland forgotten her. Opera buffs followed her progress and sometimes were able to attend her performances in Britain. She was invited back to her native Limerick for a concert recital and was happy to renew acquaintance with school pals. There was, I remember, some disappointment when her concert programme did not include "I dreamt I dwelt in marble Halls" and "Scenes that are Brightest"; otherwise she charmed her audience by her vocal technique and musicianship. She was proving a worthy successor to Joseph O'Mara and Catherine Hayes.

The DGOS mounted a new production of *La Traviata* for her and for the first time Irish opera-lovers saw her give one of her most compelling and touching performances in the Gaiety Theatre. For years they had been hearing and reading much about the soprano, but now in their eyes she had lived up to their expectations. I still remember the prolonged applause at the final curtain, as though people were anxious to release their emotion after what had been her particularly moving death scene in the opera.

I have seldom seen her look as happy as on that occasion, as relatives and friends kissed and hugged her afterwards in the crowded foyer. It's the kind of moment every singer dreams about. For Suzanne it was especially unforgettable as among the audience was Veronica Dunne, who had had faith in her voice from the beginning.

She was back in Dublin in March 1989 at the invitation of the DGOS to sing Norma. Irish people had not heard her Elvira in *Puritani*, a source of regret to the soprano, but now at least they would see her in her other famous bel canto role. In my view, the DGOS missed a chance here; they should have mounted a special production of *Puritani* for her.

Norma was presented in the National Concert Hall (the Gaiety Theatre was unavailable) and was a critical success. Suzanne sang with a delicacy and fine musical sense and displayed an imposing stage presence. 'Miss Murray gave a performance of operatic richness that towers over anything else I have seen in 20 years of DGOS productions', commented Michael Dervan in the *Irish Times*.

Fanny Feehan in the *Sunday Press* stated that it was the best Norma she had seen in Dublin or anywhere else, mainly because of the soprano's remarkable singing in the title role and Angela Feeney's outstanding performance as Adalgisa.'

Suzanne was by now a freelance artist and much in demand. She sang Norma at the New York City Opera, with Richard Bonynge conducting, Amelia in *Maschera* and Elvira in *Puritani* in Vancouver, and Ophelia in *Hamlet* in Pittsburgh. She began also to get engagements in Germany. 'I like working for German opera companies', she said. 'Working with a company there is very different from working in Britain. There are no prima donnas, no tantrums. There is a long rehearsal period and the work is much more detailed, much deeper than in Britain.'

Between concerts in Ireland for Barra O Tuama, the enterprising Cork impresario, and operatic engagements at the Aix Festival, she guested with Welsh National Opera in its new production of Puccini's *La fanciulla del West* and scored one of the biggest triumphs of her career.

Hugh Canning wrote in *Opera*: 'Suzanne Murphy's Minnie surely ranks with the finest interpretations of the role anywhere: she sang her music tirelessly and with unusual delicacy – her bel canto training – in the lyrical moments. She gave a touching and convincing portrait of the improbable gun-toting hostess who has never kissed a man. This fanciulla is a huge success and deserves to be seen and heard throughout the world.'

The question began to be asked once more in operatic circles, both in Ireland and Britain, as to why Covent Garden continued to ignore her talents. An appearance there would have seemed a just reward for all the hours of pleasure she had provided elsewhere for opera-goers. Was the reason simply a reflection of the idiosyncratic casting policy at the Royal Opera House? Or was it more political than that?

When I discussed the matter with Suzanne during one of her concert visits to Dublin, she was philosohpical and expressed the view that she was not the only soprano who happened to come into that category. 'I think there are at least two or three more in Britain,' she said, 'but it's something one cannot do anything about. Opera house managers or intendants either want you or they don't. I never thought about it much, I must confess, as I am exceedingly busy singing all over the place; not of course that it wouldn't be nice to sing Norma, Elvira or Tosca there.'

She did sing there with Welsh National Opera in *Falstaff* but that is not really the same thing.

The question surfaced later when Dame Gwyneth Jones' Minnie in *La fanciulla del West* was panned by the London critics, with Rodney Milnes in the *Times* particularly critical of her performance. Again, it seemed that Covent Garden management had erred in not calling on the Irish soprano.

Furthermore, questions were asked after she had sung the title role in *Tosca* for Welsh National Opera in October 1992. She stood in for the injured Marion Vernette Moore and showed that her singing and acting were ideal for the part. Hugh Canning was to make the comment in *Opera*: 'Toscas as good as Miss Murphy's do not grow on trees these days and hearing her in Cardiff made one wonder again why the Royal Opera had to go trawling the operatic outback of the United States to come up with the unremarkable Elizabeth Holleque in their most recent revival?'

Throughout her years with WNO, Suzanne Murphy had never lost touch with Veronica Dunne; indeed, when she was preparing her Tosca she had talked to her about the role. When Veronica was retiring from her post at the Dublin College of Music it was Suzanne, aided by her friend, Angela Feeney, who conjured up the idea of having her ex-pupils and current pupils give a concert for her.

It turned out to be a fitting tribute to a woman who had helped so many young singers to the concert and operatic platform. Marie Walshe, Andrew Murphy, Lynda Lee, Nicola Sharkey, Therese Feighan and Mary Callan-Clarke sang arias, duets and trios while Suzanne Murphy and Angela Feeney were heard in arias by Wagner, including a duet from *Lohengrin*. At the end of the evening Veronica Dunne joined the performers on the stage of the National Concert Hall and the capacity audience stood in silence as her recorded voice filled the hall in "I dreamt I dwelt in marble Halls".

It was a fitting tribute to Ronnie, as she is affectionately known in Dublin. "All of us owed her this", remarked Suzanne Murphy to me afterwards, 'and we're delighted that the box-office receipts will go to fund a bursary for an up-and-coming singer.'

To the surprise of many people, Suzanne hasn't married nor had children. There was a time when she very much wanted children. It is one of her abiding regrets.

In the meantime, her popularity as a concert artist has been growing and she brings to her singing personality and temperament. When she sang in 1990 in the Margaret Burke Sheridan centenary concert at the National Concert Hall, Dublin, critic John Allen noted, 'Suzanne Murphy was at her compelling best. It's wonderful how, even in concert, she identifies completely with the dramatic content of whatever she happens to be singing. Without any distracting body histrionics, she uses eyes and mouth to rivet you with the intensity of her storytelling. For the first time in years I wasn't bored with Desdemona's long narration from the last act of Verdi's *Otello*, and the "Ave Maria" that followed was heartbreaking in its resigned calm.'

She has remained as busy as ever. She sang Alice Ford in Peter Stein's much acclaimed new production of Verdi's *Falstaff* for Welsh National

Opera, Abigaille in *Nabucco* in Modena and Piacenza, and she was already looking forward to the world premiere in Washington in 1994 of Dominic Argento's new opera, *The Dream of Valentino*, in which she was cast as Valentino's secretary and was praised by the critics.

Strangely, she had neglected the recording side of the business, but in 1992 made amends with an album of Puccini and Verdi arias. Suzanne would have to wait, however, until the autumn of 1993 for commercial success in this sphere, and this came about in an unusual way. Her brother, Michael Murphy – he is manager of Limerick's magnificent new University Concert Hall – suggested that for her next album she include the popular Limerick song "There is an Isle", and she agreed; not only that but it formed the title of the album. She would also include other favourites such as "Galway Bay", "Kathleen Mavourneen" and "I dreamt I dwelt in marble Halls".

Before long, it proved a chart-topper in Ireland, mainly because of the technical quality of the album, the sympathetic musical backing by the Welsh National Opera Orchestra and Suzanne's judicious choice of songs, a number of which were classically arranged by Julian Smith, who also conducted the orchestra.

In September 1993 she was in Limerick for the gala celebrations to mark the opening of the new concert hall, and in the course of the evening sang "There is an Isle" with the audience happy to make up the chorus. It was a nostalgic occasion, with Veronica Dunne and her husband, Peter, coming from Dublin. Suzanne was in good voice and opened her programme appropriately with "Dich, teure Halle" from *Tannhauser* to confer her blessing on the new hall. "O hall of song" is one singing translation of the text. 'I give thee greeting. All hail to thee, thou hallowed place!'

Limerick, her native place, had waited a long time for its new hall; fittingly, its greatest soprano since Catherine Hayes had given her own welcome in song.

Chapter Eleven

Louis Browne

STARDOM AT SADLER'S WELLS

'All I ever wanted to do was to become a singer', declared Louis Browne, who in the Forties grew up in the town of Athlone and that kind of goal was understandable. John McCormack had been the perfect example of the local boy made good and even then his fame was undiminished and locally he had many admirers.

Young Browne, who had been born 160 yards from the house where the great tenor was born, had other reasons to remember him.

'My aunt Molly Curley had a huge collection of McCormack's records and my greatest joy as a kid was to go to her house and play the gramophone. I'd spend hours listening to old 78s, though I must admit that as a boy there were other singers I liked better than McCormack. However, as I became more mature I began to realise the wonderful vocal skill he possessed. No other singer could communicate better, and in his very early songs I recognised his Athlone accent. I grew to love his voice, the images he painted with words, his superb interpretative powers and the bell-like purity of his tone.

'He recorded at his best between the years 1910 and 1920, and this is particularly true of his operatic recordings. My aunt Molly Curley had met him through her husband's brother who was Bishop of the Diocese of St. Augustine, Florida, and later Archbishop Curley of Baltimore. He had helped John McCormack in America and both men, when holidaying in

Ireland, stayed at my aunt's house in Athlone. Inevitably someone would say to McCormack, "Give us a song, John," even though there was no piano.in the house, but he sometimes obliged with an Irish ballad.

'I'm told that on one of his visits my aunt made such a fuss of him that Archbishop Curley was impelled to good-humouredly rebuke her, but she was quick to reply, "Sure there are lots of bishops, but only one John McCormack!"'

Years later when he toured the west coast of America with a group of Irish singers, Louis was reminded of the friendship between the McCormacks and the Curleys. On being introduced to Lily McCormack he said he was Louis Browne from Athlone and that Molly Curley was his aunt. Lily McCormack looked at him and her eyes lit up. 'Oh ... Molly!' she exclaimed. 'She used to send butter to John and myself during the war when we were living in Dublin.'

Growing up in Athlone, he was made aware of McCormack's enduring fame. Everyone had either attended school with the tenor or sat beside him, but for all that he was the singer every boy who had a note in his head wanted to emulate. Despite deprivation and food shortages the war brought to the country, Louis never went hungry. His father farmed a mile from the town and the family lived off the produce with bacon, eggs, potatoes, butter and fowl readily available. Working on the land during his school holidays gave him a sense of real freedom and enjoyment.

As a boy soprano he had begun to be noticed. At the age of 12 he sang Schubert's "Ave Maria" and "My Singing Bird" on Radio Eireann. His father's people were musical, though on his mother's side it was not so, except that she had a great-grand uncle who piped his way from Athlone to Cork. At this time Athlone could be classed as a musical town with its energetic musical society, church choirs and the Marist Brothers' School, which enjoyed a fine reputation in this respect.

On reflection, Louis Browne says that the school exerted a big influence on him, since during his time there the headmaster inaugurated musicals and he himself took leading parts in *Maritana* and *Trial by Jury*. Before his voice broke at the age of 14, he remembered travelling with his mother to Dublin and taking a bus to Greystones where he made recordings in Peter Hunt's studios. 'I have still those recordings of "Hear My Prayer" and "O For the Wings of a Dove" and they're not bad at all!'

One of a family of five – he has one brother and three sisters – his mind had not changed by the time he had sat the Leaving Certificate – he was still determined to be a singer. He recalled that his voice was 'a bit raw' and needed professional training. At the age of 19 he decided to go to Dublin, and his mother gave him the money to pay his initial fee at the College of Music. He tended to be shy and unassertive and lacked self-confidence. He was afraid to tell his pals he was taking singing lessons for fear they would ridicule him. To support himself, he worked for a company selling furniture, but soon he moved to various other jobs. Singing remained his only real interest and he could not wait to become a professional singer.

He joined the Rathmines & Rathgar Musical Society and sang the tenor lead in *The Yeomen of the Guard* and he made new musical friends. As his idol, John McCormack, had done before him, Louis Browne won the gold medal at the Feis Ceoil; it was the proudest moment of his life. Shortly afterwards he did an extensive tour of North American cities with Kitty O'Callaghan's Festival Singers, a talented group that included Patrick Ring, Arthur Agnew, James Cuthbert, Kitty Corcoran, Austin Gaffney and harpist, Sheila Larchet. It was his first taste of the professional side of singing and he cherished the experience.

Back in Dublin, he began to sing at functions, and though the money was paltry – no more than £2 or £3 – facing an audience increased his confidence. On one occasion at a lawn tennis club dinner he sang Wallace's "Let me like a soldier Fall" and was disappointed when no one in the function room appeared to listen. Heather Hewson, the piano accompanist, said to him afterwards, 'If they're not going to listen, I suggest you sing as if singing to one person. My father once gave me that advice.'

He picked out the smiling face of a woman at a table in the corner of the room and directed his next song at her and it seemed to work. What he didn't know was that she happened to be Mairead Piggott who passed singers for auditions in Radio Eireann. A few days later she 'phoned his voice teacher, Maura O'Connor, and said, 'I heard Louis Browne sing the other night; would you send him into me?'

It was his entrée to broadcasting. He was featured on the popular Din Joe variety programme, singing light classical songs and ballads. Next, he was engaged to do a series of Sunday night programmes with the Casino Orchestra which was popular with listeners; later he was introduced to Dermot O'Hara, the conductor who took him on for a series with the Radio Eireann Light Orchestra at the Phoenix Hall.

'Dermot must have heard me sing with the Casino Orchestra", he recalled. 'Seemingly, he used to terrorise young singers by his autocratic manner, but he was alright to me. I remember he handed me a page of music and on it was written, "Watch the conductor." I did just that and found singing with the full orchestra was a valuable experience.'

It was this recognition by Radio Eireann of his vocal promise that gave him renewed hope, for at times he despaired of making a living from singing. 'I don't think I would have kept on without this support. During one of the DGOS's seasons, he went round to James Johnston's dressing room in the Gaiety Theatre and was accorded a cordial welcome by the veteran tenor. 'He was still wearing his Cavaradossi costume, but he listened to me and was encouraging and gave me names and addresses in London'.

It was a meeting, however, with Norman Meadmore, an English guest producer with the R & R that opened a door to him. Meadmore, who had worked with the D'Oyly Carte Company, arranged an audition for him at the Guildhall School of Music and Drama in London. He must have made a good impression, for he was told a scholarship was his provided he settled in London. Louis Browne did not hesitate to pack his bags and leave the uncertainty of Dublin behind him.

In the late 1950s there were a lot of talented young singers at the Guildhall, among them Benjamin Luxon, Donald McIntyre, Delme Bryn Jones and the cellist, Jacqueline Du Pre. To the young Irish tenor, it was the place to be. He was able to study different aspects of opera and acquire insights into acting, as well as learn new vocal techniques. He made his school debut as Fenton in *Falstaff* and went on to sing Cavaradossi in *Tosca* and Basilio in *The Marriage of Figaro*.

He worked with Arthur Reckless, a well-known vocal teacher and adjudicator. Reckless arranged for him to sing in oratorios and concerts outside the school and spoke highly of his tenor voice which by now had a potentially good range. During his two years at the Guildhall, he could say he had learned a good deal about all facets of singing, including intonation, phrasing and interpretation. He was relieved that what he called the 'raw edge' in his voice had gone.

By 1960 he decided it was time to make a move and auditioned for the Glyndebourne Festival chorus. He was recalled for a second audition and was taken on. The chorus, he soon discovered, was made up of very talented young singers, including Ann Howells, Ryland Davies, Elizabeth Harewood and Francis Egerton, and the standard was consequently very high. Because operas were sung in the original language, Glyndebourne acquired the reputation as an outstanding training ground for young singers.

'I would recommend Glyndebourne to any young singer', Louis Browne says today. 'I got the chance to understudy roles and in my second season sang a minor part in Strauss's *Capriccio*. Discipline was a priority and from the very start singers were made aware of this.

'I remember I was met at Lewes railway station by chorus master, Peter Gellhorn, and from that moment you were left in no doubt that you weren't arriving for a picnic. Peter was German-born and a strict disciplinarian and on the first day of rehearsals he laid down the rules for us. I can still hear him say in a firm tone, "Rehearsals are from 10 in the morning 'til 1 o'clock, but that doesn't mean you arrive at 10; we sing in actual fact our first note at 10 sharp. We break for coffee or tea at 11 and resume 15 minutes later. Not a minute after 11.15, not a minute before. Then we work on 'til lunchtime and break at 1 o'clock".'

Rehearsals continued for the month of April. With two other members of the chorus, Louis Browne rented a cottage some distance from the opera house, and as one who had spent his boyhood on a Westmeath farm he appreciated the beauty of the English countryside and the Sussex Downs. He was intrigued by the history of the Glyndebourne Festival itself and the stories of its eccentric founder, John Christie, who in 1934 – its first year – presented *The Marriage of Figaro* and *Cosi fan tutte.*

It soon dawned on him that summer that Glyndebourne was as much a social event as an opera festival; the place exuded an air of grandeur and not a little affectation, though this was not present in the music staff or among those employed on the administrative side. He was amused to learn that some of the corporate people did not always return after the customary long interval, not because they wined and dined too well, but due to their lack of real interest in the operatic performance.

'One of the operas they couldn't fathom at all was *Pelleas et Melisande*', he recalled, 'and after picnicking on the lawns they'd sneak away for a walk and return when the performance was over. Of course they were in the minority; the great majority knew their Mozart and Strauss and enjoyed the productions tremendously. As a young singer, working beside international stars, it was a marvellous experience and something was bound to rub off – and it did. Apart from their voices, they were expert actors and a joy to watch.'

It was the best paid opera chorus in Britain, the members being in receipt of a special subsistence allowance. Louis Browne was genuinely sorry to leave it, but he reckoned it was again time to move on. He auditioned for Sadler's Wells Company in London and was employed on a junior principal's contract. It was hard work, as he quickly discovered. Between rehearsals and actual stage performances he had little spare time to himself; nor was he paid during summer holidays and so was obliged to make up the loss of earnings by singing in concerts or on radio or television in Ireland. He sang the title roles in *Faust* and *Le Comte d'Ory* for Neath Opera Group in its summer seasons at the Adelina Patti Theatre Craig-y-nos, an experience he remembers with delight.

Operas at Sadler's Wells were sung in English. He was soon to discover why it was called 'Australia House'; it was due to the increasing number of Australian-born singers on contract to the company. 'I found that they possessed unusual confidence in their own ability, with the result that one of them once remarked to me after a rehearsal, "Louis, you'll have to get more like us, otherwise you're not going to make it." They were outgoing and popular with the rest of the members. I remember there was a certain New Zealander who didn't believe in formalities or the Englishman's reserved approach. Sometimes he'd pop his head into the boss's office in the morning and exclaim, "How are you this morning, eh?" The chap failed to realise you didn't do that kind of thing in jolly old England.'

He had graduated by now to senior principal tenor with the company and was singing leading roles such as Almaviva in *The Barber of Seville*, Ernesto in *Don Pasquale* and Prince Ramiro in *Cinderella*. Before long the critics began to take notice of the name of Louis Browne. In *Opera* magazine's review of Rossini's *The Thieving Magpie*, Harold Rosenthal wrote: 'The most important cast change was one for the better - Louis Browne replaced Donald Pilley as Giannetto. Mr. Browne sings this kind of music elegantly and although the role was somewhat abbreviated, he made a positive impression in it.'

Likewise, when the company toured *Don Pasquale*, the leading Wolverhampton critic commented: 'As Ernesto, the dispossessed nephew, Louis Browne was admirable. His voice has the right weight and timbre, and he uses it most effectively. He was at his best when heard and not seen, during the serenade in Act III. This was fine singing.'

Significantly, the critics praised the charm he projected, as well as his stylish singing and clear diction. Nor did his flair for comedy go unnoticed. In fact, he was amused to find his name in this respect linked with that of Dudley Moore. He was singing the young Count Ory - the seducer of the abbess and her nuns -in Birmingham, when one critic observed, 'Louis Browne, a kind of Dudley Moore, made a splendid job of Ory, firm voiced if slightly heady here and there, and graciously comic.'

It became one of the tenor's favourite roles at Sadler's Wells, although

John Higgins in the *Financial Times* noted his performance as Almaviva in the *Barber of Seville* and stated in the course of his review: 'The lovers, both new to me in their roles, were Louis Browne and Jennifer Eddy. Mr. Browne has a very light and clear tenor and he made a very decent shot at Almaviva, a role which has defeated British singers – and Commonwealth ones, for that matter – for more years than I care to remember.'

More than one critic commented on his diction as of 'exemplary clearness' and were impressed by the feeling he injected into his singing. At this time in the middle Sixties he broadcast regularly on BBC radio programmes and when time permitted, was heard on RTE.

As his contract tied him exclusively to Sadler's Wells Company, it became a source of frustration to the singer. When his brother was to be married he asked for leave but was reminded by the management that he was listed to sing Almaviva on that night. It meant that he had to pay out of his own pocket for a replacement, in this case Ryland Davies. Occasionally, though, he was able to fit in outside engagements like the *Verdi Requiem* and Rossini's *Stabat Mater*. Singing in the *Verdi Requiem* with the Liverpool Philharmonic, conducted by Sir Charles Groves, afforded him one of his abiding musical memories.

Missing out on other attractive offers, however, galled him. Colin Davis wanted him for Berlioz's *The Trojans* and privately approached Sadler's Wells management, but the conductor was told that the tenor was unavailable for the dates mentioned. Louis Browne did not hear about Davis's approach until someone remarked to him, 'I hear Colin Davis was disappointed you couldn't sing for him.'

Naturally he was upset, yet he knew that protesting served little purpose. Looking back, he wonders if after all security is the best thing for a singer; contracted to an opera house he found limited one's freedom of choice and could be an obstacle to progress. Freelance singers, in his view, tended to be better networkers and were more business-like in their approach.

Money was a perennial problem at the Wells, mainly because some singers felt they were underpaid for the heavy workload pushed onto them. Louis Browne was in agreement. 'It was a living wage, no more. As principal singers in the company we negotiated our own salaries, so we did not know what our colleagues earned, though we had a pretty good idea that it wasn't enough. During the course of a week, I would sometimes sing two or more leading roles either in London or on tour and it could be demanding, yet I can say that singing always came first. I was enjoying myself working with colleagues like Denis Dowling, Harold Blackburn, Derek Hammond-Stroud, Patricia Kern and Howell Glynne. And the camaderie and spirit in the company was excellent. I wouldn't have missed it for the world.'

Touring could be arduous and stressful, particularly when rail or air schedules went wrong. Once, he was singing with the company in Edinbugh and later that night he and the bass, Howell Glynne, boarded a plane for London's Heathrow, but due to fog it was diverted to Manchester where they decided to travel by all- night coach to London. 'I remember I got home about 10 a.m. and immediately 'phoned Sadler's Wells and asked to be excused from rehearsals and this was agreed. On another occasion, I was singing in Newcastle-on-Tyne and again took an all-night train to London, arriving home very tired. In a few hours, however, I was rehearsing a new production and the producer was being difficult with his stage instructions, and thinking that he was picking deliberately on me, I went up to him and explained how I had travelled back to London the previous night. He tried to brush me off but I was having none of it. Sometimes these people could be a bit arrogant and one had to be firm with them.'

On another occasion he was singing Almaviva at the Grand Theatre, Leeds, when he was approached at the first interval by the company manager who said politely to him, 'Sit down, Louis, I've something to tell you, something I didn't want to tell you before the curtain went up tonight. You are on to-morrow night in *Orfeo*.'

The score was almost new to him, so that after the performance of *The Barber* had ended, he hurried back to his hotel and began to study the music. Touring, though, could have its amusing moments, as he once discovered in Glasgow. On arrival there one afternoon he and the Australian baritone, Robert Bickerstaff, finding the hotels full, hurried off in search of 'digs'. After a few unsuccessful attempts to find anything suitable, they eventually spotted a man coming out of a guesthouse and enquired about it.

'Very good', the man replied, 'and so is the food.' The door was opened by a large woman with a friendly Irish accent and she offered to show the singers the remaining room available. They followed her up the carpeted stairs to the third floor, where she pointed to a vacant room. 'That's the only one I've got left', she said, making no apology for the advanced age of the two iron beds. They agreed to take the room – they had scarcely any other option as they were taking the stage in *Carmen* in less than two hours. At least, mused Bickerstaff who was to sing Escamillo in the opera, 'the place is clean.'

Later that night the tenor and baritone shared a hearty laugh as the gangling Bickerstaff, who was all of 6 feet 5 inches tall, was obliged to sleep with his legs partly dangling over the end of the bed. 'I can still see those legs', recalled Louis Browne, 'and Robert helpless to cover them in the small bed.'

To relax after performances on tour, he and other members of the company would sometimes go to late-night jazz clubs for a drink. He made many good friends in those touring days, but what he remembered most was the enthusiasm shown by provincial audiences. 'I can vividly remember the tremendous applause on one occasion at the Opera House, Manchester after we had performed *Don Pasquale*. It was one of those nights when everything went right for us, musically and otherwise. And Osbert Lancaster's set designs were always a delight.'

With Sadler's Wells concentrating on operetta as well as opera, he acquired a real love for it. Wendy Toye's hilarious production of Offenbach's *Orpheus in the Underworld* provided him with his favourite character role, that of John Styx, but he came also to enjoy Lehar, Johann Strauss and Sullivan. The London audiences, he felt, welcomed operettas as a kind of delightful diversion from opera.

When the company eventually moved from Sadler's Wells in the late Sixties to the Coliseum and was re-named English National Opera, Louis Browne thought the move was perfectly justified. 'Personally, I welcomed the change and so did the majority of the company, mainly because of its excellent acoustics and its larger size. I enjoyed singing Rossini, Donizetti and Mozart roles there and the rapport with the audience was excellent.'

But to the singers, the Coliseum came to be known as 'The Factory'. 'I suppose we thought of ourselves as workers going into a factory churning out a product – in our case opera', he said. 'Musical standards, however, greatly improved there and we attracted consistently big audiences.'

In 1973 he decided to leave the company. He was getting married to Theresa Dogham, a Clonmel woman, and he reckoned it was time to go freelance and improve his earnings. It was a decision he had no reason to regret. Between concert and broadcasting engagements he was kept busy, and he guested on a number of occasions with English National Opera. After the birth of their son and daughter, he moved with the family to Ireland, chiefly because he wanted to bring them up there.

He became the first artist to sing at Dublin's new National Concert Hall, and his albums such as 'An Evening in Ireland' and 'The Meeting of the Waters' sold exceedingly well. His voice was still in exellent shape and he attributed this to the way he had looked after it. In conversation, he talked about John McCormack, Dermot Troy, Charles Craig and Alfredo Kraus, whose artistry never ceased to amaze him. He felt that the tenor had not got the recognition he deserved and that Pavarotti, Domingo and Carreras stole all the limelight. 'I head Kraus once at a concert in London', he said, 'and I considered him a magnificient stylist. He never forced his voice and this, I believe, is one of the reasons why he is singing in his 60s. Young singers should listen to his recordings and learn from him.'

He had happy memories of tenor, Charles Craig, who was a colleague at the Coliseum. Once after singing Ernesto in *Don Pasquale*, he was visited in his dressing room by Craig who warmly congratulated him on his performance. 'He needn't have done it', Louis Brown says today, 'but besides being an outstanding tenor Charles was a generous man. So too was Dermot Troy. From our first meeting at Westminster Cathedral in London we got on very well. He invited me to his home where I met his wife, Eithne, and a visiting baritone, John Shaw. The funny thing was that the three of us smoked like chimneys, which in hindsight wasn't a very wise thing for singers to do. I had heard Dermot sing at Glyndebourne and Covent Garden and considered him a polished artist who was destined to go places. He was also, it seemed to me, exceptionally intelligent and was able to complete *The Times* crossword in under five minutes. He had an infectious sense of humour and was an excellent conversationalist and showed a genuine interest in people.'

Wherever he goes, Louis is invariably asked about John McCormack whose records he still plays for pleasure. 'Of course John was unique. The feeling he brought to a song has never been surpassed and that is why you hear his records played year in, year out. I like to remember him when his voice was still a high tenor, not when it dropped an octave or two. His recordings at his peak were incredibly good. I wish, though, he had not recorded when his voice had virtually disappeared. But he will be always remembered by those people who want to hear a song beautifully sung.'

When I reminded Louis Browne in the 1990s that most of his contemporaries were no longer singing, he smiled and said, 'Yes, I am aware of that. A few of them are now teaching singing, others have retired gracefully. I have been fortunate in that my voice held up. Looking back, I never had any serious trouble with my voice; indeed, I missed only one operatic performance in my life and that was due to a virus I picked up on tour.'

With Peter McBrien he decided to form the Irish Concert Artists, which features Irish and overseas singers in concerts at the National Concert Hall, and they also staged concert versions of operas, notably *Tosca* with guest stars Suzanne Murphy and Dennis O'Neill. It has afforded Louis Browne great satisfaction to be able to put something tangible into singing. As he says, 'Ireland has many fine young singers nowadays and it's nice for Peter and me to be able to give them a chance to be heard.

Nobody knows better than myself the frustrations they can experience when there are no opportunities available for them.'

Chapter Twelve

Bernadette Greevy

WEXFORD TO BUENOS AIRES

Bright gold discs hang from a bracelet on her wrist, and on each is neatly inscribed the names of operas such as *Werther, Ariodante, Samson et Delilah, Herodiade* and *L'Isola Disabitata*. The discs, explained Bernadette Greevy, were mementoes from her late husband Peter Tattan and were given to her prior to her appearance in each of the operas.

In any conversation with her, she tends to hold out her hand proudly as though eager to explain the symbolism of the gold discs. They evoke memories, too, of her husband who rarely, if ever, missed her performances. She has a necklace with more discs and with names like *Luisa Miller, Orfeo ed Euridice* and *Don Carlos*.

To a younger generation of Irish music-lovers her name is associated more closely with Mahler than Verdi and this is understandable for in more recent years she has concentrated on recital or concert work rather than opera. Yet opera has played an important part in her career. As she told me, 'My whole theory is that opera is very much a part of a singer's career. In most cases singers do little else. I would never, however, have been satisfied with that. The discipline of recital work has helped my operatic performances and, as a person, singing opera has been great for me. But it is only part of my career. Opera is not the be–all and the end–all.'

Maddalena was the first professional role she sang and that was in the

DGOS's spring season of 1961. She admitted she was young and very inexperienced in the ways of opera. With her father in the Gaiety Theatre audience, she was feeling slightly nervous, and he was unacquainted with the character of Maddalena, a woman of easy virtue.

'I remember that Italian tenor Antonio Gallie was singing the Duke of Mantua and I'm afraid he gave me a hard time. As he made advances to Maddalena, he pulled at my blouse and at that moment I could imagine my father mumbling to himself, "What is that fellow doing to my daughter?" No doubt he was a bit shocked. For my part, I didn't really understand the character I was playing; my main concern was to sing the role as best I could.'

Up to then she had performed only in school musicals such as *Blossom Time* and *Lilac Time* and some Gilbert & Sullivan. Born and reared in Clontarf, a bracing suburb of Dublin, she was the sixth of seven children. Her earliest recollections are of her house, then surrounded by green fields and playing 'house' with her sister Pauline, either in the back garden or on the road. Her school years at the Covent of the Holy Faith, Clontarf were happy. She remembered there was lots of music, choir exams and operettas. Sister Fedelma encouraged her to sing as a child, and music was also an integral part of home life. 'We could all sing in the Greevy family.'

Growing up in Clontarf in those days was a joy. 'During the long summer holidays we used to go for a swim in Dollymount every day, come rain or shine, armed with sandwiches and flasks of cocoa. St. Anne's Estate, formerly the residence of Archbishop Plunkett, was completely out of bounds to us when I was a child. It was then known locally as "The Lords", and to venture into this mysterious and exotic place was the very essence of adventure and daring. Today St. Anne's is a wonderful park for family outings and possesses the most beautiful rose garden in Ireland.'

The social nerve-centre of Clontarf in her teenage years was the local tennis club. Clontarf had two: Eason's, now sadly defunct, and Oulton Road, still in operation, where she said she played very little tennis but 'had a whale of a time' socially. To get to either of these clubs one had to pass the crossroads at Seafield Road and run the gauntlet of the assembled male talent invariably gathered there.

'That took some nerve, I assure you, but to this day I get a pang of sweet sadness every time I pass the spot,' she recalled with a laugh.

There were other memories such as the blackberry picking expeditions in Malahide, organised by her father. They had all to go and pick them and afterwards her mother would make 'fantastic jam' in big stone pots.

There was no surprise expressed by her friends when she decided to become a singer. As she later explained, 'I ended up being a singer because I suppose I did that better than any of the other things. I would love to have been a painter. And I'd love to have gone to a university and done an English degree as the thought of writing appealed to me. But my childhood was dominated by Feiseanna and musicals and everyone told me my voice had potential.'

By the time Bernadette Greevy had left school she had won the Plunkett Green Cup, the Lieder Cup and the Contralto Gold Medal at the Feis Ceoil in Dublin. She began to take singing lessons with Jean Nolan who was highly regarded in her field. 'Jean was very good for a beginner like me,' she said. 'She gave me an idea about repertoire as well as good advice about the path I should follow as a singer.'

That path led to the Wexford Festival in the autumn of 1962. Dr. Tom Walsh cast her as Beppe, the gipsy girl, in Mascagni's *L'Amico Fritz*, with Veronica Dunne singing Suzel. In some respects it was a notable season, for the Radio Eireann Symphony Orchestra was making its debut at the festival and it marked the last appearance there of Wexford's favourite artist, tenor Nicola Monti who in the previous 10 years had sung in Wexford in five different operas.

In retrospect, Bernadette Greevy says as a newcomer she was immediately struck by the professionalism that surrounded the festival. Singers counted it an honour to sing there and both designers and producers strove after perfection. She herself with the other principals rehearsed assiduously with Bulgarian producer Michael Hadji Mischev and conductor Antonio Tonini. To the amusement of the musicians in the orchestra, she learned to mime the violin and sing at the same time. Working with experienced Italian singers such as Nicola Monti and Paolo Pedani was a joy and an education. It was, she thought, an excellent place for a young singer to pick up operatic tips. Monti, who would record later with Maria Callas in Milan, was she noted a charming personality with no hint of ego. 'I could see that he was a great favourite with Dr. Walsh.'

L'Amico Fritz was a critical success. 'It was a great festival start for me,' says Bernadette today. 'I couldn't have asked for a nicer part.'

Singing in the intimate Theatre Royal was a new experience for her and acoustically she found it excellent. The second production that year was Bellini's *I Puritani* and it tended to steal the limelight due to a stunning performance by soprano Mirella Freni as Elvira.

It was not an easy time in Ireland for talented young singers hoping for an international career. Most of them had to support themselves, either in Dublin or London. Bernadette Greevy was no exception. She was by now studying at the Guildhall in London and supporting herself by working as a cosmetician for Elizabeth Arden. Earlier, she had applied for financial support from the Arts Council in Ireland but her request was turned down. It hurt the pride of the young contralto and it was something she would not easily forget.

However, she was more fortunate than many of her colleagues. In 1964, she made her recital debut at the Wigmore Hall and won the coveted Harriet Cohen International Award for outstanding artistry and the Order of Merit of Malta. Her co-winner was the pianist Vladimir Ashkenazy. It was the spur she needed to raise her self-confidence, yet even then she had no desire to settle permanently in England. Her decision surprised not a few of her colleagues who considered Ireland 'too small for her talent'.

It is accepted that singers need a modicum of luck during their careers. Bernadette Greevy secured it through inspirational conductors, notably Sir John Barbirolli and Tibor Paul. 'Barbirolli taught me *The Dream of Gerontius*, the *Verdi Requiem* and *Messiah*. He got me to think about words, which have been so important, if not the most important thing to me all my life. It was a wonderful training and a great bit of luck, and I wonder if he had lived would my life have taken another direction.'

Barbirolli was, she found, very relaxed in his approach to music, the complete opposite to Tibor Paul, the Hungarian disciplinarian at RTE. She remembers him with affection for taking an interest in her as a young singer. 'He would have given me the toughest boot out if I didn't fit in to what he had envisaged for me. He gave me a hard time, but it was reward-ing. It made you realise that you were in a very tough profession and that the world owes nobody a living. He was a dictator, if you like, but we needed that in Ireland at the time.'

Paul introduced her to the works of Gustav Mahler, in particular to *Das Lied von der Erde* – the composer's vision of the universe – and the song cycle *Kindertotenlieder*, and later on to his magnificent symphonies. The music made an immediate and profound impression on her; it was indi-vidual in style and extraordinarily expressive. With her natural production of tone, innate understanding of the musical phrase and a genuine warmth of expression, she overcame the technical difficulties with the ease of a born musician.

'Singing Mahler's music soon became part of me,' she said. She was thinking perhaps of *Das Lied von der Erde* and the last song of the work, "Abschied", one of the longest songs ever written. Sung with depth and feeling it can become a haunting and heart-breaking farewell. Bernadette Greevy says she has never failed to be deeply touched by the experience, no matter how often she has done it.

It was a time in Dublin when Mahler was virtually unknown, but Tibor Paul, who in musical terms was a crusading spirit in the same mould as Bruno Walter, felt the majesty of Mahler's music had appeal for every-one. Yet it was a slow initiation process in Ireland. Bernadette Greevy is delighted that she was in at the beginning of the renaissance, as she described it to me. 'I was to see a day when a Mahler symphony would pack the National Concert Hall. In the Nineties I was one of the singers in the performance at the Point Centre in Dublin of his Eighth Symphony, which was for us all a memorable occasion. Mahler has been my greatest friend all my life. He wrote so much that I could sing.'

If she had met him would they have got on?

'A very interesting question, or should I say, match-up. He was a strange individual it would seem. As a young man he was very self-opinionated, but I kind of like that. I'd say we'd have wonderful times and dreadful times. What a great pity, though, that he never lived to see *Das Lied* performed. As you know, it took place in 1911, the year of the composer's death.'

The year 1966 was to be eventful for her. When her first solo recording of Handel arias was issued, *The Gramophone* concluded its review with the simple message: 'More please!'

Shortly afterwards she married her childhood sweetheart Peter Tattan, who by then was a sales representative with a Dublin tobacco company. He had an interest in classical music and regularly attended symphony concerts. She had no apprehension about getting married. 'I was in love with Peter and felt I could manage marriage and my singing career without difficulty. Peter was understanding and knew by then what singing entailed. Of all the boyfriends I had, he was the one who was different from the rest. I always had it in the back of my mind that if I ever married Peter would be the man.'

Later on she would say, 'He was never intimidated by my success, in fact my achievements gave him the utmost pleasure. We were equals in marriage and that is as it should be.'

After their son Hugh was born her husband suggested that perhaps it would be a good idea if they moved to England. He had a job lined up for himself and was anxious to move for her sake. But Bernadette was reluctant to make the move. She already had made a conscious decision that she wanted to enjoy the quality of life in Ireland and also to bring up her son in that environment. Although aware of the travel cost it entailed making Dublin her career base, she had another reason. 'I wanted to prove – to myself more than anyone else – that if you're good enough you can live where you like. You are what you are. And I'm Irish. There was a certain thing I needed here . I needed a family back-up'.

Peter Tattan had hoped that going abroad would bring his wife greater recognition and provide her with more opportunities and money. Nonetheless, when she said no he accepted the decision as final.

Privately, she had been disappointed that Wexford Festival had offered her nothing since 1962; it was now 1969. I remember her telling me at the time, 'I can see no reason why I hadn't been asked back. The excuse will be that there wasn't a suitable part for me, but I don't go along with that. Glyndebourne Festival Opera has mounted operas for Janet Baker and other English singers.'

By now Dr. Tom Walsh had retired from the festival and Brian Dickie was the new artistic director. The operas announced for the 1969 event were Verdi's *Luisa Miller* and Haydn's *L'infedelta Delusa*. The production of the Verdi work was plagued by misfortune. The tenor Georgio Mereghi was taken ill and was replaced by fellow Italian Angelo La Forese. When Spanish soprano Angeles Gulin was forced to withdraw at short notice the entire production was threatened with cancellation, but a replacement was found in Lucia Kelston from Milan.

Bernadette Greevy was second choice to sing the role of Federica. She welcomed the chance, however, to return to the festival. Despite the cancellations she found a good atmosphere at rehearsals, though in the circumstances they were more hectic than usual. More misfortune was on the way. While driving to Dublin to meet his wife the conductor of the opera, Myer Fredman, from Glyndebourne, sustained injuries in a road accident, after his car skidded. On the first night he conducted in severe pain.

The production received mixed reviews from the English and Irish critics, though they did agree it was a suitable opera for Wexford. Bernadette Greevy was happy with the outcome. As Mary MacGoris in the *Irish Independent* put it, 'Miss Greevy managed to make the most of the rather nondescript role of the Duchess and sang with beautiful smoothness, ease and feeling.'

My own recollection of the evening was of dull stage designs and over-loud singing by tenor Angelo La Forese, who must have thought he was singing in a large Italian provincial opera house. There were compensations, however, in Bernadette Greevy's noble bearing and beautiful voice; the same could be said for Silvano Pagliuca, whose powerfully controlled singing as Count Walter delighted the audience and generated real Verdian fire.

'I loved singing Verdi's music,' Bernadette later told me. 'He writes so well for the voice and, of course, you must give it heart. Listening to the great choruses in his operas, the singing always seemed to me to pour out from the deepest recesses, such are their grandeur and nobility. As with Mozart, a singer needs a very good vocal technique to sing Verdi.'

It would be another eight years before she would sing again at the festival, which to me at least seemed a long time for an artist of her calibre. Thomson Smillie was by then the artistic director and the operas for that year were Massenet's *Herodiade*, Gluck's *Orfeo ed Euridice* and a triple bill of Italian works, Cimarosa's *Il Maestro di Capella,* Ricci's *La Serva e L'Ussero* and Pergolesi's *La Serva Padrona*.

In the previous years she had been kept busy with oratorio, concert and operatic engagements. In 1976 she had sung in a performance of Tippett's *A Child of Our Time* conducted by the composer. She had toured Russia and Finland with the Bournemouth Symphony Orchestra and sung with the DGOS as well as with Welsh National Opera in *Werther, Faust, Rigoletto* and the *Barber of Seville* respectively.

She had always been fascinated by the French operatic repertoire and regretted that the DGOS inexplicably tended to neglect it. So the thought of singing the title role in Massenet's *Herodiade* that autumn of 1977 filled her with enthusiasm. Although the opera is nowadays overshadowed by Strauss's *Salome*, it was nevertheless considered an ideal choice for Wexford which thrives on a diet of the lesser known works of first - and second class - composers. Herodiade was first produced in Brussels in 1881 and contains considerable passion in the music.

Rehearsals were not long in progress when Bernadette Greevy realised she was working with an unusually talented cast that included two Australians, Malcolm Donnelly (Herode) and Eilene Hannan (Salome) but only one French singer, the tenor Jean Dupuoy, as John the Baptist. It was, however, the conductor Henri Gallois who made the biggest impression on her. 'Naturally being French he understood the score superbly; he was also a brilliant musician and joy to work with.'

Singing in the opera was an unforgettable experience for her. The production itself was hailed as a resounding success by the critics, with most of them enthusing about conductor Henri Gallois who inspired the RTE Symphony Orchestra to playing of exceptional quality. Elizabeth Forbes in the *Financial Times* summed up: 'He ensured an idiomatically French performance from a cast of singers only one of which was French. Bernadette Greevy's ringing tones proved ideal to the role of Herodias; if she did not earn the taunts of "Jezebel" hurled at her by John the Baptist, she at least brought a striking presence to the part.'

'Everything about the opera appealed to me,' recalled Bernadette Greevy. 'Although I considered the character of Herodias a bit crazy, I had some lovely music to sing. I was so happy with this production.'

Later when a concert version of the opera was being planned for New York's Carnegie Hall she was engaged to sing Herodias. The promotors had, it seemed, searched for the most recent performer in the role and it happened to be Bernadette. During rehearsals, however, both Montserrat Caballe and Nicolai Gedda unexpectedly withdrew from the cast and were replaced by American singers.

To Bernadette Greevy, it was a disappointing start. She had eagerly looked forward to working with Caballe and Gedda, particularly the latter. 'I had collected his records for years and wondered what it would be like to sing on stage with him. 'But even without the two stars the concert version drew a packed audience to Carnegie Hall and she greatly enjoyed the experience.

By the time she was back again in Wexford in 1982 a new era had dawned for the festival. The artistic director was English-born Elaine

Padmore and she decided to mark the 250th anniversary of Haydn's birth with a production of *L'Isola Disabitata*. It is a rather static piece of theatre and it failed to excite festival audiences in the same way as did Massenet's *Griselidis*, the second opera that year, when the magnificently-voiced young Russian baritone, Sergei Leiferkus was the talk of the town.

The critics differed on the Haydn production. John Higgins in the London *Times* commented, 'There is precious little action in this tale of Constanza and her kid sister Sylvia who, apparently abandoned on a desert island, are reunited with husband and friend. There are, of course, a handful of elegant arias, but the final quartet the only concerted number in the score, seems a long time coming.'

'The opera was charmingly sung and acted by Bernadette Greevy and the rest of the cast,' stated Felix Aprahamian in the *Sunday Times*. While she enjoyed working with the international cast and tasting again the unique flavour of this festival, Bernadette came away, however, without the same abiding memories inspired by *Herodiade*. Had her expectations been too high?

Personal tragedy struck in the following year, 1983. On 3 March her husband Peter died unexpectedly. She had gone out for half an hour to her sick mother. When she came home she found him dead on the landing. He had earlier suffered a heart attack in 1980 but seemingly had recovered well. She was stunned by his death. For a long time one of the deepest wounds was that in his dying moments she was not there to cradle him. 'I'm told that it was so quick that there was nothing I could have done.'

For months afterwards she could barely bring herself to go out of the house. 'I was suddenly stripped of my confidence. I suffered greatly both physically and mentally for a long time. In truth, I hadn't been prepared for this kind of grief. Peter and I had been closer than ever before because he had given up his job and was devoting his time to managing my affairs. He had amazed me in fact by the way he went about getting me international engagements, sometimes for years ahead.'

For the first time she was aware of how a singer's career could be affected by personal grief. Gradually she pulled out of the gloom, mainly due to friends and colleagues. Fred O'Donovan, chairman of the National Concert Hall, along with Frank Murphy, manager, decided it was time to do something for the singer in an effort to restore her confidence. It was a year after her husband's death and they eventually persuaded her to give a recital.

It was a master stroke. Everyone rallied round and the recital was a success in every way. 'I'm sure it helped to restore my self-confidence,' Bernadette told me. 'It proved to me that I had still got my nerve. I was able once again to walk out on an empty stage to face an audience. And I had enough pride in my work to be able to continue with my career.'

Peter Tattan, before his death, had negotiated a tour of New Zealand for her and now she decided to take it on; not only that - she decided to bring her son Hugh along with her. She met again the renowned German conductor Franz-Paul Decker; their first meeting had been in Auckland and he was interested in her voice and regarded her as a leading interpreter of Mahler's music. The meeting marked a milestone in her future career.Back in Ireland the year 1985 was to be a particularly busy one for her. She sang Princess Eboli in *Don Carlos* for the DGOS and I can vividly remember the prolonged applause after her movingly-sung aria, "O don fatale" in Act IV. Recital and concert work followed, and in the autumn it was back to Wexford once more to sing the title role in Handel's *Ariodante.*

The opera has long been accepted as one of the composer's greatest, with its well-drawn characters, straightforward plot and glorious music. As far as I remember, it was produced in Wexford without fuss and conde-scension. The critic Desmond Shawe-Taylor regarded it as the hit of the festival. Unfortunately for Bernadette Greevy, she was suffering from a sinus infection and could not in the circumstances make the most of the heroic title-role, something she seriously regrets.

Soon she was off on a tour of China. She had accepted an invitation by the Chinese Ministry of Culture and during her stay there gave recitals and masterclasses. This proved more arduous than she could have imag-

171

ined as she had to demonstrate every point she made. As she was to explain, 'Seemingly, the most important service a teacher can render to a student in China is to demonstrate each point. So in my masterclasses I had to be a soprano, tenor and bass as well as a mezzo. It was very exciting to see such an open attitude to the teaching of singing.'

On the tour with her were her son Hugh, Jane Carty, RTE producer and Dr. Havelock Nelson who retains happy memories of the visit. 'We were greeted at Peking airport by the Irish Ambassador and a contingent of officials from the Chinese Cultural Department and driven to our hotel in great style, Bernadette and I in a Bentley and the other two in a Rolls-Royce.'

Apart from being Bernadette's accompanist at the recitals and masterclasses, he was expected to give talks on music, including folk music. Fortunately, he says, she was able to help out by dancing a number of jigs and reels by way of demonstration.

Despite a busy concert and recital schedule, she found time during the Eighties to make successful recordings, among them Handel arias, two Handel operas - *Orlando* and *Ariodante* - Bach arias, an LP of well-known Thomas Moore melodies and Elgar's *Sea Pictures*, which the critic Ivan March nominated as his record of the year in *The Gramophone*, November 1981.

She was also kept reasonably busy in the opera house. For the DGOS she sang Laura in *La Gioconda* and Delilah in Saint-Saens' *Samson et Delilah*, and though vocally in command of the role of Delilah her lack of sensuality in the portrayal suggested that it would never be an ideal vehicle for her temperament. Certainly not in the same way as Orfeo in Gluck's *Orfeo ed Euridice*, which was tailor-made to her more sadate style.

I remember reading an interview she gave to the *Irish Times* in which she stressed the importance of the beauty of sound in connection with opera. The piece had recalled what the former *Irish Times* critic Charles Acton had once observed - that Miss Greevy 'does not naturally portray emotion in movement' which could be taken to mean the singer's slight stiffness on stage.

English critics, I have noted, tend to interpret it differently. They have invariably preferred to see it as her natural dignity and nobility on stage, virtues that are particularly useful in baroque opera. She has talked to me about her yet unfulfilled ambition to sing *Carmen*. She had, she felt, some revelations to make about the gipsy's character. Throughout her early career she had been asked to sing the role but declined because she reckoned the time was not right for her.

'I felt it was a part you did at a certain stage of your career, and I had not reached that point. When the time did arrive in the late Seventies, and afterwards, the opportunity did not seem to be there.'

Would her temperament suit the role? Again the question of passion and sensuality arises, though when one examines the career of Spanish mezzo Teresa Berganza and how she deliberately avoided the role of Carmen for years because of certain inhibitions in her own make-up, yet later took it on to popular acclaim, there is no reason to believe that the same thing could not happen in the case of Bernadette Greevy, who certainly has the looks and voice to get inside the gipsy character.

She did, however, appear in acclaimed performances of Britten's *The Rape of Lucretia* with the Orquesta Ciutat de Barcelona, and she has happy memories of Covent Garden. She sang there with Thomas Allen and Ann Howells in Debussy's *Pelleas et Melisande* which afforded her much personal satisfaction. And she went back there to sing for Kenneth MacMillan's ballet *Das Lied von der Erde*. 'I was the only non dancer in the Royal Ballet's presentation. I wore all black and sang Mahler's music from the side of the stage.'

The early Nineties saw the continuation of her love affair with Mahler. Franz-Paul Decker invited her to Argentina as one of the distinguished panel of singers for performances of the complete cycle of the composer's symphonies. For the Dublin mezzo soprano it was to be a memorable experience. 'It was incredible,' she said. 'I performed with the Ouequesta Filarmonicade Buenos Aires at the Teatro Colon with Franz-Paul Decker conducting and before an audience that nearly bowled the singers over. I have never experienced the same kind of spontaneous emotion in Ireland.'

The critic of the newspaper *Especta* made a revealing comment: 'Among the many performances of "Das Lied von der Erde" heard in Buenos Aires during the past 40 years only Earl Bohm's in 1951 compared with the ideal reached in this performance under Maestro Franz-Paul Decker. Miss Greevy's beautiful vocal quality, thorough involvement and impeccable musicianship helped to make it possible.'

She would be returning to Buenos Aires until the completion of the Mahler cycle in the mid-Nineties. I could see what it meant to her; such acclaim was like a breath of fresh air, a marvellous stimulant. In Ireland she hasn't always received the acclaim or recognition she undoubtedly deserved. In another way she is reminiscent of John McCormack in that she has been honoured by the Vatican, when Pro Ecclesia et Pontifice was conferred on her and the title of Dame Commander of the Holy Sepulche. She was also given an Honorary Doctorate of Music by both the National University of Ireland and Trinity College, Dublin.

While music has taken her around the world, at home with her son Hugh - now employed as an artist - she has always been mother first. 'I've done some things right in my life, you know, and that is one of these things.' Unlike Edith Piaf, she has her regrets. She is proud of Ireland and her decision to stay in the country throughout her career, but she conceded to me that if she had based herself in London or Vienna she would now be financially secure in her middle years, which she is not.

Religion has been important in her life. She is quite a traditional Catholic who, in her own words, has raged against God at times but has come 'creeping back'. She once confided to the *Irish Times* when asked if she took on 'a full relationship with another man', would she want it to be a married one, and her reply was: 'I don't know. I would find it very difficult to walk away from my upbringing, even at this stage. And I would be walking away if I just lived with someone'. She admitted that doing without the physical intimacy of married life was dreadful. 'It is the loneliest life. You see, Peter and I had a great life together from all aspects of life. I couldn't half do it now, have some kind of working relationship with someone. It would have to be completely close.'

Her Dublin masterclasses provide her with undeniable stimulus - and a sense of challenge. She has the intellect and qualifications to impart musical knowledge to aspiring young singers. Looking back over her life she will tell you, 'Oh, it's been a desperately disciplined life. You have no idea. And I have spent hours and hours of my life learning, memorising. There is no short cut to that.'

Today she is proud that she has been able to preserve her voice. She admits she was blessed with a strong and reliable vocal instrument, yet it seems against all the rules that as she gets older she finds her voice in better shape than ever. But the realist in her surfaces when she adds with a smile, 'And that's going to be the next and final shock in my life, when I'm no longer vocally secure.' But in a display of typical determination she was preparing in the Autumn of 1994 to sing the title role in a semi-staged performance of *Carmen* at the National Concert Hall which would be conducted by Franz-Paul Decker; she was thus achieving one of the greatest ambitions of her lengthy career.

Travel has always appealed to her and flying to the Argentine or Spain still remains a tonic. On her return she likes nothing better than her home in Howth Road and occasionally walks around Howth Head, alone or with a friend. And there is something else, as she once explained when asked to write about her private world: 'My garden is my refuge and strength. I love to potter around while my son Hugh is cutting the grass, and when the work is done and the pots of geraniums and begonias have been arranged and rearranged for the umpteenth time, I can still sit and reflect and be completely private. It is from this source of stillness that I can dig deep and find peace and new strength to continue to live in what is to me an alien world now that Peter is no longer with me.

'But you see, I am a Dub, imbued with the inherent resilience and instinct for survival of that unique band, and a Dub I shall remain, living as all we real Dubs do on the northern shores of Anna Livia Plurabelle.'

Chapter Thirteen

Elizabeth Connell

A DUBLIN CELEBRATION

Elizabeth Connell arrived in Dublin on the weekend of 25
September 1993 for a dual celebration. She was, as she told me in
the Gresham Hotel, coming of age not only as a professional singer
but as an Irish citizen. There was another reason why the soprano was in
Ireland: she was due to sing Isolde in a concert performance at London's
Royal Festival Hall of *Tristan and Isolde* and reckoned 'a weekend fix of
Irishness' would do her a world of good.

A woman of wit and charm, she vividly recalled her professional debut
as Varvara in Janácek's *Katya Kabanova* at the 1972 Wexford Festival.
Artistic Director Brian Dickie had offered her the role after it was found
that the Czech singer originally engaged was unable to get a travelling visa.
'I was thrilled to be asked', says Elizabeth today. I'd love to do the part, I
told Brian Dickie, and almost immediately studied the score to ensure that
it was right for my voice.'

She welcomed also the opportunity to earn some money. At the time
she was studying singing at the London Opera Centre under the renowned
baritone Otakar Kraus and had picked up some useful stagecraft and vocal
technique, but she was eager to gain real operatic experience. Although
she was a mezzo-soprano Kraus had said to her, 'Your sound is that of a
soprano, probably a dramatic soprano, but you can't be a dramatic soprano
at twenty-one. So study as a dramatic mezzo and later you'll be able to

make the change.'

It was an exciting time to be in Wexford. Producer, David Pountney, was about to start his Janácek series and working with him on *Katya Kabanova* was, Elizabeth Connell soon discovered, at once challenging and rewarding. 'I threw myself heart and soul into rehearsals and I experienced for the first time the thrill of singing beside a truly international cast of professionals. And the money was good, too, enough to keep me going for at least six months.'

The Czech opera was the big success of the season and according to one London critic she 'made an exchantingly roly- poly Varvara, sweetly, openly sexy, and she sang like a dream.'

Elizabeth Connell remembers that it rained a good deal in Wexford but that didn't bother her; what amazed her was the way the whole town entered into the spirit of the festival, with people lending voluntary assistance where needed. Artists were greeted warmly in the streets and in the hotels, and to add to her joy news had come through that she was accepted as an Irish citizen, which entitled her henceforth to an Irish passport. Before leaving Ireland, she visited Omagh, County Tyrone where her grandfather's people (on her mother's side) had lived, and met relatives she had never seen.

She, herself, was born in Port Elizabeth where her father, of Yorkshire stock, was a wool buyer who had settled in South Africa. Both her parents were musical and young Elizabeth studied the piano from an early age. 'There was always a lot of vocal music lying around. It was in contralto or mezzo keys, so I sang it like that.'

She attended different convent schools and was attracted to choirs and if given a little solo to do tended to sing quietly and blend with the choir, otherwise she sang 'very loudly'. But it was at home that her voice was first discovered by her sister and three brothers who always remembered her singing about the house or at the piano. 'I was always singing, it was my greatest pleasure, and when it came finally for me to think of what I was going to do when I left college there was no question about it – I wanted to be a singer.

178

'My family being a bit conservative thought it best that I have something to fall back on, so I went to Witwatersrand University in Johannesburg and studied for a bachelor of music degree and a teacher's diploma and later taught for a year-and-a-half. They were happy years, years I can recall with undoubted pleasure. I remember I was sitting for my final examinations at college when President John Kennedy was assassinated and his death became a talking point. Up to then I had been the most apolitical student, mainly because I had so much work to do, which left me with no time for involvement in South African politics.'

One day she set out to audition for a chorus part in *The Bartered Bride* but somehow missed the audition and turned up instead at the soloists' audition. 'I was offered the part of Ludmila, the Bride's mother, and decided then and there to become an opera singer. My teacher said that I needed further vocal education and experience in stagecraft. I'd sung in a few operas at university and had seen performances of *Nabucco* and *Traviata*, but that was all. Eventually I got a scholarship from Anglo-American for the London Opera Centre.'

Her mother, whose name was also Elizabeth, accepted Elizabeth's decision without protest. 'My mother was a frustrated musician and I think she saw in me an opportunity to have a performer in the family. She encouraged me, though like my father she had no clear idea what the career of an opera singer entailed. At the London Opera Centre I realised I knew nothing and so had a lot to learn. I kept my mouth shut until I could open it intelligently. I studied very hard with Otakar Kraus and he being Czech was of great help to me when I was offered the part of Varvara at the Wexford Festival.'

Shortly before leaving the Opera Centre, she had done auditions for various opera companies in Britain, including the Glyndebourne chorus. She was invited to join the chorus for the production of Verdi's *Macbeth*, but to her surprise Equity would not give her a work permit because she was South African. It was on the suggestion of a colleague that she decided to claim her 'natural right to Irish citizenship' and set about getting her papers in order. Ever since arriving in Britain, Elizabeth grew more con-

179

scious of her Irish connections and placenames such as Omagh, Belfast, Buncrana and Lurgan struck a chord in her.

'I knew my mother would be proud of my decision', she recalled, 'and for my part it seemed a natural thing to do. When I wrote to my mother, she gave me her blessing and suggested that I visit Omagh and Belfast when I had the time. I have never regretted my decision and carry my Irish passport everywhere I go.'

As an Irish citizen, she was now able to accept offers in Britain, but it was to Australia that she turned to after her stint at the Wexford Festival. She auditioned for Edward Downes who was to be the new musical director of Australian Opera and was offered a two-year contract which she jumped at as it promised to provide regular work and a variety of parts. To Elizabeth, it was a dream come true and she regarded it as a very useful platform for the take-off of her career.

Her arrival in Sydney coincided with the opening in 1973 of the city's magnificent new opera house. The event would be celebrated with a production of Prokofiev's *War and Peace*, in which she had a small part; it is an event she recalls today with pride.

'I was so thrilled to be part of what truly was operatic history, and after that I was given some wonderful roles like Rosina in *The Barber of Seville*, Amneris in *Aida*, Santuzza in *Cavalleria Rusticana* and Venus in *Tannhauser*. This improved my self-confidence enormously and of course boosted my repertoire as well.'

After two years in Sydney, she returned to London in 1975 and was offered a contract with English National Opera. It was not long before Coliseum audiences took to what critic Elizabeth Forbes called the 'electrifying excitement of her singing' which she felt resulted from the mezzo's highly dramatic approach. Occasionally Elizabeth Connell had been accused of 'going over the top and attacking roles too fiercely', as in the case of Azucena in *Il Trovatore*, but vocally she never lost control. Her Eboli (*Don Carlos*), Herodias (*Salome*) and Waltraute (*Gotterdammerung*) were also to win critical acclaim.

Although she would prefer to have sung these operas in the language in which they were written, she felt a 'job was a job'. On occasions, though, she sang Eboli or Azucena in English at the ENO and in Italian in France or Holland. She made her Covent Garden debut in May 1976 as Viclinda in Verdi's *I Lombardi*, following that with Federica in the same composer's *Luisa Miller*.

She was engaged to sing Kundry in *Parsifal* at the Holland Festival with Edo de Waart conducting, and so impressed him that he insisted she sing Ortrud that summer in *Lohengrin* at Bayreuth. When she got there, he for some reason or other, had cancelled, but she went on to have a wonderful success in the part.

'That launched me internationally', she says, 'and when I returned to London I decided to give up ENO and became a freelance singer.'

Earlier, she had travelled to Sydney to sing her first Lady Macbeth. 'In those days I'd sung the part as a mezzo', she recalled, 'leaving out the D flat. Then, with the ignorance of youth, I never found it difficult. I just did it. Now, I realise that it's really quite hard.'

Gradually she began to venture into what she described as 'sopranos' territory' with roles such as Sieglinde and Donna Elvira. Her voice, she noticed, had become more like a soprano's: lighter in texture and more at ease in the higher register. On reflection, she says, 'I can almost tell when it actually happened. After singing Marie in *Wozzeck* in Bonn I returned to Bayreuth where I was the cover for Kundry and I had to sing it at rehearsal. While I was singing I thought to myself, "This is wrong, this is a false sound I'm trying to create." I hoped the soprano would get better as I knew I shouldn't be singing it. After that I cancelled all my repertoire, including a Parsifal in New York for my Met debut. This created some bad feeling, when I cancelled something before I'd been even there, so although I reckoned it was the right thing to do it put me out on a limb.'

She prepared for her change from mezzo to soprano in a methodical way and for a time spoke as little as possible and did not sing at all. Interviewed later by Elizabeth Forbes for *Opera*, she said: 'I was absolutely quiet, so that my voice didn't know what to do. Then I started talking freely again and gently, gently, working for just ten minutes at the piano. I began to sing. The voice came out high, light, pure. Unfortunately, by that time I no longer had Otakar Kraus (who died in 1980) to help me, but he was totally vindicated. So I eased myself into the soprano repertoire. My first engagement was an unknown Cherubini opera (*Anacreon*) at La Scala – how could anyone have been more fortunate? The second was at La Scala again, doing *Cosi* with Riccardi Muti. I thought, if I can get through Fiordiligi at La Scala, then I definitely am a soprano!'

The change meant that she would be working harder than ever, learning four or five new roles a year. In the summer of 1983 she sang Elettra in *Idomeneo* at the Salzburg Festival and this was followed by Elizabeth in *Tannhauser*. A year later she sang the title role in *Norma* in Geneva, but retains mixed feelings about it. 'I was happy singing the role, I wasn't so happy in the circumstances surrounding it, as I didn't quite see eye-to-eye with the producer or the conductor. I'd had high hopes for the dramatic interpretation of Norma, but it was a matter of whether the cloak flowed beautifully or not. I'd high hopes for the musical side too, but the conductor and I, though we got on perfectly well in other operas, in that case it just didn't work.'

From then on she would tackle some of the greatest soprano roles, notably Leonora (*Trovatore*) and Leonora (*Fidelio*) at Covent Garden, Reiza (*Oberon*) at the 1986 Edinburgh Festival and Donna Anna (*Don Giovanni*) in Philadelphia. The latter is a role she very much likes though she admitted that temperamentally she preferred Elvira in the same opera. Always an astute observer, she found singing in America a different experience to that of Europe. 'Over there', she explained, 'you've got to enter the business of pleasing the patrons – if you don't, they're not going to give money next year. You've got to go along to the little dinners to be looked at rather like the animals in the zoo. The singers themselves are expected to take part in the fund-raising, which is not expected in Europe. Here you've got to sign the autograph books and the pictures at the stage door – you've got to play the game somewhere, but it's different in America.'

Inevitably, she was attracted to the title role in Luigi Cherubini's

Medea, which is based on the ancient Greek tragedy Medea. The opera had been virtually forgotten until 1952, when a young soprano called Maria Callas sang the role in Florence and caused a sensation. Since then, the part of the sorceress who seeks to destroy the Corinthian hero Jason and their two sons on the eve of his wedding to someone else, has been regarded as a huge challenge to any dramatic soprano. Elizabeth Connell welcomed the chance to sing it with Australian Opera in 1987 and scored a personal triumph. 'One of the most stupendously sustained displays of vocal art that the Sydney Opera House has ever heard', said one awed critic.

Although she is an avowed admirer of the art of Maria Callas, Elizabeth disagreed with the critics who held that it was the Callas connection that made singing Medea so difficult. 'I don't think so at all', she told me. 'After all, Maria did Tosca, and sopranos aren't scared off by that. It is more the physical and technical demands. Once Medea is on stage, she dominates the drama entirely. And Cherubini has this habit of writing low lines, then suddenly shooting up to the top of the register. The technical preparations to overcome this are quite tremendous.'

It was by now April 1989, and she was preparing to sing in a concert performance of *Medea* at the Queen Elizabeth Hall, and although this would naturally restrict her dramatically, she was looking forward to making her London debut in the role. Many of her former ENO admirers turned up for her performance which was described by one distinguished critic as 'shattering'.

With the likes of Amelia, Lady Macbeth, Senta and Ariadne central to her repertoire, she stresses that the demands of the job require constant attention to keeping the voice in top condition, with singing lessons and coaching sessions high on her list of priorities. 'As a soprano, I have double the amount to sing, more high notes and often the pressure of being the "name" part. The stress is almost incalculable, so the ideal has to be about slow and steady progress. But whoever follows the ideal path to a career? For all that you plan, things don't always turn out as you would like them. By sheer luck, I had about eight years as a dramatic soprano before moving to soprano and then building up the ultimate of doing the

Brunnhildes and the Isoldes and the big Verdi bashes. I'm very happy with the deck that I've been dealt.'

Travel appeals to her enormously. Jetting from place to place causes her little stress nor does it affect her voice. Blessed with a light-hearted and jovial disposition, she makes friends easily and says she loves to go back to places, as people in the shops tend to remember her; and she likes to return to apartments where she has stayed before for it 'feels a little bit like home. I think that's the test, if you're asked back.'

She agreed there could be clashes of temperament in the opera house, but she always tried to get on with her colleagues. 'You can easily become affected by other people's insecurity and then the whole situation can become a nightmare, with everyone rushing out and cancelling. So a quick eye to judge the situation is necessary, but a sense of humour is perhaps the most important. For instance, if you don't like the costume or feel one doesn't suit you, there's no need to tear it off and chop it into little pieces. You've got to be tactful and say, "Don't you think it should be a little more like this?" Get them to think it's their idea – so many designers just produce a pretty garment, with no thought of the person inside.'

Talking to Elizabeth Connell you quickly realise how much a professional she is and how little ego counts with her. Her answers are brisk and there are few traces of self-doubt in her make-up. When I asked if she spent much time at home with her operatic characters, she replied, 'I don't believe you have to bring a character home with you. If you're professional, you can get into a role five minutes before you go on. But that implies a great deal of concentration and preparation. In my case, the interpretation begins at the earliest note-learning stage. If there is a difficult note to sing, I ask myself why the composer has written this? What does it tell us about what the character – as in the case of Medea – in feeling? So, by the performance, the technical and interpretative are completely integrated.'

As often as not she is likely to say no to an offer. Although she sang Senta in *The Flying Dutchman* for her debut for Paris Opera, she had no intention of concentrating on Wagner to the exclusion of Verdi. As she said, 'If you specialise in Wagner the voice can get into a Wagnerian rut and doesn't fit other music, though I find after singing Verdi his music enhances the Wagnerian sound. I try to keep singing a variety of roles.'

She has kept away from the Puccini repertoire because 'I think you've got to be awfully sensible and know your voice and its colour and what it can do. From the way I hear my voice, I hear it as not particularly a Puccini voice – more a classical- sounding, clean voice, can you say? It's not a flat voice, though it can be loud.'

By now her name had become synonymous with Lady Macbeth, a perfect role, she says, musically and dramatically. It's a role she has sung all over the world, in Czech, Italian and English. And her Macbeths have included the leading baritones of the day, among them Renato Bruzon who is reckoned as one of its greatest interpreters. He and Elizabeth have sung in the opera so often together that they don't need rehearsals. Once she got an urgent summons to Rome where the soprano singing Lady Macbeth had been taken ill. Elizabeth arrived a few hours before the curtain-up, had costumes fitted, and waited in her dressing room to be called. Suddenly the Italian conductor tapped on her door. 'You know this piece?', he said nervously. 'Yes, I do', she assured him. 'So do I', came his relieved reply.

Bruzon was her Macbeth and the performance, she remembered, went without a hitch. She now sings the role as soprano and admits that every time she performs it finds new depths of meaning. Her interpretation depended on her Macbeth. 'I may play it as an equal marriage partner, or a dominating partner, or even as a sexy partner. No matter what way I approach it, the music remains the same and wonderful to sing. It is one of her favourite parts.'

She does not see herself singing Strauss' Salome because the subject matter appals her. And she has vowed never to sing the role of Marie in Berg's *Wozzeck*, after her first experience in the part. 'I was so unhappy that I couldn't even console myself by thinking of the money.' She was upset at the Met when told after a performance of *Macbeth* that a man in the audience had committed suicide and at that moment was inclined to attribute the tragedy to the curse of Macbeth.

She has sung with the famed triumvirate of tenors, Pavarotti, Domingo and Carreras. Singing with Pavarotti at the Salzburg Festival in Idomeneo- was, she has no doubt, one of her happiest operatic experiences. 'Luciano is a great colleague, helpful and good-humoured. As Idomeneo, I remember he sang the recitatives in a totally dry un-Mozartian way, yet to me it was a revelation and lent much more weight than normally to the meaning of the words. The conductor was James Levine and it was really a memorable production.'

Having experienced success at Bayreuth, she felt that as a festival it surpassed Salzburg for warmth and friendliness.' The reason is simple', she said. 'Everybody comes to Bayreuth to pay homage to Wagner and submit their egos to the great composer. Wagner is the star, the unrivalled genius. While Salzburg is more international in scope, it is in my opinion, a less friendly place. Everybody is a star in their own right at the festival, and that includes singers, conductors, producers and designers, with the result that egos are to the fore, unmistakably so. I feel more comfortable in Bayreuth and with its vivid reminders of Wagner everywhere.'

To Elizabeth Connell, Pavarotti fitted comfortably into the Mozartian atmosphere of Salzburg. As an actor, she felt he was perhaps underrated. 'He may not be a good mover on stage, but he can act convincingly with his eyes and expressive face and through the colours of his voice. I sang with Jose Carreras in *Trovatore* and I was struck by the intense passion he puts into his singing; he can be a most exciting artist. Singing with Placido Domingo in *Luisa Miller* was an experience, too, for me; he has a most attractive tenor voice which is beautifully focussed and his musicianship is never in doubt. As a person, though, Luciano Pavarotti stands apart, mainly I think because of his warmth of personality and sense of humour.'

She agreed that singing with exceptionally talented colleagues can improve one's own performance, and this was the case at Covent Garden in the summer of 1993, when she sang Odabella in Verdi's *Attila*, with

Samuel Ramay in the title role and the baritone Giorgio Zancanaro as Ezio. John Allison in *Opera* described her Odabella as 'fiery, bright-toned and able to ride the ensembles with ease.'

When she sang Leonora in *Fidelio*, also at Covent Garden, the critics also stated 'she was able to ride the orchestral tumult with ease.' Does she ever regret the villainous mezzo roles, in particular the Verdi ones? 'Yes, sometimes. I did "O don fatale" at a concert in Holland, but though it was lovely to sing I realised it was two tones too low for me and the sound is not right. But who knows, when the top notes go and the voice naturally thickens, then I may return to my favourite mezzo parts.'

There are occasions when she can be disappointed, as when she gets excited about bringing to life some forgotten masterpiece and then finds her enthusiasm is not shared by her colleagues. It is the idealist speaking: the woman is on stand-by even when she is on holiday. 'I took a few days off once to visit friends in San Diego and enjoy myself. At the opera house they were doing *Fidelio*. The soprano fell ill; I went on at half-a-day's notice, with an hour's rehearsal, and everything miraculously gelled. It's funny to think I was in Geneva sometime ago rehearsing the same role for seven weeks.'

She is now accepted world-wide as an outstanding dramatic soprano, particularly in the big Verdi roles. 'I like singing his music, he understands the voice, just as Puccini does. The music they write brings out the beauty of the voice and you tend to give of your very best in Verdi operas. It's also, it seems, very satisfying for audiences.'

Home for her is a mock-Tudor house in Kew Gardens, its garden brimful with lavender, cosmos, wisteria, laburnum, climbing roses and even a bottlebrush to remind her of Australia. I'm a happy person', she will tell you. 'I always tended to be happy. I've been able to sing in all circumstances because singing is to me so fulfilling.' The words come out with a lilt and she smiles that infectious smile that can light up a room. She makes no secret that adaptability is an asset to a singer, indeed essential. 'When I'm in Italy, I speak and eat Italian; in Germany I become a good German and never cross against a red light; in New York, I always eat out and in Sydney, the first thing I do is to get a car.'

In spite of her love affair with travel, she says home is special, a place of quiet, for recovery, for learning, for retreat. Elizabeth is a voracious reader and also does embroidery. She admits she is a good cook and even finds time to write short stories. 'I just can't wait to retire', she joked. 'But they won't let me.'

It was in the summer of 1993 that she spoke for the first time about her recurring illness. Four years ago in Geneva she was feeling 'a peculiar kind of tiredness, a total lassitude'; doctors there quickly diagnosed her problem, the auto-immune disease, lupus or 'wolfe' in English. She explained that it took many forms, one a form of arthritis which was very painful; in her case it attacked her kidneys. There was a total lassitude, and hundreds of other horrible little things that happened to one with it. But she tried to be courageous. 'If you accept it with a cheerful grace and think, "I'm going to beat it" – well, a positive attitude works. I don't know why, but it works.'

The condition flared up when she was in Sydney doing *Macbeth* and the doctors who treated her were, she remembers, fantastic. It is a condition that can be controlled, though it is life-threatening. 'Everybody has to have something in their lives and lupus is what I've got. Fortunately I've never had to cancel because of it.'

On her return from Dublin to her home in London, she wrote me: 'I loved my weekend in Dublin and Wexford. I felt I had really come of age.' Elizabeth had renewed acquaintance and seen again the Theatre Royal in Wexford's narrow street where 21 years before she had made her operatic debut. 'Hard work, but great fun!' is her verdict so far on her career. Keeping her friendships all over the world is important to her, and she is determined to write a book about her parents, or 'their love story' as she describes the project. She has been collecting material in Ireland, England and South Africa. During the war her father was pilot and was shot down in Italy and had all sorts of adventures there. She's going to explore the terrain and hopes to meet the people who helped him to escape back to the Allies. He died in the late 1960s, but Elizabeth still has in her possession his log book and pictures of his squadron.

She tends to preface sentences with the words, 'Being Irish', and when I first approached her about a profile for this book, she enthused, 'Being Irish, I'd love to be included.' It was the happiness in her brimming over, as though eager to be one of the chosen bunch.

Chapter Fourteen

John O'Flynn

AUDITIONED IN ROME

'I want you to come to an audition and meet three people from Ireland,' said Paolo Silveri, who will be remembered by Dublin opera buffs as one of the most distinguished baritones to have sung with the DGOS.

John O'Flynn, a pupil of Silveri's in Rome, was clearly puzzled. Eventually when he met the party, two of them were actually from Ireland – Col. Bill O'Kelly, chairman of the DGOS and Donnie Potter, a committee member; the third was the Rome- based conductor Napoleone Annovazzi, the society's musical director and a popular figure in Dublin's operatic circles.

O'Flynn thought it ironic that he was auditioning in Rome for an engagement in Dublin. Together with Silveri, he sang a duet from *Don Carlos* and was later informed he would be engaged for the DGOS 1974 spring season at the Gaiety Theatre. He had decided only the previous year to take up opera as a career, but felt he was making progress with Silveri.

For the Dublin season he would sing the roles of Monterone in *Rigoletto*, Bonze in *Madama Butterfly*, Zuniga (*Carmen*) and Pietro (*Simone Boccanegra*) and although relatively minor parts he was pleased to be gaining operatic experience. Indeed, he was to be agreeably surprised by the reaction of the critics.

One particular critic declared that his portrayal of Bonze was 'truly terrifying and quite the best performance of this part I have seen.' Robert Johnson in the *Irish Press* agreed with his colleague, and added that as an actor/singer he showed distinct promise. His Monterone in *Rigoletto* was described by Charles Acton in the *Irish Times* as very impressive. 'John O'Flynn has a fine resonant voice and sang the part with all the passionate force needed.'

It afforded the singer personal satisfaction that the DGOS was presenting a short season at the Cork Opera House, thus enabling him to sing before his own people in opera for the first time. The DGOS's annual visits to the city with Italian opera was by now a tradition and the productions were well supported by the public. In that May of '74 Verdi's *Boccanegra* was being staged for the first time in Cork and with a particularly strong cast.

John O'Flynn recalls that the opera was not generally well known there though Verdi's operas were always very popular. Robert O'Donoghue was overwhelmed by the production, as he was to state in the *Evening Echo*. 'The opera will long remain in my memory as one of the most profoundly beautiful events I have experienced in any season of opera at any time. The same composer's *The Force of Destiny*, performed here last season, left an indelible memory, surpassed for me only on this occasion by a composition I would rate as Verdi's best, his most daring and ultimately most satisfying.'

Singing before enthusiastic Cork audiences brought back a flood of memories to John O'Flynn. As a boy he had accompanied his parents to the old Opera House and seeing *Rigoletto* there for the first time was to prove a shattering experiences, especially the final scene when the hunchback Rigoletto discovers his dead daughter Gilda. It was, however, when he first saw Mario Lanza in the film of *The Student Prince* that he wanted to become a singer.

He remembers visits to his home nearly almost every week by his uncle Father O'Flynn who ran The Loft in Cork, where aspiring actors learned speech and drama, mostly the works of Shakespeare. Young

O'Flynn found his uncle a splendid transmitter of knowledge and a wonderful teacher who had very interesting theories on speech.

After finishing primary school, he was sent as a boarder to Clongowes Wood College in Newbridge, Co. Kildare and was doing well academically until he fell ill before his final year. He was sent home to Cork to recuperate and decided to study for his Leaving Certificate there. Up to then he had no great love for Irish, but under the tutelage of Father O'Flynn he became more involved in the language and grew to love it.

He enrolled at University College, Cork, but despite pleas by his parents to stay long enough so as to gain his degree in philosophy, he left after just one year to join the Abbey Theatre in Dublin. He stayed only six months, having had a brush with Ernest Blythe, the managing director, over the question of the Irish language. 'I was not the only actor to differ with him on this issue,' he later said. For the next two years he freelanced in Dublin but eventually decided to try his luck in London. By now he had made his mind up to be a singer.

He found in Lorenzo Medea, one of the best voice tutors of the day; he was of Spanish origin and had studied with six masters of the golden age of singing. 'I found the man absolutely splendid, particularly in the area of vocal technique. He decided I was a basso cantato. It was now the early Sixties, an exciting time in London. After a few months, I was cast in West End productions of *The Student Prince* and *Man of La Mancha*.'

He was prepared to sing anywhere to gain experience and support himself. In 1972, he was one of the 16 singers engaged to entertain passengers on the *Northern Star*, a luxury liner that cruised the Mediterranean, North Africa and the Caribbean. Twice nightly they presented potted versions of popular musicals in a 500-seater theatre, an experience which he found exceedingly useful to his musical development.

A year later he decided to study opera and got an introduction to Paolo Silveri and counted himself fortunate to be taken on as one of his pupils at Rome's Conservatorio di Santa Cecilia. To support himself, John O'Flynn taught English and when he could, attended performances at Rome Opera House. He stayed there almost three years and came away with only one regret: 'Paolo worked on my voice as a bass and I think in hindsight that this was a mistake. I was inclined to consider myself a baritone with access to the bass range.'

On his return to London, he auditioned for *The Marriage of Figaro* and believed he had dashed any hopes he had of singing the role of Figaro due to a very poor audition. To his complete surprise, however, he was successful. Touring the production under the aegis of Festival Opera provided him with one of his most outstanding early musical memories. He remembers the cast as young and enthusiastic, with conductor Nicholas Braithwaite and the Northern Sinfonia Orchestra doing full justice to Mozart's marvellous score.

The group had two main objectives: to take operas to areas that normally did not get much full-scale opera, and to help young singers who had just left their training schools and needed experience before joining one of the five national opera companies. Throughout the tour the production received generally good press notices and for the most part John O'Flynn could be pleased. When the company played at Billingham Forum, for instance, the local critic wrote: 'The title role was taken by John O'Flynn and his was a virile and masterly performance. Though the part is scored for a baritone, his voice seemed to be that of a bass-baritone. Not only did he capture all the vocal inflections that the part demanded but his acting was equally good.'

Looking back, he says he was encouraged by his success in *The Marriage of Figaro* for it proved to him that he could hold an audience as actor and singer. Later in 1976, when he sang Crown in a concert version of George Gershwin's *Porgy and Bess* at Pancras Town Hall, he won praise for projecting convincingly the 'primeval strength of the character'.

Shortly before 1980 he went to Germany in search of work and based himself in Munich. It was to prove a depressing experience. To gain an audition at an opera house one had to first go through an agent who either recommended or rejected you. It was, he thought, a cruel system. 'I remember going along to one centre in Munich for an audition only to find sixteen other singers in the same room. A few of them had travelled from as far as Japan and Australia and as far as I could judge some had good operatic voices, others should not have been there at all. Half way through a particular aria an auditioner might say, "Next, please." Breaking through the system was almost impossible.'

Despite the tyranny of the system, he managed to get some concert engagements in Germany and when he moved northwards life became more pleasant, especially in the social sense. Meanwhile, he hadn't been entirely forgotten in Ireland. Artistic director Elaine Padmore engaged him to sing for the first time at the Wexford Festival of 1983 as the Prefect in Donizetti's tuneful opera, *Linda di Chamounix*, with the experienced lyric tenor Ugo Benelli cast as the girl's lover.

From the first day of his arrival in the friendly town, John O'Flynn was taken by the sheer enthusiasm of the townspeople for their festival and before long he sensed a fine *esprit de corps* among the cast and production team of the Donizetti work. Italian soprano Lucia Aliberti was singing the title role; she had delighted festival-goers four years previously in *Crispino e la Comare*.

The other operas presented in that 1983 year were Marschner's *Hans Heiling* and Wolf-Ferrari's *La Vedova Scaltra*, but it was soon obvious that *Linda di Chamounix* was the hit of the festival. Furthermore, John O'Flynn was to emerge with a growing reputation. It was 10 years since a Donizetti opera had been produced in Wexford, so the audience welcomed it with open arms and on this occasion the conductor Gabriele Bellini achieved a good balance between stage and pit.

Marese Murphy, an Irish critic who knew her Wexford better than most of her colleagues, covered the festival that year for the *Cork Examiner* and singled out John O'Flynn for his assured singing and dominant stage presence. 'He is having a substantial success at this year's event,' she told her readers, adding: 'This is his first appearance at the festival and his voice – mature and strong with rich bass tones – is perfectly schooled to suit the resources of the tiny Theatre Royal.'

'I enjoyed the whole thing immensely,' John later told me, as we discussed in a wider sense the charges of elitism sometimes levelled against the festival. He assured me that as far as the artists were concerned the question of elitism did not enter into it, but was quick to add, 'There is this terrible perception that opera is elitist; that is from an outsider's point of view. From the singers and musicians side, opera is an everyday chore but also a very exciting way of living, even though it's demanding musically. On the contrary, it can be enjoyed by almost all sections of a community; in Ireland at least that has been the case for generations. What makes opera elitist is the price of a ticket, and in the case of Covent Garden and some other leading houses the ordinary opera lover is virtually locked out as they cannot afford to pay £75.00 for a stalls ticket. Wexford is cheap by comparison and most times the opera buff gets good value.'

He remembered the tour early in 1983 of Massenet's *Griselidis*. The opera had been presented with great success at the festival with a star cast that included the much talked of Russian baritone Sergei Leiferkus as the Marquis de Saluces. For the Irish tour the cast was changed with John O'Flynn singing the Devil and Virginia Kerr, Sean Mitten and Brendan Kavanagh filling other key roles. The tour had been made possible by an Arts Council grant, but to John O'Flynn it was badly publicised and consequently did not attract the good attendances it deserved.

'Musically it was considered a success,' he said. 'Naturally I was disappointed as were my colleagues to have to sing to small attendances. Nonetheless, I have always thought that where possible Wexford should tour its finest operatic showpieces, even if this means with all Irish casts. I enjoyed singing in *Griselidis* enormously.'

In fact, Wexford was to prove a lucky place for his talents. He was back there again in 1985 to sing Stromminger in Catalani's *La Wally* and Alaska-Wolf Joe in Kurt Weill's *The Rise and Fall of the City of Mahagonny*. Working with an international cast in the latter and the production team of Simon Joly (conductor) and Declan Donnellan (producer) he found extremely stimulating at every level.

Dr. Tom Walsh's festival had successfully established itself on bel canto productions and brilliant singing by Italian principals; *Mahagonny* was a different matter. It is a long way from the escapist tradition of romantic opera; its growing popularity was due to Weill's melodies and Brecht's dark drama. The use of jazz in a work was new to Wexford and dressing the cast in anonymous 20th century garb an interesting feature. Mahagonny in the opera is a mythical American city, founded on avarice and cupidity by criminals with the central theme about capitalist corruption. Someone succinctly described it as 'a modern mystery play'. Essentially, though, it is a sharp satire on the American dream.

Soon after rehearsals began John O'Flynn became absorbed in the work. In retrospect, he says, 'I thought it one of the most exciting shows I had the privilege ever to play in. The approach of director Declan Donnellan and designer Nick Ormerod was tremendously exciting and I remember when we were rehearsing a lot of the cast and chorus who were used to the more conservative approach to an opera, were getting terribly worried because the production team were leaving it so long coming down to the blocking of the show. But of course the whole thing came together absolutely beautifully; they were wizards at their job; they did it in a particular way and it worked. I simply loved playing in it, even though at the beginning I found Weill's music difficult.'

Unfortunately on the opening night in the Theatre Royal Theodore Spencer, who was cast as Jimmy, had to live by personality alone, as laryngitis killed off his voice. To John O'Flynn this was particularly disappointing. 'I had admired his work at rehearsal and his singing and acting were first rate.'

Oldtimers in Wexford were somewhat aghast by the show. Watching on stage a wonderful line of punkish sluts in slit leather skirts was more than many of them could take and prompted one of them to say to me at the interval, 'Doctor Tom wouldn't go for this kind of thing at all.'

The role of Alaska Joe called on all John O'Flynn's stagecraft and experience, for in Act II he has got to box Trinity Moses, propagandist for the new city, in the boxing ring. A younger generation of festival-goers found the show irresistible, in particular the lively dance routines and the catchy

197

songs. 'It was a novelty in Wexford and appealed to a cross-section of people,' says John O'Flynn. 'I agree it wasn't Bellini or Verdi, yet I felt that
secretly some festival-goers at least welcomed a revolutionary kind of
operatic work.'

'This *Mahagonny* is an example of what Wexford can be like at its best:
a show got on the road briskly, stylishly and against many odds,' stated
Hilary Finch in the London *Times*.

At the time I thought it a pity that the show could not have transferred
to the Olympia Theatre in Dublin, as I believed that it deserved to be seen
by a much larger Irish audience than could be accommodated in Wexford's
intimate Theatre Royal. John O'Flynn shared the same opinion and had
no doubt that Dublin would have acclaimed Sherry Zannoth's thrilling
Jenny Smith.

He would return to Wexford the following year to sing character roles
in Thomas's *Mignon* and Humperdinck's *Konigskinder* and as an artist never
failed to be stimulated by the sheer professionalism of the festival and how
singers of different nationalities merged their talents and personalities to
ensure first-rate productions. He noted the popularity of the Operatic
Scenes, first introduced by Elaine Padmore, where young singers were
given the chance to sing leading roles in avant garde as well as more popular opera in the friendly atmosphere of White's Hotel.

Back in Cork he was contracted to sing with the newly-founded Cork
City Opera. The company catered mostly for Irish artists either working
in Ireland or overseas. To John O'Flynn, it was an excellent idea and was
deserving of Arts Council support which regrettably it failed to receive.
He sang in *Carmen*, *Trovatore* and *Boheme* and felt a decent standard was
achieved in spite of lack of money. He was particularly impressed by the
vocal artistry of baritone Niall Murray who at the time was singing on the
Continent; his voice was resonant, well-focused and possessed fine range
as he displayed in the aria Il Balen (*Trovatore*).

The company was to provide opportunities for such as Peter McBrien,
Frank O'Brien, Therese Feighan, Mary Hegarty, Angela Feeney and

numerous other singers. It received reasonably good support from the Cork public, but John O'Flynn felt that without proper funding it was doomed. As he argues today, 'Opera is expensive to mount and to stage really well, so Cork City Opera had a major problem from the outset. I do feel, though, that even in the short time it operated the company achieved quite a lot musically. Its demise was a loss; perhaps the organisers were too ambitious in view of the inadequate funding. In hindsight, a single opera each season might have been a wiser proposition. For Irish artists it was of course another severe blow and meant the loss of more opportunities for singers.'

He decided in the Eighties to settle in Cork and try to do something practical to further music in the city. Partnered by the talented young conductor Donal O'Callaghan, the Irish Opera Repertory Company was set up and again because of funding limitations, it was decided to concentrate on operetta and the more popular musicals. I remember I travelled to Cork for the company's production of *The Gipsy Baron* and found there was quite a buzz in the Opera House on opening night. The show was colourfully costumed, admirably sung and afterwards John O'Flynn was quietly confident about the future. As he said, 'In time we hope to put on *Traviata* and *Boheme*.'

He was understandably cautious, however, for working on the management side he quickly recognised the risks involved, something he says stage artists cannot be expected to appreciate. Funding became their constant headache. *South Pacific*, for example, was considered a sparkling presentation and drew excellent houses to the Opera House, yet it failed to make money. It was the same story in the case of *The Student Prince*.

To the O'Flynn/O'Callaghan partnership, it was bitterly frustrating, but they were determined to keep the company afloat and provide Cork audiences with enjoyable shows and singers with opportunities to perform. By January 1992, however, the company was in debt and a decision was taken to wind it down. It was decided to end with two farewell concerts. Ironically, in February of the same year the company received a special award from Cork Arts and Theatre Critics in recognition of outstanding achievements. Meanwhile, discussions continued about the future of IORC. 'We wanted to continue,' recalled John O'Flynn, 'and tapped every possible source. Cork Opera House offered us a scheme whereby a successful run of *Oliver* could hopefully wipe out our remaining debts. We had no choice but to accept, on a once-off basis. Three hundred "workhouse boys" were auditioned, thirty were selected.'

Oliver opened to excellent reviews, with John O'Flynn's Fagin being acclaimed, but booking remained sluggish. Sixteen performances played to average box-office business, with the result that the receipts were insufficient to clear IORC's existing debts. Cork Corporation came to the rescue in May with a grant of £14,700. John O'Flynn and his fellow director at last saw a flicker of light at the end of the tunnel. In the summer of '92 the company moved into a new office and studio at Kinlay House, Shandon.

IORC had survived against the odds. Early in 1993 *The Mikado* was presented at the Opera House and although rated a worthy production did not get the public support it deserved. Was television exerting too big an influence on Corkonians? It is accepted that symphony concerts do not always get decent support in the city, but wasn't Cork music-loving enough to enjoy musical shows and opera?

It is a factor that worries John O'Flynn, who still says that it is imperative that Cork continues to have 'live' entertainment of a high quality. He acknowledges that the city has suffered in the economic sense and has a grave unemployment problem, but he remains optimistic. 'I firmly believe that people will leave their TV sets and come out to see a good show. If I were to think otherwise, then what is the future musically for Cork?'

Apart from striving to keep IORC in operation, he finds time to give private vocal tuition. He is eager to assist young singers in a profession that he describes as tremendously difficult and not always rewarding. 'I would love to create an operatic theatre in Ireland so as to help young singers to avoid the terrible road that people of my generation were obliged to follow. I would be happy doing that. It is what we are working towards in

IORC.'

His versatility has stood him well. He can still be persuaded to take a 'straight' role in the theatre or act as compere at shows in Cork or at the National Concert Hall. For instance, he once sang and acted as MC at a celebrity concert in Cork that featured the rising Italian tenor Mario Malagnini and won applause for his professionalism and original touches. On another occasion at the National Concert Hall he was the narrator for a show of Viennese music and Kay Hingerty writing in the *Cork Examiner* remarked, 'John O'Flynn's very arrival on stage was a party sensation. He dropped his top hat, scarf and cloak around the microphone, and kept us informed (and sometimes mischievously misinformed) with his inimitable elegant stage ease.'

If there is one subject that sparks passion in the singer, it is the question of the local Opera House. When there was a suggestion in 1992 that it might be sold to an 'outside' impresario and 'carved up' so as to provide for a disco, he was horrified by the sheer audacity of the proposal before the Corporation. At a time when other European cities were thinking of building new opera houses, it would be, he told me, a sacrilige to destroy the existing one in Cork. 'We don't want it divided into two small theatres. We need the Opera House, as it's the only venue that one can stage opera for a large audience.'

He was relieved that the proposal got nowhere; instead, refurbishment work was carried out at the Opera House, which lent new hope for the future. But John O'Flynn will not be happy until it is packed again for operetta and opera.

Chapter Fifteen

Angela Feeney

'BUTTERFLY' IN BELFAST

For Angela Feeney it promised to be a night to cherish. In that May of 1985, she was making her operatic debut in her native Belfast and the prospect seemed exciting, if not daunting.

On the opening night of *Madama Butterfly*, in which she was cast as the tragic heroine Cio-Cio San, the Grand Opera House was packed not only with the music-lovers but with her relatives and friends.

'It was a great occasion for me,' she recalled. 'I was singing my favourite role before my own people. My father Bill must have seen every rehearsal of the opera, and my sister Una was in the chorus. I knew that out there in the auditorium would be people who had helped me in my career, among them the hundreds of friends who on different occasions paid a pound each in order to give me cheques amounting to £600 on the first occasion and £800 later, both the proceeds of concerts they had organised.

'Since I took up opera as a career it has always been a dream of mine to come back to sing a major role in Belfast. Two years previously, I had sung Leonora in *Il Trovatore* in Cork Opera House and my parents made the long journey to hear me sing. I assured them that one day I would make my Belfast operatic debut at the Grand Opera House. I have met singers who could not always depend on their families for support; I was lucky as my parents supported me from the outset of my professional career as a singer and I'm grateful to them.'

Now it was to be a night mixed with emotion and nostalgia. When the final curtain came down on *Madama Butterfly* the audience rose and applauded enthusiastically, as if determined to acclaim one of their own. As Angela Feeney and the rest of the cast stood centre stage some members of the audience threw flowers at their feet.

The scenes backstage shortly afterwards were equally reassuring as her family and friends tried to shake her hand. James Johnston struggled through the crowd and greeted her proudly with the words, 'Aye, you're a great wee lass.' Everybody, it seemed, wanted to share the soprano's success.

'It was absolutely fantastic and exceeded my expectations', she recalled. 'I thought I was in good voice on the night, but then the music in *Butterfly* is really wonderful, and it also helps when you believe totally in the character; it hasn't always been the way with me, for some operatic characters are, to say the least, absurd creations.'

The critics had come in force to the Grand Opera House, and despite the reservations expressed about the production, Angela Feeney's performance attracted excellent notices. I particularly liked the way Hilary Finch caught the mood of the occasion: 'When a daughter of Belfast returns to make her operatic debut in her native city, as Angela Feeney did this week as Butterfly, then the celebration goes on for at least as long as the pubs remain open.'

Alfred Burrowes in the *Irish Times* echoed the views of the majority when he wrote: 'Ms. Feeney was the lustrous star of the evening, outshining some lesser lights. Her first entry was quite stunning: unbelievable angelic sounds blossoming as the colourful procession moved stagewards. She seems unable to sing other than beautifully; her singing of "One Fine Day" won a prolonged ovation.'

'ANGELA FEENEY RETURNS TO BELFAST IN TRIUMPH' was the heading over Charles Fitzgerald's review in the *News Letter*, and he went on to state, 'Her performance brought a deserved series of standing ovations in the packed Opera House last night, when the audience includ-

204

ed many singers and friends who had started with her in their careers.'

The *Irish News* described the soprano's performance as 'extremely moving' and said the production was a triumph for Opera Northern Ireland. But no one appeared to notice anything untoward happening to tenor Riccardo Calleo (Pinkerton) at the end of the love duet in Act I.

Discussing the occasion with Angela Feeney in Dublin in the Nineties, she recounted for me the incident with an obvious hint of amusement. 'To my dismay', she said, 'Riccardo, who was I heard later prone to fainting, fainted in my arms just before the curtain came down at the end of the love duet. It was a weird situation really. He was placed on the floor behind the curtain and a doctor was called. You can imagine the panic with no Pinkerton for the last act! Fortunately, he recovered quickly and was able to finish the opera. Was I relieved!'

Singing had always been part of the Feeney family. As a child at home in Whiterock, off the Falls Road, she remembered joining in sing-songs at Christmas time with her two sisters and four brothers. Her father had a beautiful baritone voice and sang in a local choir but never got voice training; he was a great fan of Jeanette Mac Donald and Nelson Eddy. And they had a distant relative, Sheamus O'Doherty, who emigrated to America at the turn of the century where he was reputed to have enjoyed a successful career as a tenor; he also made a big name for himself as a singing coach.

Angela's talent was spotted at St. Rose's Secondary School in Beechmount by music teacher Anna Blake. While still at school she went with classmates to a film version of *La Traviata* and was absolutely captivated. 'I was only thirteen and I remember everyone in my class was laughing at me because I was taking the music so seriously. It was an old movie, yet seeing the costumed singers and the orchestra made it all seem very theatrical. I had never experienced anything before like it and quickly became hooked. After that experience, I decided that opera would be my life.'

Growing up she was conscious of living in a city divided religiously and politically, and being one of the few Catholic students at the Belfast College of Music, she experienced some degree of prejudice. 'I was having singing lessons at the time and was entered for festivals. The adjudicators were usually from Britain and although I won awards I found I was never asked to sing at the end-of-term concerts. Others, who had got only second or third prizes in competitions were invited to sing.

'This hurt me at the time and made me wonder if I was good enough. I was increasingly puzzled and could only attribute it to some form of prejudice on the part of the college authorities. As far as I knew, they were non-Catholics. It was a small thing and I didn't let it deter me. I simply loved to sing and enjoyed the School of Music and my singing lessons.'

Her father was a docker, but people at the School of Music thought he was a doctor, so she found she was more readily accepted. Unlike some other Catholic families who did not seem to be aware of the public grants and scholarships available to their children, the Feeneys knew what students could claim and their full entitlements in the educational field.

Around this time she joined a folk group and so was able to subsidise her singing lessons. She enjoyed the experience of singing before audiences and this gave her considerable confidence as a performer. When she eventually got a job in the civil service she used to boast facetiously to her friends, 'I don't have to worry; I'm in a good pensionable job.' But she had no intention of staying in the Department of Customs and Excise.

Music was still her life's ambition. In order to improve her sight-reading, she played the trumpet in a local brass band and they went on to win the all-Ireland Brass Band Competition. Friends in the south advised her to contact Veronica Dunne, and she did not delay any longer. 'One Saturday I took the train to Dublin and auditioned for her. After I had sung "The Sun whose Rays" from *The Mikado*, she asked me what time I could be with her the following Saturday. We arranged for a lesson at 3 p.m. I had turned eighteen and my voice was a high soprano, a bit more dramatic than lyrical.'

Veronica Dunne advised her to give up her civil service job and concentrate full time on singing. In a typically generous gesture, she invited

Angela to come to Dublin and live in the Dunne family home. 'I think in time Ronnie Dunne became my second mother. She got me singing engagements and advised me to join Irish National Opera, which I did and worked on the stage management side. It could be hard work as we did three performances every second weekend and some of the smaller halls were not geared for opera. As the company performed with piano, we encountered pianos that were in bad shape and this was no help to us. When Lady Dorothy Moulton Mayer heard about this she very kindly donated a piano which was toured around Ireland in a padded horse box. We managed, however, to do operas like *The Bartered Bride, Don Pasquale, La Boheme, Don Giovanni* and even *Fidelio*. In retrospect, I think it was really astonishing, but I enjoyed working with Suzanne Murphy, Joe Dalton, Frank Dunne and the others.'

To Angela's surprise, Veronica Dunne considered her a mezzo- soprano and thus encouraged her to sing mezzo roles. But after a while she reverted back to soprano. Like other pupils before her, she felt she had done her stint in Ireland and it was time to move on. Veronica Dunne agreed that she should go to Munich. It came about in an unusual manner.

Tenor Kenneth Neate, who was in charge of the foreign students at the Bavarian State Opera Studio in Munich, was in Dublin producing *Tannhauser* for the DGOS and met Veronica Dunne.

Years before, they had sung together in *Boheme* at Covent Garden. She asked him to come along and hear Angela Feeney sing.

Neate, a very good judge of a young singer, listened attentively, then without any hesitation, said, 'I'll take her. She is right for Munich.'

'Ronne gave us the confidence to believe that we were as good as anybody else', Angela Feeney would later say. 'I know I felt that way when I finished my studies with her. The thing that is actually missing in Ireland is the belief that you can do it. Ronnie gave us that, and that makes such a difference at the beginning of your career. And, of course, she gave us a basic technique that has stayed with us and helped us through changes of repertoire, through the voice changing and growing.'

During her first six months in Germany, she was homesick. It was the first time she had been away from home for a long period and found it difficult to settle in her new surroundings. She remembered crying a good deal and on her own admission spent most of her Belfast grant on telephone calls to her parents and to Veronica Dunne in Dublin. But realising the opportunity she had got, she was determined to stick it out. Gradually she settled and began to master the German language, something she told me she found at first extremely difficult. Ken Neate was proving helpful to her and she sang her first operatic role under his direction.

She was also encouraged by her results in class; in her first year she was adjudged the best vocal student - there were two other awards for instrumentalists. She was by now enjoying life at the Studio and felt she was making definite progress. In December 1980 she met Nikolaus Gruger, a professor of French horn, based in Munich. A week later, to her great surprise, he asked her to marry him.

'I said yes straight away. I just knew he was for me. He was very well read, great fun to be with and, of course, we shared a mutual interest in music. Nico, as I called him, had been to Ireland and loved the country, especially the Glens of Antrim. After Christmas we got engaged and that August got married. I was twenty-five and had signed a contract to sing with the Bavarian State Opera, so my career was assured.'

Her son was born a year later, but after a short rest she resumed singing. For the most part she had concentrated on Mozart's music at the Opera Studio, or as she would joke later, 'until it came out my ears!'. Because of the large stage in the opera house, which at first sight tended to frighten her, she took some time to adapt. Artistic standards, she soon realised, were incredibly high and the guest star policy in operation ensured that Munich opera-goers heard some of the greatest names in opera.

Rehearsing a small part in *Elektra* alongside such stars as Birgit Nilsson and Astrid Varnay was a marvellous experience for her. 'I thought they would be stand-offish to young singers like me, but to my surprise they invited me to their table during coffee breaks. I remember Birgit Nilsson was upset because the management had only given part of the opera score to those in minor roles; she wondered why we hadn't got the full score. They were wonderful colleagues and always eager to help beginners. I was to discover also that some of the biggest names in our business could be the least confident and secure about their own ability.'

In time she became a principal herself and sang Cio-Cio San, Gretel, Euridice, and Fiordiligi in *Cosi fan Tutte*. And she made occasional guest appearances in Hamburg and Frankfurt. In the 1980s she sang Leonora in *Trovatore* for Cork City Opera, as well as Mimi, a portrayal that Veronica Dunne would say came nearest to her own interpretation of the Puccini role.

Around the same period, she joined English National Opera and her first role with the company was Nedda in *Pagliacci*. It was a strong cast, with Malcolm Donnelly as the malign Tonio and Alan Woodrow as Canio, with Silvio sung by Alan Opie. *The Times* critic commented: 'Angela Feeney is a mannered Nedda, bright of tone but getting too few words across, though in her duet with Alan Opie's fresh-voiced Silvio a semblance of more passionate feeling began to emerge.'

During rehearsals for her next opera at the Coliseum, *The Bartered Bride* I met her in London and she seemed satisfied with her work up to then for the company. 'I love singing at the Coliseum', she told me. 'The house is big, so is my voice, and I am able to give it full scope. They tell me the acoustics are very good and the audience can hear every word.'

Singing the operas in English she found could be restrictive, though she never thought about this aspect when she sang the title role in *Rusalka* in what she regarded as 'a fabulous production' by David Pountney. It was, she said, a thrilling experience.

She scored an undoubted success in the Smetena opera. Although on the night I found the staging disappointing, especially in the visual sense, the singing by the principals and the chorus was admirable. Christopher Grier summed up in the *Evening Standard*: 'Smetana called *The Bartered Bride* a comic opera and so it is, but rather in the same sense as *Albert Herring*. As portrayed by Angela Feeney, Marenka's anguish and subsequent outrage at the conduct of her sweeheart Jenik (John Treleaven) is for real and very touching.'

She was earnestly hoping to sing Mozart at the Coliseum and got her opportunity midway through the run of *Don Giovanni* when she was asked to take over the role of Donna Elvira from Felicity Lott. She admitted it would be a daunting experience, but she need not have harboured any real fears. The reviews were more than favourable, though in the eyes of one London critic Jonathan Miller's stage set was gloomy.

'The new donna Elvira of Angela Feeney is effortful, but with only the occasional shrillness marring her fine flexibility and clean attack, she convincingly presents a spinsterish bossyboots of a character, enough to make any Giovanni recoil', wrote Edward Greenfield in the *Guardian*.

Later, in her review for *Opera*, Hilary Finch thought that the most revealing transformation of the evening lay in Angela Feeney's performance. 'Whereas Felicity Lott's Donna Elvira made one reflect that perhaps she and Josephine Barstow (Donna Anna) should switch roles, Miss Feeney's more muscular soprano redressed the vocal balance with well-integrated power and proper precision of attack.' And she added: 'Here was an Elvira really capable of tearing out Giovanni's heart: beyond the prim exterior was a passion and appetite that was a match for his. Miss Feeney must be persuaded to take time off from Ulster and Germany rather more often.'

Working in London meant fairly lengthy periods away from her home in Munich, but her husband, Nico, and their young son William were able from time-to-time to join her in London. Separation from them was, she confided to me, the hardest part of her career, though there were times when there was no other alternative. Were they planning to have more children?

'I'm afraid not.' Angela confessed. 'I don't think it would be fair to Nico as he would have the ultimate responsibility of caring for them in my absence. Combining motherhood and a career in singing is difficult and one has got to take the practical view. I have a wonderful husband and a healthy child and that is very important to me. Munich is a beautiful city in which to live and although in my business you have lots of competition from singers from many nations, it is a good thing for you to know that if you succeed you have succeeded against the best. You know also you are getting somewhere.'

Now, as a freelance artist, she sang Butterfly in Berlin opposite the Italian tenor Mario Malagnini. She was disappointed when she had to pull out of Opera Northern Ireland's production of *La Traviata*. Shortly after her arrival in Belfast she experienced throat problems and was confined to bed.

'Angela was terribly disappointed', recalled Lyn Callaghan, the company's spokeswoman. 'This would have been her debut as Violetta and it was very sad for her. She was especially looking forward to singing again in her home city.'

But she never lost touch with Belfast. She returned to sing with her old group, St. Agnes Choral Society, when it was celebrating its 30th anniversary with a concert in the Ulster Hall. She was to prove the star attraction; or as Charles Fitzgerald put it, in the *News Letter* she 'stole the show.' She sang Rusalka's "Song to the Moon", a great favourite of hers, but the *piece de resistance* was, he said, her singing from *Madama Butterfly*. And he had not often heard, he said, Gershwin's "Summertime" from *Porgy and Bess* sung with such feeling and superb control, making it the great moving song it was.

'I came home to enjoy a bit of a party with my musical friends', Angela told me later. She is an exuberant person who likes nothing better than to bring joy to her family and friends. When, for example, she sang in Wexford in the early 1980s in the festival production of Verdi's *Un Giorno di Regno* with a star cast that included tenor Ugo Benelli, the celebrated Italian bass Sesto Bruscantini, and soprano Licia Aliberti, she had in her own words a thrilling time.

Husband Nico travelled with her and apart from the opera, they both enjoyed the social atmosphere and everything about the town itself. 'I want to return again', she told me, 'and I hope it will happen.' Indeed, I was disappointed that she was not recalled to sing in the operas by the

German composer Heinrich Marschner. But she tends to be philosophical about such things and hopes her turn will come round again.

Throughout her career, she has kept in touch with Veronica Dunne, sometimes telephoning her in Dublin for some advice on a particular operatic problem. She was thrilled when Ronnie, as she likes to call her, was at the National Concert Hall for the acclaimed production of *Norma* in 1989; not only that, but the Norma, Suzanne Murphy, happens to be one of her best friends in the business.

Ian Fox, writing as the Irish critic for *Opera*, summed up: 'It was exciting to welcome home two Irish singers in the female roles. Suzanne Murphy is a Norma of international stature but I have never heard her sing with such brilliant tone and accuracy. Angela Feeney was a rich-toned Adalgisa, singing in the role's original soprano register, and the voices blended superbly in the marvellous duets.'

It was a source of regret that Dublin music-lovers had to wait so long to hear Angela Feeney in a major operatic role. The DGOS should have, to my mind, engaged her to sing roles suited to her impressive dramatic soprano voice. Living in Germany had probably something to do with it, for Irish artists working abroad tend to be easily forgotten.

However, she was kept busy with recording, television and the opera house. She recorded *Tiefland* with Rene Kollo and Eva Marton and was among the casts of opera screened on German television. One of the highlights of her career was undoubtedly being the co-organiser of the National Concert Hall tribute to Veronica Dunne in the early Nineties. She aptly described it as 'Ronnie's night.'

Her parents travelled from Belfast for the unique occasion, and she was able to say to me after the concert, 'Think of the number of singers Ronnie has made employable – I mean, most singing teachers would have maybe four or five, but there were something like nineteen soloists here to sing, all her pupils. It's incredible.'

Significantly, Angela Feeney has not lost her Belfast accent and was emphatic when she told me, 'Nico and I plan to retire to lovely Ballycastle in County Antrim.'

In the summer of 1994 she was back in Belfast for a very special event – the launch of the Angela Feeney Classical Bursary Award, which in the future would help students from the city to advance their studies. 'We must support our singers and instrumentalists, there is such an abundance of them,' she told me, 'but sadly the financial back-up is not sufficient.'

She had recruited an impressive panel of judges and an award-winning concert would be held in 1995. Their target was £3,000 and there was already a worthy donation from the Arts Council of Northern Ireland. 'I've waited a long time to organise something like this,' Angela said, 'and it has been very exciting to see it grow and, of course, there's great interest as it has never happened before in the Falls Road.'

It was simply her way of saying 'thank you' to the Belfast people who made her singing career possible.

Chapter Sixteen

Frances Lucey

AUDITIONS IN MUNICH

At the age of 22, Frances Lucey paid her own air fare to Munich to audition for the Bavarian State Opera Studio. When she was asked to return for a second time she again dipped into her own pocket. In retrospect, the soprano says, 'I was determined to try my luck in Germany.'

She sang five different pieces at the auditions, but the only Mozart she had was Pamina's aria from *The Magic Flute*. When Heinrick Bender, head of the Studio, heard this he turned to Frances Lucey and protested, 'You're too young to be singing that aria, it is too heavy for you.'

'But you must hear it', she begged. I don't know any other Mozart.'

Her 'bullying tactics', as she laughingly calls them today, worked and Bender was silent as she began to sing. Afterwards, he exclaimed, 'You sing it beautifully ... but you are still too young to be singing it.'

Frances thought: 'I'm damned if I've come all the way to Germany and am not allowed to sing Mozart.'

It was 1986 and she had prepared diligently for Munich. Everyone in her family sang but she was the only member to take up singing professionally. On leaving secondary school she didn't know what to do with herself.

'There was a lot of medicine in our family', she said, 'and that was a possibility. But around this time I met Ronnie Dunne and she asked me to sing for her. To my astonishment, she said to me, "You can make your living from singing." I had only sung a few scales and I wondered how she could have come to such a quick judgement.'

Frances Lucey says with pride and joy that she was born in Dublin's Coombe, a place immortalised in song by the great Jimmy O'Dea. Later as she began to take private lessons with Veronica Dunne she gradually told herself, 'Singing is for me.' Her enthusiasm was fired by Ronnie and she began to believe in her own ability. As she says, 'Ronnie has a dream and she manages to pass it on to her students.'

At the same time, she decided to study music at University College Dublin. Taking singing lessons with Veronica Dunne early in the morning and lectures during the day was, she found rather arduous. Her confidence grew, however, after she had sung Susanna in a College of Music performance of *The Marriage of Figaro*. Anthony Hughes, her music professor at UCD, heard her sing and when eventually she was leaving the college said to her, 'Go and do it.' It was the final push for her, she said, to get on with a singing career.

Hughes organised an audition with one of the London music teaching colleges and she was accepted, but after some soul-searching she decided that Veronica Dunne's methods were still right for her voice and decided to stay with her for another two years. In Dublin she began to do concert work and welcomed the opportunity to sing in Poulenc's *The Carmelites*.

When the time arrived for her to make a decision about her future, Veronica Dunne said, 'Go to Germany, Britain is too full of singers.' Through Angela Feeney she got the address of the Bavarian State Opera Studio. She successfully auditioned and went to live in Munich. There, she joined eleven students in the Studio, the numbers divided evenly between Germans and foreigners.

Heinrik Bender, who conducted as well as giving voice lessons at the Studio, was convinced that Frances was a coloratura soprano. She wasn't certain. 'Actually I don't think I'm pure coloratura. The Germans are terribly keen to slot you into a special box which I find dangerous. At this time, I thought of myself as a lyric soubrette.'

She studied with Astrid Varney, a former brilliant exponent of the Wagner and Strauss repertoire; she also worked on her concert pieces with Arleen Auger. After a year, she was joined at the Studio by another Dubliner Andrew Murphy. One of the key advantages of membership was the opportunity to improve on one's German.

The other advantage was that the Studio company brought opera on tour to little-known venues outside Munich and Frances sang in performances of *Don Giovanni*, *Cosi fan tutte* and *The Marriage of Figaro*. By now she was happily settled into the life of Munich, had her own apartment and unlike some other opera studios, students received a small personal allowance.

Her financial circumstances improved when she was taken on in the parent company, the prestigious Bavarian State Opera. She counted herself extremely fortunate to be taken on, as the company had not enlisted a student from the Studio for some time. She was now paid a respectable salary and her lifestyle was enhanced. Although she was still attached to the Studio, she was called on to sing small parts with the Bavarian State Opera.

To Frances Lucey, the Munich Opera House was a wonderful place to sing and the most beautiful house she had sung in. Soon she was meeting some renowned guest stars, who included Domingo, Kraus, Cappuchilli, Pavarotti, Lucia Popp, Gwyneth Jones and Ann Murray.

'I began to sing a good deal with Ann and off-stage we became good friends. When she sang Cherubino there was always a hush in the house and, at the end of her performance, she usually got rapturous applause. Ann is such an outstanding actress. I must have seen her Cherubino more than twenty times but I still want to laugh at it. Fame has not spoilt her; she is very much a Dubliner and over coffee we like to exchange Moore Street stories. As an artist, I've come to admire her artistry tremendously. It takes a lot to reach her position in singing.'

By now her own career had taken off. She sang a number of Mozartian roles, including Despina, Papagena and Susanna and scored a personal triumph in Wolf-Ferrari's *The School for Fathers*. When she sang

Zenia in Russian in *Boris Godunov* she found the language difficult to master and does not count this opera as among her happiest experiences. Benjamin Britten's *Peter Grimes* was a different matter.

'We sang the opera in English and I remember that the Munich audiences loved it. Rene Kollo gave a riveting interpretation as Grimes. He has a magnificent voice and his acting is superb. I regard him as among the finest of the guest stars.'

She noted a competitive atmosphere in the opera house, which she said was understandable because of the guest star system, yet in her experience the clash of temperaments was less than one might expect. All the same, she felt that one needed to be 'a bit of a diplomat' to avoid them.

'There have been moments during rehearsals when I thought that some artists had been incredibly patient with conductors, she explained. 'Some of them could be provocative as well as difficult. I've sung quite often with Gwyneth Jones and I can recall one particular operatic rehearsal with orchestra when the conductor roared at her, "I'd like to be able to understand at least one word now and then you're singing." The cast and chorus were present and I considered his attitude surly and unfair. But Gwyneth - who, incidently, happened to be friendly with him - kept singing in German and the conductor made no further comment. Actually I got on well with this man and he used to call me "Lucey", as most Germans like to address me. But he had a very quick temper.'

It struck her on more than a few occasions that the guest star policy as operated by German opera houses could have its disadvantages. From time-to-time she saw jet-setting stars arrive at rehearsal with insufficient knowledge of the music, with the result that there was usually a scramble to get it right before opening night. On the otherhand, a star like Domingo or Mirella Freni would always arrive word and music perfect. Munich audiences had favourites among the stars and showed it by their applause.'

Frances Lucey drives her own car in Munich and finds the city invigorating. Her family has travelled from Dublin occasionally to see her perform new roles. She might have married a German bass but broke off the romance. 'I suppose with both of us thinking of our careers it didn't help, or to be more precise, it made us think twice. I reckoned at the time that it wasn't the right moment for me to settle down, although he was keen to marry me. You do travel quite a bit in this business and it's a factor that must be considered. What I do know is you've got to be a very self-contained person, for on tour you can be alone in hotels, so you must be able to enjoy your own company and pass the time positively.

For example in 1991 she sang at the Semper Opera Dresden and toured Japan as a soloist with the Munich Philharmonic and with the NHK Orchestra under Wolfgang Sawallisch in *Die Zauberflote*. Touring appeals to her temperament. 'I think it's good to visit new places, particularly if you're attached to one company like the Bavarian State Opera. It tends to keep one fresh and involved and obviates the risk of staleness. I've enjoyed singing in other places.'

Returning to her family in Blackrock, Co. Dublin always affords her a special thrill. In the spring of 1992 she was engaged by the DGOS to sing Oscar, the Page, in Verdi's *Un ballo in Maschera* at the Gaiety Theatre. Irish opera buffs could be forgiven for forgetting about her, as it was to be her first professional performance in the city.

It was an auspicious occasion for the spirited soprano. Although the production itself was not well received, she was singled out. Critic Michael Dervan told *Irish Times* readers: 'There are three good reasons for going to *Un ballo in Maschera*. There's the spectacular agile and musically true singing of Frances Lucey as the frolicking Page. Ms. Lucey's voice does not sound particularly large, but she uses it with such poise and precision in her exuberantly frothy characterisation that it never seemed to lack in projection.'

In *Opera*, Ian Fox commented: 'The most rounded performance came from the young lyric soprano Frances Lucey who provided a pert if at times hyperactive Oscar; she sang with splendid tone and musicality and is developing into a fine artist.'

'Frances Lucey was a maddeningly mobile Oscar but she sang with quite delightful clear tone and agility', observed Mary MacGoris in the *Irish Independent*.

Since the producer was to blame for her 'hyperactiveness' on stage, Frances Lucey, when we met the following afternoon, expressed her obvious pleasure at the spontaneous reception she had received from the audience on the previous night. Her parents and relatives were at the Gaiety Theatre to share her success.

'I think they all knew what to expect from me', she said.' My parents had seen some of my successes in Munich and knew I could do it. It was nice to be singled out by the critics for usually with *Ballo* they tend to concentrate on Riccardo and Amelia.'

Elaine Padmore had also been among the audience. She was on the lookout for someone to sing the role of Emmy in the 1992 Wexford Festival production of Marschner's *Der Vampyr*. Before the week was out she had decided that Frances would suit the part and the singer herself told me she was thrilled to be going to Wexford.

Someone quite rightly described *Der Vampyr* as 'a sort of Don Giovanni with blood'. It is based on Polidori's short story, product of his famous sojourn with Byron and the Shelleys by Lake Geneva in 1816. Lord Ruthven, the bloodsucker of the title, is required to dispose of three maidens – an hysteric, a peasant and a haughty aristocrat – within 24 hours if he is to gain another year on earth. He does well enough, only just missing on the third.

As Emmy, one of the maidens, Frances Lucey achieved a personal triumph; all the more welcome because throughout the festival's 41 years there have been too few Irish individual successes. William Weaver in the *Financial Times* echoed the thoughts of the majority when he stated: 'The young Irish soprano Frances Lucey enjoyed a well-earned triumph. Clean and pure, the voice poured out freely, naturally; the words were distinct, the phrases sensitively shaped.'

More than one critic praised her excellent German; indeed, her German experience as a whole stood her well, for she was singing in a high-powered cast that included William Parcher as the Vampire, Walter

McNeill (a Glyndebourne Alfredo) and the outstanding Daniela Bechly. What I personally liked about her performance was her confident and unforced delivery and the bright charm she brought to the part.

'Miss Lucey is the discovery of the festival', proclaimed Andrew Porter in the *Observer*, and no one disagreed with the claim. Perhaps it will stir Wexford to search for more 'discoveries' among the new-wave Irish singers such as Regina Nathan, Mary Hegarty, Marie-Claire O'Reirdan, Cara O'Sullivan and a dozen others.

It's worth noting that the real success of the '92 festival was not *Der Vampyr* but Mascagni's *Il Piccolo Marat*, an opera rarely performed since the early Thirties. It is the kind of full-blooded work that Dr. Tom Walsh would love to have staged.

Apart from her appearance in *Der Vampyr*, Frances Lucey gave a song recital during the festival's second week, when her programme consisted of songs by Schubert, Duparc, Chausson and Vaughan Williams. The audience in White's Hotel enjoyed her delightful presence, pure soprano tone and easy interpretative skills. For a young singer, she had come a long way in mastering the difficult, if subtle, art of concert singing.

A vivacious personality off-stage, she told me how much she had enjoyed her Wexford stay. Again, family and friends had come to hear her sing and when I met her in the Talbot Hotel for coffee, she enthused about the acoustics of the Theatre Royal, the warmth of the audiences, and the fine playing by the National Symphony Orchestra. Already she was looking forward to a return visit if, as she whimsically remarked, 'the festival will have me!'

Shortly after she returned to Munich she was contacted by her agent; would she like to sing Rosina in Paisiello's *Il Barbiere di Siviglia* in Wexford in 1993? Her decision was required as quickly as possible. It was after all a plum role with gorgeous music. No sooner, however, had Frances heard about the Wexford part than she was offered a series of performances in a contemporary opera in Salzburg. It wasn't the main festival at Salzburg, it was the Landestheater, but she knew that anything in Salzburg attracted a lot of attention, especially a new work.

'The agency that brought me that work is very important', she said, 'and I thought, "Oh God, if I turn them down I'll never hear from them again." And twenty-one performances. You couldn't help saying to yourself that, financially, it would be a lot more worthwhile than Wexford. But I knew that in my heart of hearts I would prefer to sing this piece.'

Paisiello prevailed and she arrived in Wexford with high hopes to sing in an opera that was very popular until Rossini came along 30 years later with his more sparkling version of *Il Barbiere*. The other festival operas were *Cherevichki*, mounted to celebrate the centenary of Tchaikovsky's death, and *Zampa* by Ferdinand Herold.

It was an unhappy time for the soprano. Lucy Bailey's production of the Paisiello's work created a very poor impression and nowhere suggested that it was opera buffa. People walked out of the dress rehearsal, some others asked for their money back; this was unprecedented festival behaviour. Worse was to come, when the critics, Irish and overseas, panned the production. Rodney Milnes actually left at the interval and next day in the London *Times* commented: 'Paisiello's *Barbiere di Siviglia* constituted one of the most disgraceful happenings I have witnessed in an opera house. Or rather the first half was: at the interval I made no excuses and left.

'This *Barbiere* is amiable, routine and inoffensive, inevitably overshadowed by Rossini's masterpiece. But it doesn't deserve to be kicked to death, which seemed to be the aim of the producer Ms. Bailey. A series of glum surrealist images replaced meaningful direction, and as number-after-number was greeted with either thunderous silence or an embarrassed splatter of applause, the singers realised they were dying the death, and the humiliation of singers is not a spectator sport in which I would wish to participate. How could this have been allowed to happen?'

When I talked to Frances Lucey in the foyer of the Theatre Royal during the interval of *Zampa* a few days later, she looked far from her exuberant self and no doubt wished she was in Salzburg. 'It's a wacky production', she said, obviously being as diplomatic as she could. Vocally, she had acquitted herself brilliantly, a fact recognised by the audience on the opening night. For the festival it was a *cause celebre*, with artistic director Elaine Padmore going on RTE (radio) to defend the production against sharp criticism by *Irish Press* critic John Brophy who claimed that the producer was guilty of 'sexual harassment of the audience'.

Frances Lucey declined to talk on the programme on ethical grounds – *Il Barbiere* was still running at the festival. But she did say again to a researcher that the production was 'wacky' in her view. The new President of the festival, Dr. A.J. O'Reilly said he did not find the production offensive, but actually enjoyed the music. Nonetheless it became one of the biggest talking points in the 40 years of the event. But Wexford at least could claim to have achieved success with two out of the three operas.

Frances Lucey made the most of her stay in the town. Friends and relatives made the journey from Dublin hardly knowing what to expect after all the bad publicity. 'I felt for them', she told me later. 'How can you try putting people – especially your own family – off an opera. See the funny side of it if you can, I told them?

After Wexford, it was back to Munich, to a hectic schedule that passes for a normal life at the Bavarian State Opera. All kinds of everything from Kurt Weill's *Mahagonny* to Bach and Mozart. And because she's young and energetic and wants to diversify and have a bit of fun, solo concerts by Gershwin and Cole Porter. She did a spot on a four-hour show for German television which also featured Montserrat Caballe and the Swingle Singers.

She was no longer haunted by the memory of Paisiello's Barbiere di Siviglia or with meeting people in Wexford's narrow streets wanting to commiserate with her for being in that opera. Her innate Dublin humour has a habit of surfacing on these occasions. After her success in *Vampyr* at the 1992 festival, she was quoted as saying later, 'I've been living off the rave notices for months.' What she said after Paisiello's *Barbiere* was simply, 'Forget it!'

And by the time we met again in Dublin in the summer of 1994 Frances had almost forgotten about the experience. She was, in fact, preparing to go to the United States to look round the operatic scene and attend some auditions. At the time she was enjoying a deserved six week vacation from the Munich opera where in the previous weeks she had covered the role of Cleopatra in Handel's *Julius Caesar*. Although she was not called on to sing, she was thrilled to learn such a major role which has eight good arias for the soprano.

'Ann Murray sang a stunning Caesar,' she said. 'It's one of her greatest operatic parts. Ann is now a mega star and it's amazing the control she has over her voice.'

Frances was also studying the role of Rosina in Rossini's *Barber*, a role often sung by sopranos in Germany, and she hoped to get the opportunity to sing Gilda in *Rigoletto*. She expressed regret that she got so few chances to sing the French repertoire, though one of her future engagements is the part of Sophie in *Werther* with Ann Murray as Charlotte.

Peter Jones had by now taken over at the Bavarian State Opera and she noticed that he was employing a number of British artists. 'He's a dynamic personality,' she said, 'and I get on well with him.' And since the end of the Berlin Wall there was also an influx of singers from East Germany.

'A singer needs patience,' Francis mused. 'I mean, it may take a long time before you are allowed sing the role you've set your heart on. It's really up to the director or conductor. I've been lucky so far, though once or twice I missed out on parts because a director wanted somebody else.'

One suspects, however, that the vivavious Dublin soprano has the right temperament for the job and is confident that she'll find total fulfilment as a singer. She's extending her concert and oratorio repertoire, but she made no secret of the fact that she'd like to divide her time between Munich and America.

Chapter Seventeen

Thomas Lawlor

SULLIVAN TO MOZART

'If you want a career, you have got to go to London, we can't teach you any more here', was the well-meaning advice of singing teacher Maura O'Connor to her star pupil Thomas Lawlor at the Dublin Municipal School of Music early in 1960.

He was adjudged a promising light lyric baritone with a voice of rich timbre and expressive tone. Moreover, he had graduated from University College Dublin with a degree in English, philosophy and politics, which was apt since his grandfather was Labour TD for Dublin's South Central constituency, and also a trade union official. His parents did not encourage him, however, to pursue a career in singing as they regarded his teaching post at St. Fintan's High School as far more important. 'The thought of me giving up my job was anathema to my mother', he says today.

But Maura O'Connor had no such misgivings. She had sung in concert and oratorio with Arthur Reckless and decided to write to him at the Guidhall School of Music and Drama, pointing out Thomas Lawlor's potential. Reckless informed her of the availability of a scholarship at the school and urged her to enter her pupil for it. It was actually for a tenor but if none was deemed up to standard it would be awarded to an alternative voice. There was an added proviso - competitors had to be British or from the Commonwealth.

After he had sung for the panel of judges, the chairman explained to young Lawlor the rules of the trust that applied to the scholarship, and carefully added, 'I think I am right in saying Mr. Lawlor that your country left the Commonwealth in 1948?'

'Yes, that is correct', Lawlor replied; then he suddenly proceeded to sweep into a long speech about how art and music should transcend mere national boundaries and political considerations, to which the panellists laughed and said they would bear it in mind if the question of giving him the scholarship arose.

A month later, to his surprise, a letter arrived from the Guildhall, informing him that he had won the Sam Heilbut Major Scholarship, which was a cash prize and would cover all his tuition fees. He was in his early twenties and considered it a marvellous opportunity. 'I had no hesitation in giving up my teaching job, but my parents were still not sold on my ambition to become a professional singer.'

Gradually he discovered that the scholarship money did not provide him with an entirely comfortable lifestyle, so from the second year onwards he arranged all his classes and lessons for two-and-a-half days each week and with the spare days did some teaching for London County Council. He was at last able to eat properly. During his first year at the Guildhall, he had been coming out in biles from eating bread and jam.

'I went in one day to Arthur Reckless for singing lessons', he recalled, 'and must have had some biles on my skin for he took one look at me and warned me I wasn't eating properly. Instead of a singing lesson, he took me out and bought me a decent lunch. Arthur used to call me "Lawless Thomas" and I nicknamed him "Reckless Arthur". I think he enjoyed my Dublin wit and I can say the same for his English sense of humour'.

Near the end of his time at the Guildhall, when he was thinking of what to do next, Arthur Reckless said to him, 'I was at a dinner in the Mansion House last night and sitting next to me was Frederick Lloyd, general manager of D'Oyly Carte, and he told me the company was looking for a baritone.'

It was customary for students at the Guildhall to sing for guests after dinner functions there for about £10 a time and on this night a young baritone called Brian Donlon had been engaged. Lloyd was impressed. 'I like his voice', he said to Arthur Reckless, 'we could do with him.' Reckless agreed but added, 'I've a better baritone for you, Freddie; he's an Irish singer called Thomas Lawlor. I want you to hear him.' Lloyd said, 'Ask him to 'phone me in the morning.'

Next day Lawlor went to the Savoy Theatre for an audition and afterwards was offered a contract. 'I counted myself very lucky', he says. 'In fact, I could not easily complain the way things had turned out so well for me. Arthur Reckless had been, however, an excellent teacher and had helped me during my three years there to win awards for singing oratorio, opera and English song.'

It was an exciting time to be joining D'Oyly Carte. He renewed acquaintance with Sir Malcolm Sargent, who normally conducted G & S first nights at the Savoy. Earlier he had worked with the celebrated conductor at the Guildhall. At the time Sargent was recording all the Savoy operas and it was coming to the end of the series with the *Yeomen of the Guard* only left to record.

Lawlor was cast as the second Yeoman, which is a combination of two parts, tenor and bass, but to save money the director asked him to sing the two of them. The memory was to remain with him. 'I didn't mind singing the bass part, as that was okay, but you can imagine how I felt at 10 o'clock in the morning in an empty hall trying to sing tenor with Sir Malcolm conducting the Royal Philharmonic. It was the most awful experience and even to this day I cannot listen to the recording because it reminds me of that morning.'

Singing with the company afforded him real enjoyment and personal satisfaction. He found that contrary to general opinion the G & S style did not restrict singers. As he later said, 'There was a lot of mythology about the way G & S singing and acting were stylised and that there was a very strict way of doing things. In my experience this was not the case. For the nine years I worked with the company most of the stage business was introduced by the artists themselves.

'In the case of the police sergeant in *The Pirates of Penzance* I first went on as an understudy, never having had a rehearsal, and among the audience was the British Queen Mother and other members of the royal family. I remember I introduced some new business to the part and when I saw it played some years later I happened to be seated beside the then head of D'Oyly Carte productions. When I asked him where the stage business came from, he replied, "That's traditional G & S, it has always been there." He was surprised when I reminded him that I had been the innovator. The truth is that you had a lot of latitude and I never remember anyone sitting on me.'

Touring was a major part of the company's programme. For 48 weeks of the year the company toured Britain, America and Canada. Throughout the 1960s Thomas Lawlor sang principal baritone and bass-baritone roles and found that interest in the operas never seemed to wane. As his voice darkened and became more bass- baritone he began to find that parts such as Giuseppe in *The Gondoliers*, Strephan in *Iolanthe* and the Captain in *HMS Pinafore* were taxing his voice; or as he put it, 'I was find-ing it more difficult to sustain the tessitura in these parts and I wanted to drop them altogether if I could. When Donald Adams told me he was leaving the company, I wrote to Bridget Carte, who was then the last remaining link with the famous Carte family, and explained to her that my voice was dropping lower and lower and would she agree to my taking over Donald Adams' bass roles in future.

'I had a letter back from her a few days later and it's still imprinted indelibly in my memory. I remember she wrote: "Dear Mr. Lawlor, I quite understand that you are having difficulties vocally with the roles you are playing at the moment and that Mr. Adams' roles would be far more suitable both vocally and artistically for you. I thoroughly agree, but I do love you in the costumes you wear now. Please continue to sing these roles".'

He wasn't flattered; if anything he became more frustrated. He made up his mind to leave the company. It wasn't an easy decision for him, as he was enjoying a good lifestyle, was buying his own London apartment and driving a big car. And he had particularly happy memories touring with the D'Oyly Carte. He did five six-month, coast-to-coast tours of the United States and Canada, appearing in all major cities of North America. In 1968, while singing at the Central City Opera Festival in Colorado, he was honoured by the city by being named an Honorary Citizen. During his tours of America he took part in many of the well known 'chat shows' on television. 'Before I parted on amicable terms with the company I needed somewhere else to go to', he recalled. I got an agent who arranged an audition for me with Glyndebourne Festival Opera and I was successful. The company offered me small parts in the festival productions and some larger ones on the spring and autumn tours.'

He arrived at Glyndebourne in the early 1970s to rehearse for the spring tour. On his own admission he was feeling insecure, even apprehensive, as he was going into an altogether new area and could not be sure whether he could make a success of it. To the singer himself, it was a big cultural change but he discovered there was a brotherhood among artists that operated when they were faced by new circumstances. Most important of all, he was able to draw on his world-wide experience with the D'Oyly Carte and secretly found that he was often able to act international singers off the stage. He counted this a morale booster and an undoubted fillip.

The first part he sang at Glyndebourne was Zaretsky in *Eugene Onegin* – and in Russian to boot. With the assistance of the company's expert language coaching staff, he surmounted the problem. When he was cast as Osmin in Mozart's *Il Seraglio*, he found there was a good deal of spoken dialogue, so he decided to master German and attended the Goethe Institute in London. However, when he returned later to Glyndebourne for rehearsals, by now considering himself fairly fluent in the language, the German lady coach surprised him, 'My God, Lawlor, whatever has happened to your German ... it is terrible?' As he said, that 'took me down a peg or two.'

One of his favourite roles was the poacher in *The Cunning Little Vixen*, a Jonathan Miller production that he considered brilliant. He also enjoyed singing the chief of police in *The Visit of the Old Lady*. The character was a Hitler-type figure, an absolute fascist, and for the part he wore a magnif- icent full- length leather overcoat and was so taken by it that he said to the producer John Cox, 'I'd love to have that coat.' But Cox was quick to reply, 'No, you're not ... I'm going to beat you to it.' Both men, however, were too late: the management had already sold the costumes of a compa- ny in Stockholm.

During the summer months, he had rented a cottage near Lewes, but after a couple of seasons bought a small house in the town which he shared with his wife and their adopted child Frances. The English countryside appealed to him and there was, in his view, something delightfully distinc- tive about Glyndebourne, from the Georgian grandeur to the manor itself to the tennis courts and gardens.

Yet the idyllic setting suggested something else to Thomas Lawlor. 'Maybe I am wrong, but in my opinion one was always made feel that the singers were regarded as among the lowest form of animal life there and that if the management could do without us they would. We called it the most picturesque prison in Britain because it was a seven day a week job; I mean you'd have rehearsals and performances on a Sunday. I don't know how the management got away with it; in fact, they got over the Sunday performances by claiming the operas were being presented for some kind of club, which was absurd since the Lord's Day Observance Society for- bade Sunday performances in the theatre. I remember once performing for the Catholic Stage Guild at Drury Lane on a Sunday night and the extraordinary thing was that we could sing but couldn't move. That was what the law stipulated.'

It struck him occasionally at Glyndebourne that some of the interna- tional guest stars looked upon their engagements there as a kind of paid holiday and didn't seem to have the same investment in the place as the British artists, who tended to regard it as their market and wanted to excel in order to keep working. To Thomas Lawlor, it was a showcase for free- lance singers like himself and he counted singing there crucial to his career. More importantly, the house never deviated from the old Christie philosophy of ensuring that each new production was as near perfect as possible. This was one of the joys of working in the house, for you were made to realise that excellence was the overwhelming aim.

Nevertheless, he found the old theatre 'a dreadful place in which to sing' due to its dry acoustics, a fact he said that was borne out in radio broadcasts from Glyndebourne. Sometimes he was amused by the types who went there for opera, especially the 'corporate customers.' During our conversation, he was reminded of a story retailed to him by a friend who happened to be sitting behind a couple at a performance of *Capriccio*. The lady was beautifully jewelled and gowned and at one point leaned across to her partner and whispered something to him. Seemingly, her partner's reply, made in a very loud stage whisper, was, 'It's culture my dear Cynthia ... just sit back and let it wash over you dear.'

Behind the scenes, Glyndebourne was in his view a very competitive place for singers, in particular for the men and women of the chorus. All were talented singers and in those days the best of them were chosen to sing principal roles on tour with the company. 'I could see that this heightened competition among them and made everybody sing consistently well. Dermot Troy always spoke very favourably about the chorus and considered it a superb training ground for voices and stagecraft. But it was of course only part of the uniformly high standard of singing in the house and everyone worked hard to meet those all round standards. I was introduced to Mozart's operas there and counted singing in them pure joy.'

Nonetheless he was never the one to harbour illusions about his profession. Describing his departure from Glyndebourne, he said, 'One does not leave Glyndebourne, Glyndebourne ceases to call you. It is one of those places where your face fits for a certain time and then you move on. That is the way it works. It's understandable: the management wants new faces, so do the opera buffs who visit there in the summer months. Indeed, one realises in this business that there is hardly such a thing as loyalty; I mean, you can work yourself to the bone for a company but when the time comes it will tire of you. It happens all the time.'

Yet he could say he had found the experience both stimulating and fulfilling. For about five months in the year he had worked at the Glyndebourne opera house and on tour with the company and had sung a variety of roles, including Alfonso in *Cosi fan tutte*, which was a particular favourite of his due to its rich comic undertones. He had always found Mozart's music wonderful to sing and his operatic characters roundly drawn and containing depth. During his time at Glyndebourne, he had already guested for English National Opera in performances of *Iolanthe*, *Traviata* and *Julietta*, and sang Figaro in a Kent Opera production of *The Marriage of Figaro* and *Fidelio*, his portrayal of Rocco in the Beethoven work winning critical acclaim.

Inevitably, his path led to Covent Garden. He would remember his debut as Benoit, the landlord in *La Boheme* for a number of reasons. For a long time he had admired the soprano Katia Ricciarelli, both as a beautiful soprano and beautiful woman and looked forward one day to meeting her. But the image she created at rehearsals took him by surprise. As Mimi, she rehearsed with a fur coat draped over her shoulder and wore sunglasses. It struck him she found rehearsals something of a bore, as other stars did and a waste of valuable time - and money.

Placido Domingo, who was singing Rodolfo, was friendly and unpretentious. He would arrive for rehearsals with a smile in the morning and more than once slapped Lawlor on the back with the words, 'How are you feeling this morning, Tom?' They would chat for a few moments about everyday things. Domingo personified the confident and secure superstar and was more friendly and forthcoming than the lesser known members of the cast.

To Thomas Lawlor, the tenor's performance as Rodolfo was magnificient, at once warm-toned and very human. He was struck by his musicianship and powerful stage presence. Whatever reservations he had about Ricciarelli as a woman, her Mimi was a match for his Rodolfo.

Despite the stellar cast and the glamour surrounding the production, Lawlor came to hate the production. In his experience it was the least theatrical performance he had sung in for more than 30 years. The Swiss conductor was no help. A small, unfriendly man with a mocking manner, he took a dislike to the South African soprano singing Musetta, something that Thomas Lawlor found unforgiveable, as he himself regarded her as an outstanding artist undeserving of such rude treatment. The conductor's attitude tended to sour the atmosphere at rehearsals.

After seven months at Covent Garden, he moved north to Leeds to guest with the newly-established Opera North. He was cast as Jupiter in the old Wendy Toye production of *Orpheus in the Underworld*, being only the third artist to sing the role in that long span of 25 years; before that it was shared by Eric Shilling and Derek Hammond Stroud.

He was invited to join the company on contract and it heralded a happy phase in his career. The city of Leeds appealed to him and it became abundantly clear that Opera North was filling an operatic void. He sang leading Mozart, Rossini and Puccini roles and among his most memorable was that of Somarone, the ludicrous music-master in Berlioz's *Beatrice and Benedict*, which he found enormous fun. It was an ideal repertory company, in fact, pure theatre, and with everyone, including singers, designers and directors committed to a single goal. Singers did not just come and go - they belonged to the company, so loyalty entered into it.

For six years he was a member of the company; after that his contract was not renewed. 'The artistic director decided - in my opinion in his lack of wisdom - that he wanted to cast his operas from the world and not from within the company itself', he explained. 'He had eighteen principal singers on contract and gradually they were whittled down. I was one of the last two left on contract - the bass John Tranter was the other - and our contracts were not renewed. After that, Opera North went the way of most companies with singers coming and going without the same attachment, as we had, to the house. And I'm afraid a few of them fell below the standards we had set.'

Nonetheless, he was invited back regularly as a guest artist, but he admitted it was never really the same again. He wasn't short of engagements, however, and played in the movie version of the *Mikado* for Warner

Brothers, and *Cox and Box* for Brent Walker Films. Artistic Director of the Wexford Festival, Elaine Padmore, cast him as Don Carlos in the Prokofiev's opera, *The Duenna*. He revealed his versatility when he scripted and presented *A Dales Walk* in the BBC television series *Favourite Walks*, produced by Mike Weatherley. Regular walks through the Dales had, he said, inspired him to write.

The series attracted good press notices and a big viewership, which soon afterwards prompted him to write a six-part series on opera aimed at popular taste, but unfortunately the scripts got left on the shelf due to 'economic reasons'. He is hopeful, though, that one day the series will be screened.

As an experienced and versatile freelance artist, he continued to be in demand. He enjoyed his performances with English National Opera at the Coliseum where he sang principal roles in *La Traviata*, *Julietta* and *Iolanthe*, and for English Music Theatre Company, the successor to Benjamin Britten's English Opera Group, he peformed in the world premiere of *Tom Jones* by Stephen Oliver, and *La Cenerentola*. One of his most satisfying musical moments was, he said, playing the role of Pooh Bah in the *Mikado* at the Westminister Theatre in London's West End.

Tom Lawlor – as his colleagues and friends call him – is not one of those artists who takes malicious joy in stating that he doesn't read the critics. He will tell you that for the most part he has got excellent notices throughout his lengthy career in opera and operetta. 'To be absolutely honest', he says, 'most singers – and actors, too – say they don't read the critics, but of course they do. How can you escape not reading them when, as in the case in some opera houses, the press reviews are hung next morning on the notice board. Who's going to ignore someone saying a marvellous – or nasty – thing about oneself?'

'I remember there was one critic on a London daily paper who for some strange reason or other never liked anything I did, but then he never liked what a lot of good people did, and that included Jonathan Miller. There is a story told that when Miller was introduced to this particular gentleman in the foyer of Covent Garden, he grabbed him by the collar and told him in no uncertain manner what he thought of him.'

Approaching the late 1980s he began to interest himself in operatic direction and coaching. He was engaged as Artistic Stage Director for a large community theatre group, The Castleford Gilbert & Sullivan Society in Yorkshire, and during that period he directed their four major productions, *Yeomen of the Guard*, *Princess Ida*, *HMS Pinafore* and the *Mikado*. He also became an adjudicator member of the British Federation of Music Festivals. Since 1989 he has been attached to the vocal and dramatic faculty of the Bay View Summer Conservatory of Music in Michigan and told me he found working there with students challenging and very satisfying. He has also taught in the opera departments of the Royal Academy of Music as well as Trinity College of Music, London. He admitted that he was finding teaching and coaching opera students more intellectually challenging than performing. He regarded the transition as a development in his musical education and expressed disappointment that he had not been invited by music colleges in Ireland to lecture to the growing number of opera students in the country.

Tom Lawlor retains his Dublin wit and exuberance of spirit and nowadays divides his time between England, the United States and Ireland. When asked in December 1992 by the DGOS to play the jailer Frosch in *Die Fledermaus*, he quipped, 'The part is a non- singing one ... maybe they're trying to tell me something!'

I remember he brought touches of O'Casey's Joxer to the part and when afterwards I suggested - knowing his love of acting - that he might like one day to play Joxer in an Abbey Theatre production of Juno and the Paycock, he chuckled. 'Gosh, it's not a bad idea, is it?'

Chapter Eighteen

Patricia Bardon

THE 'TWO RIGOLETTOS'

Patricia Bardon is admirably equipped for the life of singer, possessing voice, beauty and personality. Born in Dublin in September 1964, she enrolled at the College of Music at the age of 15 and began her studies with Veronica Dunne. In her mind she had no doubt what she wanted. Her mother's side of the family were all basses and contraltos and as a child she had been advised at school to have her voice trained.

'I even thought of singing jazz and blues', she recalled. 'Opera didn't concern me, but Ronnie Dunne said to me, "I'll change your mind about that". And of course she did.'

At the age of 18, she represented the Republic of Ireland at the Cardiff Singer of the World Competition and surprised not a few pundits by winning second place. 'Useful experience', was how she describes the Cardiff venture. A single-minded young woman, she is not easily carried away.

Singers, they say, need luck and in this respect Patricia Bardon was luckier than most of her colleagues in Ireland. When Diner's Club International asked Veronica Dunne to nominate a young singer who in her opinion merited a Diner's Club credit card, she was the one she named, which in effect meant that for the next three years her travel expenses and certain other extras were covered.

After her good showing in Cardiff, she got concert engagements in

Dublin and elsewhere in the country and this prompted her to get an English agent. In the autumn of 1983 she made her operatic debut with the DGOS, singing Maddalena, which is considered a good part for a mezzo-soprano. Next, she sang Olga in the society's new production of *Eugene Onegin* and got favourable reviews. Performing on stage gave her an overwhelming feeling of satisfaction and well-being. When the DGOS engaged her to sing Orpheus in Gluck's *Orfeo ed Euridice* she appeared somewhat young for such a mature part, one that for long had been associated with Kathleen Ferrier in England. Yet at this time her voice was more contralto than mezzo and was ideally suited to Gluck's music.

The critics gave her a mixed reception, but Patricia Bardon contends that she was ready for the role and wasn't too young. 'I counted it a valuable experience', she said, whimsically adding, 'I think, though, if I saw myself on video I'd crack up completely.'

She admitted that at the outset of her career in opera she was worried about her acting. 'It took me sometime to come to terms with it. I found that if I went headlong into it my voice invariably suffered, so I tried to balance both and before long began to feel far more at home on stage.'

Starting out on her operatic career, she said she was cautious, even terrified of being thrown into something that was too big for her, but it didn't happen like that and she was usually offered the right parts. Astra Blair, her agent then, was careful about the roles she sang and warned her off some others. Welsh National Opera cast her as Flosshilde in *The Ring* and she felt Wagner's music suited her voice really well. She sees herself singing more of the composer's works in the future. 'I feel my voice is big enough to cope with his music and I sometimes sit at the piano and play a few of his arias. Although I sang the part in English, it was a splendid experience.'

Patricia also sang Olga in *Onegin* for WNO and felt in no way over-awed by the operatic scene in Britain. Because she was often ten to fifteen years younger than other members of the cast, she felt she had to prove herself. On reflection, she says she achieved the breakthrough in Opera North's production of *The Trojans at Carthage* at the Grand Theatre, Leeds.

'At this time, in the middle eighties, I felt I was singing very well. My voice had acquired more flexibility and though I had started my career as a low contralto I was now developing the top of my voice and in this respect I was being helped by some brilliant conductors and producers who were really inspiring to work with.'

After dealing with the principals in the cast of *The Trojans*, Martin Dreyer in *Opera* commented: 'The lesser roles could easily pale in such a centralised work. But I fell for Patricia Bardon's beautiful Anna, an unexpectedly rich, almost distracting voice of enormous promise.'

This was the type of critical comment her voice was attracting. Concert work and oratorio took her to the Continent and the United states where she sang in Beethoven's *Missa Solemnis* and was singled out as 'the best soloist on the night', with one critic commenting on her 'gorgeous, burnished mezzo.'

Nearer home, at the St. David's Hall in Cardiff, Patricia Bardon experienced one of those evenings that singers only dream about. She remembers the warmth of the reception, the prolonged applause, the sense of satisfaction the performance of Mahler's *Ruckert Lieder* afforded her. 'I remember coming off the stage feeling so fulfilled', she told me later.

The experienced critic Kenneth Loveland was deeply impressed and began his critique: Just occasionally there crosses one's path a young artist so obviously gifted that one feels safe in prophesying a future of rich fulfilment. Patricia Bardon has everything going for her: the looks, the musicianship, the voice. Particularly, the voice. She was billed as a mezzo, but she is never that. Miss Bardon is that animal at present threatened with extinction, the true contralto.

'Not, in the old-fashioned sense of a booming vocal battleship, but in range and colour. She has a wide compass, and though both ends of the register need to develop, the notes are there awaiting the full release that will come in the right hands, in which she certainly seems to be at the moment.

'The actual sound is deep velvet. It is unkind to attach a label to a young singer so soon, but the blend of youthful freshness with a surprisingly mature sound last night reminded one of the first contact with the young Kathleen Ferrier. One sensed, too, an awareness of musical nuance, and a genuine feeling for words.'

It was a useful assessment of her voice at this early stage of her career. She was aware that the ends of the register needed to be developed, but told me at the time that she was working hard on that aspect of her singing. Loveland's praise might have turned the head of a less balanced singer, but with Patricia Bardon there was never any fear of that happening; she can be self-critical and likes critiques to be constructive and the critic capable of analysing a performance expertly. She reads the critics and in conversation I found she likes to discuss certain technical points they may have raised.

She received further acclaim at the Ulster Hall in Belfast when she performed Mahler's *Kindertotenlieder*. One critic reminded his readers that Janet Baker had recorded what many regarded as the definitive account of these splendid songs, yet he wanted to compliment this young Irish mezzo for the depth of her penetration of this demanding score, apart from her ability to communicate with her listeners by her charming platform manner.

It was true. She cut an impressive figure on stage, combining beauty and elegance and her German was usually impeccable. Talking to her in London, where she has settled, she made it clear that she wanted to divide her time between concert work, oratorio and opera. Under new agents Ingpen & Williams she sang the *Verdi Requiem* in Brussels, *Elijah* in Bilbao, Janacek's *The Diary of One Who Disappeared* in Barcelona, and the Mozart *Requiem* in Madrid.

It was with Opera North, however, that she won further fame as Helen in a new production of *King Priam*. Once more, the critics stressed the riches of her voice and the depth of feeling she projected. Her acting continued to show improvement, a fact noted by some critics who earlier in her career had found her stage craft somewhat amateurish. What pleased her most of all was that she was continuing to make progress, as she said, on 'all fronts'.

Not every singer looks forward to almost constant travel, but Patricia Bardon was happy to go where the work was, whether this happened to be Amsterdam where she performed Stravinisky's *Threni* or touring Spain singing six performances of *Messiah*. She considered it a valuable way of gaining experience and extending her repertoire.

However, it was at the Royal Opera House Covent Garden that she discovered what she once described to me as 'an incredible atmosphere', something that obviously made a deep impression on her as a singer. She first experienced the feeling when she sang the minor role of Wowlke in *La Fanciulla del West*. It was her introduction to the house – a house she felt that was steeped in tradition – and she felt it from the moment she strode through the stage door earlier that evening; and backstage again she was reminded of the renowed singers, from Tetrazzini to Callas and Ponselle to Sutherland, to have sung there. Being young, she found it a little difficult to identify with them, as though such greatness was almost unattainable. But in another way it had an inspiring affect and fired her imagination. Furthermore, the house staff were very supportive to newcomers, which made the experience all the more pleasing.

When she returned there in 1991 to sing Maddalena in a star-studded *Rigoletto* cast the same atmosphere prevailed, except that the swift cast changes proved to her disconcerting. From performance to performance she never knew who her next Duke in the opera would be. 'I remember singing once with Giuseppe Sabbatini, then with Franco Farina, and later again with Georgi Tscholakov. It was the same with the Rigolettos: I found myself on different occasions singing opposite Leo Nucci, Piero Cappuccilli and Matteo Manuguerra, all splendid in the part but strangers to me. It can be off-putting meeting them for the first time on stage without a rehearsal, yet it was again a fine experience for me and enhanced my self-confidence.'

Despite the stars around her, her Maddalena did not go unnoticed. David Murray summed up in the *Financial Times*: 'Patricia Bardon's Maddalena was a great asset, articulate and penetrating and sexy.' John

Higgins in *The Times* noted that she was 'a sultry hooker of a Maddalena', a reference that amused the singer who had never before been described in such sexy terms.

In the autumn of 1992 she was engaged by English National Opera to sing the same role at the Coliseum, in a revival of Jonathan Miller's mafiosa version and which is set in New York. Patricia Bardon had no hesitation in telling me that the ENO production gave her the greater satisfaction, although it was sung in English. 'The Miller version is a riot', she recalled, 'but at the same time it's challenging and completely different from the conventional *Rigoletto* I sang at Covent Garden. At the Coliseum, I was a waitress in Sparafucile's bar but still a tart. The response by the audience was incredible and they seemed to have no trouble identifying with the new setting. Musically, it is such a perfect opera that it can work anywhere.'

In his review of the revival for *Opera,* John Allison made the point, 'Though the updating from 16th century Mantua to mafia-controlled New York in the 1950s is ingenious and in many ways fresh, it is a rather generalised view which takes little account of the deeper layers within the opera, or of Verdi's characterisation. Instead of a Duke who abuses his power Miller offers a sleazy criminal - a much less disquieting statement than the one the composer was making.'

To Patricia Bardon, the Miller concept worked and was very exciting for an audience. For her own part, she had more freedom playing Maddalena. It was a question of which version appealed most to an opera lover and as far as she could discern there was support for each. She had sung beside a seasoned ENO cast, including tenor Arthur Davies and baritone John Rawnsley (in the title role). Allison was taken by her strong singing, which he thought on this occasion was particularly welcome in the light of what had preceded it.

As a young singer, Patricia came to the view that the most talented stars could be the nicest to meet. 'I have found this to be true, for example, of Pieri Cappuccilli and Leo Nucci who gave me the impression that they had nothing to prove. Working with people like them can be inspiring and you can certainly learn from them. They are actor-singers of the highest calibre and control the stage.'

Watching them get inside a role in this respect fascinated her, and she enthused about Philip Langridge's portrayal of Aschenbach in Britten's opera *Death in Venice* at Covent Garden, describing it as a memorable experience. 'In retrospect, I regard it as the most amazing performance I've ever seen in an opera house.'

While Callas had been always the diva she most admired, there were others that enormously impressed her, among them Ann Murray. 'Yes, I admire Ann greatly. She is a tremendously rounded performer and she's what I call the complete package. Watching her perform on stage, you can sit back and relax, for you don't have moments of angst. I'm sure that is what being a professional is all about. I saw her in Handel's *Alcina* and adored her performance.'

She expressed admiration also for Mirella Freni for her durability as an artist and her courage in refusing roles she deemed unsuited to her voice. To Patricia Bardon, though, Maria Callas was the supreme artist, a true diva as she combined marvellous dramatic flair with vocal splendour in her halcyon days. 'I would love to have seen her on stage in *Norma*, *Tosca* and *Medea* or have been around to attend her masterclasses at the Juilliard School in New York. Will there be another like Maria? It's very hard to say.'

Patricia leaves you in no doubt that singers who are either bad-mannered or pretentious are anathema to her. 'They make it unpleasant for everyone, but thankfully they are in the minority. Most of my colleagues are professionals who get on with the job of singing to their best ability.'

In April 1992 she was back at Covent Garden, singing Hedwige in Rossini's *William Tell*, the biggest role she was yet to sing in this house. 'I count it a highpoint so far in my career', she later told me. A long opera, she appeared in Acts I and IV, with a big scene in the latter act. She could be well pleased with the response of the critics. Max Loppart in the *Financial Times* stated, 'Patricia Bardon's rich-toned Hedwige adds lustre to every scene in which she takes part.'

For her own part, she was happy about her performance, though she found the opera itself, here sung in French, rather heavy. Like everyone else, though, she was interested in the performance of American tenor Chris Merritt in the demanding role of Arnold. While she does not consider the voice itself beautiful, she found it extraordinary insofar as he can hit the high Cs and hold them. 'It's a naturally high voice', she said, 'and it struck me that he could go on all night pouring out those high notes.'

Next, she was off to Wales to record *Eugene Onegin*, singing the role of Olga, and with a cast that included Thomas Hampson as Onegin and Kiri Te Kanawa as Tatyana. She felt privileged, she said, to be part of such a brilliant cast. It was her first major recording and she and the other singers spent most of nine days in a studio in Swansea, with Charles Mackerras conducting the Welsh National Opera Orchestra. She admitted that at first she was somewhat apprehensive about recording, but soon felt at ease and began to enjoy the experience. 'I've never felt out of my depth with anyone in the business as long as I can hold my own singing I'm happy.'

It was during her assignment in Wales that Matthew Epstein, general director of WNO, said to her, 'Pat, you should start singing some fast music, I mean Rossini.' She was surprised to hear this for some people thought she wasn't particularly suited vocally to Rossini's music, though this was not the way she looked at it. She sang two arias from the composer's *Semiramide* and almost immediately the new ENO musical director Carlo Rizzi, as well as Epstein, were impressed. At this time they were thinking of a new WNO production of the opera and were apparently making tentative casting plans.

Later, Epstein told her that he had had a phone call from Marilyn Horne who was scheduled to sing Arsace in *Semiramide* in Venice saying that she was unable to go on; she had injured her knee and was hospitalised. He suggested to Patricia Bardon that she go to Venice to audition for the part.

She went home and had a ring from her agent telling her that flight arrangements had been made for her to fly to Venice next day. There, she was auditioned by John Fisher, musical director at Teatro La Fenice, and afterwards to her surprise asked when she could begin rehearsals. She arranged to take an apartment in Venice and in due course was joined by her mother May.

Singing the title role was the Italian soprano Mariella Devia, an experienced Rossini singer and a name familiar to La Scala and Metropolitan audiences. Patricia would share the role of Arsace with Ewa Podles and sing two performances in that November 1992. The conductor was the American Henry Lewis.

To her disappointment, she had practically no rehearsal and actually didn't get a run through with the orchestra, a fact that made her debut all the more daunting. 'Naturally I was anxious', she said. 'I was told there would be a number of important Italian and foreign agents at my first performance, so I considered it inexplicable to be asked to go on without rehearsal time with the orchestra.'

Something unexpected happened also on the night to increase her anxiety. The audience booed the tenor Luca Canonici and showed their hostility to him in no uncertain manner. To Patricia Bardon, it was uncalled-for behaviour and undeserving and she was upset.

'It's a funny feeling to be on stage when an audience is loudly booing one's colleague in the cast. He was an Italian tenor and although his voice is not really suited to Rossini, he did his best. As the booing continued, I was terrified and felt very nervous. Being the only foreigner in the cast, I said to myself that if the audience is going to boo anyone it will probably be me'.

During her second performance, the tenor was booed even more loudly than before, but on this occasion Patricia was prepared for the demonstration. Afterwards, she felt angry about it. 'In my view no singer, however inadequate, should be treated like this. Besides being off-putting to the rest of the cast, it introduces a strained and ugly atmosphere into the theatre. I felt very sorry for Luca Canonici and I hope it will never happen to me. If they considered him that bad they should have reserved their boos at least until he had finished singing; I think he would have understood how they felt.'

Despite the added strain, she was satisfied with her own performances, especially the great duets with Mariella Devia. The music lay within her voice and she was now anxious to sing more Rossini. Writing in *Opera*, Julian Budden opened his critique with lavish praise for Mariella Devia in the title role, describing her flexible technique as faultless, though he feared her lack of inches might debar her from commanding roles, but the vocal and dramatic authority was there.

Budden continued: 'She had an excellent partner in Patricia Bardon, the second Arsace (indeed, her duet with Miss Devia stopped the show, and rightly). Gifted with a rich, dark contralto which she combines with an effortless mastery of coloratura (something that no singer of her type would seem to have attempted fifty years ago), Miss Bardon carried off the trouser role with considerable bravura. If she can lighten her upper range and overcome a habit of dwelling fractionally too long on sustained notes, she may well prove the Marilyn Horne of the Nineties.'

The critic did not pull his punches with regard to tenor Luca Canonica, and stated: 'The only serious miscasting was Luca Canonica as Idreno. He has a number of assets – a pleasing timbre, youthful looks and an engaging stage presence – but a florid technique is not among them. I would have gladly foregone his aria in Act 2; and so evidently, would the audience.'

When I talked to Patricia Bardon later, she could hardly disguise her satisfaction about her triumph in Venice. It prompted her, I believe, to travel on to Milan for an audition at La Scala. Although Riccardo Muti was not present, she said 'everyone else seemed to be.' In the room she sat facing three members of the Scala music staff who asked her what roles she had sung – and where. They were especially interested in her Semiramide in Venice. Afterwards she sang arias by Rossini (*Tancredi*) and Massenet (*Werther*).

She felt the audition went well and while in Italy acquired an Italian agent and is now thinking of getting an American one.

When I met her in London early in 1993, she looked relaxed. She admitted it had taken a long time to build up the kind of confidence she now possessed. 'I feel that my technique is very secure', she reflected. 'I know what lies within my voice and I know when to say no to a particular part. It takes a long time to feel totally comfortable on the operatic stage; every opera is a new experience and makes new demands on one. I remember how I felt before I sang in Jurgen von Rose's new opera, *Dream Palace* in Munich. I feared that it was going to mess up my voice, but it didn't turn out that way at all: my voice was never in such good shape after it. I think if you're technically secure you can sing a whole variety of roles. Occasionally, when I've a problem, I ring Ronnie Dunne in Dublin and ask her what she thinks. Her advice is usually sound and I still, of course, value it.'

She was aware by now, too, of Veronica's Dunne's perception of marriage in relation to singers like herself. Patricia agreed there was some advantage in being single as a singer, if only for the fact that there was less emotional pressure caused by partings for operatic engagements or family commitments. Yet, it was in her view unwise to generalise and claim you can't have a successful singing career if you happen to be married.

'I'm in favour of singers marrying one another', she said, 'for at least we can appreciate the problems and the great demands on us as singers. I'll probably end up marrying somebody in the business, though not necessarily a tenor or a baritone, but I'm not in any hurry. I'm enjoying myself and coping with the pressures of an international singing career.'

Part of her enjoyment stems from the variety of her work; she is now a busy concert and oratorio artist as well as a rising operatic star. Although she finds that opera takes up a lot of rehearsal time, it is on her own admission her first love. 'I certainly love the excitement of a gala night and the satisfaction that singing well can mean to me. I feel I've so much more to do and that too is a challenge.'

And her biggest challenge to date? That came at the Champs Elysees, Paris late in 1993 when she sang the title role in Handel's rarely performed opera, *Orlando*, premiered in 1733 and though it won critical acclaim at the time, it ran only for ten performances. Patricia Bardon sang five performances in Paris and will this year sing it again in Antwerp and New York. 'I consider the role of Orlando as the single greatest challenge of my career,' she told me. 'Apart from the difficulty of the extreme florid arias, the mental deterioration into total madness proved to be a very satisfying character study. I was happy with the way the critics received my performance.'

She is looking forward to singing Carmen in the future, but at the age of 30 she is in no hurry. Vocally the role holds no fears for her, she says, and she sees the real challenge in the acting and dancing and the projection of Carmen's fiery temperament. 'Yes, I want to do the opera, but only when the time is right for me.'

Veronica Dunne, who still takes a great interest in her career, believes that Patricia will one day make an outstanding Carmen, although she warns her not to rush into it, saying, 'Since I've sung the role I know the pitfalls. Some modern international mezzos who have sung it too early in their careers are now paying the price.'

Patricia Bardon also hopes to sing more Wagner and Verdian roles such as Eboli and Amneris. Her diary is fairly full and in the summer of 1994 she sang a Mahler concert at the Edinburgh Festival and adores the composer's music for the voice. 'My schedule for the moment is wild,' she said with a typical laugh from her London apartment, which I took to mean that she has little time to herself. In fact she would be soon off to Cardiff to rehearse Welsh National Opera's new production of *Beatrice & Benedict*. In an overcrowed profession she is among the fortunate ones, which to me at least is no surprise; indeed she has still, I feel, to reach her full potential.

Chapter Nineteen

Alison Browner

ACCLAIM IN WEXFORD

It was no fault of Dublin-born mezzo-soprano Alison Browner that her name was not better known in operatic circles in Ireland in the early 1990s. Like some other of her gifted Irish colleagues she was singing successfully on the Continent and though she sang at the Wexford Festival in 1988 in a double bill of operas by Gazzaniga (*Don Giovanni*) and Busoni (*Turandot*) she was still not a star in the eyes of the Irish.

In 1991 Elaine Padmore, the festival's Artistic Director, invited her to sing the role of Aurelio in Donizetti's *L'Assedio di Calais*. It was another neglected opera taken off the shelf and dusted down in the hope of reviving its popularity. Few Wexford Festival-goers would have heard of its existence, yet as events were to prove, it did not deserve to be overlooked for so long.

Written in 1836, the plot concerns the siege of Calais in 1347 when Edward III's terms of surrender demanded that six of the citizens be handed over for execution. As one would expect of an early 19th century opera, the story is seen not from a political viewpoint but from the human side. Festival audiences loved Donizetti's exciting and flowing melodies, the opera's stirring choruses and the brilliant team of the principals. Director Francesca Zambello had brought alive the feelings of despair and sacrifice in a movingly dramatic manner.

For Alison Browner, it was a personal triumph. In the trouser role of

Aurelio, she cut a military bearing and sang in true bel canto-style, at once warm and lyrical. The opening of Act II, in which husband and wife console each other in the besieged city, is the musical gem of the score. It's a duet for soprano and mezzo of the kind lovers of Donizetti's music adore. Ann Panagulias, fresh from her impressive Natasha in San Francisco's *War and Peace*, blended beautifully with Ms. Browner.

Hilary Finch in *The Times* was prompted to write: 'The opera shows Wexford casting at its best. The tiny Theatre Royal flatters the smallest voices, but Alison Browner is something else besides. Germany has heard more of her so far than Ireland; her intelligent and richly expressive Aurelio is the dominant memory, although this is by no means a single-star opera. Ann Panagulias's Eleanora, Victor Ledbetter's Mayor Eustachio and Elizabeth Woollett's Isabella of England all made their mark under the sympathetic baton of Italian bel canto expert Evelino Pido'.

Richard Fairman in the *Financial Times* summed up: 'Alison Browner was a marvellous Aurelio, effortlessly fluent. It hardly seems right that an opera ignored for a century and a half should leave its audience so elated. Wexford has found a winner and Donizetti's reputation as a composer of serious operas stands immeasurably enhanced.'

Off-stage Alison Browner is a single-minded and vital person and she attributed the success of *L'Assedio di Calais* to thorough preparation and to a director and conductor who had a thorough knowledge of bel canto-style. 'I found the whole thing exciting', she told me, 'and the response by the audience wonderful.'

Her tour-de-force performance caused one to regret that Ireland hadn't seen her more in opera. In a way the Wexford Festival does serve a useful purpose in being able to engage talented artists like Alison Browner without running a financial risk, as would be the case with the DGOS Opera Ireland. From my long experience of Wexford, I've seldom seen a singer make such an immediate impact as this young Irish mezzo-soprano. She brought a real buzz to the Theatre Royal, where, incidentally, she adores singing, and for days afterwards had festival-goers talking about her performance. Wexford, used to vocal excellence, can be slow at times to acclaim visiting artists, so Alison Browner could be proud of her achievement.

In May 1990 she had won acclaim at Covent Garden, where she was engaged to sing title role of Rossini's *La Cenerentola*. She had already sung the role in German, but this would be her first time in Italian. As she was being recalled at the final curtain and accorded sustained applause, Dubliner Hugh Maguire, Leader of the orchestra, must have been tempted to shout *brevi*, for some years before Alison had played violin in the Irish Youth Orchestra, of which he was principal guest conductor.

For the Dublin girl, it was a night to remember. Dining with friends afterwards in a nearby restaurant, she was asked what it was like for her to appear on a stage on which stars like Sutherland and Pavarotti had sung. In a light voice, she replied, 'Well, I knew in a general way that it was going to be a big occasion but, honestly, when it came to it I was prepared for it in the normal way and felt nothing more than the usual nervous tingle. I was nervous, though, when I went out to take my curtain call as I had no idea how I was going to be received.

'The whole experience of working here was quite wonderful, and I'll always remember the way I was welcomed and helped by everyone at Covent Garden. I've already been asked back to do *Idomeneo*, but that depends on whether Mannheim will release me.'

At the table, surrounded by admirers she was happy but obviously still tensed up after the performance. She held a glass of champagne in her hand, a rare enough event in her life. 'I drink only very occasionally: it makes my voice descend too low.'

She had a busy schedule before her. Next morning, she would fly to Mannheim to sing in *Elektra*, an opera which she admitted she 'absolutely hated'. Two days later it was back to England to rehearse *Idomeneo* with Eliot Gardner; this would be performed twice in the same week in Paris. Sandwiched in between these performances was Mozart's *C Minor Mass*, the prospect of which excited her.

The London critics had praised her *Cenerentola*, although, today Alison confesses she was perhaps somewhat overawed and could not fully appreciate the occasion. Writing later in *Opera*, Rodney Milnes stated: 'Two changes of cast for the final performances of the run made the world of difference. Irish mezzo Alison Browner's warm, velvety tone proved ideal for the title role, and her technique equal to anything that Rossini threw at her. In time she may find more delight in her virtuosity - she is in no sense a show-off any more than Cenerentola is, but her triumph could sparkle more - and extra penetration in the lower register, which is all there and seamlessly joined to the rest but comparatively gentle. Rather that, though, than the artificial baritone register favoured and then hurled at us unsparingly by some other Rossini mezzos. A fine house debut by Ms. Browner, and well in character.'

It was a more relaxed Alison Browner I met in Dublin in 1993. Vivacious and good-humoured as ever, she sipped her coffee and was happy to recall for me the events that had shaped her life as a singer. For example, at twelve she knew she wanted to make a career in singing and was lucky, she says, to have been surrounded by encouraging voices. By the time she sat for her Leaving Certificate in Crumlin she had started taking singing lessons from Anne-Marie O'Sullivan at the College of Music.

Before that, at school, she had been helped by Cait Cooper, who recalled that Alison had a grand sense of musical style. Cait was a big help to her. Earlier, as a child, Alison had been taught singing by Leo Maguire and her first musical guardian was Mother Cecily in Loreto Convent, Crumlin, who thrust a violin into her hand when she was only bridge-high to a cello. Later on she joined the Goethe Institute Choir where she was constantly encouraged by Cait Cooper. With the choir she learned about oratorio, but knew nothing about opera. She is a cousin of former DGOS baritone, J.C. Browner and her family take a close interest in music.

After sitting for her Leaving Certificate in 1974, she began to regard music more seriously and continued her lessons once a week with Anne-Marie O'Sullivan. 'I was always mezzo', she says, 'and Anne helped me to discover music.'

When Trinity College, Dublin, started a new honours course in music she enrolled – there were only six others in the class. She regarded it as a very academic course, comprising music composition and history, but felt it was most useful to her. During her four years in Trinity, she still studied singing with Anne-Marie O'Sullivan, who occasionally advised her to go abroad to continue with her studies. In 1978, she graduated with a B.A. music degree.

But where was she to continue her vocal studies? The problem, Alison Browner remembers, was solved by her teacher. 'By chance, Anne had been listening to German baritone Hans Hotter on radio and suggested I try to get him to take me on. It looked no easy task. I was twenty-one, somewhat shy, and maybe wasn't as courageous as some of the young Irish singers of today. Admittedly I was well qualified and had my Higher Diploma in teaching as well as in music and English, but I hadn't learned to speak German at college and wondered how I'd fare without the language in Germany.'

She applied to numerous colleges and eventually was given an audition by the Royal College of Music and succeeded in winning a three-year scholarship. At the same time Cait Cooper urged her to apply to the German government for a scholarship and with her application forwarded tapes of arias by Rossini and songs by Schumann. The authorities in Bonn were impressed enough to inform her that she could sit an official entrance examination. 'I considered this rather vague', she recalled, 'but as luck would have it there was a German baritone called Claus Ocker doing masterclasses at Dublin's Royal Irish Academy of Music and since he was also professor of singing at the Hochschule in Hamburg, Jane Carty, of the music department of RTE, suggested that I apply to him there. They offered an attractive scholarship and I travelled to Hamburg for an audition and was accepted. I had an instinctive feeling that Germany was the right place for me, so I decided not to accept the London offer. I also told myself that it would be wrong not to go to Hamburg just because I couldn't speak German.'

Alison was lucky again when Brian Boydell asked her to sing at a function in Trinity College during which a wealthy German entrepreneur was scheduled to make a presentation to the college for its restoration of buildings on the campus. When she told him that she was bound for Hamburg, he invited her to stay for a few weeks with himself and his wife.

'I couldn't believe it', she says today. 'I flew to Hamburg a few weeks later and arrived at the airport about 10 o'clock at night. Since I couldn't speak a word of German, I had written my benefactor's address on a piece of paper and on arriving at the railway station from the airport handed it to the taxi driver. Seemingly, to get to the address we had to go through the notorious red light district and as I sat uneasily in the back seat I thought to myself: If the taxi stops now and I have to get out, what am I going to do? To my relief, the taxi drove on at some speed and eventually the driver stopped outside a building that in the half-light looked like a palace. I stayed there for two weeks and was treated like a royal guest.'

It was by now 1979 and soon she enrolled at the Hochschule with Americans, Japanese and Germans and studied there for a year, with special emphasis on opera. Whenever Anne-Marie O'Sullivan was in touch with her she enquired about Hans Hotter and if Alison had approached him. By this time Alison had met Wilhelm Gries, a young fellow student at the college. In the previous year he had made his escape from East Germany and was now eager to become an operatic tenor. Since she was making only slow progress in learning German Alison found it sometimes difficult to understand her boyfriend, but she did manage to convey to him her eagerness to meet Hans Hotter. Gries acted quickly. He discovered Hotter's home address in Munich and one afternoon drove there alone in the hope of seeing the popular baritone.

Hotter, who was in his dressing gown, opened the door to him. Gries said nervously, 'Can I speak to you, sir?' Hotter looked at him and as Gries began to explain that he had come to see him on behalf of his Irish girlfriend, he was invited briefly inside. The famous singer must have been impressed by Gries' earnestness, for he agreed to see Alison Browner within a week.

No one was more surprised than Alison herself. She was also elated by

Wilhelm Gries' enterprise. When eventually she met Hans Hotter at his home, he was cordial and tried to make her feel relaxed. He was by now in his late sixties but obviously in good health. 'I remember he wanted to know about my background in Dublin', she recalled, 'and why I was so anxious to be a singer. Then he sat at the piano and accompanied me in some Lieder and in a Rossini aria. After a pause, he said, "It is a very good voice. I am glad to see you have got no major problems with your voice, but there are, shall I say, one or two things that we have got to work on. You understand? You continue to sing as you always sing; you are one of the lucky ones.'

He enquired about her years at Trinity College in Dublin and how her studies in Hamburg were progressing, as though to satisfy himself further before making a final decision. Alison would learn later that Hotter always adopted this detailed approach as he regarded the pupil-teacher relationship as a personal thing. Before she left his elegant house, which he shared with his wife Helga, he told her he was prepared to give her voice lessons whenever he could. Alison hardly knew what to say. And she was delighted for another reason – his connection with Richard Strauss. She had been told that he had studied with the great composer, which meant that she could go over Strauss roles with him.

At this time Hans Hotter was professor of singing at the Conservatoire in Vienna, but Alison wasn't keen to go there. In the meantime, she had heard that the Studio of the Bavarian State Opera was looking for mezzos and she auditioned and was accepted. Wilhelm Gries had by now moved to Munich and was taking lessons with a Swiss tenor, so they could continue seeing each other. 'We had a lot in common outside of music', she said 'And we had lots of fun together.'

Whenever she had enough money, she went along to Hotter for a singing lesson; he divided his time between Munich and Vienna. He could be very demanding and once made her sing an aria a dozen times to get it the way he wanted. The lesson was normally of an hour's duration - never any longer. She was aware this was comparatively short, certainly by comparison with Elizabeth Schwarzkopf who was known to spend six hours over one lesson. Singing teachers, Alison always felt, should not take over one's life. There were singers, she knew, who would not move an inch without consulting their teacher.

'My work with Hans Hotter has been very rewarding', she says. 'He will never tell you how good you are, but rather what you have to learn. The biggest danger I see in the world of opera today is for voices like mine – I'm not a screamer – to be used in the wrong way. I haven't a big voice, I've a good voice, a healthy voice, and the problem is that audiences listen to videos and watch television and think that if you don't scream your guts out they've been cheated and complain they didn't get their money's worth. You have got to be cautious and not be led by public opinion.

'During his long career, Hans Hotter has sung heavy Wagnerian roles, roles that demand a big, powerful voice, but he once told me that the only way he could continue singing them was by being careful with his voice. As he put it, "I sing Wagner for a long time because I have good technique. I preserve my voice. I do not shout." His advice to me was to let other singers scream their heads off, but you ... you sing with your natural voice and never let yourself want to do something that your voice isn't right for. If you can sing Mozart properly you can sing anything.'

When he said that a singer to sing Lieder had to be a true musician, she presumed he was right. And his approach to teaching was, she felt, summed up in his words, 'Just as the performer needs to gain the audience, the teacher needs to win students by being human, not weak, but having trodden the same path which they maybe finding so difficult.' He emphasised that much more was expected of today's singers, in the way of acting but he was quick to note that this can be learned, particularly for opera.

She was now 24 and decided it was time to audition for German agents who would decide to which of the country's opera houses she would be sent for audition. Eventually she auditioned in Berlin and Frankfurt and other German houses, but finally settled for Darmstadt, near Frankfurt, mainly because of the opportunities it afforded her to sing important roles. If she had chosen either Berlin or Munich, she knew it would be a case of minor roles only. She signed a two-year beginner's contract at Darmstadt and was delighted by the faith shown in her by Hans Drewing, the Musical Director.

Looking back, she says it was a particularly happy period of her life. She was in love with Wilhelm Gries and they had fixed their wedding day. Before that, however, they discussed amicably their future roles in the marriage. To Alison Browner this was of crucial importance to their future, the difference perhaps between frustration and happiness. 'I felt that where there were two singers in such an intimate union, it was better for one to step aside, otherwise in my view it doesn't always work. You can't have two big egos needing permanent boosting. Wilhelm, who was keen to teach, anyway, decided to step back. Neither of us have regretted this move.'

The opera house in Darmastadt accommodated 1,000 people and to Alison was ideal for her voice. Hans Drewing was sympathetic to her and helped her along. 'Hans helped to build my confidence; I needed that help. He was at nearly all the stage rehearsals to oversee the parts I was singing like Charlotte in *Werther*, Dorabella (*Cosi fan tutte*) and Ottavia (*L'Incoronazione di Poppea*). Not only that, he didn't hesitate to correct me either vocally or dramatically. Musically, he was a big influence on my career.'

She fitted in some concert engagements and made guest appearances at the Frankfurt opera and sang one of the flower maidens in *Die Walkure* at Bayreuth, conducted by James Levine. After Darmstadt, she moved to Mannheim, which was a different experience from Darmstadt, much more demanding and new singers had to be prepared to step into a role at very short notice. 'I remember singing Orlofsky in *Die Fledermaus* without a single orchestral rehearsal and no stage rehearsal at all. It was fun doing the role but it was kind of nightmarish as well. On another occasion, we were rehearsing the *Barber of Seville* while Figaro was downstairs rehearsing another opera. If I hadn't had the experience of Darmstadt behind me I'd have found it extremely hard to cope.'

Her biggest success in Mannheim was Octavian in *Rosenkavalier* and this, Alison says, was partly due to Hans Hotter's excellent coaching of how to approach the part. Five weeks' rehearsals with an outstanding cast was another contributory factor. And she also got good advice from an old repetiteur at the opera house who had pointed out to her that the orchestra was a big one, but added, 'You must not worry about that: the sign of good singers is that they sing through an orchestra and don't try to get over it. If your technique is good, there is no problem. With Donizetti it is different - you've got to sing over the orchestra; with Strauss it is a mass of sound and if you try to sing over it you will have yourself sung out after twenty minutes.'

It was advice that she has carried with her to every role. At Mannheim it wasn't always easy and she admits that on occasions she had to stand her ground against attempts to miscast her in operas. 'I know what I can sing, and for that I can thank Hans Hotter. He taught me more than anyone else to know my own voice and so know the roles I should not sing. It's easier to know the ones you want to sing.'

To Anne-Marie O'Sullivan, Hans Hotter was the ideal tutor for Alison Browner. She had first heard his magnificent voice on radio and was instantly impressed. Later, she talked to soprano Margaret Marshall, a pupil of his, whom she had met on a music course and she had enthused about his methods. 'I knew then he was the right teacher for somebody of Alison's calibre. She was so fortunate he agreed to take her on.'

She remembered vividly their first meeting. 'I was teaching at the College of Music when one day this young girl arrived with a fiddle under her arm and asked if she could see me. I said, yes. She said she had been told about me and wondered if I could take her for singing lessons. I listened to her sing and almost straightaway agreed to take her on. Her mezzo voice sounded mature for her age and had a lovely quality. Alison was very intelligent, though at the beginning she didn't quite know what she wanted. I could see she enjoyed music and playing the violin, but she was not obsessional about being a singer. She coped very well subsequently at Trinity College with the two disciplines - music and academia.'

They worked together for seven years and Anne felt she had had an important influence on the young singer. 'We were able to communicate at a very high musical level, and I could not say that about everyone who came to me. By the time Alison was twenty her voice was that of a coloratura mezzo and of beautiful texture, yet it was not a big voice by any means. With her good looks and slim appearance, she was well suited for a career in Germany where the combination of voice and appearance can be decided assets. As Violetta, for example, you must look thin and fragile, not fat and robust.'

Voice teachers have a habit of attending their ex-pupils' big operatic and concert engagements, if only to measure a singer's progress. For Anne-Marie O'Sullivan, Alison Browner's Covent Garden debut in *La Cenerentola* was one of the most exciting musical occasions of her life. She deliberately avoided meeting the singer before the performance for fear of making her feel in any way nervous. As she sat in the crowded opera house memories inevitably flooded back. 'Hearing Alison sing brought me back fourteen years, to a time when I remember she was actually reluctant to sing opera. But gradually she got over that and by the time she went to Germany I had introduced her to roles such as Cinderella, Rosina, Charlotte and Dorabella. Listening to her sing on the Covent Garden stage was not all that different: the voice was as flexible as ever and the coloratura notes simply poured out of her. It made me feel so good, for I had believed in her outstanding talent from the outset, and here I was present at one of her finest moments.'

When they met and hugged each other after the performance, Alison was as usual her witty self, surprisingly calm for so heady an occasion, but of course delighted by the overwhelming audience reception. It struck Anne-Marie O'Sullivan that the singer was always wonderfully at home in costumed roles and could be directed to excel in any part in her repertoire. By comparison she felt that recital and concert work inhibited her and suppressed her innate buoyancy.

They were to meet again in Dublin for another happy event. By now Alison's son was born and christened Benedikt, a name which she said all her in-laws could 'easily pronounce'. The couple had set up home in Limburg (between Koln and Frankfurt) where Alison's husband Wilhelm had got a teaching post. Soon she opted to become a freelance artist and found that she had enough engagements to fulfil her. Working with John Eliot Gardner and his English Baroque ensemble was a stimulating experience, as he was, she discovered a perfectionist musically. And she was able to accept more and more engagements in other European opera houses and thus extend her repertoire. Hard work had not affected her quick wit and lively personality. 'Alison has done very well in the world of mezzos', said Anne-Marie O'Sullivan. 'As long as she has her voice and her Trinity degree in music she'll never want.'

Anne might have also added her ex-pupil's enduring love affair with Ireland, for Alison Browner eagerly looks forward to visits home with her husband Wilhelm and their six-year old son Benedikt. In the summer of 1994 she was back to give a Lieder recital at the Kilkenny Arts Festival, accompanied by Breda Zakotnik, from Salzburg, who regularly gives courses in Austria and overseas on music interpretation. Apart from the pleasure she gave in the atmospheric St. Canice's Cathedral in songs by Mendelssohn, Schubert, Schumann and Wolf, the occasion was special for Alison as she told me afterwards in Butler House, where she was staying with Wilhelm.

'I am re-discovering the joys of Lieder singing and having Breda as accompanist is so wonderful for me. Before I left Dublin for Germany fourteen years ago I did a considerable amount of Lieder singing, but afterwards concentrated on opera. Now I want to divide my time between opera, oratorio and Lieder. I agree that I'm singing to a selective and fastidious audience when I sing Lieder, but that doesn't lessen the joy for me. I intend, for instance, to sing more of Hugo Wolf's songs and I'm lucky that Breda is an authority on the composer.'

Alison, who would be returning to the '94 Wexford Festival to sing in Rubinstein's *The Demon*, had put on weight, a fact she made light of in Kilkenny with a hearty laugh, though her voice is in fine shape. She wants to sing more Strauss and Rossini, but she is happy and relaxed with the way her career is progressing. 'There have been ups and downs,' she admitted, 'but every singer experiences them. Nowadays I am inclined to pick and choose; if an operatic director or conductor is not right for me I'll say no to a new production. What's the good in going through torture at rehearsals with difficult people? There are plenty of places where I am wanted as a Mozart, Rossini and Strauss singer, so I don't experience any air of desperation when I look at my diary. It helps, too, that Wilhelm has a good job in Germany so we have what you might call some security. I tend to keep to the venues in Europe that like my voice, though I'm off to South America next year. I would also like to sing more opera in Ireland, but in Dublin that doesn't seem possible.'

Other outstanding Irish artists abroad might be tempted to echo the same sentiment.

Chapter Twenty

Virginia Kerr

'THE AIR IS CLEAN IN CLONEE'

Home for Virginia Kerr is 'Sunnybank', a charming Edwardian house near the village of Clonee, County Meath. Here, removed from the hectic concert and operatic scene, she can truly relax. It is a convenient house, too, being only 25 minutes by car to the National Concert Hall and 30 minutes' drive to Dublin airport. The soprano has undoubtedly the best of two worlds.

In every way it is a home for her. She was born up the road from 'Sunnybank', where her father was a well-known horse trainer. The 80-year-old house had belonged to a local farmer and when it came up for auction Virginia Kerr nearly let is slip through her hands. 'My solicitor was bidding for me. When it came to a six-figure bid, he stopped. I got a fright and immediately gave him a nudge. "Keep bidding, for God's sake!". He did, and by the end of the auction the house was mine.'

She had set her heart on it. 'I love the place. Not only has the village happy memories for me but it's a magical world to come back to after performances in Britain or on the Continent. And, as I always tell my friends, the air is clean in Clonee – that's crucial for my voice.'

In conversation, she leaves you in no doubt that she would never want to live anywhere else. She has three cats, of whom Pushkin is her favourite. If she ever wanted to farm there are outbuildings and a few acres of land. Without trying to appear sentimental, she told me, 'The moment the plane touches down at Dublin airport I feel that almost indefinable sense of homecoming, a longing inside me to get back as quickly as possible to Clonee. I'm away a lot from home these times, but I do try to get back as often as possible.'

Sharing 'Sunnybank' with Virginia is the conductor Colman Pearce, who bought most of the paintings that adorn the walls of the house. He admits that at first he found it difficult adapting to country life because of the extra travel it entailed, but gradually regarded distance as no real obstacle. As he says, 'I suppose you could say that both of us are homebirds.'

In the 1980s Virginia left London for good having lived there for almost nine years. 'I had no intention of sitting by the telephone waiting for something to happen. I came back to Dublin and was lucky to find concert and operatic work.'

From an early age she had shown promise as a singer. As a boarder at Mount Sackville Convent, where she went after her mother's death, she was taught singing by Sister Peter. 'When I was fifteen, Sister Peter put on an operetta. I had done piano previously, but I went along under sufferance. When Sister told me she would like to train me, I thought of the whole thing as a way of getting off studies, but I soon got hooked.'

She went on to win every feis and competition she entered for and the next stage was studying with Michael O'Higgins at the Royal Irish Music Academy while working in her father's business. She was enjoying herself and music meant a lot, but she didn't put her all into it. Not until she won the Player-Wills Bursary in 1974.

Virginia Kerr chose to study at the Guildhall School in London, where she met Rudolf Piernay, a strict German disciplinarian who was held in awe by his students. He was to have a powerful influence on her musical career. 'One of the wonderful things about him was that he spoke about seven languages, including Russian and Czech, so he let you off the hook for absolutely nothing', she recalled. She herself is relatively fluent in German, French and Italian.

At the end of her Guildhall studies, having participated in college operas and competitions and recorded for BBC Radio 3, she became seriously ill with thrombosis and glandular fever. She was 24 at the time and it looked like her career was coming to a premature end.

For two years she was unable to sing and began to lose interest in music. Even when she went back to Michael O'Higgins, her singing teacher at the R.I.A.M. in Dublin, her heart was not in it. 'I started working in a restaurant and was having a good time. I had a singing lesson every morning, but I didn't see much point in the whole thing. I'm sure that Michael was disappointed with my attitude, though he surprised me one day when he suggested that I give my coming-out recital.'

However, when he died in the middle of the preparations Virginia was almost ready to give up. It was her accompanist Jeannie Reddin along with Father Owen Murphy, the head of the Adult Education Institute, who organised the recital for her. 'If it hadn't been for them I don't know what I'd have done.'

Looking back, she doubts whether she would actually have given up singing altogether. 'I don't think I was prepared to go that far, although I was in a depressed state after the attack of glandular fever. I was lucky, too, in another respect, my voice was not affected when I returned to singing after eighteen months. I was terribly relieved naturally and very grateful.'

Performing some years later with Irish National Opera proved an inspiration to her. She came in near the end of INO's days and remembers singing Donna Anna in *Don Giovanni* in towns in the west of Ireland. 'We'd drive out of Dublin on a Friday afternoon and a few hours later would arrive in a small town where we'd have something to eat. If you were lucky, the local hall had heating, if not the cast sang in the cold. For young singers it was practical training as you were often performing under almost impossible conditions. I don't think we worried about niceties like acoustics or whether a production visually looked well. I'll always remember how attentive were the audiences and the warmth of their reception to us. In my book, bringing opera to the people could have its compensations.'

With the demise of Irish National Opera, singers like herself experienced a musical vacuum and Virginia felt that something must be done.

Winning the Golden Voice of Ireland competition was an incentive and along with a friend – Joe Browne, a baritone from Gorey – discussed the possibility of forming their own opera company.

Browne shared her enthusiasm and suggested that *The Marriage of Figaro* should be their initial choice. The new company was aptly called Young Irish Artists and rehearsals began within a few weeks. Virginia was not unaware of the risks she and Joe Browne were taking, but was more concerned that the company was about to fill a void in the Irish operatic world.

'There was nothing else for young singers at the time', she recalled. 'Few of them got a chance to sing with a professional orchestra or work with a professional conductor or director. Ben Barnes was beginning to direct at this time and agreed to take charge of *Figaro* for us. I remember it as a fantastic period, as the birth of any new company can be. Jim Golden, chairman of the Wexford Festival, let us come in under the festival umbrella in that May 1981, which of course was a great feather in our caps. It meant also that we could have the Theatre Royal for three consecutive nights; and festival director Adrian Slack was most helpful to us. Prionnsias O Duinn laid his reputation on the line when he agreed to conduct an *ad hoc* orchestra, and the Arts Council gave us a grant.'

She admitted, however, that it was nerve-racking for her, as she soon learned that combining company business and singing was no easy task. She was lucky with the singers available. Figaro would be sung by Joseph Corbett, Susanna by Nicola Sharkey, with Paul Kelly filling the role of Basilio. She cast herself as the Countess and Joe Browne was the Count. Monica Frawley agreed to design the set. Final rehearsals were held in Wexford's Theatre Royal.

To Virginia's relief on the first night word was conveyed to her backstage that the house was full. At least I can pay the orchestra, she thought. Not knowing how the opera would be received, and obviously nervous, Jim Golden left the Theatre Royal before curtain-up and went off for a meal and a drink. Two hours later he arrived back to hear, as Virginia Kerr put it, 'the rafters being lifted off the roof of the theatre' and with that he dashed into her dressing room and threw his arms around her, saying excitedly, 'We did it!

'We did, Jim', she replied, still in a state of emotion. She had found the closing scene of the opera unbearably moving. 'I'll never forget the feeling singing "Dove sono" and at the end the spontaneous burst of applause', she recalled. 'It was a wonderful atmosphere as the whole theatre took up the applause. It was my first taste of what it could be like in an opera house.'

For the following two nights the same enthusiastic scenes were repeated, as if Wexford audiences were intent on giving Young Irish Artists a vote of confidence. The veteran *Irish Times* critic Charles Acton summed up, 'In many ways it was a triumph of an idea. The singers were all young Irish artists, and one aim was for them to show that we have young singers with the vocal and dramatic talents to stage professional opera properly and with a future. And not just a make-shift hall, but in a theatre whose context is opera of international standard. They came very close to a complete success.'

Other Dublin critics had come to Wexford with no idea of what standard to expect; all, without exception, had gone home agreeably surprised. If it wasn't Anna Caleb's delightful Cherubino, it was Randal Courtney's convincing Bartolo, and Virginia Kerr was rather pleased with the notices she got. She said she decided to stage *Cosi fan tutte* in the following year, but again experienced worrying moments as she looked around the Theatre Royal's auditorium and spotted more than a few empty seats. With the Arts Council having been unable to donate the same amount as the previous year, money was in short supply. Virginia Kerr wondered once more whether she would have enough to pay the orchestra, but admirers of the company's work rallied round to save the day.

Two years later the company presented *The Carmelites,* and although Virginia did not sing in the opera, she remained the driving force behind it. After that, the company began to disband. She herself was getting engagements increasingly abroad. Joe Browne could not afford time off from his business commitments and both Anna Caleb and Nicola Sharkey were in demand elsewhere, and soon Frances Lucey would be off to Germany.

'I think we lasted as long as we needed to', Virginia Kerr says today. It had been a good and happy experience and everybody learned something from it. And there were others, like Ronnie Dunne, who are now pre-pared to carry on the idea where we left off.'

It was inevitable that her impressive press notices would attract the DGOS. She made her debut with the society as Micaela in *Carmen* and went on to sing the slave girl Liu in Puccini's *Turandot,* a role she counts as among her most successful. But it was in her next appearance with the society, as Leila in Bizet's *Les Pecheurs de Perles* that her name came really into prominence.

In the December of 1987 Mike Ashman was engaged by the DGOS to direct the opera and Virginia would remember it for the 'business' he demanded of her in various scenes. For instance, in the first act she was raised some ten feet above the stage in an iron swing and remained sway-ing there until the curtain fell. In the second she had to chase in floating draperies around and over a ring of short lighted candles set on the floor; and in the third act she was obliged to skip her way over a stage-full of prone bodies in a full-length strait jacket which curtailed her use of her arms and balance.

Despite the restrictions imposed on her, the critics agreed that she sang 'surprisingly well'. Mary MacGoris in the *Irish Independent* said she sang with 'beguiling warmth' but felt Mike Ashman's 'whizzes and notions' hadn't much relevance to the opera. In the *Irish Times*, Michael Dervan called her performance 'riveting', while John Brophy in the *Irish Press* commented on the 'courage' of Virginia Kerr, whom he said 'lived dan-gerously' in this production.

Discussing the presentation with Virginia, I recalled the reaction of the critics and the stage demands different operatic directors can make these days on singers. 'Personally', she said, 'I loved Mike Ashman's daring approach. I'll try anything as long as it doesn't affect my voice or my singing. At the same time you have to be strong enough to say to a director, "This doesn't suit me. I don't agree with it. Can we do it another way?" More often than not you'll get your own way, but if you go into a rehearsal with a bullying attitude or looking for a fight, you'll not get your own way. When in doubt I usually say, "I'll try this, but I don't think 'twill work", and I find I get my way. Once, I remember this soft approach failed. We were rehearsing a Richard Jones' production of *The Valkyrie* and he had eight of us on stilts. I couldn't see the point of this and pointed it out to him. He persisted, though, and we did perform on stilts. Not only did I find it difficult and risky, but virtually impossible to sing. I was surprised we didn't all fall off the stilts.'

'Opera is essentially a music form and I don't believe that directors should dominate the scene. It should be a question of compromise, with the singers also having a vital say. I have worked with some talented directors, among them Mike Ashman, Ben Barnes, Patrick Mason, Ian Spink and the German mezzo soprano Brigitte Fassbaender who directed me in Leeds. She was a joy to work with and a great influence on my career. She's a real singer's director and I'm afraid she spoilt me. Where else can I hope to find a woman of operatic intelligence as her?'

Patrick Mason had directed her for the DGOS in *Don Giovanni*, in which she sang Donna Elvira. She respects his musicianship and enjoyed enormously working with him. Mason had set the opera in the early 1960's Rome and aided by designer Joe Vanek, evoked the La Dolca Vita atmosphere of the period brilliantly without betraying Mozart or librettist Da Ponte. Unfortunately on the first night in the Gaiety Theatre, Virginia Kerr was striken by a virus but bravely carried on and in the circumstances sang extremely well. She counts Mason's direction and the production itself as one of her happiest operatic memories.

So also is *Jenufa* in which she sang the title role for Scottish Opera Go Round in 1988. This production, featuring seven singers and a pianist, was first toured by the company in 1986 and was an immediate hit with audiences in rural areas, including islanders.

The singers, pianist and technical crew went from place to place in a minibus. Virginia was making her debut with the company and has no hesitation in describing the experience as memorable. As she recalled, 'It was one of those special moments in a singer's life that only happens very rarely. We toured the Highlands and lowlands for ten weeks and although it was a small-scale production, it abounded in imaginative touches. The reaction of audiences was fantastic. As we know, Janacek based the opera on true Czech tales and in the Highlands, for instance, the Scottish folk seemed to identify with the characters and conflicts. Our pianist was Dubliner Brenda Hurley and I thought it was an inspired touch having her dressed in black peasant garb playing at the piano. The critics raved about her performance.'

So successful was the production, that it was decided to bring it to the Brighton Festival where it won the classical music award and later it was performed at the London International Opera Festival and again swept the top award. The London critics came in strength to see Matthew Richardson's production. Tom Sutcliffe in the *Guardian* stated: 'Ms. Kerr's handsome Jenufa is quite outstanding, strapping both in voice and frame, capable of colours and control that reveal the hidden strengths in the role.' *The Times* critic Noel Goodwin observed: 'In the title role, Ms. Kerr adds an expressive vocal freshness to her tall graceful presence, the livid scar inflicted on Jenufa's cheek, reinforcing the dignity with which she comes to terms with her foster mother's infanticide.'

What Virginia finds most satisfying about Janacek's operas is the remarkable union of music and drama. The mood was similar in Britten's *The Turn of the Screw*, which she performed with Midlands Opera Company in Birmingham and Opera Theatre Company in Dublin. 'I find that Janacek and Britten can create a chilling sense of realism with the music matching the drama. I find it challenging emotionally and vocally.'

With the parent company Scottish Opera, she sang Donna Elvira in *Don Giovanni* and covered *Salome* for the company. While singing a small role in Janacek's *Katya Kabanova* at Glyndebourne in the early nineties, and covering Nancy Gustavson in *Katya*, she received an urgent message from

Scottish Opera to say they needed her that night to sing Salome.

'It was the first time I'd been asked to go on as a cover', she told me. 'I had rehearsed the part previously with the company, but as I flew into Glasgow I had no idea how it would go now. What worried me was the dance sequence. How could I be sure that I could do it well in the circumstances? It worried me and in a way this was a good thing, for I put aside any worries about the vocals. On the night everything went well for me and I got a lot of congratulations. Next morning I was on the first plane south as I had to go on stage later than morning at Glyndebourne, singing my lines and plucking my chicken.'

The Glasgow experience reminded her forcibly that it was difficult, even if one was so inclined, to get above oneself in opera. As she put it, 'I mean, one night I'm singing Salome and the audience is going crazy because it's my house debut; the next morning I'm down in Glyndebourne rehearsing a small part in an empty theatre and no one is interested in the fact that I'd sung a star role on the previous night. All they are interested in is what is happening for them.'

She is not sure that she would want to sing Salome again, though she's happy the part is now in her repertoire. Directors, she said, were casting Salome and other heavy operatic parts a lot lighter nowadays. In their eyes casting overweight sopranos in these parts did not work visually anymore. 'To my mind, the days are gone when one stood and sang and did little else on stage.'

To the soprano, it is a good thing that those days are virtually vanished. She is inclined to see opera as a complete package, where a singer must be able to sing, act, dance and even walk a trapeze. For sopranos or mezzos to allow themselves to grow fat was nothing but an excuse to over-eat. Audiences wanted credibility in the opera house, their Mimis thin and vulnerable, their Leonoras (*Trovatore*) more robust but not fat. Directors were meeting their wishes.'

Her next role for Scottish Opera came about in an unusual way. She was covering Jenufa in the company's new production and one afternoon was rehearsing when Judith Weir, the composer of *The Vanishing*

Bridegroom, a new opera, was invited into the theatre to hear her sing Janacek's music. After listening for a while, Judith Weir said, 'Yes, she's the one.' She hadn't totally finished writing the soprano role but now intended to gear it to Virginia Kerr's high soprano voice.

The story of The Vanishing Bridegroom is an interweaving of three Highland folk tales. The bridegroom who is spirited away by the fairies in the central story also appears, along with his bride, in the ones which frame it, just as the Devil who (complete with horns and tail) appears in the final scene likewise has parts to play beforehand.

Virginia rehearsed for seven weeks with Ms. Weir in attendance at all the rehearsals. Contemporary music appealed to her and she had sung a good deal of it in Dublin. 'I'm so glad', she said, 'that Judith Weir has written an opera that isn't plink-plonk, where you can't find your note and you can't sing your note anyway. It's a very tuneful piece, a lot of it folky and there's beautiful chorus writing, wonderful harmonies; it's not like anything I've ever heard. And it's nice and high for me. Judith writes well for the voice. People are going to be very taken by it.'

After a successful premiere at the Theatre Royal, Glasgow, where Scottish audiences loved the idiomatic libretto and music, the opera was given a single performance at Covent Garden in December 1990. For Virginia Kerr, this was a real highlight and her first introduction to the famous house. With the production geared for smaller stages in Scotland, the size of the Covent Garden stage posed a problem that was not altogether resolved.

Writing in the *Evening Standard*, critic Paul Griffiths referred to this fact when he stated: 'The impression made by cast was a little less than in Glasgow, but only because the house was too big for the piece.'

Virginia Kerr emerged with an enhanced reputation and she still retains happy memories of the opera. In between operatic engagements, she found time to appear in concerts in Ireland. When she sang in the second of the BBC's Summer Invitation Concerts at the Ulster Hall in Belfast, one critic wrote, 'I have never heard Virginia Kerr in finer voice.'

In January 1992 a new challenge awaited her in Leeds where she was cast by Opera North in Austrian composer Franz Schreker's *Der Ferne Klang*. The opera, the composer's second, had an ecstatic reception at its 1912 Frankfurt premiere, and travelled not only to opera houses in central Europe, but also as far as Russia and Sweden. But Schreker's star waned, largely because of the pressures of Nazi power: as a Jew, he was dismissed from his Viennese posts, performances were disrupted, and he died, disillusioned, in 1934.

What made the Leeds experience unforgettable for Virginia Kerr was the chance it gave her to work with producer Brigitte Fassbaender. She described her approach as inventive, intelligent and inspiring. 'In a way Brigitte has spoiled me for other directors. She was a sheer joy to work with. She's a real singer's director and she influenced me enormously.'

One of her next engagements brought her to Malta and to one of the most beautiful opera houses in which she had ever sung. This was in Valetta where she would sing Musetta in *Boheme* and the Countess in *The Marriage of Figaro*. 'The theatre itself is small', she said, 'but it's exquisite with lovely boxes and an ornate interior. Acoustically, I could find no fault and as for the Maltese, they simply love opera. I was told that both Caruso and Gigli in their day counted it among their favourite houses; in fact, Gigli claimed that if he could satisfy Maltese audiences he could do so anywhere. I agree with him, for they are a very discerning audience and know their opera.'

She was to see the volatile side, though, of the Italians in *Boheme* and was amused by Rodolfo's tantrums as he accused Mimi backstage of trying to upstage him. 'Tenors can feel insecure', she said, 'and can sometimes be impossible, either in the opera house or on the concert platform. And for Italian tenors – they can be the worst prima donnas of all. They're not above flirting on the side and acting the Romeos.'

In Glasgow and Leeds she had found it very different. In these companies singers got on with the job and for the most part temperament didn't enter into it, except occasionally. Thinking back, Virginia Kerr said that working on *Der Ferne Klang* (The Distant Drum) was a happy experience; everybody got on well and for weeks ate together and often went round in groups. It was an extraordinary feeling of camaraderie. On the other hand, she remembered rehearsals of operas when casts didn't pull together and that left a bad taste. Yet she did not see this as altogether surprising.

'The life of an opera singer is a funny business', she reflected. 'I suppose you could say it is also an unnatural career in as much as you live close to other singers for weeks and weeks and suddenly it is all over, the production ends. You may go away and not see these singers again. While you are with them you sometimes see their best and worst sides and this, too, can be revealing. It can also be a miserable existence when things fail to gell in a production and you end up disappointed or bitterly frustrated. I remember Adrian Slack once saying to me, "Don't wear your heart on your sleeve in opera" and he was right, for if you do you'll be hurt. I mean, you can't afford to become totally involved with other singers around you because after a while you leave them, so you've got to remain slightly detached.'

She felt that the world of opera had become much more competitive, but she tried not to think of it in that way. If she thought of competing all the time it would, in her opinion, be very stressful and one would probably end up constantly looking over one's shoulder. 'I feel there's enough work out there and all anyone can do is their best. I've always aimed for the highest artistic standards and it is up to others to say if I achieved them. Opera is a demanding career, often entailing very hard work. Rehearsing *The Valkyries* for Scottish Opera was arduous, painstaking work, so was getting the dance sequences right in *Salome*. It simply means you've got to be as fit as an athlete with the stamina of a long distance runner.'

While singing in *Der Ferne Klang* in Leeds she was spotted by a German agent and recommended for a role in the Leipzig production of *Johnny Speil Auf* (Johnny Strikes Back). It was after the reunification of Germany and she was to spend three weeks in the city, returning later for more performances of the opera.

To Virginia Kerr, first impressions of places can be important and in the case of Leipzig she liked what she saw and the citizens seemed proud and upright. Later, when she visited Brigitte Fassbaender in Munich she was able to compare the contrast between East and West Germany, with the wealth of the western section astounding. Leipzig, for example, was experiencing social violence new to them and running inflation was also having dire effects.

Nor had the opera house escaped. Apart from first nights, attendances were down considerably. At a performance of *Elektra*, sung by a star-studded cast, she was amazed to find the house half empty. Normally it accommodated 1100 people, but on this occasion there could not have been more than 200 present. Virginia attended in all nine different operas and picked out many empty seats in the auditorium. The reason, she was told, was a lack of money, though she wondered if Leipzig had a glut of opera.

For *Johnny Speil Auf* the cast included two Americans as well as German singers. It was accorded a warm reception by the audience. Virginia Kerr enjoyed the experience and playing the role of a flighty diva had its compensations. Having only one rehearsal, however, with the orchestra was in her view unsatisfactory and she hated to think how an inexperienced singer would cope in such circumstances. In that way the German system could be daunting, if not frightening.

Returning to 'Sunnybank' and the quietness of Clonee is, she says, the perfect tonic, indeed a kind of renewal before she gets another call from Germany or elsewhere. In between her travels, she sang Elvira in Rossini's *L'Italiana in Algeri* for DGOS Opera Ireland at the Gaiety Theatre, and in 1993 made a big impression in the central role of the Governess in Opera Northern Ireland's touring production of *The Turn of the Screw*. She remains one of Ireland's true operatic professionals.

Chapter Twenty One

Peter McBrien

SINGING WITH THE STARS

Anyone who has heard him sing Germont or Sharpless will agree that Peter McBrien's strong, resonant baritone is undeniably one of the best operatic voices Ireland has produced for a long time. Moreover, it is a voice that could cope just as well with the music of Wagner or Richard Strauss.

'If Peter had decided in his twenties to go to Germany, I've no doubt he would have made a success there as a singer', was Veronica Dunne's firm belief.

Why then did he decide to remain in his native Dublin when many people, including his musical friends, expected him to try his luck abroad? When I broached the question to him he showed no hint of surprise, obviously expecting it to be asked.

'I was approached twice with offers to go to England as well as Germany', he admitted, 'but for various reasons I turned them down. On the first occasion, I was competing at the Feis Ceoil and the adjudicator, who happened to be a well-known English baritone, suggested that I go to London where he was confident I'd establish a successful operatic career. He said he was prepared to manage my affairs there. Perhaps it was because of over-caution on my part, but I declined to take up his offer, in spite of the fact that he showed great faith in me.

'Later, when I was married with a daughter and was a member of the

RTE Singers, my vocal teacher Michael O'Higgins came up with the German suggestion. He had been to Bayreuth with a number of his students and met the Intendant of an opera house near the festival town who asked him if he could recommend a promising baritone in Dublin. Michael mentioned my name and the Intendant seemingly talked about an early audition.

'I gave the idea certainly more thought than the London invitation, but again I hesitated, mainly I remember because it would have meant uprooting my family and for me giving up a well- paid job. Furthermore, I had no guarantee that I'd be a success in Germany, although Michael O'Higgins had no time for self-doubts, in fact did everything to encourage me to think again. At heart I loved Dublin, so it wasn't easy for one in his early thirties to leave a friendly city and one's friends. My work at RTE also afforded me ample time to take up other singing engagements.'

Thereafter, the question did not arise and he was satisfied to make a contribution to the operatic life of his own city and country. As a boy he studied the violin with Michael McNamara at the Dublin Municipal School of Music, and on Sundays sang as a boy soprano in the Jesuit church in Upper Gardiner Street.

The choir consisted of 20 men and 30 boy sopranos and people came from as far as Skerries to hear them sing at Mass. While young McBrien enjoyed singing, he wanted to make the violin his career and was encouraged by his teacher. His mother, a musical woman, had other ideas. Her son's voice broke sometime after his sixteenth birthday, which was considered late, and when it returned at about the age of 19 it was baritone. To Mrs. McBrien, it possessed a lovely quality and hearing Peter sing delighted her.

One day she spotted an advertisement in a daily newspaper for two scholarships, one vocal, the other instrumental, and said to her son, 'Why don't you apply for the singing scholarship, Peter?'

Since he was still committed to the violin, she wrote for a form to the newspaper and filled it in herself. To her surprise, he won the vocal scholarship. He was sent a list of singing teachers at the college but their names

PETER MC BRIEN... IN THE TITLE ROLE OF VERDI'S 'RIGOLETTO' WITH THE DGOS

LOUIS BROWNE...
AS ALMAVIVA IN ROSSINI'S
'THE BARBER OF SEVILLE'
AT SADLER'S WELLS

IN A BEL-CANTO IN THE SAME
THEATRE

ELIZABETH CONNELL...BECAME AN IRISH CITIZEN TWENTY-TWO YEARS AGO AND IS PROUD OF HER IRISH PASSPORT

AS ODABELLA IN COVENT GARDEN'S EXCITING PRODUCTION OF VERDI'S 'ATTILA' (1993)

HUBERT VALENTINE... DUBLIN-BORN TENOR RUNS
POPULAR CLASSICAL MUSIC RADIO SERIES IN AMERICA

INSET: VALENTINE OFF-STAGE

IN THE TITLE ROLE OF GOUNOD'S 'FAUST'

DR TOM WALSH...

FOUNDER OF THE WEXFORD FESTIVAL IN 1951

BRENDAN CAVANAGH...

SANG WITH THE STARS – A TRULY RELIABLE ARTIST

MARY SHERIDAN – OPERA SOPRANO OF NOTE

MICHAEL O'HIGGINS...RESPECTED

VOICE COACH

TENOR JOHN CAROLAN...

FINE LYRIC VOICE

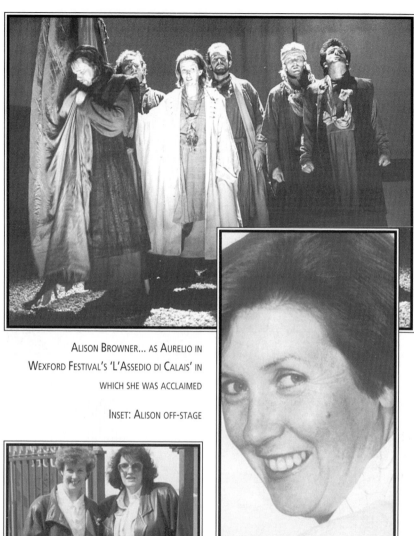

ALISON BROWNER... AS AURELIO IN
WEXFORD FESTIVAL'S 'L'ASSEDIO DI CALAIS' IN
WHICH SHE WAS ACCLAIMED

INSET: ALISON OFF-STAGE

ALISON WITH HER FORMER SINGING TEACHER ANNE-
MARIE O'SULLIVAN OUTSIDE COVENT GARDEN
OPERA HOUSE AFTER HER TRIUMPH IN 'LA
CENERENTOLA'

MEZZO-SOPRANO PATRICIA BARDON... IN THE TITLE ROLE OF HANDEL'S OPERA 'ORLANDO', PARIS, 1994,
IN WHICH SHE WON CRITICAL ACCLAIM

Soprano Angela Feeney... returned to sing Butterfly in her native Belfast, with James Johnston among the full 'house'

Tom Lawlor... came to grand opera via Gilbert & Sullivan performances with D'Oyly Carte

Virginia Kerr... likes the clean air of Clonee

JOHN O'FLYNN... IN THE RING IN WEXFORD FESTIVAL'S 1985 PRODUCTION OF KURT WEILL'S 'THE RISE AND FALL OF THE CITY OF MAHAGONNY' IN WHICH HE SANG ALASKA-WOLF JOE

MARIE-CLAIRE O'RIORDAN... ACCLAIMED FOR HER DGOS PERFORMANCES

MARY HEGARTY... CAUGHT THE 'OPERATIC BUG' IN HER NATIVE CORK

WITH ERIC ROBERTS (FRANK) IN THE DGOS'S 'DIE FLEDERMAUS' AT THE GAIETY THEATRE

REGINA NATHAN... SANG MIMI IN THE DGOS PRODUCTON OF 'LA BOHEME'
OPPOSITE STUART NEILL'S RODOLFO

Bruno Caproni...
the Bangor-born baritone
as Masetto and Angela
Gheorghiu (Zerlina)
in Covent Garden's
'Don Giovanni', in which
Ann Murray sang
Donna Elvira

FRANCES LUCEY... GUARDING
AGAINST THE COLD IN WEXFORD

AS THE PAGE OSCAR WITH
MAURIZIO SALTARIN
(RICCARDO) IN THE DGOS'S
'UN BALLO IN MASCHERA'

THERESE FEIGHAN... SANG AT THE SALZBURG FESTIVAL

KATE MCCARNEY... IS ALWAYS DELIGHTED TO SING IN HER NATIVE BELFAST

did not mean anything to him, though he was intrigued by one - Viani - which he reckoned was foreign and decided to select him. Peter McBrien says today that it was a wise choice and he learned a good deal about vocal technique and interpretation from him. Later, he would go on to study with Michael O'Higgins.

By now he was a member of the RTE Singers, whose repertory was very extensive, and annual overseas tours became an exciting feature of their programme. 'It was great experience for a singer,' he says, 'for not alone were there some fine voices in the group but we sang music by a host of composers, from Monteverdi to Britten.'

The arrival in Dublin of the famous English baritone Denis Noble to teach at the R.I.A.M. resulted in a number of Irish singers, including Peter McBrien, seeking lessons with him. Noble had sung at Covent Garden in the late 1930s and after the Second World War had visited Ireland as a guest star. An outgoing and friendly individual, he was popular in Irish music circles. He was now devoting all his time to teaching.

Peter McBrien had a special reason for going to him. Around this time in the Sixties he was tormented by music people saying his voice was tenor. He became worried, fearful, too, that he was not a baritone and, therefore, running the risk of damaging his voice. He asked Denis Noble for advice.

Noble could be forthright. He seated himself by the piano and remarked with a touch of cynicism, 'So they're telling you you're a tenor?' After a slight pause, Noble added, 'Well, listen to this.'

To McBrien's astonishment, the veteran baritone went up a scale and sang a high C. 'The windows of the Academy nearly fell into Westland Row.'

Noble then turned away from the piano and asked McBrien aloud, 'Am I a tenor? ... No, I'm not. I'll ask you something and it's this - can you live up there in the tenor region?'

Peter McBrien nodded his head. Noble stressed to him the dangers of changing from baritone to tenor and the vocal strain involved. He stayed with Noble for some time and believed he was the right teacher for him. As he said, 'Sometimes you spent half the lesson getting the history of Denis

Noble himself, as the man loved to reminisce about his Covent Garden years and the great artists he had met. Once, as I began to sing "Di Provenza", he raised his hand and said, "Oh, Peter, I used to do a marvellous job on that. Wait and I tell you about the first time I sang with Nelly ...". You were supposed to understand that he was referring to Dame Nelly Melba.'

On another occasion, McBrien came for a lesson but before he began to sing, announced, 'Denis, did you hear the news ... Thomas Beecham has died?' Denis Noble looked at him and sighed, 'Oh, no, Peter!' He turned his back towards the window and took out his handkerchief, as if to cry. In a moment, though, he wheeled round and said, 'That's enough of that ... Tommy wouldn't like it!'

To McBrien, he was not only a character but a lovable man, and for a retired singer in his seventies his voice was in surprisingly good shape. Working with Noble had fired his love of opera and he saw himself singing Verdi, Puccini and even Russian roles.

His chance to sing with the Dublin Grand Opera Society came about in an unusual way. Robert Johnson, the music critic of the *Irish Press* telephoned him one afternoon to say he had been talking to Col. Bill O'Kelly, chairman of the DGOS, who said he was looking for someone to sing Duncairo in *Carmen*. Johnson recommended McBrien, at which the Col. said, 'Send him down to see me.'

He sang for him and immediately afterwards the Colonel remarked, 'Great.' The contracts were signed even before the singer left the room. Looking back, Peter McBrien felt that Col. O'Kelly could easily be misunderstood. 'From the outset I hit it off very well with him. There were others, however, who did not always see it his way. Bill could be abrupt and off-putting; this I expect he inherited from his army days when he got things done his way. When he came to the DGOS he expected his orders to be carried out, and though his approach meant that things were done, he apparently clashed on occasions with singers and producers. To his credit, he did succeed in holding the society together and few will deny that his heart was in opera. Bill wanted Dublin to have the best there was and in this respect he worked miracles.'

The Sixties, he believes, were the golden years of opera in Dublin, a decade notable for the remarkable voices heard at the Gaiety Theatre, although the era had begun in the middle Fifties when singers of the calibre of Paolo Silveri, Caterina Mancini, Plino Clabassi and Virginia Zeani sang in the big Italian seasons. To Peter McBrien and other young Irish singers, it was a spur to them as they listened to outstanding artists and studied their technique and stagecraft. With the coming of the Sixties more names were added, such as Piero Cappucilli, Ebe Stignani, Giuseppe di Stefano, Margherita Rinaldi and Giangiacomo Guelfi. Etched in his mind are Cappucilli's towering Count di Luna, Stignani's awesome Azucena, Gobbi's subtle Scarpia, Zeani's radiant Lucia, Maria Caniglia's engaging Tosca and Labo's brilliantly sung Rodolfo.

When Italian baritone Giangiacomo Guelfi arrived in Dublin to sing Scarpia and the title role in *Nabucco*, Peter McBrien sang the Sacristan in the *Tosca* performances and was soon to conclude that Guelfi's was the most powerful baritone voice he had ever heard on the Gaiety stage, but it had the saving grace of having an appealing tonal quality and fine flexibility. His Scarpia was an intimidating character, a man who would not think twice of torturing his own brother. He carried the same authority and commanding stage presence into his Nabucco and Gerard in *Andrea Chenier*. 'I had no doubt in my mind that I was in the presence of a great actor-singer.'

During those years the spring season of Italian opera often comprised six productions, including *Turandot*, *Chenier*, *Boheme*, *Otello*, *Traviata* and *Nabucco*, with conductors like Napoleone Annovazzi, Ferdinando Guarnieri and Tibor Paul. Scenery was transported from Italy, with the result that visually the productions looked acceptable. Emphasis, however, was on the voice. 'In those days', says Peter McBrien, 'opera buffs could hardly name a producer for you or designer, but ask them about singers and they'd know a lot about them. There was a traditional way of presenting opera and no one tried a novel approach. The public wanted exciting voices and settled for that.'

He remembers long queues outside the Gaiety Theatre with people clamouring for tickets, and it was obvious, too, that opera meant glamour and generated excitement. 'I'm sure it was the same kind of excitement you'd have found at the time in any Italian city where Silveri, Gobbi or Stignani were on the bill. When, for instance, Giuseppe di Stefano was engaged by the DGOS to sing Mario Cavaradossi, there was a rush for tickets at the Gaiety box-office, yet many people were to be disappointed. The society could have filled the theatre twice over. Everyone, you see, had heard about the tenor's performances with Maria Callas at La Scala and naturally wanted to hear him. But on the night I think it was Gobbi's Scarpia that stole the show.

'Singing with these artists, in my view, was an education; they made it look easy only because their artistry and technique were superb. I used to say, hopefully, to myself, "I hope some of it rubs off on me". Admittedly there were a few "mere mortals" among them, but Dublin was getting the cream of Italy's singers and the DGOS could be thanked for that.'

Among the Irish artists singing with the DGOS was tenor Patrick Ring, who one evening went along to see *Rigoletto* at the Gaiety and, as he was to tell Peter McBrien next day, was astounded by a young Italian tenor in the role of the Duke. 'You've got to hear him', urged Ring. 'His name is Luciano Pavarotti.'

McBrien was to share the same view as his colleague, and today says, 'I remember the voice soaring to the heavens, almost effortlessly, and it had a lovely lyric quality. You were left in no doubt that you were listening to a great star of the future.'

He sometimes wondered if tenor Brendan Cavanagh's value to the DGOS was fully appreciated by opera-goers. 'Whether it was singing Spolleta in *Tosca* or Gaston in *Traviata* or a score of other roles, Brendan was thoroughly reliable. He has graced the Gaiety stage with the best and I never saw him give a bad performance. He is a singer I've long admired for his dedication and love of opera. They are not easy to come upon nowadays.'

During those decades when opera prospered, the DGOS could rely on support from Kerry folk and as well as from Donegal people. For my own part, I once met a famed Kerry footballer in the Gaiety foyer discussing with Dublin friends Paolo Silveri's unforgettable performance as the jester in *Rigoletto*. Peter McBrien says it was a time of widespread interest in opera and the singers were stars who signed fans' autographs in hotels and shops. 'I remember people having their favourite tenor or soprano and on no account would they miss their performances. It was great fun and people enjoyed being part of it.'

As a singer, he was rarely if ever 'resting'. Concert engagements took him to the Continent and to America and in the 1970s he joined Irish National Opera and became part of that happy band of strolling singers who brought opera to the provinces, singing principal roles in *The Barber of Seville*, *Traviata*, *Don Giovanni* and Verdi's *Falstaff*. The public's response in the small towns surprised him. 'Their enthusiasm was heartening to us singers; in fact, on some nights the halls and theatres were too small to cater for all the people clamouring to see us. We performed with piano and without chorus, but did have stage sets and props. I sang many performances on tour of the Don in *Don Giovanni* and contrary to our expectations audiences didn't consider the opera too long. They loved the Don's amorous antics, as they did Figaro's swagger in *The Barber*. Paddy Ryan was a producer who often worked wonders in inadequate conditions. From the singers' point of view, the whole thing was worthwhile, if only because it gave a number of them, including Suzanne Murphy, an opportunity to sing leading roles and they made the most of it.'

He continued, meanwhile, to sing with the DGOS, taking on more important roles, including the title role in *Rigoletto*. It was the winter season of 1987 and the golden days of the Italian 'greats' had long passed, mainly because the society could no longer afford their fees. Instead, the casts of the three operas that season – *Don Pasquale* and *The Pearl Fishers* were the others – featured Irish, English and Italian singers. In fact, the Duke in *Rigoletto*, Ingus Peterson, was Russian-born. The part of Rigoletto, the tragic hunchback, is one of Verdi's most testing characterisations requiring abundant vocal stamina and acting ability above the ordinary to carry it off successfully. Apart from some difficulty with the high tessitura, Peter

McBrien made a brave shot at the role; his wasn't an introverted Rigoletto but a man with strong paternal instincts where his daughter Gilda was concerned. It was a moving performance combining pathos with anger in convincing measure.

'It was tiring but I enjoyed singing the part,' Peter told me later. 'It's not something you'd want to sing too often in the one week, but it does contain some of Verdi's finest operatic music.'

He had already achieved success with the society as the elder Germont in *La Traviata*, a role that perhaps suits his voice even better than *Rigoletto*. He showed himself, however, to be a most reliable artist, a fact that the DGOS recognised by repeatedly engaging him for a variety of exciting roles. He made no secret of his genuine enjoyment of opera, though he found time to fit in oratorio and concert performances. A versatile singer, he was in demand all over the country and also toured in Europe and America. It was inevitable, contends Peter McBrien today, that money would begin to dictate matters and that in time Dublin would only see the superstars in concert and not in operatic performances Soon superstars like Pavarotti, Domingo and Carreras would command huge fees; indeed, even those singers in a league below them would be too expensive for the DGOS.

For a time in the 1980s the newly-founded Cork City Opera made its mark with interesting productions of *Trovatore*, *Carmen*, *Boheme*, *Cav & Pag* and *Madama Butterfly*. He sang Dancairo in *Carmen* and Sharpless in *Butterfly* and both productions were rated popular successes. The Cork venture, he believes, was a worthy one and gave employment to talented Irish singers such as Frank O'Brien, Mary Hegarty, Therese Feighan, Angela Feeney and others, but realistically it could not be expected to work on such an ambitious scale with the inadequate funding available. The company underlined the fact, however, that a city the size of Cork should have its season of opera annually. To Peter McBrien, the *Carmen* production showed what could be done. Directed by Tom Hawkes, choreographed by Domy Reiter Soffer, and conducted by Robin Stapeleton, it excited local audiences, especially

Gillian Knight's *Carmen* and Enrico di Guiseppi's Don Jose, whose "Flower Song" brought calls of bravo.

'I was sorry to see the company disappear', he says, 'because it was another opportunity lost to young Irish singers. I think we all looked forward to the prospect of singing in Cork.'

Back in Dublin he sang Germont for the DGOS, a character role suited to his resonant baritone, and his Marcel also won praise, turning out to be one of his best operatic portrayals. He found singing in *Tannhauser* a most rewarding experience and considered Ken Neate's direction outstanding. 'Ken, to my mind, succeeded in making the relatively small Gaiety stage look twice its size. I enjoyed singing in German and it's a great pity really that Wagner's operas are so neglected nowadays in Dublin.'

Elaine Padmore engaged him to sing a poet monk in the 1984 Wexford Festival production of Massenet's *Le Jongleur de Notre Dame* and the cast included Brendan Cavanagh, Virginia Kerr and the celebrated Russian baritone Sergei Leiferkus. Peter McBrien also took part in the Operatic Scenes and as far as I can remember made his mark with arias in Russian. He enjoyed working in the festival atmosphere, though to my mind he should have been given more important operatic roles there.

By the late Eighties he had teamed up with Louis Browne to form Irish Concert Artists and the company quickly carved a popular niche for itself at the National Concert Hall. Their concerts were well supported and the guest artists were sometimes international. In more recent times the company has staged concert performances of opera, including *Tosca* in which he sang Scarpia, thus fulfilling a longtime personal ambition. Dennis O'Neill was Cavaradossi and Suzanne Murphy sang Tosca. Peter McBrien persuaded Brendan Cavanagh to come out of retirement to sing Spoletta.

He himself was back on the Gaiety stage in the winter of 1993 singing the character role of Benoit in DGOS Opera Ireland's production of *La Boheme* and his cameo performance received copious praise from Mary MacGoris in the *Irish Independent*.

Today he also finds time to give singing lessons, but one suspects that he is essentially a performer. When I asked him about his eventual retirement, he shrugged his broad shoulders and quickly dismissed any such suggestion. Had Louis Browne warned him of my question?

'I haven't given a thought to it', Peter McBrien mused. 'I'm just too busy.

Chapter Twenty Two

Therese Feighan

SALZBURG FESTIVAL DEBUT

When mezzo soprano Therese Feighan was engaged to sing in Monteverdi's *Orfeo* at the 1993 Salzburg Festival it was on her own admission, a dream come true. She would be joining that small and very select coterie of Irish artists to appear there, which made it in Therese's eyes an honour.

The festival was celebrating the 350th anniversary of Monteverdi's death and his masterpiece, *L'incoronazione di Poppea* would also be staged. Predictions that Monteverdi would turn off the traditional public were to be proven wrong. Booking for the two productions was very brisk from day one at the box-office.

Therese Feighan arrived in Salzburg in the last week of June to begin nearly six weeks' rehearsals. These would take place in a large studio building outside the city which normally accommodates all the festival operatic and drama rehearsals. Sets were built to opera house specifications and by the time casts performed on the first night at the official venues they were familiar with their stage surroundings.

Although rehearsal time was long she enjoyed the experience. 'I had been looking forward very much anyway to singing in Salzburg and when I got there I settled in quickly, so rehearsing wasn't a chore. We worked hard every day but the atmosphere was pleasant and the opera came together with no great difficulty.'

Opening night was 30 July in the courtyard of the Salzburg Residenz in the heart of the city, only a few minutes walk from the Grosses Festspielhaus. Apart from the stage which is covered, the rest of the courtyard is open to the sky and in that way operas risk being cancelled in unsettled weather.

Such was the case at the premiere when a downpour of rain caused the cancellation of *Orfeo;* instead, it was transferred to the Mozarteum, a lovely old theatre used mostly for festival concert and recital performances. Gerard Mortier, artistic head of the festival, decided that *Orfeo* be performed in a concert version. Therese Feighan admits that she and the rest of the cast were disappointed by the unexpected turn of events and particularly that their big first night was ruined. 'It was the last thing I expected', Therese said.

However, the subsequent performances of *Orfeo* were presented at the Residenz where, she says, the acoustics are excellent. Therese was unable to sing on the third night because she contracted a flu virus and her understudy took over. She was back, however, for the rest of the run. Musically the opera got favourable notices from the critics, though some of them were not taken by the production itself which they felt did not do justice to Monteverdi.

I caught up with the opera on Sunday 22 August. As I join the crowds on their way to the Salzburg Residenz the air is uncomfortably humid and I figure that rain cannot be far off. Is my journey from Dublin to be in vain and the performance cancelled?

It will be another 45 minutes before the doors are opened but already people's eyes are ominously cast skywards. There is a foreboding look about the black rolling clouds. Momentarily a mini bus draws up at the door behind us with members of the *Orfeo* cast and as it is driven into the court-yard Therese Feighan smiles and waves at me. Artists at the festival are, I learn later, looked after very well by way of transport and accommodation.

My worst fears are soon confirmed when light drops of rain begin to fall and gradually get heavier. I am reminded of my experience years before at Arena di Verona when rain washed out the performance of Verdi's *Aida.* By now hundreds of people are gathered near the main entrance door, most of them holding umbrellas high over their heads. Their solemn, unsmiling faces tell their own story. We are told that the doors will not open until the rain ceases altogether.

Eventually the miracle happens and before long we are being ushered into the courtyard. Our seats are either damp or wet from the rain. It is already 30 minutes behind official starting time for the opera. It is not the most pleasant way to enjoy a performance but we are grateful that it is going on at all and hope and pray that the rain stays away.

The director, Herbert Wernicke, has set the opera in modern times with the participants in modern dress. The members of the cast are part of a banquet for the wedding of Orfeo and Euridice - 'bored music lovers', as one critic put it, 'in place of Thracian nymphs and shepherds'. They spend most of the evening gorging themselves at a long table in the background.

Because of her height I can easily pick out Therese Feighan, but perhaps more so on account of her stunning full-length dress. She moves with elegance and sings Monteverdi's music stylishly and confidently, especially her big aria in Act 4 as she pleads Orfeo's cause; this in fact turns out to be a vocal highlight.

Just when it seems the performance is to end on a triumphant note the rain returns with a vengeance. First, the orchestra stop playing and most of the musicians put their instruments hastily away and hurry from the pit. The cast remain standing on the stage with a forlorn look, as though hating being cheated of their final act. In no time at all members of the audience leave their seats and hurry away. At that moment I join the cast on stage and sympathise with Therese Feighan and the English tenor Laurence Dale who has sung the role of *Orfeo* with conviction.

'How awful that it's turned out like this for you', Therese says. 'The thing is you can never trust the Salzburg weather'.

Later over dinner she talked of the satisfaction it gave her singing in Salzburg. 'Music takes precedence over everything else here', she said. 'It's the single most important thing, so high standards are expected of singers, but you're paid well, very well. I've found the experience exciting and working with Herbert Wernicke has been a joy. I do want to come back here and hope I'll be invited.'

In all she sang twelve performances of Orfeo and was so taken by the dress she wore as Proserpina that she made enquiries about purchasing it and was told she could have it for £1000 sterling.

'I was nearly tempted to fork out the money', she said with a laugh, 'but then I thought I wouldn't be going to that many dress dances so as to justify indulging myself.'

To Therese Feighan, Salzburg is a very special festival, notably because of the number of international singers it attracts. 'I have never worked with so many talented people before and that goes for everyone from directors to designers to singers. You cannot help but give of your best in such surroundings. I am talking from an artist's point of view, of course. I am not sure how the public regards the high ticket prices and this intangible thing they call elitism. I do know that people enjoy their opera and drama and recitals at the festival and it's astonishing the number of visitors who come here from all over the world. Yes, I would love to be asked back.'

Singing hadn't been Therese Feighan's first love. She had fancied herself as a ballerina but was too tall, so her mother encouraged her to take singing lessons. Standing 5 ft. 11 ins., she was self-conscious about her height and the conflicting advice she was getting. 'I know mezzos who are taller than me; tallness is not that rare among professional singers. I feel that it can be an advantage as well as a disadvantage.'

She found this to be the case early in 1991 when she was singing the title role in Handel's *Tamberlane* for the Opera Theatre Company in Dublin; it is a trouser part and as the tyrant in the opera she was expected to dominate the stage and so she did. There are other roles, however, she wants to sing, Rossini for example, though she fears height could be a disadvantage.

Therese can be candid about herself. 'As a person I'm very volatile. I suppose I'm a perfectionist, which can be a bad thing insofar as you're not prepared to leave things well alone. After a performance I tend to go into a corner and lapse into a self-critical mood. Even the sense of pride and relief that you should experience when something goes well for you is, in my case, often tempered by a desire to do better.'

Early in 1992 she sang with the English tenor Anthony Rolfe Johnson in Monteverdi's *Orfeo* for English National Opera and as they were about to go on stage he turned to her and said in a whisper, 'I'm so nervous, I'm terrified.' It was a shock to her, coming from someone she admired for his outstanding artistry. 'You can't be?', she whispered. 'Yes, I am, I've to push and push myself to make my performance better.'

For a long time she remembered his words. 'It struck me that no matter how good you think you are you can always do better and so win over more people in the audience.' When she auditioned for ENO in 1989, the company offered her the cover in Debussy's *Pelleas et Melisande* and although she wasn't called on she learned a great deal about opera, in particular how to study a role, approach a music score and about stagecraft.

'I had always been pretty good on the technical side but musically I was a novice. I decided I had so much to learn and I was lucky as the ENO provides excellent coaching.'

Prior to *Orfeo* she had understudied Orlofsky in *Die Fledermaus* and when Ann Howard became indisposed was called on twice to sing the part. 'I'll never forget it', she recalled, 'I was nervous, but my ENO colleagues were terrific. They cushioned me and lifted me along, and though I had done my preparation, this support was a real fillip to me. Unfortunately the critics were not in on these particular nights so I got no second opinion.'

Working with director David Freeman in *Orfeo* was, Therese Feighan says, a turning point in her career. Freeman introduced a routine of mind and body exercises that consisted partly of yoga, breathing, limb stretching, leg strengthening and mental concentration that she soon discovered made her voice more secure. 'David asked us in rehearsal, for example, to dwell our minds on a single subject and this tended to improve our concentration. I began to sing much better and after the run was over I continued with the exercises in my flat.'

His direction of the Monteverdi work was important to her for another reason. She learned to use stage space and to move with more ease and was no longer cowed by the large-sized Coliseum. As *Orfeo* is totally stylised and set in the 14th century, they were directed to walk and move at a slower pace and this became almost natural to them after the first few rehearsals. It was part she could see of Freeman's desire to achieve a sense of total realism by stripping away all semblance of artificiality. 'The thing is that David is not happy until he has pushed and pushed you until you discover the real core of the music. I have never experienced with anyone else the same feeling of musicial fulfilment.'

Later on she would return to the Coliseum to sing the Third Lady in *The Magic Flute* and cover the role of the Composer in *Ariadne auf Naxos*. Therese admitted that understudying could be frustrating in one sense because it made one impatient to go on, but at the same time she found it a deeply satisfying way of learning a new role. Mindful of the fact that one could be called on at a few hours' notice, even less, it meant that one had to be thoroughly prepared. She said she was particularly happy to cover Octavian in *Der Rosenkavalier* for Welsh National Opera as it gave her very useful insights into the Strauss role.

Musically her only ambition is to improve as a performer and be given the opportunity to sing more Monteverdi, Strauss, Handel and Rossini. Singing Mozart she finds incredibly difficult as well as exhausting. 'I find it tough, tough, tough. I suppose it boils down to the fact that his operatic roles - at least some of them - do not lie well for me.'

We returned to the question of height and she partly attributed her limited repertoire to this fact, though she hoped to go on expanding it. She was by now an experienced concert and oratorio performer. She sang in Elgar's *Sea Pictures* with Welsh National Opera, Haydn's *B Minor Mass,*Bach's *Christmas Oratorio* and Handel's *Messiah*. Singing in concert and performances of Meyerbeer's *Il Crociato in Egitto* in Dresden and Stuttgart and *Rodelinda* at the Batignano Festival sometimes made her wonder about the anxiety complex that afflicted so many singers. Was it because of their over-anxiety to do well? On occasions she was aware of the feeling in herself, though as far as she knew it had never affected her performances. She was more likely to be affected after watching performances by renowned artists when she was inclined to ask herself, 'How can I ever aspire to be as good as them?' In fact, it was while singing in the Dresden concert that she was assailed by this feeling. 'I remember I felt quite humbled by the brilliant singers around me and suddenly was reminded of how much I had still to learn. Yet I knew I could not afford to get a hang-up about it or else I would be totally intimidated and maybe suffer a loss of confidence.'

The more she travelled the more she realised the enormous industry that opera had become and felt one could be quite easily swamped by it. Nonetheless she believed that this need not be and that the industry would always have a place for dedicated and talented people. She was more concerned by the prospect of opera slipping away from them due to such factors as elitism, exorbitant ticket prices, lack of inspiring new composers, and the huge cost of mounting opera itself.

Therese Feighan is in favour of singing opera for the most part in English so that the masses can understand the plots and enjoy what they've paid to see. As she says, 'I've had people come up to me after performances and say, "We're so glad it was sung in English". As for surtitles, I don't believe they are the answer since many people find it hard to keep their eyes focused on them.' She saw the benefit of opera in English when touring with *Tamberlane* for Opera Theatre Company. It was a revealing experience. The enthusiastic response by the Tralee audiences, for example, to Handel's music was very reassuring to the singers. In her view, part of the enjoyment derived from the fact that people understood the words and, therefore, the plot. She hopes that people in the Irish provinces will be given the opportunity to see much more opera. 'From what I could gather, there is a hunger for opera in the towns and cities outside of Dublin.'

Therese Feighan has happy memories of growing up in Dublin. Her family was, however, more attuned to traditional music, though her mother played light classical pieces on the violin. After leaving secondary school, she took a degree in English and Spanish at University College Dublin and soon began teaching in Templeogue. While she thoroughly enjoyed the experience, she began to acquire a deeper interest in music and singing. One day she decided to go along to Veronica Dunne who agreed to take her for singing lessons.

Fitting in her teaching with singing lessons wasn't easy. Usually Therese attended lessons at weekends or early in the morning. Eventually, she became a full-time student at the College of Music and gave up teaching altogether. She financed herself by working in city restaurants and found that other singers were supporting themselves in the same way.

Within a few months she won first prize in the 1983 Golden Voice of Ireland and that gave her the spur she needed. Something else also helped her to make up her mind. 'I found the Therese Feighan on stage was more me than the person going shopping, which began to convince me that singing was for me. Feeling at home on the stage was important to me and made me feel relaxed which was good for my singing.'

Five years' singing tuition with Veronica Dunne had given her confidence in her own ability and soon she was performing small parts with the Dublin Grand Opera Society. She sang Mercedes in Cork City Opera's production of *Carmen* and today very much regrets the demise of the company. 'With some assistance from the Arts Council and more private sponsorship I think it would have survived. The idea was good and having a professional opera company in Cork made sense to singers.'

In the year 1986 she moved to London. It was a competitive new scene for her and she supported herself by taking day jobs and in the evening posted letters to operatic companies. Both the Welsh and the Scottish companies gave her auditions, but she knew in her heart she wasn't ready at the time. 'I really hadn't enough self-confidence to face the international field, and although I could always technically sing well - thanks to Ronnie Dunne- I didn't give a good impression, I think, of myself. I felt insecure and lacked confidence in my work as a performer. I'm sure this showed at auditions.'

On reflection, she counts those early months in London as 'a rather painful experience', yet in another way she regards them as beneficial since she was learning the hard way. She never lost her belief in her own vocal ability. Her trouble, she says, stemmed from an inner fear of not succeeding as an artist and this worried her no end. 'I had given up a secure teaching post in Dublin and taken a risk; now I wondered whether I was right or wrong.'

She was conscious of being an outsider in Britain, or as she likes to describe it, 'someone who hadn't gone through their educational or music systems and so could not expect the authorities there to take her in trust unless she had something exceptional to offer.' She confessed it was a period of highs and lows for her, but all the time she convinced herself that it was only a matter of time until she got a 'break'.

A successful audition for the Pavilion Opera Company gave her renewed hope. She was cast as Orlofsky in a stylish production of Johann Strauss' *Fledermaus* and for the next few months toured all over Britain, bringing the operetta to some picturesque country mansions. To Therese Feighan, it was a delightful way of gaining experience and, for a virtual beginner, exceedingly useful musically.

Next, she got the chance to taste bel canto when she sang Alisa in *Lucia di Lammermoor*, and although only a minor part, she hoped that one day she would be asked to sing in the same composer's *La Favorita* and Bellini's *Norma*. Singing on a regular basis, she found, improved her voice and boosted her self-confidence.

If Pavilion productions were modestly performed with piano accompaniment, it was a different matter with Opera 80, her next assignment. The company toured with an orchestra and engaged some very talented directors, designers and conductors. Performances also attracted scouts from the big London opera houses.

She received encouraging notices for her Marcellina in *The Marriage of Figaro* and Madama Larina in *Eugene Onegin* and thoroughly enjoyed the tour. The final performances were given at Sadler's Wells Theatre in London. Later, she returned to Dublin to sing Suzuki in the DGOS production of *Madama Butterfly* and found the Puccini role vocally satisfying.

In the years 1987 and '89 she achieved another ambition when invited to sing at Wexford Festival, being cast as Dorothe in Massenet's *Cendrillon* and as Arbate in Mozart's *Mitridate*, which was brought to London's Queen Elizabeth Hall shortly after the festival. Therese felt indebted to Elaine Padmore for her appearances at the festival. 'Elaine has been a great support to me through my career', she said. 'She is one of the people who has believed in my voice and that pleased me. A singer needs support like this as it can be interpreted as an act of faith in in a singer's ability. As for Wexford, it's sheer magic, particularly the atmosphere the festival generates. One gets the feeling that new operatic ground is being broken because people are seeing unknown operas. Elaine Padmore has left her stamp on Wexford and I've no doubt she's going to be a difficult act to follow.'

With the approach of the 1990s, Therese began to be increasingly busy visiting Spain and Italy for concert work and travelling to Batignano to perform in her first Handel opera, *Rodelinda* which she said whetted her appetite for *Tamberlane*. She would like to tackle certain Wagner roles but wonders if her voice would be up to them.

Despite the glitter and glamour surrounding the world of opera, she says that she is determined to live as normal a lifestyle as possible. 'I believe it's the only way you can succeed in this business. I try to give everything to my singing while at the same time endeavouring to get on with normal life, otherwise I could drift into a dream world.'

Today she lives happily in London, though she would like if possible to work more on the Continent, especially in the Netherlands. Occasionally she will 'phone Veronica Dunne for a chat about Dublin if she encounters a problem with an operatic role she is preparing. 'I know that Ronnie will put me right',

Chapter Twenty Three

Regina Nathan

MOVED BY MIMI

They met and fell in love in Maynooth College, once an exclusive seminary for aspiring priests, but by the 1980s its doors were open to young men and women seeking general university degrees. Regina Nathan came from Dublin and was studying French and music, Ennis-born Joe Lynch was taking mathematics and music.

Regina, dark and handsome, had been a boarder in the Mercy Convent in Ballymahon, Co. Longford and was fortunate that it had a proud tradition for music and singing. During terms the nuns presented school operetta in which Regina took part. 'I enjoyed best that side of my education there', she recalled, 'and I found the sisters very helpful.' They realised she had a sweet and pure-toned soprano voice and encouraged her to sing.

At the age of 16 she did an outside scholarship for the College of Music in Dublin and on the adjudicating panel were Frank Heneghan, the college head, and Nancy Calthorpe, who was in charge of vocal studies. Regina was successful and this entitled her to an hour's singing lesson each week with Nancy Calthorpe.

'Both Frank and myself came to the same conclusion about Regina's voice', said Nancy. 'We agreed that it was of lovely texture and full of potential. I was delighted to have her. I'd been lucky with the calibre of my students, first with Ann Murray, then Ethna Robinson and now Regina.'

After leaving the Mercy nuns, Regina enrolled in Maynooth College but continued with her singing lessons at the College of Music. To Nancy Calthorpe, she was a quick learner and very intelligent, though on occasions they had 'little run-ins' because she felt that Regina was being lackadaisical and was capable of giving more. However, as a teacher-student relationship it was generally positive and harmonious.

'At the outset I worked on breath control with her and was very careful not to push her voice, so I selected music that I thought was right for her', says Nancy. 'At the same time I knew she could sing more complex pieces and in a higher register than I was giving her, but that would have been a dangerous course to follow. I sent her to Sligo to do the feis and she won almost every competition. I remember that one of the arias she sang was Micaela's from *Carmen* and adjudicator Colman Pearce was very taken by it.'

On graduating from Maynooth with her degree and Higher Diploma in Education, Regina Nathan was, according to Nancy Calthorpe, somewhat unsettled and unsure whether to pursue a career in teaching or in music. She was also inclined to lack self-confidence. One afternoon Regina came to her and said she had got a place in the RTE Chamber Choir and intended to take it in order to find out if singing suited her.

'I was thrilled for her sake', Nancy recalled, 'since she now had a job and would be earning money each week.'

Thinking back, Regina Nathan has no doubt that it was a turning point in her life. The choir, under Colin Mowby's direction, consisted of talented young singers like Nigel Williams and Therese Feighan, with rehearsals each day and Fridays devoted to radio recording.

After both had obtained their Higher Diplomas in Education the romance between Regina and Joe Lynch blossomed. 'We saw more of one another', Joe says, 'and you could call it a steady line.'

Soon he took up a teaching job in Dublin and with his interest in music, books and sporting activities enjoyed a full and interesting life. Seeing Regina now more assured about her singing prospects was a relief to him and he felt confident she could make it as a singer.

Meanwhile, she confided in Nancy Calthorpe of her intention to pursue further studies in London and that she had gained a place at Trinity

College of Music where she would do a two-year post-graduate course. During her time there, Joe Lynch visited her and as he usually spent his summer holidays working in England they were able to see more of one another. He believed that she had taken the right course and he was prepared to wait. 'We were in love', he said, 'and I knew that before long I'd be faced with the decision either to emigrate for good or stay in Dublin. I loved life in Ireland and had numerous friends,yet I was prepared to make the sacrifice for Regina's sake, even if this meant giving up my job.'

Her studies proceeded smoothly. After Trinity College, Regina found a place in London's National Opera Studio which, at the time, enjoyed an excellent reputation. 'I was petrified at first of the very thought of going there', she later told me. 'I lacked confidence in myself and it was not until after the second term that the fright left me. I became more relaxed and decided that this was the place for me. In Elizabeth Hawes I found an excellent teacher and the head of the studio, Richard van Allan, was also a good communicator. Gradually my vocal technique and stagecraft improved and I learned there was more than one way of doing things.' Expressing emotion, for example: she felt one had to dig deep in order to reflect different aspects of it.

After one year there she was convinced that singing, especially opera, was the life that would give her perhaps the most aesthetic satisfaction. As a person her confidence had grown and she knew what she wanted. By nature she tends to be thoughtful and one suspects there is an ascetic side to her character. If she hadn't studied singing she said she would like to have done arts and crafts, preferably in a country place. She is an avid reader of books and likes to cook when she finds the time.

When she laughs her face lights up and her eyes sparkle. Her husband Joe is a good foil, being chatty and good-humoured, someone who also has a keen perception of life and its human and social complexities. In company the pair can relax and be at ease. Regina does her own talking, Joe his, indicating independent minds. And she is not one of those singers who constantly indulges herself in shop talk; indeed in our conversation there were moments when I had to persuade her to talk about herself and her achievements. When she says that singers in Britain are not paid enough for their operatic work, you are inclined to take her seriously; she doesn't waste words. At other times, though, she can be fun and enjoys an amusing anecdote.

During her London studies, she and Nancy Calthorpe kept in touch. Regina had rented a large flat in the Richmond area and wisely invested in a second-hand piano. Once on her way to Vienna, Nancy stayed overnight with her and was agreeably surprised at how quickly she had settled into London musical life. Later, she attended her debut recital at the Wigmore Hall, an event she recalled with the utmost pleasure. 'I will always remember it for the way Regina sang the lovely Irish air "The Coolin". She sang it in Irish and unaccompanied and it sounded so beautiful. I'm sure it has never been heard there before or since.'

Regina and Joe decided to marry in 1989. Regina says she had no feelings of anxiety about going into marriage and felt that it couldn't change her attitude to singing. 'I was convinced that it was the right thing to do, though I was apprehensive about having children, and still am.' For Joe Lynch it meant an important adjustment to his lifestyle. He soon decided to give up his teaching post in Dublin and look for one in London. Although he was aware of the demands made on singers, he nevertheless felt that he would have to first experience married life before he could say for sure how he would respond to fairly regular separations due to Regina's engagements away from London. He realised he would have to prepare himself for the change and that it wouldn't be easy.

In June 1991 Regina was invited by RTE to represent Ireland at the 5th Cardiff Singer of the World Competition. Held every two years, it is a prestigious event and an important shopwindow for singers because of the huge television coverage. Her teacher, Elizabeth Hawes joined Regina in Cardiff and Joe Lynch later made the trip from London. Although she failed to qualify for the final I found that the competition brought out a refreshing side of her character, one I hadn't detected before, and it was the philosophical way she accepted defeat.

Talking to Regina afterwards back at her hotel, she seemed to take it all in good cheer and looked far from crestfallen. Elizabeth Hawes was naturally disappointed for her pupil, but told me she was reassured by the fact that Regina had sung beautifully and had received a tremendous ovation from the audience in St. David's Hall, the venue for the competition.

'She has the quality of rapture', was how Jill Gomez, one of the distinguished panel of judges, described her singing. For my part, I considered her unlucky not to qualify for the final in a year in which the competition was dominated by sopranos.

But there were compensations. Regina went on to win joint third prize at the 10th International Belevedere Competition in Vienna; in fact, of the 25 prizes awarded she won seven. Elaine Padmore, who was in Vienna, described her singing of "Caro nome" as absolutely magical, adding, 'Let me say that it would make the hairs stand on the back of your neck, it was that kind of performance.'

When he could, Joe Lynch travelled to be with his wife and she admitted to me that she found his presence a source of strength on occasions that could be stressful as well as tense. He came to Dublin for the big gala concert at the Point Centre when Regina shared the bill with none other than Placido Domingo. Shortly before the event she was supposed to sing for the tenor but contracted a bad cold, so he did not hear her until their rehearsal together. His visit caused a good deal of excitement in musical circles and on the morning of the concert Domingo gave a special press conference at the Berkeley Court Hotel. As Regina Nathan entered the foyer he walked over to her and kissed her on the cheek. When the press photographers requested a repeat, he said to them, 'I didn't do that for you.'

Appalling weather almost ruined the concert. Traffic jams built up on the roads outside the Point and many people missed the entire first half of the concert. Dublin had seldom, if ever, seen a more chaotic scene. Thankfully, the singers did not seem affected. To Regina Nathan, Domingo sang with utter conviction and sincerity. In their duets together, he ensured she would be heard. For both artists it was a triumph.

Among the audience were Regina's mother Breda - 'my greatest fan' -

and Nancy Calthorpe whose wrist was in plaster after a recent accident. She was unable to wait around afterwards to congratulate her pupil, but she need not have worried. Next day Regina and her husband Joe came round to her apartment to present her with the bouquet of flowers that on the previous night had been presented to her on stage. 'It was a lovely gesture on her part', recalled Nancy, 'but then again it didn't surprise me, for Regina is a thoughtful and generous person.'

Looking back on the occasion, Regina Nathan says, 'All I can say is that Placido is a real gentleman and a pleasure to work with. It was a great opportunity, a very exciting time, a lovely memory. Nothing much, however, happened as a result, except that people heard that I got to sing with Domingo. In terms of getting engagements from it I don't think things work that way. People came of course mainly to hear and see him, it was just great for me but it didn't open a load of doors or anything. It's something that will always look good on the CV.'

She sang Susanna in *The Magic Flute* for Glyndebourne Touring Company and was particularly happy with the people she was working with, particularly the producer. It was, however, a frightening experience in her view to be in a big role for the first time, but it got better as it went along. She enjoyed working as one of an operatic team. 'It's not you on your own, whereas in recital and concert work you are very much more exposed; you're not in character, you've no costume.'

In December 1991 she was back in Dublin to sing the same role with DGOS Opera Ireland and Mary MacGoris described her "Deh Vini" as spell-binding and that all round she made 'a delicious Susanna'.

It was a particularly busy time for the singer. She took the role of Nannetta (*Falstaff*) with Opera Theatre Company and later covered Sophie (*Rosenkavalier*) for Welsh National Opera. Recital engagements brought her to Ireland, Belgium and Paris. When I reminded her that other singers had talked to me of how luck had often played a major part in their careers, she was dismissive of the notion. 'No, I prefer to think that for the most part we create what happens in our lives.' Furthermore, while she said others tended to look only at the glamorous side of the business, she saw it differently as more of a personal thing where one was constantly striving after perfection at all levels.

When she was engaged to sing Mimi at the Lucerne Opera in Switzerland she sat down at home one evening and played Renata Scotto's recording of *La Bohème* and as she listened she cried, such was the profound affect on her. 'I knew then that Mimi was a part I wanted to sing more than any other, as though she was a part of my own self.'

She enjoyed her long stay in Lucerne enormously and her different Rodolfos were, she said, excellent tenors. The whole production went with a swing and the rather reserved Swiss audience seemed to enjoy every moment of the opera. In the winter of 1993 Dublin saw the same production with Regina Nathan as the only member of the original Lucerne cast. It proved the hit of the season and the soprano repeated her moving portrayal of the tragic heroine.

During the season, she stayed with her colleagues at the Westbury Hotel where in the second week she was joined by her husband Joe. 'I find the opera very true to life', she said. 'There's really nothing sentimental about it, I think that's where its strength lies. Mimi is just a character, it's just life, those illnesses happened to people in those days and they died just like people are dying tragically today of cancer and Aids. The music is just beautiful. Everybody feels the same who does it. Everytime you do the opera there is another dimension to it.'

By now they had purchased their own terraced house about ten miles from the centre of London and Joe Lynch liked the idea of living among a multi-cultured society. Since they moved to England nine years previously he had sometimes thought of coming back to Dublin, but for the moment he had put the thought out of his mind. He felt he wanted to do more study and that London was the place. He had come to terms with marriage to a singer, though there were still times when he would like to have been with Regina at rehearsal time and after operatic performances.

'Singing is Regina's domain, mine is teaching', he explained. 'I see myself as her ally, someone who is there to support her, so there is really no conflict of interests. It has worked for us and I'm relieved about that. For others in the same position it may not work as well.'

During the last year, Regina has changed her teacher and now has lessons with Janice Chapman. She says that going to coaches and music lessons in London can take up a lot of one's time. Hours to get there and hours to come back, so she tries to have a lot of work done first. Once the coaching starts she is happier since she knows she is well on the way. 'I'm always nervous when I'm learning something new', she said.

She is conscious of the fact that since Margaret Thatcher's time the arts in Britain have suffered and haven't been high on the list of the Tory Party's priorities. 'Things have got worse. The arts are badly funded, very badly paid, but despite that a lot of good work is done. As for singers, there's so many of them and so little work to go around, it's difficult.'

With her own work taking her more and more to the Continent it is safe to assume that Regina will not have to depend entirely on Britain for her future livelihood. It is something that she is conscious of and feels proud that her Swiss operatic debut went so well for her.

Chapter Twenty Four

Mary Hegarty

A CORK BEGINNING

Nearly a decade after singing her first opera in the Opera House Cork, Mary Hegarty reflected on the profound impact it made on her. She was cast a Micaela, a Spanish country girl in the 1984 Cork City Opera production of *Carmen* with Gillian Knight in the title role and John O'Flynn as Zuniga.

'I remember there was an incredible buzz about the whole production, and coming off stage I knew opera was for me. I uttered to myself words like, "This is it ... this is what I want to do". I was young and inexperienced and must have been a terrible actress, but I had got hooked on the excitement of the music, the glamour if you like of the show, and Gillian Knight's performance which was gripping.

'As far as I was concerned it changed my whole thinking dramatically. Up to then I was unsure of what I wanted to do. I had considered a degree in music and piano teaching as a career, but after Carmen my mind was made up. In the following year I sang Nedda in *Pagliacci* for the company and enjoyed the experience even more.'

Born in Fermoy, where her father, Paddy Hegarty, taught music in the local St. Coleman's College, she was only six months old when the family moved to Cork and made their home in a semi- detached house in Ballinlough; her father had got a new post as piano and organ teacher in the Cork School of Music.

As a child, Mary Hegarty listened to her parents play music at home and it was not long before she and her twin sister Helen were taking piano lessons from their father. As their three brothers came along, they would in time join the Hegarty music ensemble; their mother, Mrs. Nell Hegarty was an accomplished violinist.

'I probably sang my first song in public in the choir', Mary recalled. 'Dad used to play the organ in St. Patrick's Church, beside the railway station, with my mother seated by his side. It was a wonderful old organ and placed in front of it was a large bench on which my sister and I used to sit on either side of our parents. On Sundays we automatically joined in the choir singing.

'I can remember another occasion when my Dad was playing at a church wedding and the singer failed to show, with the result that the Hegarty sisters stood in. My parents encouraged us to sing and with my brothers by now having a bash at the piano the house was alive with music.'

She remembers she was only eight when she joined her sister and brothers in forming a pop group that soon became known as Double Unit; her brothers also played guitar. Any money they earned was used to buy new gear and keep a van on the road. She is amused when she looks back, as the van always seemed to be breaking down. Even today when she returns home they have lively music sessions.

During her school years, she won numerous feis awards for singing, and since her father was associated with musical presentations at the Opera House, she often attended the first nights. By now she had reached Grade 8 in the piano and was encouraged by her parents to study for a music degree, though they felt her soprano voice was good enough to be trained.

After secondary school, she decided to take singing lessons at the School of Music with Maeve Coughlan. 'I found that Maeve was good on vocal technique and was anxious that I keep a natural and open sound. She reckoned I had a future as a singer but clearly was not inclined to push me.'

It was her experience in *Carmen,* as we have seen, that finally decided Mary Hegarty's career. In addition she won the Golden Voice of Ireland Competition, and in the summer of 1985 represented Ireland in the Cardiff

Singer of the World. On reflection, she says she went to Cardiff with an open mind, anxious for the most part to perform as best she could and winning the competition was not a priority with her.

Mixing with the various international entrants, was she found a new and interesting experience. While the majority shared her own philosophical attitude, there were others who gave the impression that their lives depended on the outcome. She found such a competitive approach hard to comprehend and in the end it resulted in some sorely disappointed singers.

What did surprise her was the Cardiff reaction. People came up to her in St. David's Hall and in the hotel afterwards to sympathise with her. They were convinced the judges were wrong and a few people were annoyed by their decision.

After the semi-final, one of the adjudicators called her aside. 'You liked it up on that stage tonight?' he said. 'Well, what are you going to do with yourself?' She told him that she was going to be an opera singer. 'Then', he added, 'you will have to slow down and not try to get everywhere too fast.'

Sir Geraint Evans, the renowned Welsh bass-baritone, called her aside too. She will not reveal what he said to her. 'No, no' she protests, 'it would sound like cockiness.'

At the time many readers wrote to the *Radio Times*, complaining that she had not got through to the final. Mary did not disagree with them.

She was happy enough with the television exposure and felt singing in Cardiff did a lot for her confidence. She says she thoroughly enjoyed the experience.

Around this time the Cork impresario, Barra O Tuama began to present operatic concerts in Cork, Dublin and other big centres. It was understandable that he should show an interest in Mary Hegarty and soon engaged her to sing in Cork. Topping the bill was the rising young Italian tenor Mario Malagnini and the Romanian mezzo-soprano Mariana Ciormila. The concert presented in St. Francis Church was packed to capacity, though acoustically there were problems.

For Mary Hegarty it was a rewarding evening. She was warmly applauded for her singing of Micaela's aria from *Carmen* and again when she and Mariana Ciormila sang "Mira O Norma" from Bellini's opera. She decided that concert singing could be more demanding than opera. 'I felt more exposed and perhaps more vulnerable. It is a test of one's self-confidence and, of course, vocal technique. In opera you don't have this feeling of isolation, of facing the audience on your own. But I realised I had to master the art of concert singing since it's an important part of one's career.'

Among the Barra O Tuama sponsors was the Dublin merchant banking firm of Guinness & Mahon and prompted by the impresario it generously agreed to sponsor Mary Hegarty for three years' voice coaching in London. 'I felt it was right that she get this opportunity', O Tuama later told me. 'She possessed after all one of the most promising voices to come out of Cork for a long time.'

She was fortunate in her London coach. Josephine Veasey, the distinguished mezzo-soprano, had only recently retired and was now devoting her time to voice training. 'She agreed to take me for one hour each week', recalled Mary Hegarty. 'Basically, she thought I was doing nothing wrong and that technically my voice was fine. Later, when she attended some of my operatic performances she'd pass on helpful notes to me. She could be critical, but I didn't mind that as long as I was improving. I think we worked extremely well together.'

Next, she enrolled at the National Opera Studio in London. Students were expected to submit operatic roles they wished to study and her list included Mimi, Sophie, Norina and Rosina. By the time she left the studio she had studied in detail seven different operas and in the process learned a good deal about characterisation and stagecraft.

On joining City of Birmingham Touring Opera she was offered the role of Nannetta in *Falstaff*. She quickly discovered how important a part touring opera played in British musical life. 'We toured all over the place and usually drew very good houses. Bringing opera to the people, particularly in rural areas, is I was told a cultural tradition in England and audiences certainly seemed to enjoy themselves. As a singer, it was great experience for me. I was working with a talented company and although touring can be arduous I enjoyed every minute.'

She felt that Josephine Veasey's coaching was proving a big help. Her voice, she said, was fuller, more rounded and she was happy with the sound. Occasionally she returned to Ireland for oratorio engagements and concert work. It was noticeable that she had become one of the most popular artists on the Irish concert circuit.

In the year 1988 she achieved another personal ambition and that was to sing at the Royal Opera House, Covent Garden. Recalling the occasion for me, she tended to be amused by the fact that four of the six Flower Maidens in the production of *Parsifal* had never previously sung on the Covent Garden stage.

'I remember saying in a whisper to the others, as we were about to go on stage, "This is it, girls!" I suppose it was a bit awesome the first time, but you soon realise that a stage is a stage no matter where you are singing. Covent Garden is very much what you make of it; I think the "royal" tag puts some people off a bit, yet inside the house everyone is polite and helpful. Of course you are as a singer aware of the glory of the place and its historic significance and singing there can be a boost to your confidence.'

She was back there soon again to sing Pousette in *Manon*. Next, she auditioned for English National Opera and was asked to cover the role of Nannette and actually went on twice when Ann Rodgers was indisposed. But it was the company's new production of Richard Strauss's *Ariadne auf Naxos* that left the deepest operatic imprint on her.

Singing Naiade in a cast that included Janice Cairns, Rita Cullis and Cyndia Sieden, she says she was almost overwhelmed by the sheer richness of the music. The experience made her more anxious to sing Sophie in the same composer's *Der Rosenkavalier*. She could not complain, however, as she was seldom out of work and kept up her weekly visits to Josephine Veasey. It was noticeable by now that the coloratura side of her voice had become most attractive.

Her next move was to prove one of the most important of her career. It started when she was engaged to sing for Opera North in Carl Nielsen's comic opera *Masquerade*. The production was part of the 1990 Leeds Festival which opened in June of that year with concerts, exhibitions and street events.

It was the British premiere of *Masquerade* at the Grand Theatre, Leeds, an occasion that the Cork soprano would remember with genuine satisfaction. Despite her limited opportunities as Leonora, one of the young lovers, she managed to catch the eye of the critics, one of whom noted her 'radiance of voice', another described her performance as 'pure and poised'.

Since her arrival in Leeds, she had made a marked impression both vocally and dramatically. Her success was to continue in the company's next production, *The Jewel Box*, which was presented in 1991 to mark Mozart's bicentenary.

It was described as a 'new' opera by Mozart, when in fact it was a collection of arias and ensembles contributed by the composer to by now forgotten operas. Music critic and novelist Paul Griffiths was responsible for skillfully creating the text. 'Some beautiful music has thus been saved from the oblivion of the archive', stated the London *Times*.

Mary Hegarty recalled that at Opera North's world premiere of the work there was a real buzz in the theatre, with most of the London critics in attendance. As Colombina, one of the buffa characters, she had one big aria to sing – "Enough, It's over" – and scarcely a critic failed to praise her. For her own part, she loved the music, in particular the ensemble singing, and would like to see the opera staged in Dublin.

She was next cast as Laoula in the company's production of Chabrier's *L'Etoile*, which has been described as one of the finest examples of opera-comique. The plot is unfortunately 'gloriously complicated'. What pleased Mary most at this time was the opportunity she was getting to sing in operas of contrasting styles and set in different periods. Looking back, she says it was like a learning process. 'I wanted to try something more than Verdi, Puccini and Rossini and I was getting a chance to do so.'

The critics continued to be favourable to her. 'Mary Hegarty skillfully mixed petulance, coquetry and charm', observed the London *Independent*, while Nicholas Kenyon stated, 'The vocal lines flow and dart happily: they are caught best by Mary Hegarty's lovely Laoula.'

She was chuffed to get the front cover of *Opera* with two others of the cast of *L'Etoile:* earlier in that year, 1991 she had got the front cover with the *The Jewel Box*. In between singing for Opera North and some concert work in Ireland, she covered for Ann Dawson the role of Marguerite in *Faust* and was relieved at not being called on. 'I love the part so much that I want to go straight into it when I get the chance. I was offered it by Opera Northern Ireland but had to refuse as I was in a revival for ENO of *Ariadne auf Naxos*. I hated having to miss out.'

In December 1991 she was able to get back home for the first Christmas in three years. On previous occasions it was only for two or three days and she hardly counted it worthwhile. She had just finished what she described as 'a solid eighteen months of work with Opera North' and felt she was due a break. In Cork she would always be regarded as 'one of our own' and she knew that however famous she became it would remain like that. The family was a close-knit one and two of her three brothers Jim, Pat and Dave were involved with a pop group. Although by day a hair- dresser her sister Helen still sang with a pop group and she and Mary were as always very close. Going home to Cork was something of renewal for her after long months of operatic rehearsals and performances. By now singing was her whole life and she was very determined about it. As she said, 'If something doesn't come up, I go out looking.'

Privately her life had changed. Jonathan Murphy, a smart young London television executive, was guiding her affairs and she seemed happy. He accompanied her to Dublin when she was awarded the *Sunday Independent* music award of the year. There to celebrate the occasion with her was Barra O Tuama who had managed her prior to her departure for London. Now her diary was almost full for 1992 and even into '93.

I have seldom seen her so pleased as in the spring of 1992 when she told me she was to sing at that year's Brighton Festival. It wasn't so much the festival as the opportunity she was getting to sing Stravinsky's music. She was cast as Anne Trulove in *The Rake's Progress* and early on in rehearsals found working again with the conductor Lionel Friend a stimulating experience; she had worked already with him at ENO and admired his talent. Coming new to Stravinsky's score, she confessed she wanted all the assistance she could get. 'Lionel helped me to avoid obvious pitfalls', she told me.

The response to her singing was enthusiastic, especially that by Ronald Crichton in *The Times*: 'Among the leading soloists Mary Hegarty's Anne Trulove was a delight. One does not often find a soprano who can look like a country girl and give such an accomplished account of both the big aria at the end of Act I and the lullaby in Act III.'

Her performance invariably attracted good press notices which is something that not every singer can boast. And she was proud also of the support afforded her by her parents; her father Paddy tried to attend all her big first nights in London and Leeds. Mary was disappointed when in 1992 DGOS Opera Ireland was obliged to cancel a scheduled production of Puccini's *Turandot* because of lack of funding. She told me she had been looking forward to doing the opera; instead the society staged a concert version of *Fledermaus* in which she sang Adele.

Fledermaus turned out ironically to be the hit of the season, with Albert Rosen conducting a sparkling performance. Although she expressed misgivings about the concert version in the first place, Mary Hegarty was pleased by the outcome and thought that everyone had worked their hearts out to make it a success.

'A sparky Irish Adele', was how one critic summed up her performance. For me, she sang with agility and charm and her effortless coloratura delighted the Gaiety Theatre audiences.

Early in 1993 she surprised the audience at the National Concert Hall when she arrived on stage with crutches. A week previously she was injured while skiing on the Continent but she was determined not to let down her large Dublin following. Later in the year she achieved another ambition when she sang Mimi in a concert version of *La Boheme* at the RTE Proms in Dublin.

The one big disappointment in her life is the decline of opera in her native Cork. 'When I go back there I wonder what has happened - no

Verdi, no Puccini, no Donizetti. It is very sad. I would love to sing Mimi or Violetta in Cork if that was possible, but they tell me there is no money to stage grand opera. What is the next generation of singers going to do?'

1994 was another particularly good year for the soprano. For nearly all of the year she was occupied with operatic, concert and recital work. 'I don't seem to have a moment to myself just now,' she laughed. She still retains her lilting Cork accent and infectious sense of humour, though her recent streamlined figure took some people by surprise. She was inclined to be chubby in the eighties. Mary is now in the envious position of being able to say no to a part in opera she doesn't care to sing. 'I'm careful with my voice, I have to ensure that it lasts for a long time. I enjoy festival opera either at Buxton or Edinburgh and 1994 was terrific in this respect.'

She still finds time, however, to sing in concerts in Ireland and late in 1994 was planning to return to the Opera House Cork to sing in a new production of *Orpheus in the Underworld* for John O'Flynn's Irish Operatic Repertory Company. John has been a longtime friend and had hoped to engage her to sing for the company for some years. 'I'm delighted she was able to accept my invitation,' he told me. As for Mary, she was thrilled to be asked.

Chapter Twenty Five

Bruno Caproni

BARITONE FROM BANGOR

B runo Caproni is a burly and friendly man, the kind that one imagines would be a riot in a comic Donizetti or Rossini role. He was wearing Schaunard's costume when we met on an April morning in 1992 at reception inside Covent Garden's main stage door. It was shortly before 10.30 and he clearly was in a hurry.

'I'll show you to a seat in the balcony', he said politely. 'I've got permission for you to attend the rehearsal.'

He led the way up a nicely carpeted stairway and afterwards hurried away to be in time to take his place for the run-through of Acts I and IV of *La Boheme.* Save for a handful of people, the auditorium was empty. Before he left me, Caproni had remarked, 'Watch for the young tenor Alagna.'

It was my first experience of being in an opera house so early in the morning and I must confess it was a decidedly unreal sensation. On the previous night I had attended the opening performance of Bellini's *I Puritani* starring June Anderson and Giuseppe Sabbatini, so here I was twelve hours later in the same theatre sans the same glamour and excitement, a stark anticlimax if there ever was one. Yet in a curious way I felt privileged. Was I not getting a peep inside the *real* world of opera?

With the stage curtain drawn back, the familiar *Boheme* scene came into view: the grey Parisian attic with the poet Rodolfo looking through a window at the snow-covered roofs outside, while his friend Marcel continues to paint by his easel. Two friends join them, the philosopher Colline and the musician Schaunard.

Members of the orchestra, under Mark Ermler, are in casual attire and as they play the first notes of Puccini's music score producer Richard Gregson stands by with his eyes focused on the stage. From time to time either Ermler or Gregson halts the rehearsal to have some stage business repeated or an aria re-sung. The cast, mainly young, demonstrate no hint of impatience but cheerfully carry out orders. Bruno Caproni's lyric baritone voice projects well and it is easy to see that he's right inside the character he is portraying. And he is right, too, about Roberto Alagna: the tenor's voice is warm and secure, displaying no difficulty with range or intonation. It is only four years since he has won first prize in the Pavarotti Competition for voices, and barely two years since the Romanian Mimi (Angela Gheorghiu) was successful at the Belvedere Competition in Vienna.

At this point the director asks Caproni to repeat a short scene. 'Try it this way', I can barely hear him say. Caproni goes back out the door and returns almost immediately to repeat the scene. Once more I catch the director's words, 'That is better.'

As tenor and soprano begin to sing their love duet "O soave faniculla" at the end of the act I almost forget I am in an empty theatre, such is the beauty of the music. Alagna sings with passion and effortless high Cs, Gheorghiu with beguiling charm. Yet the pair are only half-way through the duet when the conductor waves them to a halt to explain some point. As he gesticulates with his hands they stand and listen. To an onlooker like myself it is easy to imagine frustration building up in the singers. But evidently they have been through it before.

Bruno Caproni has fitted in admirably with his Bohemian friends in the opera, showing a penchant for comedy and for a big man uses the stage well. His movements are never awkward. The rehearsal of Act I has gone without acrimony and it is 12.30 when I go downstairs to join Bruno in the Covent Garden canteen where already a queue has formed.

When I tell him that I think the rehearsal had gone well and was in fact a revelation to me, he nods his head and says, 'Good. Glad you think so. I keep telling people opera is hard work and they don't always believe me.'

As he sips his coffee I notice he takes a little time to unwind and disengage himself from the character he has been singing. He says it is a busy time for him, for apart from covering the role of Riccardo in *Puritani* he is preparing a part in *The Magic Flute*.

'I'm thirty now', he says earnestly, 'and by the time I'm thirty-five I must have a score of important roles under my belt.'

How does he feel about singing in the morning time? He replies in a soft voice: 'It's like this, you don't go night clubbing if you're on next morning. You take care of yourself and your voice. I've got used to singing in the morning and am prepared for it. Opera is a serious business, as you saw this morning. You've got to be fit and in good voice.'

I remind him I have seen his performance in 1987 at the Wexford Festival when he sang in Giordano's *La Cena Delle Beffe* and for the first time he smiles and looks more at ease. 'I enjoyed Wexford. Very professional but good fun. I'd like to go back there again.'

After a pause, he adds seriously, 'I want to sing the big Verdi and bel canto roles. I may have to go to Germany to do so.'

He has a pleasant personality and I can see why he is popular with his colleagues. He introduces me to a few of them, then turns to me and remarks, 'It's a good *Boheme* crew, we get on well, we're enjoying working together. I like that.'

I can see that it means something to him. He leaves me at 2 o'clock to get back to the rehearsals of Act IV. I had first heard about Bruno from Dr. Havelock Nelson in Belfast. Nelson explained that young Caproni came from the seaside resort of Bangor in Co. Down where his family, of Italian origin, carried on a successful restaurant business. One day they met and Caproni intimated that he wanted to be a singer but was uncertain if he was good enough. He suggested that he go along to James Shaw and see if he would take him for singing lessons. 'I reckoned that if anyone could help him it was James.'

Shaw auditioned the young baritone and was immediately impressed.

'His voice was the most remarkable I had heard for a long time and it was obvious to me that he had tremendous potential.'

By this time Caproni had moved from the family home in Bangor and was employed as a part-time waiter in Belfast. At first he had lessons once a week with James Shaw and it was soon clear that he wanted to be a professional singer.

'Normally when a young singer tells me this I act as devil's advocate', Shaw says today. 'I try to talk them out of it, as it's a rat race in which I've seen so many people become disillusioned. My usual advice to them is to hang on to their day jobs and sing in their spare time. In Bruno Caproni's case this did not apply as he had no day job of any substance, nor apparently did he want one. So I decided to encourage him as I felt his ability was far above average. He didn't read music at sight but picked it up quickly, and he's blessed with a very retentive memory.'

Caproni stayed with Shaw from 1979 to '83. Shaw was not keen for him to sing much in public as he wanted to develop the singer's technical ability to complement his vocal quality. 'Bruno was still very young - he had been only eighteen when he first came to me. Although he didn't sing in a choir, he had done some concert work and also sang small parts with the Studio Opera Group. And in 1983 he won the male section in the Golden Voice of Ireland competition in Limerick.'

In that same year Shaw felt that Caproni needed the backing of one of the major music colleges to equip him for a professional career, so in collaboration with Dr. Havelock Nelson, he succeeded in getting him a place at the Royal Northern College of Music in Manchester, as well as a grant from Belfast Education & Library Board.

'I remember how utterly thrilled I was by the news', the singer told me later. 'I owed everything to Havelock Nelson and James Shaw. I could never have made it without their assistance.'

From 1983 to '88 he studied with the distinguished voice teacher Frederick Cox and all the time kept in touch with James Shaw, telling him about his progress and his hopes for the future. In his final year he sang the title role in *Rigoletto*. His mentor made the journey from Belfast to hear him.

'I was delighted to be present for the occasion and for Bruno' says Shaw, who was most impressed by the young singer's performance. So it seems were the Covent Garden scouts, for shortly afterwards he was auditioned and offered a contract. However, he wisely decided first to go to the National Opera Studio where his scholarship was sponsored by the Friends of Covent Garden in association with the Arts Council of Northern Ireland.

Caproni's good progress continued. He made his house debut in January 1989 as Yamadori in *Madama Butterfly* and after that he sang a succession of smaller roles. James Shaw acknowledged that the baritone field was very competitive, but in the case of Caproni he had no doubts about his ability to go to the top.

'In Bruno's favour is the fact that he has a high tessitura that suits the 19th century roles, but he hasn't lost the resonance in the lower register and he's still only in his early thirties. Baritones don't often reach their vocal pinnacle until their early forties.'

Soprano Virginia Kerr speaks enthusiastically of his voice. She sang with him in a performance of *La Boheme* for the DGOS and found him vocally and temperamentally ideal for opera, especially Puccini's music. 'When I was first introduced to him he was amiable and good-humoured, but behind the smiles I could instantly recognise a young singer who was serious about his music and wanted to get on in his career. He fitted easily into the cast and I remember he listened very attentively to what the director had to say. Later, I wasn't surprised to learn of Bruno's progress at Covent Garden and more recently in Germany. He has what it takes to be a star, and that is something you can't say about all singers.'

Although he continued to receive favourable notices from the London critics, Caproni was still determined to sing the big Italian roles. He was advised that he would have to wait, perhaps for a few years more, before he could hope to get the opportunity at Covent Garden. He was in luck. As it happened, the house's casting director was German and he arranged for auditions for him at the opera house in Darmstadt, which also took in Frankfurt. He was successful and in August 1992 took up his appointment and has since sung Marcello in *Boheme* and Renata in *Ballo un Mascera*. And in December he sang a number of performances of Rodrigo in Verdi's *Don Carlos*. He was still under contract, though, to Covent Garden and returned to sing Ping in *Turandot,* a portrayal that received good notices, and later sang Masetto in *Don Giovanni.*

It was during the *Giovanni* run that he was advised by Thomas Allen who was singing the Don, that he should concentrate on his Italian repertoire and accept the new contract offered him by Darmstadt. James Shaw also advised the same thing and thought Caproni's lyric baritone was also ideally suited to the big bel canto roles.

Later, when the singer was asked in Germany to sing some Wagner, he was again advised by Shaw to avoid it. As Shaw told me, 'It would be unwise for him. He has already realised his ambition to sing Verdi and there's time in the future to do other things.'

When I talked to him in September of 1994, he was as exuberant as ever and reeled off the latest operatic roles he had sung, which included Michele (*Il Tabarro*), the title parts in *Eugene Onegin* and *Gianni Schicchi*, Germont (*La Traviata*) and Marcello (*La Boheme*). He was also receiving offers, he said, from other German opera houses as well as from English National Opera and Covent Garden.

'I'm so lucky to be able to sing these great roles at my age,' he said with a sparkle in his voice which hadn't quite lost its Northern Ireland accent. But he was quick to add that life in Darmstadt opera house was hectic, for between singing in revivals and rehearsing new roles he had little time to himself. 'We sing about twenty performances of each opera in the year,' he added, 'but honestly I don't mind the demands on me. As I said, I would have waited years in the UK to sing all these parts.'

He enquired about the musical life in Dublin and regretted that he hadn't yet sung at the National Concert Hall, an omission he hoped to rectify in the not too distant future. 'I also want to sing in Belfast again, but I haven't heard from Opera Northern Ireland lately. And, of course, I want to go back to the Wexford Festival.'

Time was the crucial factor, however. By late 1994 there was little likelihood that he would achieve all his ambitions, but then he has time on his hands and more new roles to sing in German opera houses. He is in a happy position. Bruno Caproni had come a long way in a short time from his native seaside town of Bangor, Co. Down.

Chapter Twenty Six

Marie-Claire O'Riordan

ROMANCE IN GERMANY

She was first introduced to John Fowler, a freelance American tenor in Cardiff in 1984. Today, Marie-Claire O'Reirdan derives obvious pleasure in recalling that occasion.

'Welsh National Opera was presenting *La Boheme* and John was singing Rodolfo with Suzanne Murphy as Musetta. At the time I was a member of the company and had sung with Suzanne in *The Merry Widow*. One day, after a rehearsal of *Boheme*, she introduced me to John Fowler and I was immediately taken by his amiability and good humour.

'Suzanne had a car and a few of us, including John, would visit interesting places such as Bath and Stratford. Sometimes I'd say to them, "We've a day off next week, so let's go somewhere together." Friendship is important in our profession, and in an opera company you tend to get to know your colleagues rather quicker than, say, in an office job. I know I've made some wonderful friends. Getting on with one's colleagues is also advantageous when it comes to working with them. I've found an affinity on stage between male and female singers and this can be useful in achieving a convincing and credible performance. I mean, if you're supposed to be kissing someone in a scene, or having a romantic relationship in a particular opera, it does help, in my opinion, to be on good terms with them off-stage.

'At this time John Fowler was singing Rodolfo on tour with Welsh National, but we managed to see each other. We had endless fun together, lots of laughs, and became good friends. I was enjoying my work and gaining valuable experience. I was cast as Micaela in what was considered an avant garde production of *Carmen*, but to me it was a fresh and exciting approach. However, when an opportunity arose later for me to go to Germany I decided to take it.'

The chance, she recalled, came by accident. She travelled to London to audition for an English agent and he happened to have a German agent with him. After the audition in the Wigmore Hall, the German said he knew of two house jobs in Germany and offered to fly her over the following weekend.

'I felt I had nothing to lose. Actually, I reckoned it would be both an interesting and constructive thing for me to do. To my surprise, I was offered both jobs, one in Hamburg, the other in Wiesbaden. After some soul-searching, I chose the Staatsoper in Hamburg; it was not an easy decision as I'd be going there as a virtual beginner, singing small roles, for the company operated the star system. In Wiesbaden, on the other hand, I'd be going straight into your meat-and-potatoes repertory.'

On arrival in Hamburg she found she had no place to live, so she booked into a hotel at her own expense. However, at the opera house she quickly made friends and inside a few days heard about a colleague who was leaving her apartment for six months. She agreed to take it. Among her friends were an American repetiteur and a Swedish baritone.

'We went around a lot together and I suppose I did make the mistake of speaking too much English, for if I hoped to make headway in opera in Germany a fluent knowledge of the language was necessary. Compared with Welsh National Opera, I found the Hamburg approach was totally different and I took a while to adapt.'

As Marie-Claire O'Reirdan's German improved she was able to communicate more easily with the management and her colleagues and she appreciated their different culture much better. 'I fitted into the way of things there – that's the most important thing you've got to do in a strange country', she says today. 'I'd strongly advise young Irish singers coming to Germany to learn the language before they arrive here. In my case, I learned it as I went along, which isn't the most advisable way.'

She was in Hamburg only a short time when one day she received a surprise 'phone call from America. It was John Fowler on the line; he told her he was bound for Europe where he had got some operatic engagements. In subsequent weeks, as they did sight-seeing tours of the city, dined in the evening at different restaurants, and talked about singing, their friendship deepened.

John Fowler was anxious to get as much European experience as possible and, as it happened, Germany had more than its share of American singers, so he did not feel a complete outsider. Marie had signed a beginner's contract, which was akin to being attached to an opera studio, except that Hamburg, unlike Munich, did not have a studio. The first role she sang was Barbarina in *The Marriage of Figaro*, a comic role that wasn't taxing.

It was wonderful, she thought, to be meeting at last stage and recording stars she had only read about, such as Mirella Freni, Margaret Price, Thomas Allen, Agnes Baltsa and some famous German singers and reckoned she had benefitted from working with them. 'They made singing look so easy', she said, 'but I knew this was so because of their experience and thorough approach to opera. I realised how much I had to learn and was determined to give it everything. I loved the way of life, despite the arduous rehearsals, and there was excitement about first nights that caused a real buzz in the opera house.'

Opera-going was, she noted, a way of life in Hamburg; even cab drivers were able to discuss star singers and express opinions about them. This brought opera alive and people were proud of the tradition of opera in the city. Although her income ensured that she was able to live a comfortable lifestyle, she decided in 1986 to move on and seek a new challenge.

Dusseldorf offered it and in contrast to her earlier contract in Hamburg, she was now being hired to sing leading roles; instead of Barbarina she was asked to sing Susanna in *The Marriage of Figaro*, Adina instead of Gianuetta in *L'Elisir d'Amore*, and Sophie in *Der Rosenkavalier*. She made no secret of the fact that she read the critics and was able to say that she never once got a really bad notice. She sang Lauretta in *Gianni Schicchi* and Nerina in

Haydn's *La Fedelta Premiata*.

Singing Gilda in *Rigoletto* afforded her a special thrill, since she felt it was a role that ideally suited her soprano voice and in some ways resembled Violetta, which she had already sung in a concert performance of *Traviata*. Sophie in *Rosenkavalier*, not only appealed to her because of its ravishing music – it was the first German opera she sang speaking fluent German.

In 1988, Marie achieved one of her fondest ambitions, and that was to sing at the Bayreuth Festival. 'I saw it as the Glyndebourne of Germany, but with one notable difference: it was Wagner's music first and last and most festival-goers came to worship at the Wagner shrine. The very air breathes the great composer, and as far as singers are concerned the opera house itself is a perfect place in which to sing – at least I found it so. I love going back there to sing; the place simply grows on one.'

She made her debut in a new production of *Parsifal* and has been singing at the festival on a regular basis.

With John Fowler's career becoming established in Europe, both of them managed to see a good deal of each other, despite the fact that the tenor was 'living out of a suitcase.' By the late 1980s their love had matured and they were talking of marriage.

For Marie their relationship had a few dimensions. 'I think it's a wonderful thing to have someone with which to share your success as well as your problems', she explained. 'I mean, John and I were lucky to have met and come together. We have a lot in common and I do feel that personal happiness can make a tremendous difference to one's career.'

When eventually they decided to marry, they were determined to have a relaxed wedding, not a rushed and hectic affair, and they chose a neutral venue, London. By then Marie's parents had moved there from Ireland so that they could be nearer their grand-children.

With no operatic engagements to think about, the occasion went off without a hitch. 'It's a day we remember with affection', she recalled. 'John and I wanted the day to be different – and it was. And we had a reasonable time for our honeymoon.'

Later, they made Dusseldorf their base, though John Fowler spent much time travelling to America and other parts of the world. Marie said that as singers they had naturally discussed the travel aspect and agreed that either short or long separations in marriage could be a hardship. 'We felt prepared for them when they happened', she said. 'when I went freelance and spent months at a time in Bayreuth it meant that we were separated. John was getting more work in America, so we had to work out meeting times when possible. It's just part of our business and singers have got to be realistic about it.'

Elaine Padmore engaged her to sing in Nicholas Maw's opera, *The Rising of the Moon* at the 1990 Wexford Festival. It proved to be a controversial production, with one critic from Belfast walking out of the Theatre Royal in protest and claimed the opera was 'rubbish'; none of his colleagues walked out with him, nor for that fact any member of the audience.

Despite the mild furore, Marie found the music interesting, even occasionally compelling. Earlier in Dusseldorf she had sung in a Benjamin Britten work and musically discovered echoes of his music in Maw's opera. While the production did not excite people generally in Wexford, she told me she saw no reason why such an experimental work should not be staged at the festival.

After Wexford, she was off to Monte Carlo to sing in Puccini's *La Rondine*, an experience she found worthwhile and musically challenging. In August 1991, she and her husband John Fowler discussed together where they would make their permanent home. Should it be New York? Marie was against the idea on the grounds that the city was 'ferociously expensive' and anyway neither of them were city people. Should it then be Florida? Since John Fowler liked the seasons to change, as in Ireland, they ruled out that possibility.

Eventually after considering Munich and London, they fixed on North Carolina, which was under an hour's flight from New York. They picked on a 200-year-old log farmhouse on a couple of acres, where George Washington was once reputed to have spent a night. They were close to Charlotte, a delightful city, where John Fowler had friends and relatives. To Marie-Claire O'Reirdan, life was laid back in North Carolina, although

Charlotte has a busy airport with direct flights to Paris and London.

Culturally, the city is progressive, having got a multi- million dollar arts centre, including an opera theatre. For the first time John and Marie sang there together in Gounod's *Romeo et Juliette*, which both considered very satisfying; in fact, Marie had found the opera so beautiful that she hoped she and John would sing it one day in Dublin. Already she had been contacted by Elaine Padmore, then artistic director of DGOS Opera Ireland, asking her to audition for the title role in *Martha*.

When she was engaged to sing it in Dublin in 1992, she and John Fowler looked over the Flotow score and he suddenly remarked, 'Surely you're not going to sing "The Last Rose of Summer" in German?' When Marie reminded him that the opera was being sung in German, he persist-ed, 'No, Marie, you can't sing "The Last Rose" in German to an Irish audi-ence; you must sing it in English'.

Marie suddenly thought: John is perfectly right: I must sing it in English.' As it transpired, it proved one of the highpoints of the evening in that spring season at the Gaiety Theatre. The critics, both Irish and English, acclaimed her performance. Ian Fox in the *Sunday Tribune* commented 'Marie-Claire O'Reirdan returned from successes in Germany and the USA to demonstrate just why she is in such demand. She was always a vivacious actress and stylish singer but now she can add a confidence and fullness of tone which are quite remarkable.'

Sunday Times critic Hugh Canning described her Martha as vivacious and said she shared the honours with Swedish mezzo, Ulrike Precht, a sumptuous-voiced Nancy. John Allen observed in the *Irish Times*: 'A well-balanced quartet of young singers is topped by Marie-Claire O'Reirdan making a welcome return to Dublin as Lady Harriet. Her lightish soprano broadens richly at the top and she gave a polished performance, even man-aging to soften Harriet's hard-hearted image with her winsome demeanour.'

We had decided to meet next morning for coffee in Dublin's Conrad Hotel, opposite the National Concert Hall. Marie admitted that it has been an emotional experience for her, singing before her own people. She was particularly moved by the audience response at the final curtain. 'I could hardly get over their great enthusiasm and the fact that they enjoyed my singing so much. I will always regard that as a very special moment in my career. I must confess that before curtain-up I had felt a little nervous, not knowing how they were going to take the performance.

'Martha is one of the most difficult roles I've sung, harder than Gilda because there is more coloratura in it. And you have got to place yourself in the part. I could almost feel the silence as I sang "The Last Rose"; it was quite an extraordinary sensation for me.'

A few nights later Veronica Dunne, Marie's first singing teacher in Dublin, attended the performance of *Martha* and was to remark on how Marie had paced herself so well and managed to sustain such lovely singing throughout the performance. A few years previously she had convinced Marie that she could make a career in singing.

'I think I got hooked pretty quickly', Marie told me, as she relaxed in a hotel armchair. 'I know that for the next five years I worked hard with Ronnie. She was always encouraging and impressed on me voice quality and breathing control. I think she liked to discover potential in a voice.'

Marie had made her debut as Pamina in *The Magic Flute* and later on sang Gretel in *Hansel and Gretel*. She likes to recall those early years. 'I was absolutely thrilled to be singing these parts. I wanted to do them so well that I suppose the anxiety showed. I don't think that singing is something you'd persist with unless you passionately enjoyed it. It was enough for me when Ronnie said I could go on and make a career. I have been fortunate also that my parents were so supportive.'

She accepts that it is something of a bizarre world that she and John Fowler inhabit, since there are lengthy periods when both are away from their log farmhouse in North Caroline. 'I would like to think', she says, 'that when I get to a certain stage in my career I can be selective in the roles I want to sing. I appreciate that it would be a wonderful luxury and would allow me more time to spend at home and indulge my hobbies, like reading and theatre-going; in fact, I would like to be involved in the theatre.'

As she sipped her coffee, she looked at ease and was over the excitement of the previous night's opera. But in our conversation reference to it was occasionally made, as though she was still overwhelmed by the warmth of the audience reception. She said she counted herself fortunate, or as she put it, 'I haven't had to struggle tremendously hard to get on a footing in the business. Singing has enriched my life. When I stroll through the streets of Bayreuth I know I can thank singing for bringing me to this unique place. It is a marvellous feeling to have. And, as I keep stressing, I've made great friends along the way.'

I sensed, though, before we parted on the footsteps of the hotel that she would not be truly happy until she and her husband John have performed *Romeo et Juliette* together at Dublin's Gaiety Theatre. There are elements of that legendary romance about their own lives.

However, they were offered Violetta and Alfredo by DGOS Opera Ireland in the society's new 1994 winter season production of *La Traviata* and were delighted to accept the offer. John had already sung Edgardo in *Lucia di Lammermoor* in Dublin and by now Marie was a firm favourite with Irish audiences. During that summer she had been singing in Bayreuth Festival with John Fowler busy in Europe and America. For Marie it was in her own words 'an operatic dream come true'. As she said, 'Singing Violetta is a rare privilege at any time, but to sing it with one's husband is something else. I'm, thrilled.'

Chapter Twenty Seven

Kate McCarney

MEZZO FROM ANDERSONSTOWN

'I think you've got a singing voice', remarked Mrs. Josephine McCarney to her daughter, 'and I want you to have lessons.' Kathleen McCarney, as the girl was known in Belfast, was 15 years of age and for three years had sung in musicals at her school, the St. Louise's Grammar, in the Falls Road. Sister Genevieve of the Sisters of Charity gave the pupils there lots of encouragement to sing.

'I found I loved singing', Kate recalls. 'My family were musical; my father played the traditional fiddle and my uncle Michael McCarney had a very good tenor voice and sang with St. Agnes Choral Society. The quality of his voice was so good that I think he could easily have turned profession-al and made a decent living.'

The McCarneys had moved to Andersonstown when she was two years old and she grew up in a strong Catholic background. From a very young age she can remember singing at home and was thrilled when her mother later brought her to a private voice teacher with whom she studied for a year. After that, she enrolled at the Belfast School of Music where she had lessons on four nights each week. 'I was totally consumed by singing', she says today. 'It didn't worry me that we had to pay for the lessons'.

Her entry to the school coincided with the outbreak of violence in Northern Ireland, particularly in Belfast. She was aware of the dangers of living in Andersonstown but singing eased her mind. For instance, on the day her A-levels results were due out she was unable to get to the school because of street barricades. From early morning she had been awakened by the symbolic beating together of bin lids; it was August 9, 1971, the day internment was introduced in the province.

'We were living in the middle of the Troubles', she said, but in my own case singing bridged the political divide between us. The School of Music was supposed to be in a Protestant area, but I happened to be mixing with non-Catholics there so that the religious thing didn't figure in my psyche as such. Anyway, it seemed natural for me to be attending the school.'

Her first taste of the real musical world came as a member of St. Agnes Choral Society, and singing the soprano lead Saffi in *The Gypsy Baron* she was awarded the best female voice at the Waterford International Festival. After that, she was classed as a mezzo-soprano and has continued to sing as such. To secure herself in the future, she trained as a teacher and between 1975-'76 taught in a Belfast primary school. But she was still determined to follow a singing career if she could.

Around this time she had what she described as a chance meeting with Ena Mitchell, a well-known singing teacher attached to the Royal Northern College of Music in Manchester and she suggested that she audition for the college. She was successful and for the next four years studied with Miss Mitchell and also with baritone John Cameron who had gained a good reputation as a voice coach. The college enjoyed a considerable reputation and had an impressive record for turning out polished singers.

Usually students there auditioned at end of term in the hope of joining an opera company. Kate McCarney was more fortunate than some of her colleagues and was taken on in the chorus of Scottish Opera. She would be based in Glasgow and apart from chorus work was asked to cover smaller roles.

From the outset, she enjoyed working with the company; the spirit was excellent, the artistic standard high. Eventually she sang small parts in major productions, among them *The Beggar's Opera* and felt proud to be singing in a scene with baritone Thomas Allen.

After two years in the chorus, she began a new career as a member of

Scottish Opera-Go-Round, the touring branch of the parent company and was cast in the parts of Suzuki and Cenerentola. Performed with piano accompaniment, the productions were costumed and she found that it was a unique operatic experience. The company toured from the Highlands to the border areas, bringing opera to audiences who otherwise could scarcely hope to see it. Once, on the island of Mull they performed in a circus ring. Kate remembers it was a cleverly devised production of *La Cenerentola* and it was exceptionally well received.

'I was amazed to find so many people coming up to me after the performance', she said, 'telling me how they enjoyed the evening. It was the same the following night with *Butterfly*, when the enthusiasm was even greater among the locals. These people seemed to be drained by the dramatic and musical experience and couldn't believe that the two experiences could be so different.'

During the tour, she often worried about her folks at home in Andersonstown where the Troubles showed no sign of a cessation. Sometimes her Scottish or English colleagues asked her about the situation. She sensed their puzzlement but she tried to appear optimistic, expressing the hope that some day everyone in Northern Ireland might learn to live in peace.

By 1980 she was on the move once more. She got a place in London's Opera Studio and again counted herself very fortunate to be among the 12 singers chosen. She was one of four Irish singers - the others being Dublin-born bass John Milne, Colette McGahon and Hugh Mackey. It was an excellent training ground, affording practical insights into different aspects of opera and leading professionals in the spheres of direction and design were on hand to assist. Students prepared operatic roles and for a time Kate concentrated on the operas of Rossini and Mozart.

On leaving Opera Studio, she joined Glyndebourne Touring company and was offered the role of Herma in Britten's *A Midsummer Night's Dream* and came to love the music. 'I absolutely loved singing it. I love all of Britten's operas.' She found time to slip over to Belfast to give recitals and did a *Messiah* in the Ulster Hall. It was, she thought, great to be back, even if the Troubles intensified week by week. Musical life went on and people still came out for concerts and operas. They were so brave, she often thought.

Kate McCarney, like most of her young colleagues, had to work hard to support herself. On Sunday afternoons she sang in a small trendy wine bar in London's Hampstead and enjoyed the experience. It was there she met, as she said, 'a tall, handsome stranger' who introduced himself as Jonathan May, an English singer from Windsor. Eventually they did an opera cruise together.

Organised by a London travel agent, the cruise attracted a few hundred opera buffs and the idea was to trace a historic voyage. To Kate McCarney, it was a fascinating form of entertainment. As the group of ten singers rehearsed two different operas the passengers were invited along to watch the rehearsals. In the evening the group gave concerts with a small orchestra and the whole cruise was a musical celebration.

Among the highlights were the operatic performances given ashore. *The Barber of Seville* was performed outdoors in a duke's palace in Seville,while on another occasion she sang Cherubino in *The Marriage of Figaro* in a castle. Later, back in England Jonathan May joined the chorus at Covent Garden while she travelled to Dublin to rehearse the role of Carmen in a new production of the opera by Opera Theatre Company.

The part of the Spanish gipsy woman intrigued her and she had her own ideas about it. 'I think there has to be something of yourself in the role. Each Carmen is going to be different. You can get the stereotype of the woman with dark hair and long earrings and posing with hands on 'hips, but that to me is a superficial image. There must be a lot more subtlety and depth. Sex appeal, yes, but humour, too. I consider it one of the most marvellous roles in the mezzo repertoire.'

The Dublin-based Opera Theatre Company decided to present, for touring purposes, a condensed version of Bizet's opera and called it *Carmen and Don Jose*. It was in a way a brand new reworking of the opera by director Ben Barnes, who two years previously had directed a highly-acclaimed production of Britten's *The Turn of the Screw* for the company. OTC's aim was always to present opera in a theatrical form, thereby broadening its public appeal.

For Kate McCarney the year 1988 was particularly interesting. A few weeks previously she had sung for Opera 80 the title role in the original version of *Carmen*, when the company toured England with it, so she was now naturally looking forward to OTC's new-look version of the work to be performed without choruses. Emphasis would be entirely focused on the relationship between Carmen and Don Jose – hence the new title.

All the cast was Irish. Apart from Kate's Carmen, Paul McCann was the Don Jose, with Joe Corbett as Escamilio and Regina Nathan as Michaela. When I talked to Kate McCarney after the rehearsals, she enthused about the production. 'I can't tell you how much I've enjoyed working on a project of this kind, which involves both singers and actors, and I think it's true to say that we've had a mutual fascination about each other's art. For me, it's been a great learning process watching how other people in the arts work. I can only compare it with a piece I worked on with the English National Opera, in which mime experts were employed. I'm all for integrating the different aspects of art, where it's appropriate, and I think that this theatrical version of Carmen is terrific.'

The Dublin media found Kate interesting to interview, for unlike some other singers she is uncomplicated, and for the most part is both articulate and perceptive. She admitted that travel had up to then been a highlight of her career, as she took in places that otherwise she could not have hoped to see. 'It's funny', she said, 'how people all over the world are fascinated when you tell them that you come from Belfast. When I was performing in Tel Aviv, a play was being rehearsed at a theatre in the city. It was about women living through the Troubles in West Belfast and I was called in to advise them on their accents.'

I can vividly recall the impact *Carmen* and *Don Jose* made on Irish opera-goers. I caught up with it at the Gate Theatre, Dublin, and found it an absorbing evening in the theatre. Vocally and dramatically it had much to offer, from Kate McCarney's powerful portrayal of Bizet's heroine to Paul

McCann's strongly sung Don Jose. My colleague Ian Fox, writing for the *Sunday Tribune*, stated: 'One of the most gripping evenings I have spent at the opera. This is a highly charged view of Bizet's magical score, supported by an excellent orchestra. Kate McCarney was a rich-voiced Carmen but she also created a sinuous, sexy sorceress.'

Recalling her visit with the St. Agnes Choral Society to the Waterford International Festival in 1973, Kate McCarney said, 'I was playing the part of a lovely innocent gipsy girl and here in the Gate Theatre I am back playing another gipsy, but one who is anything but innocent. I suppose you could say the story is an allegory of myself. In 1973, I was totally naive and green about the music business. Fifteen years on, I've learned an awful lot - enough to come back and sing Carmen. It's a real sizzler of a role, definitely not one for a person with inhibitions!'

She was back in Ireland a few years later when she sang Meg Page in Opera Theatre Company's touring production of Verdi's *Falstaff*. The Dublin venue on this occasion - the Tivoli Theatre - was not quite suitable and in my own view took from the enjoyment of the opera. There was much to admire in Keith Latham's Falstaff, but from an audience point of view the women stole the show, with Kate, Regina Nathan, Mary Callan Clarke and Marie Walshe giving sparkling performances.

The young cast demonstrated that Ireland could by now draw on abundant young talent and that OTC by presenting works like *Falstaff* did a fine service to opera, for otherwise such operas would not be seen in the country, either north or south.

When Kate successfully auditioned for Welsh National Opera, she was asked to cover the role of Carmen while at the same time singing Mercedes in the production. Eventually in Plymouth she had to take over at a few hours' notice from an indisposed Jean Stillwell. She remembers she was more elated than nervous. 'I really loved going on. I suppose I would have been nervous if I had come raw to the production, but singing Mercedes was a big help to me. The last act was the most difficult of all because you have to sustain the intense emotion right through to the death scene. It is a two-way thing, since Don Jose has also to sustain the drama. The music is superb and utterly matches up to the dark mood of the scene.'

She was to receive one of her best notices. Headed A DOMINANT CARMEN, the piece by a local critic stated: 'Kate McCarney's sensuous Carmen outspirits most of the other performances and she holds the stage from her first step on it; her voice captures her character, proud, bold and enticing.'

She went on to make her Covent Garden debut in the mid-Eighties as one of the orphans in *Der Rosenkavalier*, conducted by Georg Solti. Although it was only a minor role, Kate recalls the experience as being a highlight of her career. 'As I stepped onto the stage I felt I was stepping into a part of musical history. The atmosphere was great and the experience terrific. Some day I'd love to sing a big role there.'

There was another special thrill for her when a few years later she returned to her native Belfast to sing Siebel in Opera Northern Ireland's production of *Faust*. Jonathan May was also in the cast as well as in the company's *Rigoletto*. It was a *Faust* that Kate McCarney remembers with affection and pride. Apart from the satisfaction of singing before her own people, the production was hailed by the critics, the positioning of the chorus in tier formation being especially effective.

During her stay in the city, Kate did not forget her old school, St. Louise's Grammar, where once she was head girl and sang her first faltering notes. One day she went along and held an opera workshop and the enthusiasm of the children delighted her. In another way it was also a happy time for her as she introduced Jonathan May to her parents and family and had a delightful reunion. In spite of the continuing violence in the province, she was always amazed at how the people tried to live life as normally as possible. Her parents, for example, would never think of leaving the city and living instead in Britain. It was their city and would always remain so.

Shortly afterwards she covered Siebel for English National Opera and discovered it was a different style production, though every bit as successful as the Belfast *Faust*. By comparison with Belfast's traditionally-played

Mephistopheles, ENO's singer in the part - John Tomlinson - presented him as a psychologically evil character and in her view it was a frightening portrayal yet it worked well in this particular staging.

In the late Eighties she decided to change her singing coach and on the recommendation of a London colleague, Joan Rodgers, began taking lessons with Audrey Langford. 'Audrey has been a great help to me', she says. 'Temperamentally, we are suited to each other and for me it's like starting all over again.' Audrey has improved my technique and suggested a new repertoire. I've no worries about my voice, but I do think about singing better, every singer does.'

My interview with Kate McCarney took place in the Talbot Hotel in Wexford during the 1992 festival in the town. She was singing in Stephen Storace's *The Comedy of Errors* and as Lesbia she performed, in my opinion, with flair and conviction. She was thrilled to be working again with the director Giles Havergel, who once directed her in Welsh National Opera's *The Barber of Seville*, a production described by a Bristol critic as 'a hysterical romp'. Kate's impersonation of Rosina was played with 'a fine sense of cynical comedy' the same critic, David Harrison, added.

'Giles is one of the best directors I've ever worked with', she told me. 'He knows every step he is taking in an opera and has got a brilliantly imaginative mind.'

Later we continued our conversation at the Westbury Hotel in Dublin when she was singing in DGOS Opera Ireland's 1993 winter season's *Lakmé* and expressed delight at the chance of singing in French and in an opera that she adores. By now she and Jonathan May were married and living in an Edwardian semi-detached house in Tonbridge Wells in Kent. During her weeks in Dublin, Jonathan was singing Dulcamara in *L'Elisir d'amore* with English Touring Opera.

A secure private life is important to Kate McCarney. 'I consider myself fortunate to be married to Jonathan', she reflected, 'as he appreciates the pressure under which we operate and this mutual understanding is crucial to our careers and to our happiness. There are other singers who are content to remain unattached and get on with their careers; I'm not one of them. I need support. Jonathan is both husband and friend to me and I hope I'm the same to him. I'm a bit of a dreamer really, so it's nice to come home to a partner with his feet firmly on the ground.'

Her family's consistent support, especially that from her parents, Patrick and Josephine McCarney, is something she feels strongly about and in our conversation she occasionally referred to it. There are roles she wants to sing, including Charlotte in *Werther* and Marguerite in *The Damnation of Faust* as well as Carmen again. At 40, she is at the height of her career and optimistic about the future. And like Marie Claire O'Reirdan she enjoys the prospect of singing with her husband in the same operatic seasons. 'It spares me phone and fax bills!' Kate says with typical Belfast humour. For the '94 season at the Grand Opera House she was engaged to sing Olga in Opera Northern Ireland's new production of *Eugne Onegin* while Jonathan had parts in the same opera as well as in *Don Giovanni*. Before that, Kate had sung with the City of Birmingham Touring Opera and received impressive notices for her performance as Marthe and Cleopatra in *Faust*. Despite the air of political uncertainty in the province, she assured me she always looked forward to singing in Belfast.

'For me, it's like going home,' she mused. 'And I always seem to get on the good side of the Opera House audience. Yes, I do enjoy the experience, and always will. I think I can say the same for Jonathan.' ∎